Cub Scout Leader How-To Book

SUCCESSFUL IDEAS TO ADD FUN AND EXCITEMENT
TO DEN AND PACK ACTIVITIES

BOY SCOUTS OF AMERICA

33832A
ISBN 0-8395-3832-4

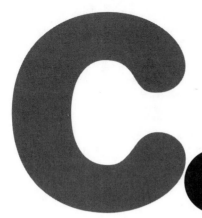

CONTENTS

Introduction

- How do I plan a skit for next month's pack meeting?
- How do I find a new game—that can be played indoors?
- How do I make papier-mâché?
- How do I make a hike interesting to my den?
- How do I plan the blue and gold banquet?
- How do I help make my Cub Scout with special needs more successful?
- How do I make pack meetings more upbeat?

You'll find the answers to these questions and countless others within the covers of this book. The *Cub Scout Leader How-To Book* has been written by and for den leaders and Cubmasters across the country. The tested suggestions you'll find for games, crafts, skits, applauses, songs, and more will add fun and sparkle to all your Cub Scout meetings and adventures.

Used with *Cub Scout Program Helps,* the *Webelos Leader Guide,* and the *Cub Scout Leader Book,* this book will enable you to plan den and pack programs that will be fun for everyone. And while boys are having fun, they will be learning, advancing in rank, and strengthening relationships with one another. That's what Cub Scouting is all about.

ACCENTUATE THE POSITIVE

This chapter deals with everything that is positive in Cub Scouting: Cub Scout ideals, advancement, awards, and good behavior. The goal of the chapter is to suggest ways for you to recognize and reward these things. Rewarding the positive encourages boys and will ensure the success of the program for both boys and adults.

THE PURPOSES OF CUB SCOUTING

Since 1930, the Boy Scouts of America has helped younger boys through Cub Scouting. Cub Scouting is a year-round family-oriented part of the BSA program designed for boys who are in first through fifth grade (or are 7, 8, 9, and 10 years of age). Parents, leaders, and organizations work together to achieve the 10 purposes of Cub Scouting:

1. Character Development
2. Spiritual Growth
3. Good Citizenship
4. Sportsmanship and Fitness
5. Family Understanding
6. Respectful Relationships
7. Personal Achievement
8. Friendly Service
9. Fun and Adventure
10. Preparation for Boy Scouts

THE METHODS OF CUB SCOUTING

Cub Scouting uses seven specific methods to achieve Scouting's purpose of helping boys and young adults build character, train in the responsibilities of citizenship, and develop personal fitness. These methods are incorporated into all aspects of the program. Through these methods, Cub Scouting happens in the lives of boys and their families.

1. The Ideals
2. The Den
3. Advancement
4. Family Involvement
5. Activities
6. Home and Neighborhood Centered
7. The Uniform

The Purposes and Methods of Cub Scouting and Ideals of Scouting

Every pack and den activity should reflect the 10 purposes of Cub Scouting, which also reflect the ideals and purpose of the overall Scouting movement. Note that the fifth method of Cub Scouting used to achieve Scouting's purpose is "Activities"—which is what this book is all about.

To emphasize the purposes of Cub Scouting, use them during the **Cubmaster's minute** at the end of the monthly pack meeting or during the **den leader's minute** at the end of the den meeting.

The den leader's minute introduces the formal closing of the meeting. To begin, ask the boys to arrange themselves in a formation, such as a circle or a horseshoe, that will signal to them that it is time to listen. Say something like, "It's time for us to close our meeting for today. But before we go, I'd like for us to think about something important." This "minute" is to be truly that—it should take only a minute or two. Then close the meeting with the Cub Scout Promise, the Law of the Pack, the Cub Scout motto, or another appropriate closing.

Cub Scout Program Helps and the *Webelos Leader Guide* have suggestions for closings that fit the monthly theme. Here are some additional suggestions:

1. Take one line from the Cub Scout Promise or Law of the Pack and ask one of the boys to explain what it means. Help him along as needed, and then ask another boy how that portion of the Cub Scout Promise or Law of the Pack was used in the den meeting that day.

2. Talk about what it means to "Do Your Best."

3. Talk about the fact that every day we have two choices: We can choose to do things that are right and help other people; or we can choose to do things that are selfish and serve only us. Our character and what other people think of us are based on these choices. In the Cub Scout Promise, we promise to help other people. Ask boys whether they will keep that promise.

4. Talk about one of our country's heroes or what makes our country strong. Here's an example: "Meriwether Lewis and William Clark were two of our country's great leaders. In the early 1800s, they and their company, called the Corps of Discovery, forged the path that linked the east and west coasts of this land. When they arrived in what would become Washington State, decisions had to be made about their return. Rather

than just deciding themselves and telling their companions what to do, Lewis and Clark let the members of the corps vote. It would be nearly 70 years before a black man could vote in the United States, and yet York, a black slave who had made the difficult trip, cast his vote with the others. The Constitution wouldn't guarantee the right of women to vote until 1919, but Sacajawea, an American Indian woman, voted with the men that day. America has been blessed with many great leaders like Lewis and Clark. Who will be next? Will it be you?"

5. Talk about incidents at school or in the community that showed good citizenship or bravery, courage, or compassion.

6. Pick out a familiar saying or song and tie the meaning into the purposes of Cub Scouting. For example, Johnny Mercer wrote in his song: "You got to accentuate the positive, and eliminate the negative." Another way to say this might be to make the most of your blessings and make the least of your troubles.

7. Give the boys an opportunity to tell one good thing that happened to them that day or week.

8. As a group, talk about what it means to be a friend, respect others, or share.

Highlighting Advancement

CEREMONY LADDER

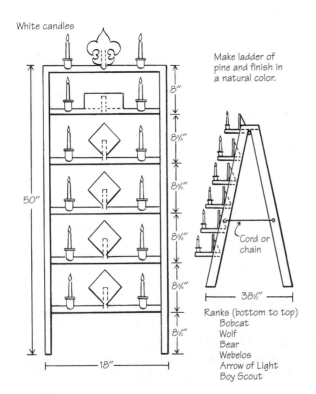

White candles

Make ladder of pine and finish in a natural color.

Cord or chain

8"

8⅜"

8⅜"

8⅜"

8⅜"

8½"

50"

18"

38½"

Ranks (bottom to top)
Bobcat
Wolf
Bear
Webelos
Arrow of Light
Boy Scout

Materials: **Ladder, badge shapes cut from wood or foam board, candleholders, candles**

You can use over and over a pack ceremony ladder like the one shown. The ladder folds for easy storage. You can make a ladder from pine and finish it with varnish or shellac, but any ladder will do. Cut badge shapes from wood and fasten them to the rungs. Burn the badge designs into the wood or use large Cub Scout insignia stickers adhered to foam board. Fasten candleholders to each rung and light each candle as that particular badge is represented in the ceremony.

AKELA'S TOTEM

Materials:
   Insignia posters
     Wood or foam board
   1-by-2-inch wood
     Nails
   Coffee can
   Plaster

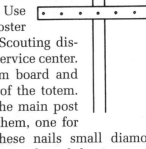

This totem can be either floor- or tabletop-sized. Use the Cub Scout Insignia Poster Set available from your Scouting distributor or local council service center. Mount them on the foam board and attach to the main post of the totem. Nail the crosspieces to the main post and hammer nails into them, one for each boy. Hang from these nails small diamond-shaped posterboard pieces with each boy's name on it. A small coffee can filled with plaster can hold the totem if it is inserted into the plaster just before it sets.

TWO-WAY CEREMONY BOARD

Materials:
   1-by-2-inch board
     Hardboard
   Paint
     Drill
   ¼-inch plywood
     Glue

This ceremony board is easy to make and can be used in many ceremonies. Cover the 1-by-2-inch board with hardboard. Paint it blue. Drill holes in the top for gold candles. The front and back sides are identical, with storage space inside. Cut the Arrow of Light from ¼-inch plywood, paint it gold, and glue it to the board.

PACK ADVANCEMENT BOARD

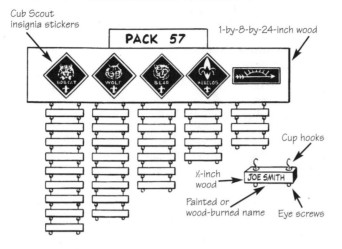

Materials:

> **1-by-8-by-24-inch wood**
> **Cub Scout insignia stickers**
> **½-inch wood for name boards—one per boy**
> **Two cup hooks per name board**
> **Two eye screws per name board**
> **10 additional eye screws**

Boys will look forward to adding their names to an advancement board. As Cub Scouts earn a rank and receive their badge, they hang small name boards under the appropriate rank as a part of the advancement ceremony.

An alternative to this advancement board is to use PVC pipe to build the frame. PVC pipes and joints create a frame that is inexpensive, lightweight, and easy to assemble and transport as well as durable.

DEN ADVANCEMENT CHART

Scout and Webelos Scout
from your Scouting distrib-
vice center. Or create one
ch boy's name on the chart
art for each achievement as
he responsibility for updat-
or the boy who has earned

and Flags

r way to record advance-
accomplishments of the
l decoration for the den
something as simple as a
vancement chart, or it can
sting of a cutout mounted
odles are alike.

With the boys' help, choose a design that "fits" the den. Den doodles can be made from wood, cardboard, foam board, or other materials; they can be a tabletop or floor design; or they can hang on the wall or from the ceiling. Include the den's number and a place for each boy's name and advancement record or accomplishment. Add something to the den doodle at each meeting, recognizing attendance, proper uniforming, and behavior as well as completed achievements towards rank. Colored beads and shells slipped onto leather lacing are common items for symbols of progress. Identify each symbol with an achievement or elective number or activity badge name.

Dens may earn simple awards (sometimes called *dingle dangles*) for a variety of things, such as perfect attendance, good behavior, participation in service projects, or responsibilities at the pack meeting. For example, the den leading the flag ceremony at the pack meeting or at school might earn a small flag to hang on their den doodle; the den that leads a song might earn a musical note made of felt.

You can find more examples of den doodles in *Cub Scout Ceremonies for Dens and Packs.*

DEN FLAGS

Den flags are simple flags that represent each den and give den members a sense of camaraderie and identification. The flag is blue and yellow with the den number on it. Den flags are available from the BSA Supply Division.

The flag may go home with a different boy after each meeting or can be the responsibility of the denner for the month. The flag can be brought to each pack meeting and mark the place where the den sits.

BASES FOR DEN DOODLE OR DEN FLAG

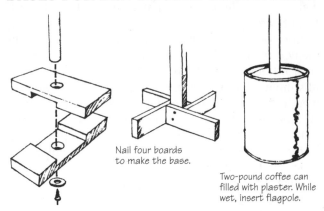

Nail four boards to make the base.

Two-pound coffee can filled with plaster. While wet, insert flagpole.

Make bases from wood or from a two-pound coffee can filled with plaster, as shown. Cover the end of the flagpole with aluminum foil and grease with a thick layer of petroleum jelly so it will slip out easily after the plaster hardens. Or use a piece of PVC pipe that has an opening slightly larger than the diameter of the flagpole. Cover the bottom end of the PVC with foil and set it into the wet plaster. It should stick several inches out of the plaster. When dry, the pole will slip easily into the PVC pipe.

Special Awards

CUBBY

The Cubby is a pack trophy awarded each month for a variety of reasons. Award it to the den with the largest percentage of parents at a pack meeting. Or award the "best-uniformed den" or "best-behaved den." The pack committee determines the award category and keeps it secret until the pack meeting. Cubby is a "traveling" trophy and should be returned to the pack meeting each month to be presented again.

Tin Man Cubby

Materials:
> A variety of cans for the Cubby parts—
>> Hat: 5⁵⁄₁₆-inch funnel
>> Head: 4¹¹⁄₁₆-inch-tall can
>> Neck: 2⅜-inch-tall can
>> Ears: Two 2⅛-inch pieces cut from can
>> Body: 12-inch-tall can
>> Upper and lower arms: Four 3¾-inch-tall cans
>> Hands: Two 2⅞-inch-tall cans
>> Thighs: Two 4¹⁵⁄₁₆-inch-tall cans
>> Lower legs: Two 3¾-inch-tall cans
>> Feet: Two 3¾-inch-tall cans
> Fabric for neckerchief
> Solder
> Tin snips

This Cubby is approximately 27 inches tall. His size depends on the tin cans used. (See the "Crafts" chapter of this book for suggestions on working with tin.)

To assemble the Cubby:

1. Cut holes in the bottom of the head and the top of the body for the neck can. Flange both ends of the neck can. Insert the neck in the head and body, and solder in place.

2. Assemble the leg parts. Flange to the ends of the thigh cans. Solder the closed ends of the thigh and lower leg cans together. Trim to fit the foot cans. Remove both ends from the foot cans and flatten to about 2 inches. Solder to the lower legs.

3. Cut holes in the bottom of the body can close to the outer rim to hold the thighs. Insert thigh flanges in the body, and solder in place.

4. Cut ears from can tops so the ridges of the tops form the edges of the ears. Cut flanges and spread them to fit the head. Solder in place.

5. To make the arms, remove the rims from the cans. Cut the upper arm cans to fit the body, flatten slightly, and solder to the body. Remove both ends from the lower arm cans. Cut off the lower rims, flatten slightly, and solder to the hands. Then push the lower arms over the upper arms and solder.

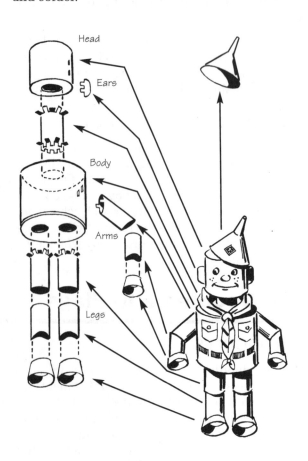

6. Tilt the funnel and solder it to the head.

7. Sand all rough spots and sharp edges.

8. Paint the Cubby to resemble a Cub Scout, and add a neckerchief made of fabric.

Bowling Pin Cubby

Materials: **Bowling pin, acrylic paint**

Paint an old bowling pin to look like a Cub Scout. It can be as simple as a head, a painted-on neckerchief, and a blue body. Or you can make a cap and neckerchief from fabric and glue them on.

WISE OLD OWL AWARD

Wise is the pack that encourages the boys, the dens, and the pack to earn the National Summertime Pack Award. To emphasize this award, a pack might offer the Wise Old Owl Award to dens and individual boys. The pack committee sets the criteria for winning the award. Each den leader keeps track of the den's activities and each boy's participation during the summer. The records are turned in to the pack committee at the end of the summer, and the awards are presented at the first fall meeting to each den meeting the criteria. Awards become more elaborate as the dens and boys exceed the basic criteria.

Wise Old Owl for Dens

Materials: **3-inch leather rounder (round piece of leather), hole punch, permanent markers or owl leather stamp, leather lacing, colored beads or feathers**

Punch two holes in the leather rounder at the edges, across from one another. Draw an owl on the rounder with permanent markers or use a leather stamp. Attach leather lacing at both holes. One is for hanging on the den flag, the other, for adding beads, feathers, etc., to indicate the involvement of the den during the summer. The more boys involved, the more den meetings held, the more elaborate the award.

Wise Old Owl for Boys

Materials: **Candy mold of owl, ring for neckerchief slide, plaster, acrylic paint**

Make plaster owls for neckerchief slides. As the plaster hardens, place a ring in it for the neckerchief to go through. When hard, remove from the mold and paint with acrylic paint.

AWARDS FROM THE HEART

Everyone needs a pat on the back to feel appreciated! These awards, suitable for both boys and adults, are quick and easy. Remember to reward den chiefs, pack leaders, and parents, too. Be sure to mention specifically what the person is being recognized for.

- **Monu-MINT-al Award:** Attach a mint to a note or certificate stating that the person has made a monu-mint-al contribution to Scouting.
- **Chalk It Up to Another Great Job!** Glue pieces of chalk to wood or foam board that state "Great Job!"
- **You Have Been the Link to Success:** Award links of a chain.
- **We Are Not STRETCHING It—We Appreciate You!:** Mount rubber bands on foam board or mat board.
- **Smooth Sailing Award:** Award a small toy sailboat.
- **Good Sport Award:** Write "Good Sport" on a baseball.
- **What a Catch!:** Award a certificate with a fish picture or plastic fish.
- **You Are Tops:** Award a toy top.
- **You Are the Best of the Bunch:** Award plastic grapes or bananas.
- **You Rose to the Occasion!:** Award a plastic rose.
- **Appreciation From Your Scouting Fans:** Award a handmade paper fan.
- **You Are Worth a Million:** Award play money or gold-covered candy coins.
- **For the Person Who Can't Be Licked!:** Award a lollipop.
- **Top Dog Award:** Award a dog chew toy.
- **Thanks…**
  —**For Leading Us in the Right Direction:** A compass
  —**For Sticking to It:** Tape or glue
  —**For Lighting Up Our Meeting:** A light bulb
  —**For Tying Up Loose Ends:** Shoelaces

TROPHIES

Materials:
> Two cans of different sizes
> Spray paint
> Coat hangers
> Pipe cleaners or plaster figure
> Small square of wood
> Stain or paint
> Foam board

Glue the smaller can to the top of the larger can. Make two handles out of coat hanger wire and glue them on the top can. Spray-paint the trophy. Glue a plaster figure to the top, or if desired, make a small figure out of pipe cleaners. Glue the whole thing to a square of wood that has been stained or painted and sealed. Attach an appropriate "plate" made from foam board.

WOOD MEDAL

Materials: 3-inch square of wood; stain or paint; markers; ribbon, leather lacing, or yarn

Drill a hole in the corner of a wood square. Stain and seal or paint the square. Use markers to decorate, indicating first, second, or third place. Attach ribbon, leather lacing, or yarn to hang around the neck.

METAL LID MEDAL

Materials: Canning jar or frozen juice lid, nail and hammer, yarn or ⅛-inch ribbon, paint

Canning jars or frozen juice lids make good medals. Begin by making evenly spaced holes around the lid edge with a nail and hammer. Paint the lids different colors and indicate first, second, or third place. Weave yarn or ribbon in and out of the holes, making the yarn long enough to hang around the neck.

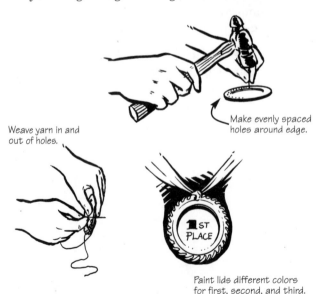

Make evenly spaced holes around edge.

Weave yarn in and out of holes.

Paint lids different colors for first, second, and third.

CARDBOARD MEDAL

Materials: ½-inch-thick cardboard; silver, gold, and bronze wrapping paper; glue; permanent marker; ribbon

Cut two rounds from the cardboard 2½ inches in diameter. Glue them together and wrap with the wrapping paper, gluing the edges to the back. Punch a hole at the edge of the circle and thread the ribbon through it for the necklace. Label the medal first, second, or third place with the permanent marker.

BRIDGES

Bridges are often used in advancement ceremonies when boys move from one rank to another or from one level of the Scouting family to another. Use the Parent and Family Talent Survey to find someone in your pack who likes to build things. You will want the bridge to be sturdy and safe. Diagrams for three possibilities are shown here.

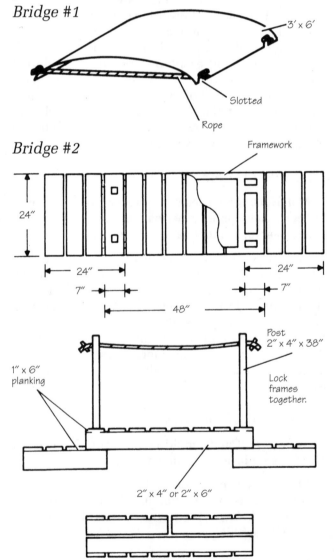

Bridge #1

3' x 6'

Slotted

Rope

Bridge #2

Framework

24"

24"

24"

7"

7"

48"

1" x 6" planking

Post 2" x 4" x 38"

Lock frames together.

2" x 4" or 2" x 6"

Self-contained storage

Bridge #3

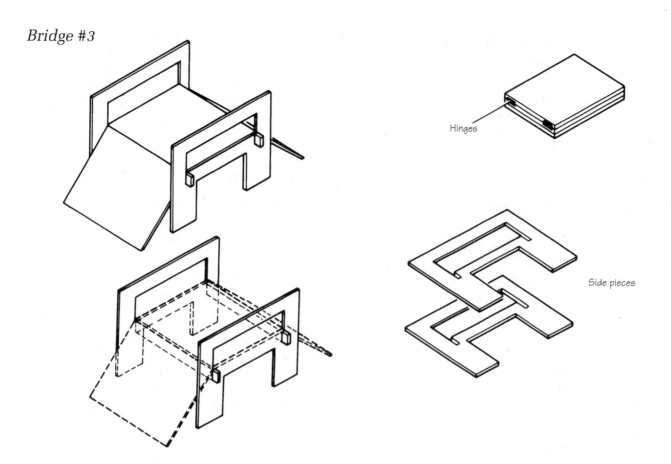

Hinges

Side pieces

Materials for Bridge #3

- ¾ inch Plywood 4 feet by 4 feet Grade A or B
- Hinges
- Paint

Hinge ramps to deck.

To store, pull hinge pins.

Sides and rails slot together to form a basic bridge structure.

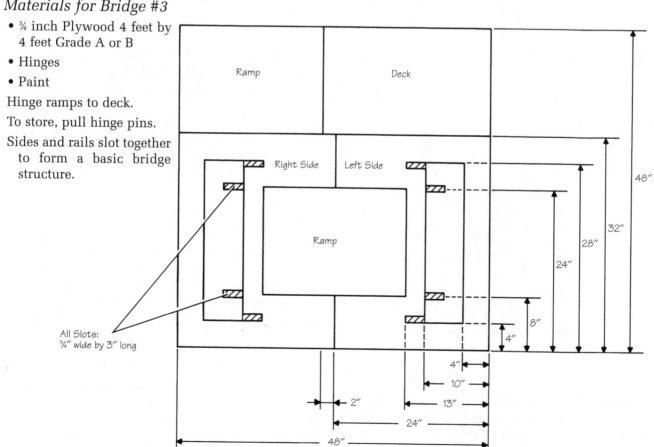

Ramp

Deck

Right Side

Left Side

Ramp

All Slots:
¾" wide by 3" long

48"

32"

28"

24"

8"

4"

4"

10"

2"

13"

24"

48"

Capture the Memories

Scouting is a series of steps aimed at the highest achievement: the Eagle Scout Award. The suggestions below are designed to help boys celebrate how far they have gotten on the road to the Eagle and to capture their Cub Scouting memories.

PATCH BLANKET

Materials: **Blanket, patches the Cub Scout has earned**

Patch blankets can display extra badges a Cub Scout has earned. Use any size of blanket that will fit on the Cub Scout's bed, and stitch the patches on it.

SCRAPBOOK

Materials:
   **Scrapbook, three-ring binder, or cardboard
      pieces wrapped in fabric
   Acid-free paper
   Hole punch
   Markers, stickers, rubber stamps, etc.
   Pictures, advancement award cards, etc.
   Double-stick tape**

Punch holes in the paper to fit your scrapbook. If using cardboard, tie it all together with ribbon, string, or leather lacing. Use double-stick tape to adhere the pictures, awards, etc. Decorate the pages and encourage the boys to write something in the book about the event or award. This is a good project to show off at the blue and gold banquet.

TROPHY SKIN

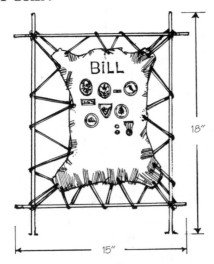

Materials: **Two 18-inch and two 15-inch sticks or dowels, four 12-inch pieces and one 90-inch piece of hemp twine, four 12-inch pieces of bell wire, one 12-by-15-inch piece of thin vinyl**

Bind the four sticks or dowels together with bell wire to form a rectangle. Be sure to make these joints as rigid and tight as possible. Cut the piece of vinyl in the shape of a skin. Punch holes around the edges. Tie the four corners in place with the four 12-inch pieces of twine, and then lace around the skin with the 90-inch piece of twine. Sew, staple, or glue badges to the "skin."

WALKING STICK

Materials: **Large dowel stick long enough and thick enough for a suitable walking stick, 12 inches of leather lacing, piece of rope or yarn**

Drill a hole through the dowel about 4 inches from the top. Thread the leather lacing through the hole and secure with a square knot. Encourage boys to attach something of significance to this loop for each milestone they wish to remember. These "dingle dangles" can be, for instance, a branded piece of leather, feathers, or beads and other trinkets. Paint the walking stick, or carve it or wood-burn it.

CAREER ARROW

What better way to recognize the Arrow of Light, Cub Scouting's highest honor, than with a decorated arrow? Purchase arrows at sporting goods stores that sell archery equipment.

Materials:
   **28-inch hunting arrow with broadhead point
      and blue and yellow feathers
   Acrylic paint or auto detailing tape
   1-by-2-inch wooden board 30 inches long
   Wood stain
   Two cup hooks
   Picture hanger**

Paint or use auto detailing tape to make 3-inch-wide stripes on the arrow for each rank the boy has achieved. Use orange for Tiger Cubs, black for the Bobcat badge, yellow for the Wolf badge, light blue for the Bear badge, and red for the Webelos badge. Add a ¼-inch stripe of gold or silver for each arrow point or Webelos compass point the boy has earned on top of the stripe that represents that rank.

Stain the 30-inch wood board and attach two cup hooks on the front to hold the arrow. Add the boy's name using permanent markers. Attach a hanger on the back.

GRADUATION PLAQUE

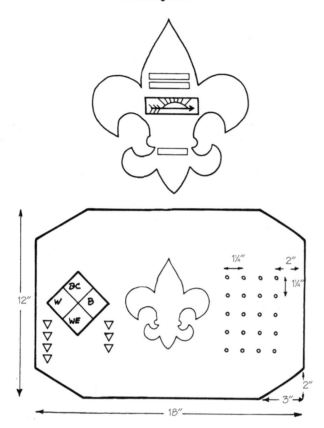

Materials:
- ½-inch plywood, 12 by 18 inches
- ¼-inch plywood, 5 by 5 inches
- Stain
- Gold paint
- Black paint or permanent marker
- Fine steel wool
- Picture hanger

Cut a plaque from the ½-inch plywood using the pattern shown. Stain and seal with clear lacquer or varnish. Cut the fleur-de-lis from the ¼-inch plywood and paint it gold. Tone down with fine steel wool. Drill or nail small holes for each activity badge the boy has earned. Glue on only the badges of rank and arrow points a boy has earned. Glue in the holes the activity badges the boy has earned. Add the boy's name, pack number, and date using black paint or permanent markers. Attach a hanger on the back.

ADD-A-BEAD NECKLACE

Materials: 30 inches of leather lacing, colored beads

Give each Cub Scout an add-a-bead necklace to wear to the pack meeting as a special and immediate recognition to take home with him. Use different colors of beads to symbolize attendance, advancement,

participation in pack and council events, etc. Feathers, eagle talons, and bear claws can have special significance, such as rank advancement. The Cub Scout can pick up the beads at the pack meeting to add to his necklace.

Add-a-bead necklaces work well for adults and den chiefs, too. Use the different colors of beads to represent attendance at pack activities, participation in training, awards earned in Scouting, tenure, the den advancing in rank, participation in service projects, leadership for district and council events, etc.

In the Public Eye

A strong, active Cub Scout pack has a story to tell, both within the pack family and to the larger community it serves. And if the pack hopes to remain strong and active, it's important that its story be told.

Good communication with the pack's parents is obviously essential because without their help the pack is bound to flounder. And telling the pack's story to the community—thus keeping it in the public eye—is an excellent method of attracting recruits.

PACK NEWSLETTER

Ideally, all the pack's parents will attend every pack meeting and keep abreast of what's going on and what's planned. But this isn't always the case, so monthly a pack newsletter is a good way to keep all pack families informed about activities and plans. You can also use the pack newsletter as an opportunity for giving boys who have advanced or done special Good Turns an extra measure of recognition by listing their names.

A pack newsletter doesn't have to be an elaborate, printed production—although with computers and desktop publishing, this is easier than it once was. But it also may be nothing more than a single typewritten sheet that has been photocopied. Every issue should include short articles covering coming events and names of boys who have advanced.

You may want to have dens contribute short articles on their activities for the month. Assign a different den member with the job of reporting each month.

Choose a pack committee member or parent to be newsletter editor, another to be typist, and a third to be the production person. Mail the newsletter to homes, or distribute it to families at pack or den meetings. (It may not be a good idea to give copies to boys to take home because they may lose, misplace, or forget them.)

Individual dens may want to have their own occasional newsletter, with all articles and production in the hands of the boys.

NEWS RELEASES

Pack activities are newsworthy. Newspaper editors and news directors of radio and television stations are interested in stories about unusual pack activities. Most newspapers don't have the resources to cover every event in every community, but they do appreciate getting factual information about especially interesting events. Neighborhood and small-town newspapers are more likely to print a story of this type than large city newspapers. But in either case, a news release, typewritten in the proper form, stands a better chance of being used than if you merely call the paper or turn in some haphazard notes.

Community-access cable TV offers another way to get your pack's story before the public. Some cable TV stations will also schedule dens or packs to produce their own TV shows.

Your pack event must compete with all the other activities that are going on in the community at the same time. If your activity has a unique angle, it is more likely that your event/news release will catch an editor's attention. Consider writing releases on such things as special service projects, special anniversaries, visits by well-known individuals, or unusual outdoor activities. But many newspapers will also use stories about recruiting drives and monthly pack meetings, with lists of boys who received awards.

First, check with an editor or broadcast news director to see whether the paper or station has a special format for news releases that you should follow. If not, follow these guidelines:

- **Timing is essential.** Deliver the news release well before the deadline. If the story is about an event that has already happened, it isn't news after a day or two.
- **The first paragraph** of a news release should catch the reader's attention. It should tell *who* did *what, when,* and *where.* Subsequent paragraphs should give further details. The least important information should be at the end of the story, so it may be cut if necessary for space.
- **Terminology.** Use correct titles, with capital letters as indicated: Cub Scout, Webelos Scout, den chief, Cubmaster, assistant Cubmaster, den leader, Webelos den leader. Always capitalize the word *Scouting.* (Note, however, that some publications will have their own style and may change your capitalization.)

- **When mentioning the pack for the first time** in the story, identify it as *Cub Scout Pack [number],* followed by the name of your chartered organization. In other paragraphs, refer to "the pack" (lowercase) or "Pack 10" (uppercase).
- **Always use the full names** of any individuals the first time they are mentioned in the news release. When only one or two Cub Scouts are mentioned (as for important awards), add the names of the parents/guardians. It is usually best not to include addresses, but if more than one town is involved, name them. Names of adult should include Scouting titles, if applicable.
- **Check with the editor** to find out whether you can use photographs, and if so, what the specifications are (size and type, etc.). If you furnish photos, try to get "action" shots, which are much more interesting than "head" shots or shots of people shaking hands. Identify all the people in the photo (left to right), giving their full names.

SCOUTING SHOWS

Your pack will want to be part of your council's (or district's) Scouting show, Scoutorama, or other exposition featuring Scouting. Getting involved will help pack families understand that they are part of the entire Scouting family—which includes Tiger Cubs, Boy Scouts, Varsity Scouts, and Venturers.

Your Cub Scouts will have a wonderful time participating. Scouting shows demonstrate to the public how Scouting serves youth and the community. Some councils hold Scouting shows each year, and others, every other year. Your pack will be informed in plenty of time and will probably be asked to provide a demonstration or exhibit. You may be assigned a booth or asked to make one.

The council will provide you with guidelines and suggestions. Here are some general tips as you prepare for a Scouting show:

- Boys should be well-trained and thoroughly familiar with the booth subject.
- They should be able to explain what they are doing, how, and why.
- Boys should be courteous and well-behaved.
- Boys should be in proper uniform (except when the subject of the booth calls for costumes).
- One boy can act as a barker to attract attention to your booth and help tell the story.
- Colorful, eye-catching backgrounds and decorations will draw people to your booth.
- Displays on the booth subject made by the boys add to its appeal and are sometimes an important factor in judging.

- Giveaways attract interest and attention. Give inexpensive prizes for participation in booth activities or games. Boys might also make craft items to give away.

- Don't sell anything at booths. The pack will earn profits from ticket sales.

- Action in the booth is important. If the boys are making a craft item, it should be simple and quickly made while spectators look on. Consider involving spectators in games and other activities.

- Each den is usually assigned a time to cover the booth. Be sure to let them know when, and what they are supposed to do.

- The den chief can help Cub Scouts in the booth while the den leader or other adults are nearby.

Types of Booth Activities

The type of booth activity will depend on the theme of the Scouting show, the criteria for judging, and the resources you have. A continuous demonstration, staffed by the boys and with plenty of action, is better than a static display. Here are some examples for booth demonstrations and activities:

Pinewood derby	Puppet show
Space derby	Kites
Bicycle safety	Skits
Costumes	Paper airplanes
Obstacle course	Physical fitness
Musical instruments	Soap carving
Beanbag toss	Turtle race
Woodworking	Bird feeders
American Indian crafts	Neckerchief slides
Model building	Block printing
Wolf, Bear, and Webelos advancement projects	Tossing games
	Masks
Cub Scout Academics and Sports	Leatherwork

Decorating the Booth

Crepe paper is one of the best materials for booth decoration. (Always use flameproof crepe paper!) It comes in many colors and can be stretched, twisted, fringed, crushed, scalloped, fluted, or ruffled. You can cover booth frames with sheets of crepe paper. Use colorful crepe paper twists, ruffles, or streamers to trim the booth.

Brown wrapping paper is also good for covering frames. Decorate it with paint, crayons, or markers before tacking or stapling it to the booth frame. Burlap or other inexpensive fabric is another type of frame covering. Lightweight posters and displays can be pinned to the fabric.

If sheet cardboard is available, use it to make sturdy booth sides. It is easily fastened to wooden booth frames with tacks or a staple gun. It can be painted with leftover latex wall paint, which adds both color and strength. Use a roller for painting large pieces. Add details over the latex with tempera or wide-line felt-tip markers. Attach signs and other lightweight displays to cardboard with tape, staples, or straight pins.

Foam board is another lightweight, strong siding for booths. Although more expensive than cardboard, it comes in many bright colors and has all the ease of cardboard. It can be cut into smaller sizes and mounted for booth signs, etc. Because it has a smooth surface and bright color, it may be better to use where there will be writing—the name of the booth or other display material.

Another alternative to wood for booth construction is PVC pipe, which has the advantage of being lightweight and easily portable. The joints and poles eliminate the need for hammer and nails, and the parts can be reused for other projects fairly easily. PVC can be painted just like wood, and siding can be glued or taped to the frame.

Be sure to include a large sign showing your pack number and the name of your chartered organization in bold letters. You may wish to post a chart showing the names of pack leaders and a duty roster of times when various dens staff the booth.

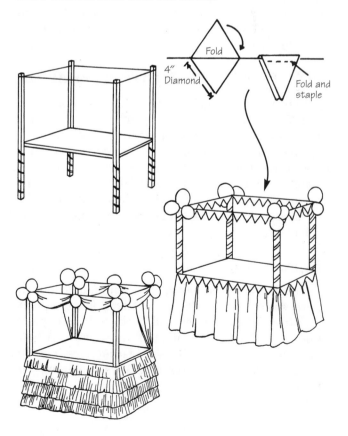

A Simple Booth

This quick-and-easy booth can be used for a pack circus or fair as well as a Scouting show.

Materials: Table, four sturdy posts or poles (6 to 7 feet long), wire or cord, crepe paper, stapler or tape

Tie or wire a pole to each table leg. Wind crepe paper strips around the poles. Tie a cord from pole to pole around the tops and decorate with paper flags or drapes. Balloons add color and can be tied together at the tops of the poles. Cover the lower part of the booth with crepe paper fringes or gathered fabric (such as an old sheet).

Boy Behavior

Positive behavior is a great responsibility and, sometimes, challenge for the den leader. It isn't easy—but it isn't impossible, either. Remember that each boy (just like all of us) has emotional needs that need to be fulfilled. These include the need to be accepted, to be noticed, to belong, to be praised and encouraged, to be safe and secure, to let off steam, to express himself, to experiment (and make some mistakes in the process!), and to have fun.

How each boy tries to fulfill these needs is what makes him unique. One boy may be timid and quiet, and another, loud and rowdy; but both are afraid they won't be accepted. Den leaders must plan ahead and be prepared to make Cub Scouting a positive experience for every boy and his family.

HOW TO ACHIEVE POSITIVE BEHAVIOR

The den meeting is a time when the den leader and Cub Scouts socialize, practice what they've learned at home, and plan for future activities. For the den meeting to be productive for everyone, it must run smoothly. A good atmosphere is essential to managing boys' behavior. Many times, that simply means recognizing and rewarding good behavior. Here are some suggestions for encouraging good behavior.

Expectations

Be sure that every boy and parent understands the purposes of Cub Scouting, the advancement system, the structure of the den and pack, and the expectations of both boy and parent in the program. A letter to parents with a follow-up face-to-face meeting within a couple of days of their son joining Cub Scouts will ensure this.

Code of Conduct

A code of conduct is a list of behavioral expectations and consequences if the code is broken. Boys, with the den leader's guidance, usually create it themselves. Three or four points will be sufficient, and they should be *positive;* the words *no* or *don't* have no place in a code of conduct. Include a final rule such as "Have fun!" Also consider including the 3 R's: Respect for others, Responsibility for yourself and your things, and Reasonable behavior. Boys should sign the code of conduct, and it should be displayed at every den meeting.

Two-Deep Leadership

A minimum of two registered adult leaders, or one adult and a parent of a participating Cub Scout—one of whom must be at least 21 years old or older—is required for all trips and outings. Two-deep leadership can also be invaluable in managing boys and their activities during den meetings. With two leaders, an energetic den can be divided into two groups, or one leader can work with a boy who is having difficulty keeping up or managing his behavior. Furthermore, a second adult provides another pair of hands when projects require adult help.

The Den Chief

The den chief is a wonderful tool for the success of a den. Although the den chief is not part of the two-deep leadership because he is not an adult, he can help manage the den by being prepared with a game, story, stunt, song, or other brief activity that provides some variety in the den program. See the *Cub Scout Leader Book* and *Den Chief Handbook* for more information on den chiefs.

Den Meeting Structure

Following the den meeting structure as outlined in the *Cub Scout Leader Book* and *Webelos Leader Guide* will go a long way to making a meeting run smoothly. Also, *Cub Scout Program Helps* and the *Webelos Leader Guide* both have detailed meeting plans for each month. Every part of the den meeting structure plays a vital role in the success of the meeting.

Leader/Boy Relationship

The relationship between a leader and the boys is central to managing the boys' behavior. For instance, if the den leader enjoys the den meeting, the boys will, too. The boys model what they see, so **be a good model** by having a positive attitude.

Be consistent and fair in all your dealings with boys. Treat them the same when they break any rules. But do this in a manner that allows a boy to keep his dignity. Give him a chance to tell his side of the story. Allow him the opportunity to apologize. He will be aware of and remember your kindness and caring. Your example of fairness will carry over into other aspects of the boys' lives.

Be a good listener. When a boy wants your attention, look him in the eye. If you are busy, look him in the eye and ask him to wait a minute. Honor his patient waiting by turning to him with your full attention as soon as possible.

Give each boy a chance to participate in discussions. To encourage boys to speak one at a time and to listen carefully, you might try a "talking stick," an American Indian tradition. Only the person holding the talking stick is allowed to speak, and everyone else must listen respectfully without interrupting. A talking stick can be a dead branch from a tree, a dowel rod, or even a shortened broomstick handle. Let the den members decorate the talking stick so that it represents them and they value it. Use markers, paints, or stickers to enhance the stick. Boys may want to hang feathers, beads, or shells on leather strips from their talking stick.

Talking Stick

When you notice a boy's good behavior, comment on it! Let him and the others in the den know exactly what you liked. Soon, you'll have all the den members copying that behavior. Comments such as "I like the way you did that," or "Good thinking," or "Now you have the hang of it" encourage and build self-esteem. The more specific you are, the more likely the communication has been effective and the activity will be repeated.

TRACKING BEHAVIOR

Keeping track of behavior helps a boy and his leader know how he is doing. Here are some suggestions.

Conduct Candle

Use the same candle each week. The denner lights the candle at the beginning of the den meeting, and the candle is allowed to burn as long as all den members show good behavior. But if a boy misbehaves or breaks the code of conduct, the candle must be blown out for the rest of the meeting. As soon as the candle burns down, the den is entitled to a special outing or special treat.

Tickets

Buy tickets at teacher or party supply stores, or make them yourself by hand or with the use of a computer. Give boys a ticket when they do something good. (Try to give each boy an opportunity to receive a ticket during a meeting.) They write their names on the back of their tickets. The tickets are placed in a jar, and a drawing is held at the end of the den meeting for a small treat (gum, candy, stickers, small toy, etc.). At the end of the month, hold a drawing for a "big" winner.

Marble Jar

Use a glass jar so it makes lots of noise when you put a marble in. Draw a line on the jar high enough so that it will take the boys six weeks or so to earn enough marbles to fill it to that point. Explain that when marbles reach the line, the den will get a treat. Drop a marble in the jar when someone in the den does something good. Make a production out of it. Celebrate with the den when they reach their goal.

Stickers and Certificates

Give big flashy stickers to boys for good behavior. Use them only occasionally, or they lose their appeal.

Make certificates by hand or with a computer. Use gold seals or other decorative stickers. You can also purchase certificates at teacher supply stores.

Super Star Pins

Decorate clothespins, one for each boy, with stars. As you notice a boy's good behavior, pin one on him. At the end of the meeting, boys with pins on can pick something from a "treat bag" filled with food items (candy, granola bars, popcorn, bags of chips or cookies, etc.) or inexpensive items that appeal to boys (baseball cards, small toys, pencils). Vary the items in the treat bag often.

Super Star Notes

These notes to parents are good for praising the boy when he gets back home. You can make your own by hand or with a computer or buy them at a teacher supply store. The boy will know you really appreciate it if you tell his parent how well he did.

Coup Stick

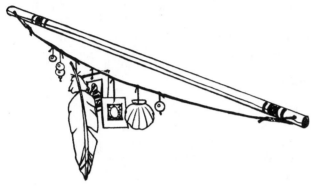

Some American Indian tribes used coup sticks ("coo sticks") as a way to display accomplishments. Items such as beads, feathers, bear claws, or eagle claws were awarded at tribal meetings for deeds of note (not unlike badges Cub Scouts earn!). These were attached to the coup stick for display, bringing honor to the coup stick owner.

Make a den coup stick by drilling a hole through a wooden dowel at the top and bottom. Loop a long piece of heavy-duty string or leather cord through the holes so it runs the length of the dowel. Award small items at den meetings for good behavior. Use beads, feathers, stamped leather pieces, stamps on poster-board pieces, etc., and attach them to the string on the coup stick. Take the coup stick to pack meetings to bring honor to your den!

LEADER SURVIVAL KIT

At times, even the best plans go awry. A bag packed as a leader survival kit comes in handy when chaos has erupted, all your planned activities for the meeting have been exhausted, or the den just needs a change of pace. Your survival kit will grow as you and your den work together and discover the things the boys like best—you will base your survival kit on those activities. The goal is to pack your bag with lightweight, multiple-use objects—and take it to every den meeting.

Here are some suggestions for your leader survival kit. Remember that each item should have multiple uses. Newspapers, for example, can be rolled and taped to become bats or batons to pass during a relay; left flat, they can become a "base" for use during a game; opened, they can act as a dropcloth for messy projects; folded, they can become hats. Newspapers can also be torn and taped and shaped into instant costumes. Your imagination is the only limit.

- Balls—a couple of tennis balls and at least one soccer ball
- Blindfolds—at least two
- Safety pins
- Duct tape
- Newspapers
- Markers, pens, pencils, chalk
- Blank paper, various colors
- Lightweight rope
- Scissors
- Balloons
- Empty 16-oz. drink bottles with caps—at least six
- Magic tricks
- Puzzles
- *Cub Scout Leader How-To Book*

CONCLUSION

A den leader who can effectively manage the boys in the den is better prepared to help them to do their best. Every boy gets the opportunity to have a rewarding Cub Scouting experience filled with adventure, success, and lots of fun in a safe, positive environment.

2 CRAFTS

This chapter is filled with hours of craft fun for you and your Cub Scouts. Besides craft ideas and tips, you will find out how crafts can be used to build a boy's self-esteem, stretch a boy's creativity and imagination, and incorporate the purposes of Cub Scouting. These "boy-tested" crafts have been used successfully by dens and packs across the country.

Why We Use Crafts

As Cub Scouts work on craft projects, they not only learn to make useful items but also get valuable experience in using and caring for basic tools and materials, learning to follow directions, using their imaginations, and developing coordination and dexterity.

Crafts can help leaders develop the monthly theme in den and pack meetings and tie the activities of the whole month together. Craft projects can be used for advancement requirements or just for fun.

Making his own craft project calls for creativity in each boy. As he embarks on his project, he may need to measure, trace a pattern, cut or saw, sand, and assemble a project with nails, screws, or glue. Crafts develop boys' ability to understand and satisfy their urge to experiment. Furthermore, physical development and mental growth are by-products of the craft program. Muscle coordination comes from lifting, moving, sawing, drilling, hammering, and pounding. Painting helps improve arm and hand control. Folding, cutting, shaping, filing, and sanding craft materials help develop eye and hand coordination.

As boys work with crafts, they learn to shape materials into useful articles. While decorating them, they also learn that useful things can be beautiful art. They gain confidence to experiment with materials and tools and learn new ways to do things. A completed craft project enables each boy to shout out "I did my best!"

Teaching Crafts to Cub Scouts

The leader's job is to stimulate each boy's interest and curiosity and to encourage him to *try*. It is important to allow the boy to create and be proud of his creation. He is making more than just "things"; he is building his mind, body, and future.

All Cub Scout leaders have different backgrounds and experiences, so their knowledge of craft techniques and tools will vary. Those with limited experience may enlist parents and other adults to teach specific techniques or to provide materials and tools.

The *Cub Scout Leader Book* provides some excellent tips for leaders working with boys on craft projects. In addition, the following steps will help leaders teach crafts:

1. Choose a project with the help of the boys. Make sure the project is something that has a purpose and that they will enjoy making.

2. Make a pattern, if needed. Have enough pattern pieces available so that boys don't have to wait to trace them.

3. Make a sample to show the boys, but remember: These are age-appropriate crafts for boys, so don't go overboard and make your sample too elaborate.

4. Gather enough materials and tools so everyone can work at the same time.

5. Teach the craft step by step:
   - Cut out parts, as required.
   - Put them together.
   - Finish it (sand, polish, paint, etc.).
   - Clean up.

6. Whenever possible, start a craft in a den meeting that boys can finish at home with family help. Be sure, however, that the family is aware of the responsibility and has any instructions and materials necessary.

7. Display the craft projects at a pack meeting.

Leaders should guard against crafts that are simply "busywork" of the "cut-and-paste" type that are below the boys' abilities and interests. Crafts should be more than mere handwork: They should be a creative outlet and a form of expression, as well as a way to learn skills. By relating crafts to the monthly theme, you give each boy a chance to live a new dream each month and to create the costumes, props, and other items to help make that dream a reality.

Sometimes, leaders think they need to have a craft project at every den meeting. But remember that crafts are only one of many activities used to accomplish the purposes of Cub Scouting. Overemphasizing crafts may discourage boys whose interests and abilities lean in other directions.

MEASURING RESULTS

Adults judge their own projects differently from boys. Adults judge the excellence of the workmanship and the quality of the project. This is because adults have had more time to develop skills, manual dexterity, and knowledge. A boy does handicrafts for fun. His effort should be measured by his own standards. Leaders and parents need to see the boys' efforts through the eyes of a Cub Scout–age boy. This requires understanding, patience, and a willingness to invest time in working with boys. Each boy is expected to do his best, and each boy's best is different.

To help measure the value and success of den and pack craft projects, ask yourself the following questions:

- Are the boys learning things that will be helpful to them later?
- Do the craft projects reflect the interests and abilities of Cub Scout–age boys?
- Do the den and pack craft projects help create the opportunity for more family activity?
- Do the boys enjoy working on crafts?
- Do they have adequate working space, tools, and materials?
- Are the boys given an opportunity to use their own initiative and imagination in planning and making projects?

HELPING THE BOY

- Encourage the natural creative urge in each boy. If you don't, the urge may disappear and be replaced by lack of confidence in his own abilities.
- Through praise, you can help the boy build self-confidence in his abilities.
- Learning by doing is important.
- Show enthusiasm for the boy's progress. Don't be overly critical.
- Show him *how*—but don't lose patience and take a tool away from him because you can do it better or faster. This will discourage him and destroy his self-confidence.
- Be patient. Remember: Boys may have to be shown over and over how to use a tool.
- Be tactful. Offer your help during difficult parts of a job by saying, "Let's work on this part together."

Resources for Craft Materials

Materials for crafts should be simple and inexpensive. In most cases, you can find scrap materials for crafts around the home.

Most communities have many resources for craft materials. Although you may have to purchase some specialized items at craft and hobby stores, you can acquire most through salvage and surplus or donation. Check telephone directories and begin looking for places where you might be able to obtain aluminum foil, burlap, canvas, clay, cord, floor covering, leather and vinyl scraps, nails, paper bags, plastic rope, sandpaper, spools, etc.

Here's a "starter" list of possible resources for craft materials. Most of the sources listed have scrap that is available for the asking, or at minimal cost. Keep your eyes and ears open for the endless list of "beautiful junk" available for recycling into Cub Scout crafts.

- **Lumber Company:** Wood scraps, sawdust, and curls of planed wood may be given away by the boxload. Make your contact and request, and then leave a marked box to come back for later.
- **Grocery Stores:** Check grocery stores for boxes of all sizes and shapes. Discarded soft drink cartons are excellent for holding paint cans.
- **Telephone Company:** Empty cable spools make great tables; use old telephones as props for skits; use colorful telephone wire for many different projects.
- **Soft Drink Company:** Plastic soft drink crates may be available at a minimal charge. Use them for storage or for projects. Also, use plastic six-pack rings for various projects.
- **Ice Cream Stores:** Use empty 3-gallon cardboard containers for wastebaskets and storage.
- **Medical Laboratories:** Look for clean paraffin and tongue depressors.
- **Gas Stations and Garages:** Tires and bike tubes are great for games and obstacle courses.
- **Wallpaper Stores:** You'll find wallpaper sample books of discontinued patterns.
- **Carpet Stores or Outlets:** Discontinued rug samples and soft foam underpadding can add to craft projects.

- **Tile Stores:** Use broken mosaic tiles for many craft projects.
- **Appliance Stores and Furniture Stores:** Large packing crates are handy for skit props and puppet theaters.
- **Newspaper Companies:** Ask about end rolls of newsprint.
- **Printing Companies:** You can never have too much scrap paper and cardstock.
- **Pizza Restaurants:** Cardboard circles are good for making shields and other craft projects.
- **Upholstery Shops and Drapery Shops:** You'll find a wide variety of fabric and vinyl scraps.
- **Picture Framing Shops:** Leftover mat boards make great awards or bases for other projects.

USING SALVAGE

Many items that are destined for the trash can be used for Cub Scout craft projects. Ask families to be on the lookout for scrap materials. If you live in a community that has a manufacturing company nearby, you may be surprised at the scrap wood, plywood cutoffs, and odd pieces of metal, cardboard, leather, and plastics that you can get just by asking. Ask families to save things such as tin cans; the cardboard rolls inside paper towels, toilet paper, and wrapping paper; boxes; tree branches; plastic bottles; buttons; cloth; pinecones; and wire hangers.

Here's a partial list of useable scrap materials:
- Bottle caps—for Christmas tree ornaments, foot scrapers, wheels, construction projects, markers for games
- Bottles—for musical instruments, containers
- Broom handles—as dowels for projects
- Cardboard cartons—for construction projects, stage props, puppet stages, storage
- Catalogs—for decorations, designs, cutouts
- Clothespins—for human figures, fastening items together, games
- Coat hangers—for wires for mobiles and other constructions, skeletons for papier-mâché work
- Coffee/juice cans—for storage, planters, games
- Coloring books—for patterns for name tags, etc. Patterns can be enlarged for craft projects.

- Corrugated cardboard—for stage props and scenery, bulletin board, shields, swords
- Ice cream cartons (3-gallon)—for trash cans, drums, masks
- Ice cream spoons—for mixing paint, spreading paste, figures
- Jars—for containers for paint, paste, and brushes; decorate them for gifts.
- Juice-can lids—for tin punch projects, awards
- Leather or vinyl scraps—for key chains, bookmarks, neckerchief slides, coin purses
- Macaroni—for stringing for jewelry, pictures, and frames
- Margarine tubs—for storing small objects (lids can be used like flying saucers in games)
- Newsprint—for covering tables, papier-mâché, flip chart, growth charts, large backgrounds and scenery
- Old shirts or pajama tops—for paint smocks (cut off the sleeves), costumes
- Paper bags and old socks—for hand puppets
- Paper plates—for plaques, masks, games
- Paper towels—for papier-mâché, clean up
- Pipe cleaners—for simple sculptures
- Plastic water bottles and milk jugs—for planters, games, costumes
- Shelf paper—for finger painting
- Soap bars—for carving
- Sponges—for painting, printing, clean up
- Straws—for holiday decorations, party favors, games
- Tin cans—for metal work, storage containers, planters
- Tongue depressors and craft sticks—for mixing paint, modeling tools
- Wallpaper—for book covers, paper for painting
- Wrapping paper—for murals, painting
- Yarn—for hair for wigs and puppets, holiday ornaments

How-To Tips

TIPS FOR PAINTING

Acrylics: Jar acrylic is more economical, but acrylic paint is also available in tubes. It can be thinned with water. Brushes clean easily with water. Acrylics are nontoxic, good for painting almost anything, and don't need a finishing coat.

Tempera: Water-based paints such as tempera are great for Cub Scouts. Powdered paint is more economical but messier. Mix powdered tempera with water and add a little liquid starch, which helps the paint go further and not run.

Cleaning Brushes: Different paints need different cleaners. For tempera, poster paint, or acrylics, use water. The boys can clean up after using these paints; adults should supervise cleanup for other media. To clean varnishes, oils, or enamels, use turpentine, mineral spirits, or kerosene. For shellac, use shellac thinner. For model paint, use the recommended thinner. For lacquer, use lacquer thinner. These solvents are flammable and should be used outside and well away from sparks and flames. *Adequate ventilation is required when working with any of these paints or solvents.*

Finishing Coats: Objects painted with tempera or poster paint will have a dull finish and will not resist moisture. For a shiny finish and for protection, spray with clear plastic or clear varnish, or finish with a coat of diluted white glue. Acrylic paint does not need a finishing coat.

Paintbrush Substitutes: For large items such as scenery, use a sponge dipped in tempera. For small objects, use cotton swabs.

Painting Plastics: For painting plastic milk containers or bottles, mix powdered tempera with liquid detergent instead of water or starch. The paint will adhere better.

Painting Plastic Foam: Some types of paint will dissolve plastic foam, so only use one that is recommended. Test it first on a scrap.

Painting Wood: It is best to give raw wood a coat of wood sealer or thin shellac before painting to prevent the paint from soaking into the wood.

Spray Painting: A spray bottle works well for spray-painting large items. Use diluted tempera or poster paint. If using commercial spray paints, be sure to read the label and follow any instructions

TIPS FOR ADHESIVES

- To save money, buy white glue in quart sizes and pour into small glue containers for the boys.
- To make heavy-duty glue, mix cornstarch with white glue until the mixture is as thick as desired.
- For small glue jobs, put glue in bottle caps and let boys use toothpicks or cotton swabs.
- Clear silicone is the best glue for plastic bottles and milk containers. It is available at hardware stores and requires adult supervision.
- Egg white is a good adhesive for gluing kite paper. It is strong and weightless.
- Tacky white glue is the best adhesive for plastic foam. A little goes a long way.
- Wheat paste (wallpaper paste) is a good paste for papier-mâché. Flour and water make a good paste too.
- Masking tape and cellophane tape can be used successfully in many projects.

MORE TIPS

- **Stuffing for Puppets:** Use plastic bags or old nylon stockings.
- **Cutting Plastic Foam:** Some types can be cut with a serrated knife or an electric carving knife. *Please note that adults should perform this procedure.* On heavier types, adults might use a coping saw or jigsaw.
- **Punching Holes in Plastic:** Use an awl or hole punch. A leather punch will work on most vinyl. *Adult supervision is mandatory.*

Theme Crafts

Consider each monthly theme for its craft possibilities. In addition to the ideas found in this book, *Cub Scout Program Helps,* the *Webelos Leader Guide,* and monthly roundtables are loaded with ideas. If the projects are fun, the boys will want to do them.

A leader may suggest wide project areas and give the boys greater freedom of choice and an opportunity to use their imaginations. For example, the theme "Things That Fly" might produce kites, gliders, planes, boomerangs, or even flying insects. Ask a boy what knights remind him of and you'll have everything from slaying dragons to building castles. If boys have an opportunity to talk about a theme and what they would like to make, they will come up with lots of good ideas. And boys will have more fun making something they thought of themselves.

During some months, all boys in the den and pack may be working on the same things, such as when the pack is preparing for a pinewood derby, raingutter regatta, or space derby. The cars, boats, and rockets for those events, however, are youth-adult projects, and boys don't work on them during den meetings. During these times, boys could work on decorations for the event.

Theme crafts may include costumes, ceremony boards, game equipment, props for skits, gifts, decorations, toys, inventions, conservation projects, nature items, and more. The following list will give you some ideas on general theme topics. You'll find details for many of the ideas throughout this book.

FITNESS
- Fitness equipment
- Beanbag toss
- Puddle jumpers
- Fitness chart
- Stilts

SPACE/FUTURE
- Rockets
- Space shuttle model
- Flying saucer
- Launching pad
- Robot
- Radarscope
- Space station model
- Star map

TRANSPORTATION
- Pinewood derby car
- Pushmobile
- Airport
- Glider
- Model train
- Cubmobile
- Model cars
- Model planes
- Helicopter

WATER/BOATS
- Model boats
- Water wheel
- Waterscope
- Raft

HEALTH/SAFETY
- Posters
- Home fire escape plan
- Emergency road signal
- Traffic signs
- First aid kit
- Nutrition chart or Food Guide Pyramid

KNIGHTS
- Costumes
- Family crest
- Banners/flags
- Castle model
- Teeterboard jousting
- Dragon

PIONEERS
- Costumes
- Homemade soap
- Homemade butter churn
- Puppets
- Quill pen and ink
- Model fort
- Old-time games

FAIR/CIRCUS
- Midway games
- Performer costumes
- Animal costumes
- Musical instruments
- Masks
- Puppets
- Noisemakers
- Prizes
- Banner/flags

NATURE
- Birdhouses
- Bird feeders
- Insect net
- Terrariums
- Bird treats
- Box garden
- Collection boxes
- Plaster casts
- Leaf prints
- Ant farm

SCIENCE
- Inventions
- Electric games
- Barometer
- Rain gauge
- Science projects
- Telegraph
- Electric buzzers
- Weather vane

COMMUNICATIONS
- Tin can telephone
- Secret codes
- Telephone directory cover
- Telegraph
- E-mail directories

Safety Rules for the Use of Tools

What is safe for one Cub Scout may be unsafe when two or more Cub Scouts are around. Any workshop must have rules governing the use of tools. Den tools include scissors, markers, low-temperature glue guns, and other craft items—not just hammers and saws.

Because accidents are usually caused by the improper use of tools, take time to teach each boy the right way to use a tool and how to take care of it. Remind him that cleaning up and putting away tools and materials are part of the job. Make sure tools and materials are easy to reach and replace.

- An adult should be present when a Cub Scout uses any type of tool.

- Use each tool for the job it is made for and the way it was intended to be used. (So, for instance, never use a screwdriver to pry or pound.)

- Never use a tool with a dull cutting edge, dull bit, or loose part.

- Most accidents occur to the hands, face, or feet. Protect the eyes. Keep fingers and hands away from the cutting edges of tools. Secure or clamp down wood that is being worked on.

- Be patient and never use force. Don't work with tools when you are tired; you need to be alert.

- Don't wear loose clothing or jewelry, which can be caught in moving parts.

- Keep the work area clean, dry, and well-lit.

- Never use electrical tools (such as a low-temperature glue gun) in damp or wet locations. *Note: It is best to use only simple hand tools and avoid power equipment when working with Cub Scout–age boys.* Adults, however, might wish to use a power tool to precut pieces of a project for younger Cub Scouts.

- Use only heavy-duty extension cords. Don't use the type of extension cord that is intended for small appliances.

- If an electrical cord has a plug with three prongs, you should plug it into a three-hole receptacle (outlet). If you use an adapter on a two-hole outlet, you must attach the adapter wire to a known ground (the screw in the middle of the outlet coverplate).

- Don't abuse tool cords by carrying tools by the cord or by pulling a plug by yanking on the cord. If the cord is frayed, don't use the tool until the cord is repaired.

- Adults should unplug all electrical tools when they are finished and put them out of reach of children. Don't leave any tool unattended. *Remember: Power tools are not to be used by Cub Scout–age boys.*

- Adults who choose to use power tools should always unplug electrical tools when changing saw blades, drill bits, or other attachments.

- Keep tools sharp, clean, and oiled.

Enlarging Patterns

You can enlarge the patterns found in this book and elsewhere as needed. The easiest way to enlarge patterns is to make a copy on a commercial copy machine and enlarge by the desired percentage.

Several types of projectors also will make enlargements. To use an overhead projector, trace over the design you wish to enlarge, using thin plastic (such as notebook page protectors) and the special marking pens designed for use on plastic. Place the plastic sheet on the overhead projector "bed," and you can enlarge it to almost any size. This is especially helpful in making posters and other wall hanging–sized drawings.

Tracing of original small drawing on 1-by-1-inch grid.

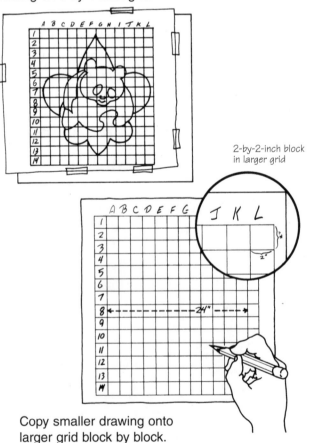

2-by-2-inch block in larger grid

Copy smaller drawing onto larger grid block by block.

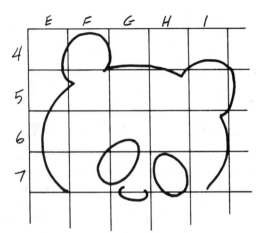

Portion of larger grid showing how to sketch block by block.

ENLARGING PATTERNS BY HAND

Here's a good method for enlarging patterns by hand. Use a ruler, tracing paper, pencil, and these simple directions:

1. Place tracing paper over the design you want to enlarge. Mark the design's outer limits.

2. Using these limits as guides, draw parallel horizontal and vertical lines on the paper to create a grid. With a ruler, make the lines the same distance apart (depending on the size and detail of the pattern).

3. Letter each top square; number them down the left side.

4. Tape the grid over the original design and trace the pattern onto the grid.

5. Decide how much of an enlargement you need. Draw another grid with larger squares to the total width and length of the new pattern. Letter and number the new grid in the same manner.

6. Copy the lines of the pattern into their exact positions in each square of the larger grid.

Managing Den Supplies

Boys will take pride in a meeting place that is consistently well-organized. You'll find that craft tools and items can easily get out of hand, so a den craft storage box is a good idea—both for organization and so that needed craft items are always available. Fill it with feathers, paper plates, puzzles, table tennis balls, tennis balls, balloons, assorted buckets and jars, paper bags, straws, and string. Also keep glue, scissors, markers, beads, and other craft items on hand. Make pencil cans from frozen orange juice or other similarly sized cans and keep them in the den craft storage box.

You can make craft storage boxes out of any material as long as they meet your needs. Sort craft materials by using an egg carton. A heavy-duty cardboard box that 10 reams of paper come in is also excellent for storage. Cut handholds, and then paint or cover with colorful adhesive-backed paper if desired. Another favorite is a plastic fishing tackle box.

HANDY TOTE BOX

This sturdy box will carry a lot of weight. Make it from two identical cardboard cartons.

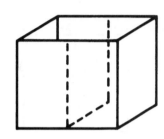

Cut one box in half, along sides and bottom. Turn pieces so that open sides are on the outside and uncut sides are touching. Tape together.

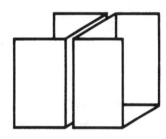

Cut out an opening for handle through both sections.

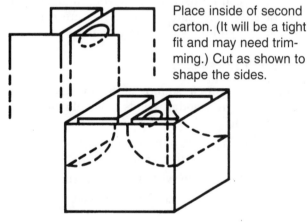

Place inside of second carton. (It will be a tight fit and may need trimming.) Cut as shown to shape the sides.

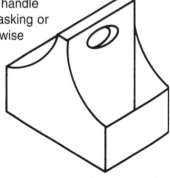

Finish cut edges where the two boxes meet and around handle hole by covering with masking or duct tape. Paint or otherwise decorate as desired.

PERSONAL STORAGE BENCH

Each boy could have his own storage bench for pencils and crayons, incomplete projects, etc. Make from 1-inch shelving as shown in the illustration. Each boy and an adult can build and decorate one in their own style. This can be the boy's seat at den meetings as well as holding his tools and materials. And these benches will stack for easy storage.

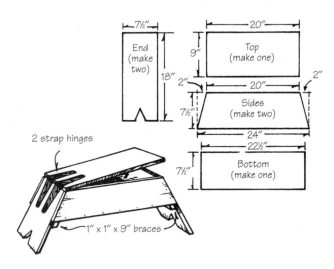

Paper Crafts

Paper can be a great medium for simple craft projects. These can be used for gathering times or filler time, or as a den craft project. They are easy and inexpensive, and boys will enjoy them.

PINWHEEL

Materials: **5-inch square of heavy paper, long heavy pin, two wooden beads, two plastic disks, dowel or pencil**

1. On a 5-inch square of heavy paper, draw diagonal lines from corner to corner as shown.

2. Cut on the lines to within ¼-inch of the center.

3. Punch holes in the center and the corners.

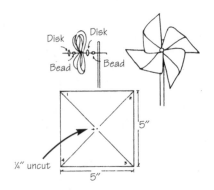

4. Put the following on the heavy pin (or a thin nail) in this order: plastic disk, wooden bead, the pinwheel corners in the order they are numbered, center of pinwheel, plastic disk, and wooden bead.

5. Push or tap the pin through the dowel or pencil.

BALOO AND KAA PAPER PROJECTS

Make the Baloo finger puppet and Kaa hanger from heavy cardstock. Enlarge the patterns as needed, and run off one pattern per boy on a copy machine or trace on posterboard. Boys can cut out and color and decorate as they want. Decorate Kaa with stripes, spots, and diamond patterns. Cut out finger holes for Baloo's "legs" (younger boys may need help cutting out the finger holes).

WINDSOCK

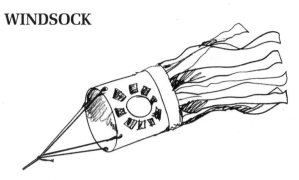

Decorate this windsock to fit any theme. Use blue streamers on gold paper for the blue and gold banquet, or red and white streamers on blue paper for a patriotic theme.

Materials: **4-by-16-inch paper, crepe paper streamers cut into 3-foot lengths, four pieces of string or yarn 12 inches long**

1. Boys decorate paper using markers, crayons, or stickers, leaving a ¼-inch edge.
2. Make a cylinder with the paper, securing with transparent tape.
3. Tape, glue, or staple streamers around the bottom edge of the cylinder.
4. Punch four evenly spaced holes around the top.
5. Tie one end of the strings through each hole, and tie the other ends together to make a hanger for the windsock.

KWANZAA MKEKA

Kwanzaa is a nonreligious holiday celebrated at the end of the year during which African Americans reflect upon their heritage, families, and communities. One of the symbols of Kwanzaa is the *mkeka,* or mat. Although preferably made out of straw, this woven paper mat will also fulfill its purpose.

Materials: **10 strips of black construction paper, 2 by 24 inches; four strips each of dark yellow, deep red, and forest green construction paper, 2 by 22 inches; transparent tape; clear contact paper**

1. Lay the black paper strips next to each other on a flat work surface.
2. Run a piece of tape along the edge of the right side to tape the strips together.
3. Using the colored strips (the traditional colors of Kwanzaa), weave back and forth through the black base, one color at a time, alternating colors in any order.
4. Pull the ends of the color weaves to make the edges straight.
5. Run a second piece of tape along the left side to hold the strips in place.

6. Cover the front and back of the mat with clear contact paper.

PAPER AIRPLANE PROJECTS

Paper airplanes are simple and always fun. An excellent resource for flying crafts that use no glue or cutting is *The Gliding Flight: 20 Excellent Fold and Fly Paper Airplanes,* by John Collins (Ten Speed Press, 1989).

A Catapult Glider

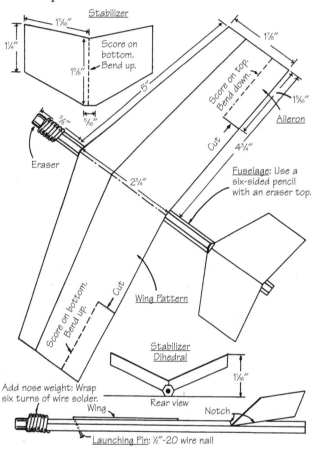

This glider will take some time to make, but it will be lots of fun and worth the effort.

Materials:
    New six-sided pencil with eraser
    Stiff cardboard (cereal box sides or posterboard)
    ½-inch wire nail
    7 inches of ³⁄₃₂-inch-diameter wire solder
    Model cement or craft glue
    5-inch length of another pencil or piece of dowel
    One or two heavy rubber bands

1. Enlarge the pattern to the size indicated and trace onto the cardboard.

2. Cut out the wing and stabilizer. For more accurate cutting, use a modeler's knife. Guide the cuts using a metal ruler as a straight edge.

3. Notch the pencil 2 inches from the end. Score the bottom of the stabilizer on the centerline and bend up. Insert the stabilizer into the notch. Check that the tips of the stabilizer wings are 1¾₆ inches from the bottom edge of the pencil.

4. Insert the launching pin (the ½-inch wire nail) on the bottom of the pencil about 1½ inches from the eraser end.

5. To add weight to the nose, wrap it with about six turns of wire solder.

6. Cut and score the ailerons at both ends of the wing. Glue the wing to the top of the fuselage (pencil).

7. To make a launching rig, notch the small pencil or piece of dowel to hold the rubber band or bands.

8. To fly the glider, attach to the launching rig, aim high, and let it go! If the glider dives out of its glide, remove some solder. If it stalls (repeatedly swoops up, dives, and then swoops up again), add solder. Hold a glider contest to see whose glider goes the farthest!

Helicopter Wing

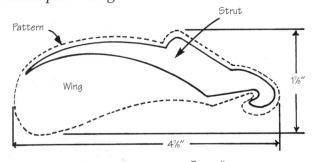

Strut

Pattern

Wing

1⅛″

4⅞″

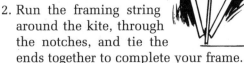

Paper clip

Materials: **Thin cardboard (from file folder or posterboard), tissue paper, paper clip, ¾-inch-wide transparent sticky tape, rubber band**

1. Enlarge the pattern to the size indicated.

2. Trace the wing strut on the thin cardboard and cut it out.

3. Place the strut on the tissue paper. Cover completely with 6-inch strips of sticky tape, overlapping them by ¹⁄₁₆ inch. Be sure to press down firmly to ensure a good bond.

4. Make a pattern for the wing and trace its shape onto the tissue paper. Cut it out.

5. To fly the helicopter wing, slide a paper clip onto the wing. You may hand-launch the wing or shoot it into the sky with a rubber band.

KITE PROJECTS

Besides being fun, successful kite building and kite flying give boys a feeling of competence. Don't worry about flaws in workmanship; in a simple kite, they won't make much difference. Refer to Elective 5, "Spare-Time Fun," in the *Wolf Cub Scout Book* for more information about kites. Also see the chapter "Special Pack Activities" in this book for kite derby ideas and kite safety rules.

Two-Stick Flat Kite

Materials: **Wrapping paper, strong plastic, or cloth; ⅛-by-⅜-inch stick, 36 inches long; ½-by-⅜-inch stick, 30 inches long; white glue or rubber cement; at least 100 feet of kite string**

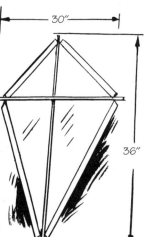

30″

36″

1. Notch the sticks in the ends for framing strings. Tie the sticks together at right angles.

2. Run the framing string around the kite, through the notches, and tie the ends together to complete your frame.

3. Measure and cut the frame cover (wrapping paper, plastic, or cloth) with a 1-inch overlap all around, except at the sticks, as shown.

4. Lay the frame over the "skin" and fold all the flaps over the frame. Check for fit. Glue down one flap at a time.

5. The lengthwise bridle string should be about 40 inches long; the crosswise string, about 34 inches long.

6. For a tail, tie 4-by-6-inch tissue paper bows about 6 inches apart on an 8-foot string.

7. If the kite dances too much or is too sluggish, add or reduce the length of the tail to correct the kite's flight.

Tissue Paper Kite

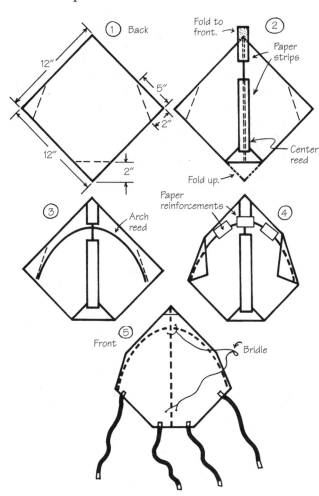

Materials:
- 12-by-12-inch tissue paper square and scraps
- Four 2-inch-by-5-foot strips of crepe paper
- Rubber cement (or egg white)
- Matchstick-thick bamboo reed
- Scissors, pencil, ruler
- 22-inch lightweight string (bridle)

1. Cut the bamboo reed into two pieces, one 22 inches long and the other 15 inches long.

2. Crease the 12-by-12-inch square of tissue paper on the broken lines as shown in illustration 1.

3. Glue the 15-inch center reed in place by covering with a strip of scrap tissue paper. Trim the reed if necessary. Glue the bottom flap up over the center reed and a narrow strip of paper over the tip, folding the corners of this strip to the front to act as reinforcement (see illustration 2).

4. Measure and cut the reed for the arch to fit as shown in illustration 3. Be sure the reed is strong, with a good natural curve.

5. Glue the left and right corner flaps over the arched reed (illustration 4). For best results, glue on one side first and let it dry, and then glue the

other side, holding it taut until it dries. Glue paper reinforcements over the intersections of the reeds midway between the center and corners (illustration 4). Then turn over kite.

6. Tie the bridle string over the intersection of the bamboo reeds and then over the center reed 2 inches up from the base of the kite. Set the angle of the bridle by tying a loop in the string, as shown (illustration 5).

7. To find the correct flying angle, hold the kite by the bridle over a table. The center reed (spine) of the kite should be tilted upward at about a 15-degree angle from the horizontal. Add the four crepe paper tails as shown.

Star Kite

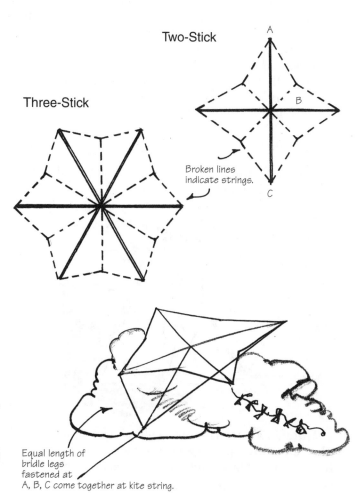

You can make two- and three-stick kites in a star shape as shown. The sticks are the same length. Tie them together and use string as shown. Glue on a paper cover. A tail, attached to one of the star points, is needed to balance these designs. Use a three-leg bridle and attach the kite line.

Kite Messenger

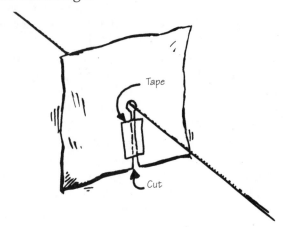

Tape

Cut

Cut a small hole in the center of a square of paper, with a slit to one edge, as shown. Slip the paper over the kite flying line and tape the slit shut. The wind will blow the messenger up the kite. To have a kite messenger race, all players send their kites up to a specific length of line—perhaps 50 yards. The messenger is then attached to the flying line and allowed to move up to the kite. The boy whose messenger reaches his kite first wins.

Hang Glider

This hang-gliding guy is easy to make, and boys will enjoy his antics in the wind.

Nose piece

Straw

Straws

Straws

Materials: Transparent cellophane tape; thin plastic food wrap; three plastic soda straws, ⅛-inch in diameter; plastic lid from margarine tub; cardstock or heavy paper

1. Trace the shape of the nose piece on the plastic lid. Cut out the nose piece and insert into three straws of equal length. The nose piece should fit tightly for better wing support and better flight.

2. Trace the pattern for the pilot onto heavy paper and cut it out. Fold the feet forward and the top down on the dotted lines as shown.

3. Make tape ringlets by folding a 2-inch piece of sticky tape lengthwise, sticky side out. Cut into ¼-inch rings.

4. Place two ringlets on each of the straws and one ringlet on the nose piece, as shown. Place the straws, ringlets down, onto the plastic food wrap. Cut around the straws as shown using a straight edge and blade, allowing about ¾ inch extra on all sides. Fold the extra width over the straws and tape down.

5. Attach the pilot to the center straw about 2 inches from the nose piece. Fly your kite and watch your hang glider fly!

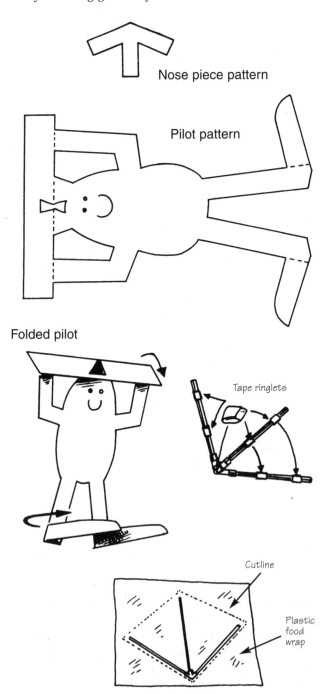

Nose piece pattern

Pilot pattern

Folded pilot

Tape ringlets

Cutline

Plastic food wrap

Papier-Mâché

Papier-mâché is a modeling material made by mixing wallpaper paste with absorbent paper, such as newspaper, paper towels, paper napkins, or tissue. Cub Scouts love the messiness of papier-mâché, and you shouldn't hesitate to tackle it because boys can make some useful items—such as trays, bowls, animals, figures, relief maps, napkin rings, masks, candleholders, and wastebaskets. Just spread around lots of newspapers for protection and cover the boys' uniforms with old shirts.

HOW-TO TIPS FOR PAPIER-MÂCHÉ

- When using papier-mâché on an object that needs to be removed after the papier-mâché dries (bowl, vase, etc.), first oil or grease the object so the dried papier-mâché shell will slip off easily. Petroleum jelly works very well.
- Count on a papier-mâché project lasting through several den meetings.
- Let objects air-dry when possible. Heat tends to make papier-mâché shrink and buckle.
- Sand objects for a smooth finish before painting. A final finish can also be made by covering with papier-mâché made from paper toweling.
- Painting papier-mâché: If using tempera paint, give the project an undercoat of gesso or thinned white latex paint first. Tempera-painted objects should be sprayed with a clear plastic finish or clear varnish for a protective overcoat. Acrylic paint does not require a base coat. You can also use household enamel or latex paint.

FRAMEWORK FOR PAPIER-MÂCHÉ

You will need some type of framework—such as chicken wire, cardboard tubes or cartons, coat hangers, or balloons—for working with papier-mâché. Make a small animal figure from a framework of newspaper rolls or cardboard rolls taped together. Use various sizes of balloons to make planets for a model solar system. Mold larger items over a framework of chicken wire bent and crushed to the desired shape.

STRIP PAPIER-MÂCHÉ

This method is good for making large masks and stage props.

1. Mix wallpaper paste according to package directions. (It should be the consistency of pea soup.)
2. Tear (don't cut!) newspaper strips about 1 to 1½ inches wide. The frayed edges will blend smoothly. Use wider strips for larger objects.
3. Dip the strips into the paste and run them through your fingers to remove excess paste.
4. Lay them over the framework, overlapping and in different directions. It is usually best to let each layer dry before applying another. You can use alternate layers of regular newspaper and colored comic strip paper so missed spots will show easily. The number of layers needed will depend on what you are making and how strong you need it to be. A final coat of torn paper towel strips will give an even textured surface for painting.
5. Place the object in a room where warm air circulates to let it dry.

WASTEBASKET

Materials: 3-gallon cardboard ice cream carton, waxed paper, newspaper and paste for strip papier-mâché, gesso (for undercoat if using tempera paint), paint

Set the carton on waxed paper. Completely cover it with papier-mâché strips, as described above. Also cover the inside of the carton. Only one or two coats are needed because the carton itself is sturdy. Let it dry completely. Sand any rough edges. Paint and decorate as desired.

VOTIVE CANDLE HOLDER

Here's a simpler version of papier-mâché.

Materials: Small glass jar, pieces of colored tissue paper, thin paste

Cover the jar with a thin layer of paste. Press layers of different colored tissue paper to cover the outside of the jar. Take care to keep the jar translucent so light can filter through when the candle is lit. Let the jar dry. Then place a votive candle inside and light it for soft, colorful light.

MASKS

Simple masks can dress up any skit.

Materials: **16-inch balloon, 36-inch-long heavy string, newspaper and paper towel strips, wallpaper paste**

1. Inflate the balloon. Tie a knot in the end and attach a string. Suspend the balloon by tying the string to an object inside or outside. Be sure it isn't near anything that will cause it to burst.
2. Cover the balloon with several layers of newspaper papier-mâché strips. Let it dry.
3. For an animal mask, add a framework for nose or ears at this time. Use a paper cup or cardboard roll for the nose, heavy cardboard for the ears. Use masking tape to fasten these to the papier-mâché–covered balloon, and then cover them with paper towel papier-mâché strips.
4. When the mask is dry, cut out a hole large enough so the mask fits over the head and remove the balloon. Cut eye holes in the proper position. Cut out a mouth or nose hole as needed. Also punch some smaller holes in the back for air.
5. Paint as desired. Add additional decorations, such as yarn hair, a hat, etc.

PIÑATA

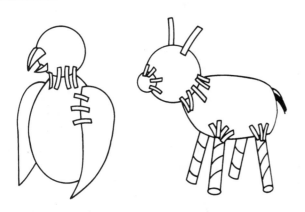

Piñatas are usually colorful animal shapes filled with candy or toys and broken open at holiday or birthday parties. For an entertaining awards ceremony, make an individual piñata from a 10-inch balloon for each boy. Put his award inside and let him break it open.

1. For the basic body, inflate a balloon and follow the directions above for making a mask. The type of animal or figure you are making will determine the size and shape of the balloons. Two or three layers of papier-mâché are adequate. Let dry.
2. Tape on additional balloons and cardboard pieces for head, legs, ears, wings, etc. Cover with two layers of papier-mâché.

3. Insert a bent clothes hanger as a hanger for the piñata. Cover with additional layers of papier-mâché to hold it in place, and then let it dry.
4. After the piñata is completely dry, cut a hole in the back to remove the balloon and add wrapped candy or party favors.
5. If desired, you can add a finishing touch of tissue paper curls. Fold 3-inch strips of colored tissue paper lengthwise and fringe as shown in the illustration. Hold several strips together and cut all at once. Turn the strips wrong side out so they will fluff up. Wrap these around the piñata, overlapping each row as you glue it on.

To use the piñata, hang it from a tree or other object so it swings freely. Blindfolded boys take turns hitting at the hanging piñata with a stick until it breaks and the goodies fall out. For an added challenge, hang the piñata from a cord or rope that someone can pull on so that the piñata moves up and down, making it harder to hit!

Printing

With some simple printing methods, boys can print holiday cards, party invitations, blue and gold banquet program covers, flags and banners, T-shirts, shields, table covers, and pictures. Only a few tools and materials are required.

Printing can be done on paper, paper bags, fabric, wood, and canvas using linoleum blocks, wood, wax, sponges, vegetables and fruits, stencils, silkscreen, crayons, and other items.

HOW-TO TIPS FOR PRINTING

- If the design is to be permanent, such as on a T-shirt or other fabric that will be laundered, use a fabric paint, oil-based paint, or ink. Acrylic paint will also work. Otherwise, use tempera paint or water-based inks.
- When printing T-shirts or other fabrics, be sure to place a newspaper pad between the front and back so the paint won't run to other parts of the fabric.

STAMP PAD

Make your own stamp pad by gluing felt to the bottom of a plastic foam tray (such as the kind cuts of meat are on when wrapped at the grocery store) and soaking the felt with vegetable dye or food coloring. Be sure to cover your clothing and work area, as some dyes stain.

RUBBINGS

This is one of the simplest printing methods. All you need is dark crayons, chalk, or pencil and thin paper

1. Find a surface with an interesting texture, such as leaves, tombstones, carved monuments, manhole covers, or tree stumps.
2. Hold or tape the paper over the surface and rub hard with the side of the pencil, crayon, or chalk.
3. Frame your rubbing with a piece of posterboard or construction paper, or put it in a scrapbook.

Another good rubbing material is a heavy, black, waxy mixture called *heelball,* available from shoe repair shops.

BLOCK PRINTING

Cub Scouts will enjoy making their own brands or family crests from these simple materials.

Materials: **Piece of craft foam or felt, printing ink or paint, block of wood, white glue, paper or fabric to print on**

1. Cover the work area with newspapers.
2. Draw a design on paper and trace it on craft foam or a piece of felt. Be sure that it will fit on the block of wood.

3. Cut out the design and glue it to the wood block. The design will print the reverse of what you see on the block, so if the design has lettering or a specific right and left, glue it to the block backwards. Let the glue dry.

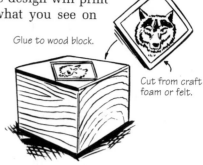

Glue to wood block.

Cut from craft foam or felt.

4. Press the block firmly onto an ink pad. Then press it firmly on paper or fabric.

POTATO PRINTS

You can also use carrots, turnips, lemons, oranges, and other vegetables and fruits for this simple printing method.

Materials: **Large potato, scratching tool (pencil, nail, toothpick), sharp-edged cutting tool (paring knife or pocketknife), paper for printing, tempera paint and paintbrush**

1. Cover the work area with newspapers.
2. Cut the potato in half so that each surface is flat.
3. Use the scratching tool to scratch a design on the potato or the cutting tool to cut out a design. Cut away all parts that you don't want to print. Blot the surface of the potato to remove excess moisture.
4. Brush the design with tempera paint. Stamp on a newspaper or paper towel to remove excess paint. If ragged edges appear on the first imprint, cut away any uneven parts of the potato that cause this.
5. Print the design on paper until it begins to fade, then add more paint and repeat.

SPONGE PRINTING

Materials: **Flat sponge about ½ inch thick, felt-tip marker, scissors, tempera paint, paper for printing**

1. Draw a simple design on the sponge with the marker. Cut the sponge into this shape.
2. Wet the sponge and then squeeze the water out thoroughly.
3. Dip the damp sponge in thin tempera paint and press it gently on the paper. The tiny holes on the surface of the sponge will not print, but the areas between the holes will leave an unusual design.

STENCILS

Experiment with your stencils on scrap paper before trying your finished project.

Materials: **Cardboard, sharp hobby knife or scissors, thick paint (acrylic, latex, heavy tempera, or tube oil paint), stiff bristle brush, paper or fabric to be stenciled**

1. To make the stencil more durable, give the cardboard three coats of shellac before using. Or make your own stencil paper by dipping bond paper in melted paraffin several times.
2. Trace a design on the cardboard or stencil paper. Cut it out with a sharp knife or scissors.
3. The paper or fabric surface to be stenciled should lie flat. The stencil should also lie flat so the paint won't spread under the edges. Fasten the stencil to the printing surface with tape or pins so it won't move.
4. Beginning on the stencil near the cutout edge, brush the paint, using a stiff brush, onto the fabric or paper. Brush away from the stencil edges so the paint won't run underneath.

Wire, Bead, and Plastic Crafts

FRAYED NERVE

Use this as a neckerchief slide or pencil topper.

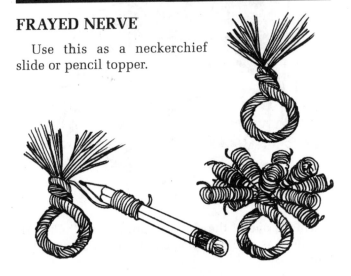

Materials: **Old telephone wire, wire strippers/ cutters, pencil**

1. Strip off the wire cover from the telephone wire so that you have small wires of different colors. Cut 12 pieces of 30-inch-long colored wire.
2. Hold the wires together and twist them in the middle.
3. Wrap the twisted part around your finger and twist the ends together.
4. Wrap each wire end around a pencil in a tight coil, and then gently slide the pencil out. Repeat until all wires are coiled.

HOW-TO TIP FOR WIRE CRAFTS

- Telephone wire comes in many colors. By stripping off the outer plastic covering, you'll find a pliable wire rainbow inside for your projects.

TRASH BAG APRON

This is one of those "Why-didn't-I-think-of-that?" crafts. Any time boys are working with messy materials, they can keep their uniforms clean with this easy apron and still have fun. Use heavy-duty trash bags, and you can reuse the aprons.

Materials: **Trash bag, scissors**

1. Fold the trash bag in half.
2. Cut a J shape from the closed end of the bag with the approximate dimensions shown.
3. Make two more cuts in the bag as shown, cutting from the bottom to make apron ties, and cutting around the J shape for the arms.
4. Wrap around the Cub Scout to help protect him from those messy, but fun, projects!

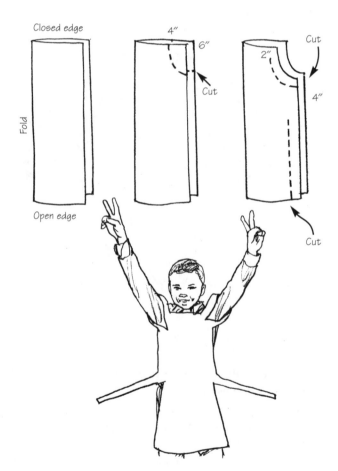

BEAD CRAFT FLAG

Plastic beads of all kinds have been used in Cub Scout crafts for years. Many patterns for bead animals and various shapes can be found commercially and on the Internet. Boys can wear this flag pin with pride.

Materials: **11 No. 2 safety pins, one gold chenille stem, 27 blue 3-mm "E" beads, 34 white 3-mm "E" beads, 29 red 3-mm "E" beads**

1. Open 10 safety pins and place the beads on them in the order shown. Close each pin once the beads are in place.
2. Put the chenille stem through the end loop of the remaining safety pin. Fold it in half and twist the tip to lock in place.
3. Feed the end loop of the beaded safety pins onto the chenille stem in the order shown. Make sure that the pins are all facing the same direction.
4. Feed the other end of the chenille stem through the top loop of the single pin as shown, and twist to lock in place. Pin your bead flag to your shirt and wear it with pride.

R = red bead; B = blue bead; W = white bead

Pin 1	Pin 2	Pin 3	Pin 4	Pin 5	Pin 6	Pin 7	Pin 8	Pin 9	Pin 10
B	B	B	B	B	B	B	R	R	R
B	W	B	W	B	W	B	W	W	W
B	B	W	B	W	B	B	R	R	R
B	W	B	W	B	W	B	W	W	W
B	B	B	B	B	B	B	R	R	R
W	W	W	W	W	W	W	W	W	W
R	R	R	R	R	R	R	R	R	R
W	W	W	W	W	W	W	W	W	W
R	R	R	R	R	R	R	R	R	R

STAINED "GLASS" SUN CATCHER

Materials: **Clear plastic lid and length of ribbon for each boy, black permanent marker, colored permanent markers**

1. Clean and dry the plastic lid.
2. Outline the desired drawing on the lid with the black marker.
3. On the opposite side, color with colored markers.
4. Punch a hole in the top and attach the ribbon as a hanger.

MOBILES

A mobile is a sculpture that moves. They are often made of balanced parts, wires, and cords connected such they move in the slightest breeze.

Cutout objects to hang on the mobile can fit the theme of the month, or use keepsakes, toy cars, table favors, driftwood, fishing lures, sports emblems, badges, or other items.

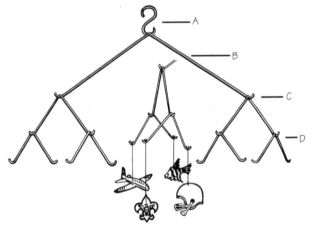

Materials: **Three wire coat hangers; cutouts (metal, cardboard, foil, wood, plastic) or other objects to be hung on the mobile; carpet thread, strong string, or fishing line; pliers; yardstick**

1. Open the coat hangers with pliers. Cut off the hook part of one hanger and use the pliers to form an S-shaped hanger *(A). Boys will need adult help for this step.*
2. Straighten all the coat hangers and cut a 36-inch length of wire from each.
3. Make arm *B* from one 36-inch length. Bend it in the middle as shown, and curve the ends up. To get both sides even, draw an outline of one bent side on a sheet of paper and use it as a pattern for the other side.
4. Cut a second length of wire into equal pieces and make arms *C.*
5. Cut a third length of wire into four equal parts and form arms *D.*

6. To assemble the arms, hang the **S** hook on the ceiling attachment from which the mobile will be hung. Hang arm *B* on the **S** hook. Then hang arms *C* on the ends of *B.* Hold the *C* arms steady while hanging arms *D* as shown.
7. Tie loops of thread or fishing line to the objects to be hung from the mobile. Make the loops various lengths, from 2 to 6 inches to give an interesting effect.
8. Hook the loops on the arm ends, one at a time. Hang about the same weight on each end so the arm will balance.

STRAW WEAVING

Use straw weaving to make neckerchief slides, belts, or shoulder sashes, depending on the amount of yarn used. Sucking the yarn through the straw will be the boys' favorite part, especially if you use clear plastic straws.

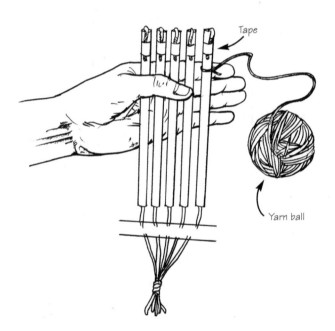

Materials: **Plastic straws; pieces of yarn, 1 yard long; small pieces of tape; ball of yarn about 6 yards long**

1. Tie the ends of five pieces of 1-yard-long yarn together in a knot.
2. Put the other end of each piece of yarn through a straw by inserting it into the straw and sucking gently. The yarn will slide through. Fold ½ inch of yarn over the end of the straw and tape it to hold.
3. Hold the straws in one hand as shown, with the end of the yarn ball tied to the straw on the outside edge.
4. Weave the ball of yarn back and forth through the straws. When you reach the edge, wrap the yarn

around the last straw and weave back the other direction. Repeat until the weaving is as long as you wish. (You can make longer weavings by tying on additional yarn.)

5. To finish, tie off the weaving yarn to the last straw. Slide the weaving onto the yarn below the straws. Cut the yarn and tie the ends in a knot.

SUMMERTIME CRAFTS

Summertime is fun time, and these cool summer crafts will add just the right cool touch.

Visor

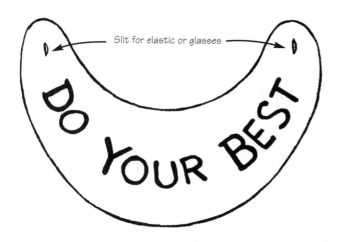

Materials: Heavy craft foam or cardstock, scissors

Enlarge the visor pattern as needed and cut out of craft foam or heavy cardstock. Decorate as desired. Make small slits as marked. For regular visors, insert narrow elastic through the slits and tie the ends together. Boys with glasses can slide the visor directly onto the arms of the glasses.

Beach Bag

Materials: 15 plastic six-pack holders, 4-inch pieces of yarn

1. Lay out the plastic six-pack holders as shown. The three six-pack holders in the center will make the bottom of the bag. The three holders above and below the center will make two sides, and the two holders to the right and left of the center will make two other sides. Attach yarn pieces as shown by the solid lines, looping the yarn through the plastic holder rings and tying

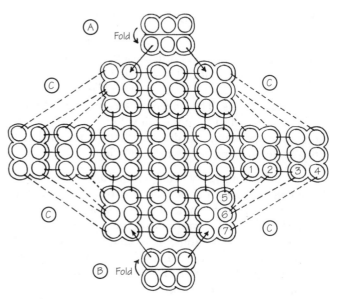

the ends together so that the open rings are linked.

2. Fold pieces A and B in half along the dotted lines as shown and loop yarn through both plastic rings and tie to the bag at the points indicated by the lines.

3. Fold up the sides to make a basket shape, tying rings 2 and 3 into ring 6 at the four points C of the diagram, as well as rings 4 and 7 and rings 1 and 5.

4. Tie all four corners of the bag together, looping the yarn through the plastic rings and tying the ends together with either a square knot or an overhand knot. Ties should be on the outside of the bag.

5. Decorate as desired, such as by attaching an art foam cutout of a yellow sun wearing orange sunglasses.

Cup Holder

Materials: Art foam, low-temperature glue gun

1. Cut a 4-by-10-inch piece of art foam. Roll in a cylinder shape, overlapping the edges ½ inch. Glue together using a low-temperature glue gun.

2. Place the end of the cylinder you just made on the art foam and draw around it. Cut out the circle and glue to the bottom of the cylinder.

3. Decorate as desired. (Decorate with the same art foam cutout you use on your beach bag for a matching pair.)

CLAY CRAFTS AND MODELING

It's a thrilling experience for young or old to twist and mold a pliable mass into a useful and decorative object. Modeling with clay or other materials gives Cub Scouts a chance to develop self-expression in three dimensions. They become aware of symmetry, texture, curve, and line; they develop a sense of form and increase their ability to shape and reshape objects by working with modeling clay.

The modeling "clay" recipes included here have been used successfully by leaders around the country and can be used to make bowls, vases, ornaments, animals, figures, candleholders, paperweights, doorstops, napkin rings, and many other useful items. You'll find most of the ingredients for these recipes in the kitchen. You can obtain sawdust from any sawmill or woodworking shop.

HOW-TO TIPS FOR MODELING

- When making ornaments or beads, be sure to make a hole in the object before it dries or is baked so that a hanger can be added.
- If the clay begins to dry and crack as you are working with it, try wetting the cracks with a finger or sponge and rubbing them away as they appear.
- Unless a recipe calls for baking, molded objects should be allowed to air-dry thoroughly. Drying can be hastened by punching tiny pinholes in the object.
- Leftover modeling clay can be stored in a plastic bag in the refrigerator for later use. Don't store for extended periods unless specified.
- Make a "tool" out of a ¼-inch dowel or orange stick cut about 6 inches long and sharpened like a pencil.
- Mixing regular clay with glycerin and then adding petroleum jelly can make permanently elastic clay. The proportion of clay to glycerin and jelly varies according to the desired consistency. For a start, try eight parts clay to one part glycerin to one part petroleum jelly. Add more glycerin and petroleum jelly as needed.
- Powdered alum will keep homemade clays from getting moldy. Add a tablespoon or two to your dough.

MODELING "CLAY" RECIPES

Salt/Cornstarch Clay

Ingredients: 2 C. salt, ⅔ C. water, 1 C. cornstarch, ½ C. water

Mix the table salt with the water in a saucepan. Simmer over medium heat, stirring constantly until the mixture is well-heated (3 to 4 minutes). Remove from the heat. Mix the cornstarch with the ½ C. cold water and add. This will make a thick, stiff dough.

Salt/Flour Clay

Ingredients: ½ C. salt, 1 C. flour, water

Combine the salt and flour. Add water, a little at a time, and with your hands, mix and knead until it is a stiff dough. (By adding ⅓ C. water, you can make a soft clay that is good for making a relief map.)

Basic Clay

Ingredients:

1 C. flour	½ C. salt
2 t. cream of tartar	1 C. water
2 T. vegetable oil	8 drops food coloring

Mix the flour, salt, and cream of tartar and set aside. In a saucepan, bring to a boil the water, vegetable oil, and food coloring. Remove from the heat and add the dry ingredients. Stir until well-mixed. Let cool and knead a bit to stretch. Stored in an airtight container, this clay will keep for months.

Sawdust Clay

Ingredients: 4 C. clean, sifted sawdust; 1 C. wallpaper paste; 2 C. water

Mix all ingredients thoroughly to the consistency of modeling clay. Add ½ C. plaster to the basic recipe for added weight to make doorstops or paperweights. *Note:* This mixture must be used right away.

Sawdust/Flour Clay

Ingredients: 1 C. flour, 2 C. sawdust, 1 t. salt, water

Mix the flour, sawdust, and salt together. Add water until the dough is thick and pliable.

Sawdust/Cornstarch Clay

Ingredients: **3 T. cornstarch, 1 C. cold water, 1 to 2 C. sawdust**

Slowly add the cornstarch to the water. Cook the mixture in a double boiler until thickened. Allow to cool, and then empty into a large bowl. Add the sawdust, a little at a time, and knead it thoroughly until you get pliable dough that is thick enough to handle without cracking apart.

Cornstarch/Baking Soda Clay

Ingredients: **1 C. cornstarch, 2 C. baking soda, 1¼ C. water**

Mix the cornstarch and baking soda. Add the water and mix. Bring to a boil over medium heat, stirring constantly. This will thicken to the consistency of mashed potatoes. Store in the refrigerator. *Note:* This clay dries white.

Bread Modeling Clay

Ingredients: **Crusts from several slices of white bread, white glue, lemon juice**

Break up the bread crusts into small pieces and mix with white glue. Add a few drops of lemon juice. Mix until it is the consistency of clay.

Baker's Clay

Ingredients: **4 C. flour, 1 C. salt, 1½ C. water**

Use your fingers to mix the flour, salt, and water together in a big bowl. If the clay feels too stiff, add a little more water. Knead for 5 minutes. This recipe should not be doubled or halved. After objects are molded, bake them on a cookie sheet in a 350-degree oven for 1 hour. Test for doneness with a toothpick.

Peanut Butter Clay

Ingredients: **1½ C. peanut butter, 1½ C. powdered milk, ¾ C. honey**

Mix all ingredients together to the desired consistency.

TWISTED NAPKIN RINGS

Materials: **Cardboard roll, aluminum foil, modeling clay, water, shellac or varnish, paint**

1. Cover a cardboard roll with foil.
2. Roll pieces of modeling clay into ropes, each about ¼ inch thick and 12 inches long. Fold each rope in half and twist as shown.

3. Wrap the clay twist around the foil-covered tube, dab the ends of the twisted ring with water, and press to seal.
4. Bake or let air-dry, depending on the type of clay used.
5. When dry, slip the rings off the tube. Give napkin rings a coat of clear shellac or varnish, or paint a bright color.

BUSY HANDS KEEPSAKE

This easy project is best for younger boys.

Materials: **2-pound coffee can lid for each boy, modeling clay, paint**

1. Smooth out a lump of clay onto the coffee can lid.
2. Boys press their hand into the clay, leaving a distinct impression.
3. Let dry. Paint or decorate as desired, including the date made and name of the boy.

CLAY MENORAH

Materials: **Salt/flour clay, alum, candles, acrylic-type paint**

1. Make the salt/flour clay above, adding a teaspoon of alum to prevent the clay from getting moldy. Mold into a base 9 inches long, 2 inches wide, and 2 inches high.
2. Coat the ends of nine candles (one larger than the other eight) lightly with vegetable oil. Insert the largest candle into the center of the base; then insert the other eight—four on each side of the center candle, an equal distance apart. Insert the candles deep enough so they can stand on their own.
3. Let dry overnight. Remove the candles and continue to air-dry.
4. Once the clay is dry, paint and decorate the clay base with acrylic-type paint.

ORNAMENTS

Materials:

Rolling pin	Modeling clay
Waxed paper	Cookie cutters
Toothpick	Paint
Shellac	Ribbon or string

1. With a rolling pin, roll out modeling clay flat between two pieces of waxed paper.

2. Use cookie cutters to cut out stars, bells, or other shapes.

3. Use a toothpick to make a hole in the top of each ornament for a hanger.

4. Let the ornaments dry or bake, depending on the clay recipe used. Paint with tempera and add a topcoat of shellac.

5. Tie ribbon or string through the hole for hanging.

MAGNETS

Materials: **Modeling clay, paint, craft magnets, glue**

1. Mold modeling clay into desired shapes—animals, flowers, etc. Make the backside as flat as possible.

2. Let dry. Paint as desired.

3. Glue a craft magnet on the back—and stick them to your refrigerator!

PINCH POT

Use the recipe for baker's clay above for this small pot.

1. Roll clay into a solid ball about 1½ inches in diameter.

2. Place the ball in your palm and slowly push your thumb into the center to within ¼ inch from the bottom while rotating the clay ball.

3. Then with both thumbs in the center hole and your fingers on the outside of the pot, hold the pot bottom away from you and press the sides out, revolving the pot in a slow circle.

4. When the sides have been pressed to about ⅜ inch in thickness, place the pot on a piece of waxed paper on a table. Work around the edge in a pinching motion with the thumbs and fingers until the sides of the pot are smooth and about ¼ inch thick. Be careful not to strain the pot by forcing or pinching too near the bottom.

5. Work from the bottom up, keeping the top edges thick until the very last.

6. When the bowl is as even and round as possible, you can vary the shape by pushing the edges inward or outward.

7. Bake on a cookie sheet in a 350-degree oven for about an hour.

8. When the pot has cooled, paint with the designs of your choice.

CLAY ALIENS

Put the boys' imaginations to work creating a friend from another planet. Anything goes for an extraterrestrial! Once the boys make their alien pal, they can pick a name and introduce their new friend to the rest of the den.

Materials: **Any type of clay recipe above; miscellaneous craft items and other small materials— beads, sequins, wiggle eyes, chenille stems, washers, small screws, wire, etc. Each boy will need a clay working tool made out of a ¼-inch dowel cut about 6 inches long and sharpened like a pencil.**

Make 1-inch balls out of different colors of clay. Each alien requires at least two or three balls of clay. Fill egg cartons with different craft materials. Boys pick assorted colors from the clay balls, take a tool, and get to work.

Candle Making

The first candles were probably made from dried rushes soaked in grease. The Romans used candles made out of beeswax. Today, you and your boys can make beautiful and useful gifts from inexpensive materials.

SAFETY FIRST

Melted wax is hot. Follow these rules so that you and your Cub Scouts will have a safe craft experience.

- Never leave children alone with melting or melted wax. *Remember:* Wax doesn't boil or steam, so boys probably won't realize how hot it is.
- Never leave melting or melted wax alone.
- Use a thermometer. Wax has a flash point of 375 degrees Fahrenheit. There is no need to heat wax above 200 degrees for any Cub Scout project.
- Don't let wax have direct contact with a flame. If an accident occurs, treat it as a grease fire. DO NOT use water. Smother with baking soda or a pan lid, or use a dry chemical fire extinguisher.
- Always use a water bath method to melt wax; that is, use a double boiler or use an old pot filled with water and brought to a boil, with a second pot or a small coffee can in or over the water in which to melt the wax. DO NOT use a microwave. The wax can splatter, and it will discolor.
- Use pot holders or pliers when handling hot pots or cans.
- If wax gets on your skin, run it under cold water immediately—then peel off the wax.
- Don't pour leftover wax down the drain. It will block the drain and require a plumber.

HOW-TO TIPS FOR WAX PROJECTS

- Always melt wax in a container over a pot of hot water, such as a double boiler.
- "Prime" the wick by immersing it in melted wax for 2 to 3 minutes. Cool slightly and then pull it straight and lay it flat to dry.
- Use crayon pieces or commercial dies to color wax. Water-based dyes and paints will not work.
- If you want to add scent to your candles, use commercial scents or oils only. Water-based scents will not work.

DIPPED CANDLES

In colonial times, every household made a supply of candles in autumn. Candle rods with rows of wicks were repeatedly dipped into big iron kettles of melted tallow. Candle dipping is still a tradition in some towns and villages in Switzerland, where the public can make candles during a candle dipping festival at the end of the year.

Materials:
  Wick or thick cotton string in 8- to 10-inch lengths to make a 6-inch candle
  Paraffin or candle wax
  Double boiler or large pot with clean empty coffee can
  Long-handled wooden spoon
  Second coffee can filled with cold water
  Chopsticks, 6-inch lengths of doweling, or unsharpened pencils for dipping sticks
  Drying rack (a clothes drying rack, a narrow cardboard box, two chairs back to back)

1. Heat water in the bottom of the double boiler. If you are using a coffee can, place the can in the heated water.

2. Break the paraffin into pieces and place it in the top of the double boiler over the water. Stir until the wax is melted and it reaches a temperature of 160 degrees Fahrenheit.

3. As it melts, you can add crayon or candle dye for color. Stir gently to distribute the color evenly.

4. Remove the upper pan of wax from the water and place it on a flat surface. Boys tie a wick onto a dipping stick and dip it into the wax. Then lift straight up, holding it for a moment to allow any large wax drips to fall.

5. Dip the candle in and out of the cold water and dry with a cloth. Hang on the drying rack to dry completely between dips.

6. Repeat the process until the candle is the desired thickness. (You can expect about 25 dips for a candle ½ inch in diameter.)

MOLDED CANDLES

You can buy many candle molds at hobby and craft stores. They are easy to use and come with instructions. Or, make homemade molds from milk containers, muffin tins, or boxes from bar soap. If using a homemade mold, you can support the wick by tying it to a pencil and lying it across the top of the mold.

Pour mold a little less than full so that candle can be easily removed.

Make wick hole with hot ice pick.

Stiffen wick by dipping in hot wax and then cooling. Poke stiff wick into hole.

CRUSHED ICE CANDLE

This is a candle within a candle. The taper includes the wick, and the crushed ice makes a lacy decorative candle.

Materials:
>   Double boiler
>   Empty clean pint milk carton
>   One 4-inch white taper candle
>   Ice (about 1-inch cubes)
>   Candle wax or paraffin
>   Crayon pieces or wax dye for color

1. Heat water in the bottom of the double boiler. If you are using a coffee can, place the can in the heated water.

2. Break paraffin into pieces and place in the top of the double boiler over the water. Stir until the wax is melted and it reaches a temperature of 160 degrees Fahrenheit.

3. As it melts, you can add crayon or candle dye for color. Stir gently to distribute the color evenly.

4. Spread newspaper on the work surface. Place the taper in the center of the milk carton. Surround the taper with crushed ice to hold it in place.

5. Carefully pour the melted wax up to the top of the taper, making sure that the candlewick extends beyond the melted wax. Leave overnight.

6. Pour water from the melted ice out of the milk carton. Then tear and peel off the milk carton to expose the square candle. (Use two den meetings, if necessary: one to pour the wax and one to remove from the mold.)

SAND CANDLES

This candle craft takes a little more work and requires a lot of adult help, but the finished product is worth the effort.

Materials:
>   **Sand—natural or colored**
>   **Container to hold wet sand**
>   **Water**
>   **Jar or bottle (It needs to have fairly straight outward sloping sides at the top so it can be removed from the sand without having the sides cave in.)**
>   **Wicking or cotton twine**
>   **Double boiler**
>   **Wax (paraffin)**
>   **Stearine (to harden the wax)**
>   **Wick tabs (available at craft stores)**
>   **Pencil**

1. Put sand in the container and add enough water so when mixed it is moist and packs well.

2. To make the mold, push the jar or bottle into the wet sand. Then remove it carefully to complete the mold.

3. Attach a wick tab to one end of the wick. Tie the other end of the wick to the pencil and suspend over the cavity of the mold with the wick tab touching the sand. Make sure that the wick is not too long and hangs straight by wrapping excess around the pencil.

4. Heat water in the bottom of the double boiler. If you are using a coffee can, place the can in the heated water.

5. Break paraffin into pieces and place in the top of the double boiler over the water. Stir until the wax is melted and it reaches a temperature of 160 degrees Fahrenheit. Add 3 T. stearine for each pound of wax. As the wax melts, add crayon or candle dye or scents, as desired. Stir gently to distribute evenly.

6. Carefully pour the melted wax into the mold cavity. (The sand may sizzle a bit, but this is normal.) Allow the wax to cool completely.

7. Scoop out the sand from around the candle to remove the candle. Brush off loose sand. Spray with clear acrylic for a nice finish.

Plaster Crafts

Cub Scouts, families, and leaders will enjoy learning to cast and finish plaster projects. Use plaster to make casts of animal footprints and leaves, picture frames, neckerchief slides, plaques, and other items.

Casting plaster can be found at most craft or hobby stores. Plaster of paris is the most common type, but casting plaster is not expensive and is more durable.

MOLDS FOR PLASTER

Commercial molds are available in many different sizes and shapes. Plastic candy molds are great for neckerchief slides. Plastic or waxed tubs and cartons make excellent molds for candleholders. Picture frames and plaques can also be molded in plastic or waxed cartons. Scoops from dry beverage mixes make excellent molds for circular objects such as happy faces or bicycle wheels.

Make a Mold

You can make your own mold by using a commercial latex molding compound available from most hobby and craft stores. Almost any nonporous object can be covered with several coats of latex, which will produce a mold.

Preparing the Mold

Molds need to be prepared to prevent sticking and to help the cast slip out easily. Use vegetable oil for all molds *except* latex. Use a soap solution of 1 C. water to 1 T. liquid detergent for latex molds. Coat the inside of the mold lightly, as excess oil or soap solution will cause defects in the cast. You don't need to prepare wax carton molds, as the wax already serves that purpose.

MIXING PLASTER

1. Fill the mold with water to determine the amount of plaster required. Pour this water into a disposable mixing container, such as a paper cup or small aluminum pan.

2. Sprinkle plaster slowly into the water until a peak forms above the surface. Allow it to set for 1 minute. Then, using a wooden or plastic spoon, stir gently to prevent air bubbles. The mixture should resemble heavy cream.

3. Don't mix more plaster than you need. It will harden quickly and can't be reused.

4. Discard extra plaster in the disposable container. *Don't pour it down the sink or dump near shrubbery.* It will clog drains and kill some types of shrubbery.

POURING PLASTER

1. To fill small molds, pour plaster immediately and work into crevices with a toothpick.

2. Fill larger molds about three-quarters full; flex the mold with your hands or gently tap against a table. You may add a layer of gauze to strengthen the cast at this point. Fill to the top and tap again to allow any air bubbles to rise to the surface.

3. If the cast needs a ring, such as for a plaque or neckerchief slide, insert it now.

4. Allow the plaster to set before removing it from the mold—15 to 30 minutes for small molds and 1 to 2 hours for larger molds.

5. Remove the cast from the mold. It should slip out easily if the mold was properly prepared.

6. Scrape or sand any rough edges.

7. Allow the cast to dry completely (a day or more) before painting.

PAINTING PLASTER

Most paint will soak into plaster, so it is best to seal the cast with a commercial spray sealer, gesso, or thinned latex wall paint. After the sealer is dry, apply any type of paint—tempera, acrylic, oil, or enamel. Tempera will leave a dull finish unless you give it a final coat of shellac or varnish.

PLASTER WHITTLING

Plaster is an excellent medium to use when teaching boys to whittle. Once they have mastered the technique, they can go on to wood.

Make small plaster blocks and let them harden. When ready to whittle, soak the plaster in water for 5 to 10 minutes. The plaster is porous and will absorb the water, making it easier to work.

PLASTER PAPERWEIGHTS

Use your imagination to create novel paperweights that will make great gifts. Carve blocks of hardened plaster or use molds to make interesting shapes.

Materials: **Mold for paperweight, plaster/water, container and spoon for mixing, felt scraps, paint**

1. Use plastic margarine containers as molds for larger paperweights and paper cups for smaller ones. Prepare the mold and plaster as described above.

2. For a turtle paperweight, use a margarine tub for the body and old measuring spoons for the head

and feet. When the plaster is set, carve the head and feet into desired shapes and glue to the turtle body.

3. Glue felt to the bottom of the turtle and paint as desired.

PLASTER SCRIMSHAW

Sailors and whalers began the art of scrimshaw in the 1860s to make the time pass more quickly at sea. They would scratch a design in whalebone or polished ivory and then fill in the lines with ink. Cub Scouts can use plaster in place of whalebone to make carvings that look like scrimshaw. Wear them as pendants or use as paperweights.

Materials:

Plaster	Waxed paper
Dark tempera paint	Shellac
Nail or sharp tool for scratching	Thong for pendant

1. Mix plaster as described above.

2. Drop globs of plaster on waxed paper. If necessary you can flatten with your fingers.

3. If you are making a pendant, use the nail or a toothpick to make a hole in the plaster for a thong.

4. When the plaster is hard, scratch a design in it with the nail or sharp tool.

5. Thin dark tempera and brush one thin coat over the plaster. Wipe lightly with a paper towel so that the dark tempera stays in the scratched design but not on the rest of your object. When the paint is dry, apply a shellac finish.

6. For a pendant, add a thong or heavy cord to tie around neck.

PLASTER CRAFTS IN NATURE

Plaster crafts can be a great way to keep boys interested during a nature hike. By seeking out the materials and possibilities for casts, they will be paying close attention to what's going on around them.

Plaster Leaves

Materials: Plastic lid, leaf, vegetable oil, plaster

1. Lightly oil the inside of the lid and the vein side of the leaf.

2. Place the leaf, vein side up, in the bottom of the lid.

3. Pour plaster gently over the leaf, without spilling over the top.

4. If making a hanging, press a hanger into the edge of the plaster.

5. Let set until hard. Remove the cast from the mold. Remove the leaf. Let it dry thoroughly.

Plaster Casts of Animal Tracks

You'll find the best tracks for casting near streams, muddy banks, or beaches.

Materials: Plaster, strip of cardboard 1½ inches wide, paper clip, disposable container for mixing plaster, disposable plastic spoon for stirring

1. After you have found the tracks you want to cast, brush away any twigs, stones, or dirt from around the tracks.

2. Surround the tracks with the cardboard strip in the shape of a ring and fasten the ends with the paper clip. Push the cardboard into the mud around the tracks.

3. Prepare the plaster as described above.

4. Pour the plaster slowly from one side to the other over the tracks inside the ring. This way, the plaster has time to push the air out, and no bubbles will be left.

5. After about 15 minutes, the plaster should be hard enough for the cast to be removed. While the cast is still damp, scratch the date and the type of animal in the plaster. When it is thoroughly dry, remove the cardboard ring.

If you will be doing the plaster casting while on a hike, have each Cub Scout carry a resealable plastic bag with ⅓ to ½ C. of dry plaster. When you find tracks, boys add a little water from their canteens or water bottles slowly and gradually into the plastic bag. Close the bag and knead until smooth. Pour into the ring as described above and dispose of the plastic bag properly.

Metal and Tin Craft

Metal is one of the basic craft materials. Have Cub Scouts begin with aluminum foil to teach the skills of designing, measuring, cutting, modeling, tooling, polishing, and finishing. Then move on to tin or aluminum cans and other metals.

TOOLS FOR METAL WORK

- **Vise**—To hold metal while working or to aid in bending material.
- **Scratch Awl**—To mark lines or designs. (You can also use nails for this.)
- **Center Punch**—To make dents in the design or to make holes. (You can also use nails for this.)
- **Ball Peen Hammer**—To pound nails, punches, chisels, or whatever you are using to impress designs in the metal.
- **Can Opener**—To open both ends of cans.

TOOLING METAL

Use this method to tool metal book covers, belts, jewelry, and other items.

Stylus

Foil

Newspaper or magazine stack

1. Sharpen a pencil-sized dowel to a point for the basic tool *(stylus)*. Sand the other end of the dowel to a flat slant. (You can also use a ballpoint pen as the stylus.)
2. The metal piece to be tooled should be flat. Place it on a soft but firm surface, such as a stack of newspapers or magazines. Tape it in place.
3. Lay the pattern of your design on the metal and trace around it with the stylus, including all the details. Remove the pattern and trace over the entire design again. This is the underside of the work.

HOW-TO TIPS FOR WORKING WITH METAL

- **Sharp Edges:** When working with tin, aluminum, or other metals, smooth sharp edges with a file and steel wool or emery cloth. Protect hands from steel wool by wearing gloves or holding it in a cloth.
- **Painting:** Remove any paper labels. Sand the surface with wet sandpaper to remove the shine and prepare the surface for painting. Wipe off with a wet sponge. Paint cans with enamel, latex, lacquer, or acrylic. If spray painting,  insert a small paper bag into the opening to protect the inside of the can from paint, as shown. Spray three light coats, letting the paint dry between coats.
- **Punching Holes:** To make holes in cans, place the can on top of a piece of scrap wood. Hold an awl to the inside of the can and punch the hole with a hammer as shown.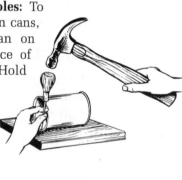
- **Joining Cans:** To join cans, cut the bottom out of one can and place on the top of another. Secure with strong glue or strapping tape.
- **Decorating Cans:** Decorate painted cans with plastic stick-on letters or dots, macaroni or seeds, tiny mosaic tiles, or scrap wallpaper. You could also cover them with jute twine or yarn.
- **Aluminum Foil Tooling:** It is easy to tool designs in aluminum foil (see "Tooling Metal" below) from frozen pies or dinners, or aluminum offset printing plates. Frame the designs and hang them on a wall.

4. Turn the metal over to the front side and use the stylus just outside the ridges, pushing the background down and away from the design. Use the flat end of the stylus for working the background that isn't close to the design.

5. Turn the metal to the backside again and work the design out with the flat end of the dowel. Continue working both front and back to emphasize details and make the design stand out.

For variation, try hammering lightly on a heavy straight pin or nail over the background, or use the coil end of a safety pin to provide a different texture.

TIN FOIL COMET

This foil comet is almost too easy and always too fun.

Materials: **One 12-inch-long piece of tin foil from a standard roll, 12 Mylar strands or curling ribbon strands of different colors**

Lay the foil flat. Place one end of the Mylar strips in the center of the foil. (You can secure with tape, but this usually isn't necessary.) Close the foil around the strips to make a ball. Toss it to a friend and you have a tin foil comet.

PINHOLE PLANETARIUMS

Boys can learn to recognize constellations with these pinhole planetariums made from 12-oz. soda cans that have pop tops.

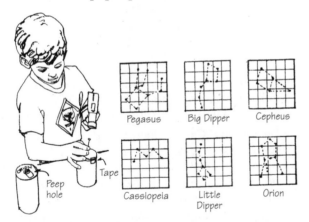

Pegasus   Big Dipper   Cepheus

Cassiopeia   Little Dipper   Orion

Peep hole   Tape

Materials:
Clean 12-oz. soda cans	**Pen or dark pencil**
Paper	**Tape**
Nail	**Hammer**
Adhesive shelf lining	

1. Make paper patterns of the constellations shown, enlarging the pattern to 2½-inch circles using the grid method (see "Enlarging Patterns" above). Mark the stars' positions with a pen or pencil.

2. Tape each pattern upside down on the bottom of a clean soda can.

3. With the nail and hammer, punch tiny holes at each star's position in the constellation.

4. Decorate the can with adhesive shelf lining, and put the constellation's name over the "peep hole."

5. To use your planetarium, hold the bottom of the can toward a strong light and look through the peep hole.

TIN CAN LANTERN

Tinsmiths used tin piercing to make items such as lanterns, charcoal heaters, and cabinets. This craft requires careful supervision by adults but makes a "keeper craft" the boys will truly enjoy.

Materials:
Clean tin can, any size
Paper, pencil, scissors
Water
2-by-4 scrap lumber
Duct tape
Hammer
Flathead nails
Small candle and holder

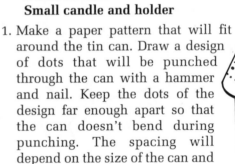
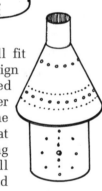

1. Make a paper pattern that will fit around the tin can. Draw a design of dots that will be punched through the can with a hammer and nail. Keep the dots of the design far enough apart so that the can doesn't bend during punching. The spacing will depend on the size of the can and the age level of the boys.

2. Fill the can almost full with water and freeze solid.

3. After the water is frozen, wrap the paper pattern around the can and tape in place.

4. Use two 2-by-4-inch pieces of scrap lumber slightly longer than the can to make a "frame" along both sides of the can. Secure the ends of the frame with duct tape. This frame will brace the can during punching and still allow it to be rotated.

5. Use a hammer and sharp flathead nail to punch holes in the can following the design. The nails must be sharp or the can will bend. Keep extras on hand and replace as needed.

6. After the ice melts, dry the can. Place a small candle and holder in your lantern. Votive candles work well.

If you want a top for your lantern, you can punch a design into an aluminum funnel, as shown. The funnels are sturdier than the cans so they won't need ice to hold their shape during the punching.

TIN ORNAMENTS

Tin ornaments are popular and traditional in Mexico. Some possible designs are shown here, but boys can use their imaginations to create others.

Materials: **Foil or aluminum trays or plates, emery board, newspapers, orange stick or dry ball-point pen, permanent markers**

1. Cut desired shapes from foil trays or plates. Use an emery board to file the edges smooth if necessary.

2. Place the ornament on a stack of newspapers. Use the orange stick or dry ballpoint pen to draw the details

3. Color the ornament using permanent markers, and punch a small hole in the top for hanging.

TIN CAN TELEPHONE

Boys love to make and use these telephones to send important messages, discuss bright ideas and private plans, and tell deep dark secrets.

Materials: **Two small empty tin cans, 20 feet of sturdy cotton string**

Cut out one end of the cans. Punch a small hole in the bottoms. Thread the string through the holes and tie knots in the ends to keep the string from pulling through. Pull the string tight between the two "phones"; one boy talks into his can and the other listens.

SIMPLE TELEGRAPH

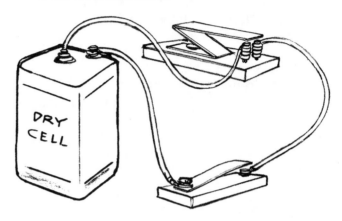

Materials:

Two pieces of wood	**Three screws**
One dry cell (battery)	**Two nails**
Two metal strips cut from a tin can	**Two wires**

1. Cut metal strips from a tin can and bend in the shapes shown for the "sounder" (the **Z** shape) and the key. (Make sure you remove sharp edges with a file or emery paper.) Screw them to the blocks of wood.

2. Put one screw underneath the key, with ¼ inch of clearance to the key.

3. Hammer in the nails for the receiver. (There should be about ⅛ or 1⁄16 inch clearance between the wrapped nails [see above] and the sounder.)

4. Wire as shown. In wrapping the wire around the nails, start at the top of one nail and work down. Then go across to the other nail and work up. Have at least eight turns on each nail.

5. When you push down on the key and come in contact with the screw underneath it, the electric current is completed and passes through the wire. This magnetizes the wrapped nails, which then pull the sounder down and make a clicking sound.

NUTS AND BOLTS CHESS SET

Materials:

Two small acorn nuts
Two ⅜-inch cap screws
Eight ⅜-inch nuts
12 ⅜-inch flat-head socket cap screws
Four ⅜-inch thumb screws
Four ⅜-inch castle nuts or castellated nuts
Two external tooth lock washers
16 ¼-inch machine screws
16 ¼-inch nuts
Epoxy cement
Contrasting paint colors

Assemble and glue the nuts and bolts together as illustrated to make enough pieces for one chess set. Paint half the pieces one color and the other half a contrasting color. Or you might make one set out of steel and one set out of brass nuts and bolts.

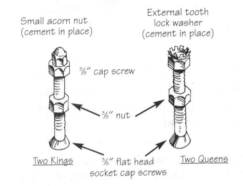

Small acorn nut (cement in place)
External tooth lock washer (cement in place)
⅜" cap screw
⅜" nut
Two Kings
⅜" flat head socket cap screws
Two Queens

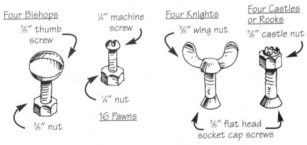

Four Bishops
⅜" thumb screw
¼" machine screw
Four Knights
⅜" wing nut
Four Castles or Rooks
⅜" castle nut
¼" nut
16 Pawns
⅜" nut
⅜" flat head socket cap screws

Leather Craft

Working with leather has much to offer Cub Scouts, including learning new skills as they create useful and beautiful items. Leather can be decorated by painting a design on it, dyeing it, tooling it, stamping patterns in it with punches, burning designs on it, or weaving or braiding through it. Don't confine your leatherwork to simply lacing together precut kits!

Leather, however, can be expensive. Look for stores that will give away leather scraps or sell bags of scraps at a low price. Scrap leather is suitable for most Cub Scout projects. You can use heavy scrap vinyl, such as upholstery vinyl, as a substitute for leather in some projects. Begin with leather tooling, one of the simplest types of leather craft. This skill requires only one tool: a *modeler* or *stylus*. Tooling projects can be completed in a short time.

LEATHER TOOLING

- With a sponge or cloth, dampen the leather on the rough side with cold water. After a short while the dampness will reach the finished side of the leather. If it looks wet on the finished side, the leather is too damp to tool. Wait until it dries slightly and the natural leather color returns.

- Place your pattern on the front side of the dampened leather. Fasten it in place with tape or a clamp. Trace the pattern with a stylus. Lift one end of the pattern to be sure the entire pattern has been transferred. Remove the pattern.

- Lay the leather on a firm surface. Use the flat end of your stylus to level around all the outside lines of your pattern and around the inside of any other lines. Always draw the tool toward you. Keep an even pressure on the stylus to prevent making deep marks in the leather. This technique brings out a darker, waxed-like color in the leather, and the depression will produce an attractive design. If the design is not clear enough, go over it again. Redampen the leather if necessary.

- When the design is finished and the leather is dry, apply a final finish of wax, saddle soap, or leather dressing.

LEATHER LACING

You can get leather or plastic lacing at your local Scout distributor or a craft or hobby shop. The *spiral* or *whipstitch,* illustrated here, is the simplest lacing stitch. It consists of running a single lace, spiral fashion, through successive holes. Always make the first and last lace a double one, to conceal the ends.

LEATHER STAMPING

There are a variety of tools and techniques for stamping leather, and you can find out more about them on the Internet or at the library. Along with your stamping tools and leather, you'll need a wooden mallet, or *maul.*

Dampen the leather on the backside as described above. Don't soak it. Place it on a hard surface. Hold the stamping tool in one hand and tap it gently with the maul. Make sure that you strike the tool carefully so that you don't cut through the leather.

BOOKMARK

Choose a design or monogram that will fit on a piece of 2-by-8-inch leather. Follow the instructions above for leather tooling or stamping to imprint your design on the leather. Cut the top and/or the bottom of the bookmark into a fringe if desired.

KEY CHAIN

This handy, easy-to-make item is a good gift for parents. Choose a design or monogram that will fit on a 1¼-by-4-inch piece of leather. Punch a hole near the top of the leather that is large enough for a beaded key chain to slip through easily. Tool or stamp your design, following the instructions above.

MYSTIC BRAID

1. Cut soft leather (or cloth-backed vinyl) to 1¼ by 4½ inches. Cut two slits, as shown, dividing the leather into equal thirds. Number the thirds 1, 2, and 3, using a light pencil mark, from left to right (Figure A).

2. Push the bottom left corner through the slit between 2 and 3 (Figure B).

3. Put strip 3 on top of strip 2. Then put strip 1 on top of strip 3, making a sandwich with strip 3 in the middle. With your fingers, work strip 3 out to the left, exposing an open loop (Figure C).

HOW-TO TIPS FOR WORKING WITH LEATHER

- Use a hard surface as a base when tooling leather. Marble is an excellent base because it doesn't absorb moisture. You can also use laminated countertop scraps (from countertop manufacturers and kitchen remodeling firms).

- Dampen all leather completely before working on it. Redampen from the backside if it dries out before you are finished.

- Note: Don't moisten leather that will have a burned design. Use a regular wood-burning set.

- If leather becomes soiled while working with it, clean it with saddle soap. Apply with an old sock or other clean rag to the entire surface and allow it to dry. Do this before applying any finish coat or wax.

4. Bring the bottom end toward you, and then insert it through the loop and pull through.

5. Rework with the fingers into a braided strip that looks like Figure D.

6. To make into a neckerchief slide, use a small stapler to staple the top and bottom ends together (Figure E). (Lengthen the pattern to make a larger slide.)

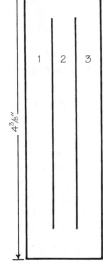

Figure A

Figure C

Figure D

Figure B

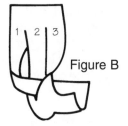

Staples

Figure E

Wood Craft

The wood craft projects in this section are suitable for Cub Scouts and leaders who have had little experience working with wood. Use the Parent and Family Talent Survey to find skilled family members who may be able to help you and your den. Also, you can contact a hardware store for more tips, tricks, and information regarding wood tools and their uses.

Before you begin, have on hand the materials and tools needed for the project. Find out what type of sandpaper is best for your project, what type of nails or brads. Use scrap wood, which is free of knots. (Knots can sometimes be dangerous when cutting wood.) Make a sample of the project before the meeting to check out the directions. Provide step-by-step instructions for the boys, but also don't stifle their creativity and imaginations.

HAND TOOLS FOR WOODWORKING

It is best to use only simple hand tools and avoid power equipment when working with Cub Scout–age boys.

- **Hammer:** An 8- to 10-ounce hammer is the best size for a Cub Scout to grip and swing. If a nail bends, pull it out. Use a wooden block when pulling nails to prevent strain on the hammer handle.

- **Screwdriver:** Use the longest one convenient for the job. Make sure the blade fits the screw slot. Keep the screwdriver and screw aligned.

- **Plane:** Teach boys to use a block plane to smooth and square wood. It is the best type to use on their projects.

- **Brace and Bit:** Show boys how this drilling tool works. Explain that a brace holds bits; some have ratchets to permit partial turns of the handle; and auger bits are wood bits measured by sixteenths of an inch. Show them how to start a bit by guiding it into place with one hand and how to secure a bit by holding the chuck and turning the handle of the brace clockwise. Have them learn to finish a hole from the underside to prevent splitting.

- **Hand Saw:** Teach Cub Scouts to use a 20-inch saw, recommended for boys their age. To start a saw cut, draw a pencil mark on the board where you want to make the cut. Start the cut by notching on the mark at the edge of the board. Steady the blade with your thumb well above the cutting edge and then draw back gently to create a notch on the mark. This is called *readying the blade.* With the blade ready, remove your thumb and begin sawing

down the pencil mark. Be sure to tilt the saw at approximately a 45-degree angle to the board when cutting across the grain of the wood. Explain that you straighten the saw handle to correct the direction of the cut. Be careful not to pinch the saw. If this happens, gently work the saw back and forth to release the blade.

- **Ripsaw:** Use this saw to cut with the grain of the wood only. Show boys how to brace the wood firmly on a sawhorse, bench, or vise. Start sawing gently, changing to light, steady strokes. Don't press. Take fairly long strokes and let the saw do the work.

- **Coping Saw:** Teach boys to use this simple saw to cut curves and odd shapes for wood. Saw with the handle either above or below the wood, setting the blade to cut on the down stroke. Use a heavy blade and a long stroke. Clamp the work securely in a vise or use a bench hook.

- **Bench Hook:** Make this handy tool for your home workshop. Use 1-inch pine. Follow the dimensions shown. To use, set the bench hook on your worktable or a chair. Butt the underside against the edge of the table or chair. Hold the piece of wood to be cut against the top block and saw with a level stroke as directed. The under board protects the table or chair top. Countersink screws or use dowels to protect the tabletop.

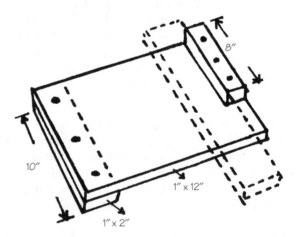

POWER TOOLS

It is best to use only simple hand tools and avoid power equipment when working with Cub Scout–age boys. Adults, however, might wish to use a power tool to precut pieces of a project for younger Scouts. See "Safety Rules for the Use of Tools" above for precautions that adult leadership should take when using power tools.

FINISHING WOOD PROJECTS

Always sand projects before you finish them. Make a sander from a 2-by-2-by-3-inch wood block and wrap sandpaper around it. Always sand with the grain, never against it or in circles. To get the best results from sanding, use a filler for scratches and holes. When dry, sand again.

You can use several finishes on wood projects: acrylics, varnish, shellac, lacquer, enamel, latex paint, or even wood stains. Apply a clear wax polish to raw wood to emphasize the beauty of the natural wood grain. *Always use finishes in a well-ventilated area.* Consider the needed adult supervision and cleanup required before you begin.

- **Acrylics:** Acrylic paint is nontoxic and good for painting almost anything, including wood projects. It can be thinned with water and doesn't need a finishing coat. Clean brushes with water.

- **Varnish:** Prepare wood with one or two coats of thin shellac or wood sealer first, sanding between coats. This will fill the pores of the wood and prepare it for varnishing. Thin varnish with turpentine, if necessary. Use shellac thinner or alcohol to clean the shellac brush; turpentine to clean the varnish brush.

- **Enamel:** Prepare wood in the same manner as for varnishing. Enamel usually needs thinning with a small amount of turpentine. If it is too thick, it will leave ridges. Two thin coats of enamel produce a colorful finish. Clean the brush with turpentine.

- **Wood Stain:** To prepare the wood, moisten it with turpentine before applying the stain. Experiment on a scrap of wood to make sure the results please you. Clean the brush with turpentine.

- **Varnish Stain:** Prepare the wood as for enamel or varnishing. A shiny varnish may be dulled by rubbing it lightly with a mixture of oil and a small amount of powdered pumice stone. Rub gently, wipe off with a soft rag, and finish with wax.

- **Lacquer:** Use lacquer the same way as for enamel, except that the brush must be cleaned with lacquer thinner.

- **Tempera:** Tempera and poster paints are not as good for painting wood projects as acrylics. The wood must be sealed so the paint will not soak in. Tempera will leave a dull finish, so you may want to give the project a top coast of clear varnish or shellac. Clean tempera brushes with water.

CAUTION: Many painting supplies are not only flammable, but also explosive. Never use them near an open flame. Be sure windows are open for circulation. It is best to use them outdoors if possible.

CRAFT STICK PICTURE FRAME

You can make picture frames out of many different materials. This craft stick frame is simple and inexpensive and looks great.

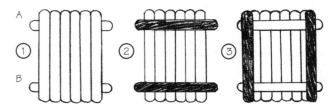

Materials: **Craft sticks, white glue**

1. Lay craft sticks A and B horizontally and line up enough craft sticks across them to cover them (the number will depend on the size of craft stick you are using). Glue in place.

2. Glue two sticks across the vertical sticks directly on top of sticks A and B.

3. Glue a stick on each side outside edge.

4. Continue alternating top/bottom and right/left sticks until they are as high as you want. Decorate as desired.

5. Choose a picture and cut it to fit and glue in your frame.

CORK HOT PLATE/TRIVET

Family members will love this usable household item. *Note:* Corks may vary in size so you may need to adjust the dimensions of the base or leave spaces between corks.

Materials:
9-inch square of ⅛-inch board
Two 9-inch-long pieces of 1 by 1 trim
Two 7-inch-long pieces of 1 by 1 trim
32 1-inch corks
Four panel nails
Wood glue
Hammer

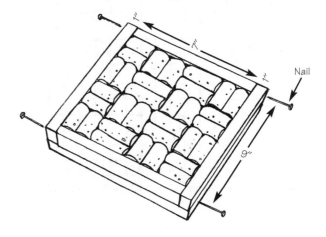

1. Use the 9-inch square of board for a base. If the base is unfinished, sand it smooth.

2. Form the pieces of trim into a square. Use wood glue on the joints before you nail them together. Glue this onto the base.

3. If desired, use a stain and finish coat on the wood frame.

4. Glue corks into the frame in the desired pattern.

BOOKENDS

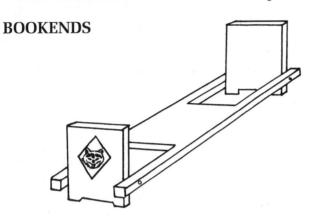

Cut these easy bookends from one piece of wood.

Materials: ½-by-8-by-18-inch board, nail, paint or varnish

Cut pieces from each end of the board according to the illustration. Nail the cutout pieces in an upright position at the ends of the remaining piece of board. Sand and finish as desired.

CUTTING BOARDS

Materials: ¾-inch wood, wood stain and paint, paste wax

Enlarge a pattern and cut out with a coping saw. Drill a hole for hanging. Sand and then apply wood

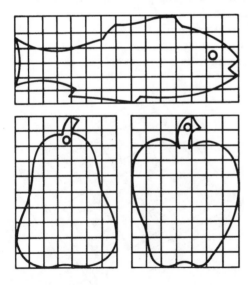

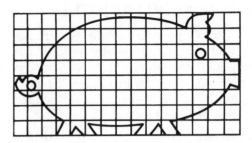

stain. Let dry and apply wax over the stain. Paint the backside as desired so you can hang it on the wall as a decoration when you aren't using it for cutting.

SUNDIAL

Many animals and plants use the sun as their natural time teller. Cub Scouts can, too, when they build their own sundial.

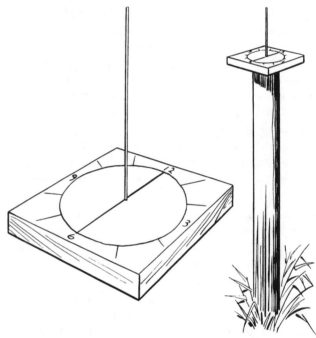

Materials: 11-inch square of wood, drawing compass to make a circle, ⅛-inch dowel 12 inches long, 4-foot post

1. Use the compass to draw the largest circle that can fit inside the square of wood. Mark the center point with a dot.

2. Drill a hole in the center to accommodate the ⅛-inch dowel. This will be the *gnomon,* or pointer, that casts a shadow on the sundial.

3. Draw a straight line through the center of the circle, perpendicular to the top of the wood block. This is the 12:00 marking.

4. Nail the sundial to the top of the post, and put it in a place that gets full sunlight. Set it so the 12:00 mark points north, or at noon (standard

time); rotate the sundial until the shadow of the gnomon falls on the 12:00 mark.

5. From 6:00 A.M. to 6:00 P.M., make a dot each hour where the shadow hits the outside circle.

6. Now you can tell the time of day simply by glancing at the sundial to see where the sun casts its shadow.

COUNTDOWN CHRISTMAS TREE

Pine wood and acrylic paint work best for this project.

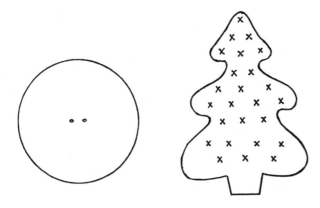

Materials:
1-by-10-inch board (large enough to support the tree pattern)
Small wooden star
25 small nails (or brass tacks with heads)
Two flathead wood screws
25 red circle candies with a hole in the center
Felt scraps
Paint, hammer, wood glue

1. Enlarge the tree and base patterns as needed and trace them on ½-inch board. A good size is a tree about 11 inches tall on a base with an 8-inch diameter. When finished, the tree will stand upright in the center of the circular base.

2. Cut out the tree and base and sand all sides and edges smooth.

3. Paint the base and tree as desired and let dry. You can add depth and interest by painting the tree green and then, when dry, using a natural sponge dipped in a lighter green paint to add highlights ("sponge painting"). Then, use an old toothbrush dipped in white paint to add snowy effects: Hold the toothbrush over the tree and tap the handle to spatter small drops on the edges of the tree ("spatter painting"). Paint the base brown and when dry, use a fine black marker to add plank lines and nails as shown.

4. Glue the star to the top of the tree.

5. Mark X's lightly with pencil where each of 24 small nails (or tacks) will go on the tree. Hammer a nail at each X. Nail the 25th nail through the star into the tree (to hold the 25th candy).

6. Drill two holes through the back of the base as marked in the center of the pattern to attach the tree. Put glue on the bottom of the tree before screwing it in place to hold it securely to the center of the base. Insert the wood screws through the base, align the tree, and tighten the screws into the tree.

7. Glue felt on the bottom of the base.

8. Count down to Christmas by hanging a red candy on the tree each day from December 1 through December 24. On Christmas day, put the last candy on the star.

SAILING SHIP

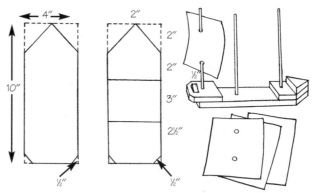

Materials:
Two pieces of 1-by-4-inch board
Heavy cardstock
Three 10-inch-long pieces of ⅛-inch dowel
Saw
Wood glue
Small hole punch

1. Cut each piece of board as shown. Save the cut corners to use as additional pieces for stacking.

2. Sand all edges smooth.

3. Drill three holes into the ship about halfway through the wood as shown: one into the center of the base, one into the prow block, and one into the stern block to accommodate dowels for the masts. (The holes should be large enough so that the ⅛-inch dowels fit into them.)

4. Stack the pieces as shown and glue.

5. Dip one end of the dowels in glue and insert into the drilled holes for masts.

6. Cut three sails from heavy cardstock and color as desired. Punch holes where indicated and slide onto each mast.

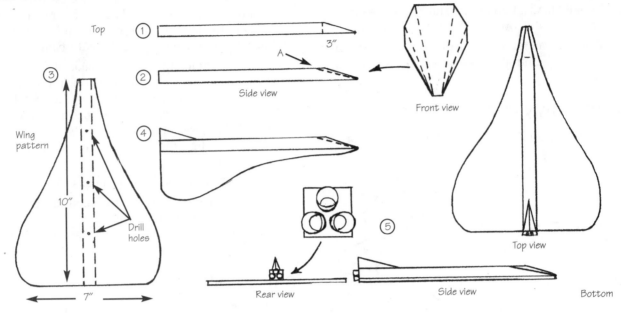

Dotted lines indicate space shuttle placement on wings.

SPACE SHUTTLE

Materials:

One 10-inch square of ⅛-inch pressed wood
One 10-inch piece of 2-by-2 wood
Three ¼-inch rubber stoppers
Three flathead screws
Wood glue
Paint

1. Enlarge the wing pattern as needed (7 by 10 inches) and cut from ⅛-inch pressed wood. Sand all edges smooth.

2. With the 10-inch piece of 2-by-2 wood, measure 3 inches back and cut the nose at an angle as shown in diagram 1.

3. Start at point A of diagram 2 and cut the angles off the tip to create the shuttle nose. Save the cut pieces to use for the tail (front view).

4. Drill three holes along the center line of the wing: one at 2½ inches from the tip, one in the center, and one at 7½ inches from the tip (diagram 3).

5. From the underside of the wing, screw on the flat side of the 2-by-2 wood piece, with "nose" ends touching as shown in diagram 4.

6. Glue together the two pieces saved from the angle cut of the front view, and then glue them to the top rear of the 2-by-2 to make the shuttle tail (top view, diagram 5).

7. Glue the rubber stoppers on the back for jet rockets (rear view, diagram 5).

8. Paint and decorate as desired.

Neckerchief Slides

As part of the worldwide brotherhood of Scouting, all Cub Scouts wear the official uniform. One part of that uniform, however, is available for individual expression: the neckerchief slide. Slides can be used as incentives, in support of monthly themes, and for completing achievements, electives, and activity badges.

You can make slides from almost any material. Here are a few ideas, but you can find many more in *Boys' Life* magazine, *Cub Scout Program Helps*, other BSA publications, pow wow books, and even on Web sites.

PLASTER SLIDES

Use poured plaster to make neckerchief slides that match the monthly theme. Find a suitable mold and prepare as directed in "Plaster Crafts" above. Small candy molds work well.

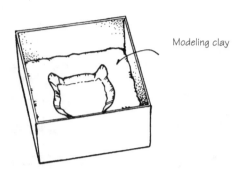

Modeling clay

Or you might make your own mold, digging your design in modeling clay in a small box to the depth of ½ inch. Remember to put a light coat of grease or cooking oil on your mold. Insert a plastic ring or 6-inch chenille stem bent in half (open side out) into the middle of the wet plaster. Don't press it all the way through, as you don't want it to show through your slide face.

LEATHER, VINYL, AND FELT SLIDES

Leather, vinyl, and felt can be great materials for slides. (For instance, see the Mystic Braid, page 2–31.) Just cut into the desired shape; glue, staple, or rivet a loop onto the back; and decorate as desired.

Elephant Neckerchief Slide

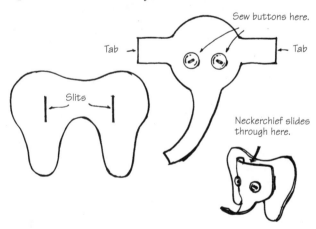

Sew buttons here.

Tab

Tab

Slits

Neckerchief slides through here.

Materials: Scrap leather, vinyl, or felt; scissors; buttons

Cut the pieces as shown. Sew on the buttons for eyes. Put the tabs through the slits and glue together.

WOOD SLIDES

You can make easy slides using slices from tree branches. Leave them in their natural state, decorate with beads or feathers, draw on wolf or bear tracks with permanent markers, or glue a small leaf to the center.

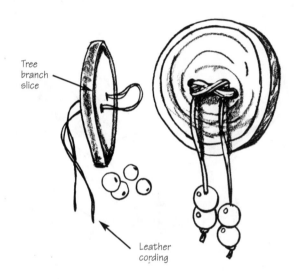

Tree branch slice

Leather cording

Or you may wish to cut shapes from thin wood with a coping saw. Sand the edges until they are smooth. Glue or staple a loop of leather or vinyl to the backside, or use a low-temperature glue gun to glue on a piece of ½-inch PVC pipe. Decorate as desired with markers, paint, stamps, glitter—let your imagination go!

PLASTIC SLIDES

You can glue a loop to the back of almost any small toy (using a low-temperature glue gun) to make an individualized tie slide of the boy's choice. Film containers with lids can be particularly useful. Boys can fill the container with materials that are important to them—campfire ashes, a small shell from the beach, meaningful handwritten words—attach a slide, and have their special memories in a safe place.

First Aid Kit Slide

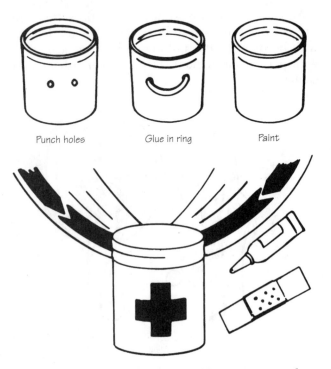

Punch holes   Glue in ring   Paint

1. Remove the lid of a 35-mm film canister and set aside.
2. Punch two small holes ¼ inch apart on the backside of the film canister. Insert a 6-inch chenille stem or ring to make a loop.
3. Paint the can white and let dry.
4. Use two ½-inch pieces of red tape to make a red cross on the front.
5. Fill the can with first aid items, such as a small bandage, a small safety pin, change for a phone call, an alcohol swipe, a small tube of antiseptic ointment, and emergency phone numbers. Replace the lid.

CLAY SLIDES

Clay is especially versatile for slides, as you can mold it into millions of different unique shapes. Here's one example.

Snake Slide

1. Roll about 2 T. of clay into an 8-inch-long rope.
2. Coil the rope around a ¾-inch dowel that has a light coating of vegetable oil on it.
3. Flatten the head and make a point on the tail.
4. When dry, remove from the dowel; paint and decorate as desired.

GAMES

Introduction

WHY WE USE GAMES

Games are part of all the fun of Cub Scouting. Skills and interests boys develop now teach self-confidence, independence, and the ability to get along with others. Children learn through play.

For these reasons, games are an important part of Cub Scouting. Games not only help to accomplish Cub Scouting's overall objectives of citizenship training, physical fitness, and character development, they have educational benefits, too. Games teach a boy to follow rules, to take turns, to respect the rights of others, to give and take, and to play fair. Some games help boys to develop skills, body control, and coordination. Some teach self-confidence and consideration for others. Games stimulate both mental and physical growth, as well as providing an outlet for excess "boy energy."

HOW TO CHOOSE GAMES

When choosing a game, you should consider three things: the physical aspects, mental values, and educational values of the games as they relate to Cub Scouting.

Consider first the *physical aspect:* the release of surplus energy. An active game should be satisfying to the strongest boy and yet not overtax the weakest. It should stimulate the growth and development of muscles. Most outdoor games meet this test.

Boys of Cub Scout age are growing rapidly. They like to run, jump, climb, lift, balance, crawl, bend, yell, chase, and hide. Generally, long walks or runs and other exercise involving endurance are not as suitable for boys of this age. (Also, boys who have had recent severe illness should not take part in active games.)

Some games are selected for their *mental values* because they have an element of excitement or accomplishment. Games can help boys develop quick thinking, alertness, and strategy. Many games offer boys opportunities to express their feelings and emotions, which is healthy.

Boys need to learn to play fair and to follow the rules. They also need to learn that they can't always be winners. Many boys of Cub Scout age have not yet learned to lose gracefully. Your task as leader is to make it clear that losing a game is not the end of the world and that a loss should be an incentive for the boy to try to improve his skills.

Some games are selected for their *educational value.* Boys' minds are more receptive to learning when learning is fun. Their interest and concentration are probably never higher than during play. Games are a way to help boys learn that rules and self-discipline are necessary and that doing one's best is important. Most Cub Scout games help in character development because they require teamwork, fair play, and consideration for others.

Consider these factors when choosing games:
- Purpose (physical, mental, educational)
- Space available
- Number of players
- Equipment available
- Skills and abilities of players

Whether the game involves group competition with team winners or individual competition or is just for fun, the results should be positive and lead to building character and helping boys grow and develop.

FITTING GAMES TO THEMES

Games don't have to fit the monthly theme, but theme games help tie the month's program together. Many of the games included here will fit monthly themes; others can be easily adapted to themes. Sometimes, all you need to do to fit a game to a theme is change the name of the game. For example, a Cowboy Relay could become a Bareback Rider Relay to fit a circus theme.

SUGGESTIONS FOR LEADING GAMES

Boys will like most games if leaders have fun leading them. Anyone can be a successful games leader by following these simple suggestions:

- Know the rules of the game and have the necessary equipment on hand. Plan not only *what* you are going to do, but *how* you are going to do it.
- Start with your best game—one that is easy to explain and enjoyable to play. In addition to bolstering your own confidence, a successful game can enhance the morale of the players.
- Make sure the space available is large enough so everyone can play. Mark off boundaries for active outdoor games with brightly colored cones.
- Remove potential hazards from the play area. Follow health and safety rules.
- Get the full attention of the group and then explain the rules of the game simply, briefly, and in proper order. Be enthusiastic.

- For team games and relay races, you must have equal numbers of players on each team. If the teams are unequal, one or more boys on the smaller team must compete or race twice.

- As a rule, Webelos Scouts are larger and stronger than first-grade Tiger Cubs and second- and third-grade Cub Scouts. For some pack competitions, it may be wise to give Webelos dens a handicap of some type to equalize the contest.

- Teach the game by steps or through demonstration.

- Ask for questions after explaining and demonstrating the game.

- Be sure boys follow the rules. Insist on good sportsmanship and fair play.

- If the game is not going right, stop it and explain the rules again.

- Don't wear a game out. Quit while the boys are still having fun.

- Have enough leaders to handle the group.

- Keep It Simple; Make It Fun (KISMIF).

Teach games to boys with the hope that they will be able to play and lead these same games independently in other settings, such as at school or in the neighborhood. Coach your den chief in leading games. This will enhance his leadership role. Find creative ways to develop leadership skills among the boys so that they may soon be able to play on their own without the assistance of a den leader or den chief.

CHOOSING "IT" AND TEAMS

There are many ways to choose the boy who will be "It" for any game. Here are some suggestions, but make up others that work for your group.

- By birthdays, starting with January 1

- By alphabet, using first or last names

- By drawing a name out of an "It" box. After a name is drawn, it goes into a second box marked "It." When all names are in the second "It" box, put them back in the first box to begin again.

When choosing teams, try one of these ideas:

- Even-numbered birthdays against odd-numbered birthdays

- First half of the alphabet against the last half

- Drawing names from a box. Each boy decorates a craft stick with his name on it and any other creative artwork he wishes. When you need teams for a game, pull out two sticks and put them in separate piles. Continue to pull out pairs of sticks, separating them into two piles, which will be your teams. When you are finished, replace all the sticks so they will be ready for the next team game.

You can also make a game of choosing sides. Have boys sit in a circle and then whisper in each boy's ear the word "Wolf" or "Bear." Then they must make the appropriate animal sound to find the other members of their team.

REFLECTING AFTER GAMES

What is *reflecting*? Reflecting is guiding the players to think about what has happened as a result of the game or activity and try to learn from it. It is remembering thoughts, feelings, and actions and their effects. It is making comparisons and contrasts. Reflecting is making sense of the game or activity by using a series of questions to fit the needs of the group. In the section below on "Noncompetitive, Cooperative, and Team-Building Games," reflecting is an integral part of many of the games.

You should ask the boys five important questions at the end of each activity or game regardless of whether the game is cooperative or competitive. Be sure to allow time for these questions:

- Did you do your best?

- Was anyone left out of the game?

- Was anyone physically hurt?

- Did anyone have their feelings hurt?

- How would you make the game different next time?

Reflecting is a learning experience for you, the leader, as well. Enjoy this opportunity to help your Cub Scouts learn by doing.

EQUIPMENT FOR GAMES

The games included in this book require inexpensive equipment or no equipment at all. You can find most of the needed materials around the house, or boys can make them during a den meeting. Here is a list of some useful items for games.

Balloons: Use balloons in the place of balls for many indoor games. (Be sure to pick up and discard all the pieces of broken balloons.)

Small Balls: Try softballs, tennis balls, table tennis balls, foam balls, or beanbags. They can be pitched, tossed, passed, batted, kicked, bounced, dribbled, carried, or rolled.

Large Balls: Rubber playground balls, beach balls, volleyballs, and soccer balls can be kicked, bounced, thrown, carried, or batted.

Clothespins: Use them as game pieces or to secure other equipment, such as newspaper or balloons.

Sticks: Broom handles are ideal. They can be used to jump over, for pushing other objects, or for batting. (Be sure that sticks won't give boys splinters.)

Tin Cans: Roll or kick them along a course or between obstacles; set them up as targets or markers; or use them to roll objects into. (Make sure that edges are clean and smooth.)

Rings: Use rubber, metal, or margarine tub lids with the centers cut out, or rope rings, for tossing over nails, pegs, hooks, or stakes. Use them to play shuffleboard or throw them into tin cans, boxes, or other containers. Curtain rod rings are useful, too.

Paper Bags: Use them for masks or blindfolds, to blow up and burst, or to wear as hats.

Ropes: Use clothesline or sash cord to jump over, spin as a lariat, or thrown as a lasso. Try rope as a marker for start and finish lines or to tie knots. For tug-of-war, use ¾-inch-diameter or larger rope, and avoid using nylon or polyethylene rope, which can more easily cause rope burns.

Newspapers: Use them as stepping stones, markers, or obstacles; roll them to make swatters or balls.

Bottle Caps: These can be markers or obstacles, checkers, small objects to hide, or objects to throw for accuracy.

Beanbags: They don't roll or bounce. Make them from old denim in many different sizes.

Store equipment for games in a den game chest, which can be as simple as a large cardboard box. It is helpful for all game materials and equipment to be stored in one place, easily accessible to the den. Your game chest can also be useful for those moments when you find yourself with a little free time and nothing prepared!

Here are some ideas beyond the items listed above that you might want to keep in a game chest:

Foil pie pans	Feathers
Chalk	An old umbrella
Toothpicks	Playing cards
Plastic spoons	Washers
Old work gloves	Paper cups
Jars	Marbles
Straws	Checkers
Whistles	A muffin tin
Golf tees	

DEN GAMES

Den games are designed for a small group of boys. Quiet games are helpful when weather prohibits outdoor activities. Active games help boys release excess energy and prepare them for quieter den activities. Most of the games in this book are suitable for dens.

Den games may be competitive or noncompetitive. Remember: Some games are played just for the fun of it. Most of these games don't need a winner.

PACK GAMES

Pack games are played with larger groups of boys, adults, and siblings at pack meetings and activities. Relay games are a great favorite. Note that shuttle relays require less space.

Pack games should include as many boys as possible—preferably all boys in the pack. If all cannot participate, select representatives from each den. Involve parents and leaders whenever possible. Boys love to see their parents or guardians participating in a game.

If you award prizes, keep them simple and inexpensive, such as suckers, bubble gum, balloons, or stickers.

Remember: Above all, pack games should be fun for everyone—those who play *and* those who watch.

Active Games With Equipment

BALLOON BATTLE ROYAL

Activity Level: **High**

Needed: **Any number of players, balloons, string**

Arrange Cub Scouts in a large circle, each with an inflated balloon tied to his ankle. On a signal, players try to break all other balloons by stamping on them, while not letting their balloon get broken. When a balloon is broken, that player leaves the game. The game continues until only one player is left.

BEANBAG SNATCH
(OR STEAL THE BACON)

Activity Level: **High**

Needed: **Large playing area, even number of players, beanbag**

Form two lines facing each other about 25 feet apart. Place a beanbag in the center. Count off the boys in each line from opposite directions. The leader calls out a number, and the opponents with that number run to the center. The object of the game is for a Cub Scout to snatch the beanbag and get back to his side without being tagged by the one with the same number from the other side. Score two points if a player brings the beanbag back without being tagged. Score one point for the opposing team if the snatcher is tagged.

BLAST OFF!

Activity Level: **Moderate**

Needed: **Any number of players, chairs**

One boy is Mission Control. The others are given the names of planets and are seated in chairs around the room. Mission Control walks around the room, calling out the names of various planets. When a player's planet is named, he gets up and follows Mission Control. When most of the boys are walking, Mission Control calls "Blast off!" and all players, including those still sitting, must find a new seat. The player left standing is the new Mission Control.

CAT'S TAIL

Activity Level: **Moderate**

Needed: **Even number of players; pieces of cloth or yarn, different colors for each team**

Divide the group into two teams. Hide several pieces of cloth or yarn—a different color for each team. One boy on each team is a Cat Without a Tail. On a signal, all players search for "tails" of their color. As each is found, it is tied to the belt of their Cat. The winner is the team whose Cat has the longest tail at the end of 5 minutes.

CHANGE CARS

Activity Level: **Moderate**

Needed: **Any number of players, chair for each player, cards with the names of different cars on them**

Prepare for the game by fastening to the back of each chair a card with the name of a different automobile. Each boy checks the car name on his chair and sits down. One player is "It" and stands in the center of the circle of chairs. "It" calls the names of two cars (e.g., Ford and Toyota), and the boys in those chairs try to exchange seats while "It" tries to get a chair for himself. The boy left without a chair becomes "It."

Variation: Use different types of transportation, such as car, plane, boat, or train, or names of animals or states in the United States. Ask the boys for other ideas of things to use.

COVER THE CHAIR

Activity Level: **Moderate**

Needed: **Any number of players, chair for each player**

Boys are seated in chairs in a circle. One player is "It" and stands in the center of the circle, leaving his chair empty. When he commands, "Move to the right," all players try to get into the chair to their right. While this is going on, "It" tries to get a seat. If he succeeds, the person who should have gotten that chair becomes "It." To confuse the players, "It" may suddenly call, "Move to the left"—and he stands a good chance of finding a place.

DEFENDERS AND INVADERS

Activity Level: **High**

Needed: **Large playing area, even number of players, slips of paper, pencils, newspaper**

Divide boys into two groups—the Defenders and the Invaders. One Defender is the Starving Captain, who sits in the "stockade" (marked with a piece of newspaper). Give each of the other Defenders a slip of paper with the name of a food and its allotted playing value: flour, 25; baking powder, 20; dried beef, 15; hardtack, 10; jam, 10; fruit, 5; sugar, 5; and corn, 5. A Leader chosen by the Invaders places his men in the Invaders' territory, which surrounds the Defenders' stockade. The Defenders surround the Invaders and look for ways to break through the Invaders' lines to take supplies to their Starving Captain in the stockade. The Invaders try to capture the Defenders by tagging them. They search their captives and confiscate any "food" found on them. After about 15 minutes of play, tally the score. The Invaders add up the value of the captured supplies. The Starving Captain figures the value of the supplies that have been delivered to him. The side with the highest value of supplies wins.

DISK FOOTBALL

Activity Level: High

Needed: Large playing area, even number of players for two teams, plastic flying disk

Divide the group into two teams, which begin play at opposite ends of a play area. Play begins with one team "kicking off" (throwing the disk). The receiving team tries to score a touchdown by passing the disk and advancing it downfield to the other team's goal line. The other team tries to intercept and score a touchdown. No player may run with the disk and no player may hold it for more than 5 seconds. Play is continuous. There are no downs.

FLYING DISKS

Activity Level: Moderate

Needed: Large playing field, any number of players, plastic flying disk for each team, three or more hula hoops or bicycle tires

Set the hula hoops or other targets up at three different spots, each farther away from the participants. The object is to throw the plastic flying disk so that it lands inside the hula hoop or bike tire. The hula hoop closest could be worth two points; the hoop in the middle, three points; and the one the farthest away, five points. Landing on the hoop or tire doesn't count.

Variation: Two teams can play against each other to see which team can score the most points in a specific time period.

POP OR PROTECT

Activity Level: High

Needed: Large playing area, even number of players, inflated balloons, neckerchief or similar piece of fabric to signify Defenders

Divide the group into two teams—the Defenders and the Invaders. Distinguish the two teams by having the Defenders tuck their neckerchiefs in their belts. Toss an inflated balloon between the two teams. The Invaders try to break the balloon by grabbing it, clapping their hands on it, or stepping on it. The Defenders try to protect it by batting it out of reach. Keep track of the time required for the Invaders to break the balloon. When it is broken, the Defenders become the Invaders. Give each team three turns as Invaders, and then add their times. The team with the least total time wins.

INDOOR SKI RACE

Activity Level: High

Needed: Large room with a smooth floor, any number of players, 12-by-18-inch construction paper for each boy

Line up boys along a starting line and give each a sheet of construction paper. On a signal, boys tear their sheets in half and place a piece of construction paper under each foot. They then "ski" to the goal line. This game must be played on a smooth floor so the "skis" won't tear.

Variation: Play as a relay, with each team member skiing to a line and back, and the next boy taking the "skis" and doing the same.

LINK PASS

Activity Level: **Low**

Needed: **Even number of players, 20 pebbles (10 for each team)**

Divide Cub Scouts into two teams facing each other. They lock elbows with those next to them in their line. Place 10 pebbles on the floor near the first player in each line. On a signal, those two boys each pick up a pebble and pass it to the next player in line, who passes it on. The players' arms must remain linked throughout the game. If a Cub Scout drops a pebble, he must retrieve it without breaking the chain. The first player may start another pebble right away. The first line to pass the 10 pebbles to the end wins.

NEWSPAPER SOFTBALL

Activity Level: **High**

Needed: **Large playing area, even number of players, softball plates, two tin cans, rolled up newspaper**

Divide players into two teams. Place two tin cans on either side of home plate and a rolled newspaper across the tops of the cans. The first "batter" stands behind the newspaper and kicks it with his instep, and the game is on. From that point, follow softball rules.

QUICKSAND

Activity Level: **Moderate**

Needed: **Any number of players, long piece of rope**

Tie the ends of a long rope together to form a large rope circle. Mark off another circle (the "quicksand") on the floor or ground, about one-third the size of the rope circle. Boys take hold of the rope with both hands, forming a ring around the quicksand. On a signal, they all try to pull as many of the other players as possible into the quicksand while keeping out of it themselves. As soon as a player steps into the quicksand, he is out of the game. The game continues until only one player remains.

SLEEPING GUARD

Activity Level: **Moderate**

Needed: **Large room or playing field; any number of players; blindfold; rock, beanbag, or neckerchief for precious object**

Choose one boy to be the Sleeping Guard. The others are Stalkers. The Guard sits blindfolded on the ground, guarding a precious object. The Stalkers form a ring around the guard about 20 feet away. On a signal, they advance as quietly as possible, trying to get close enough to steal the object without waking up the Guard. When the Guard hears an approaching Stalker, he points a finger in that direction. If his finger points at the Stalker, the Stalker is out. If a Stalker succeeds in getting the object without being caught, he is the Guard for the next game.

SPOT CHECK

Activity Level: **Low**

Needed: **Blindfold; key, button, coin, or other small object; small pad of paper and pencils; masking tape**

This game is like Pin the Tail on the Donkey—but without a tail and the donkey!

Place a small object in the center of the floor. Each player writes his name on a small slip of paper and tapes a piece of masking tape to it. At one end of the room, mark a starting line with a line of tape. One by one, players are blindfolded, turned around a few times, and told to walk to the spot where they think the object is located without actually touching the object. As each player reaches his selected spot, he tapes the slip of paper next to it. The player whose paper is closest wins.

TAILS

Activity Level: **High**

Needed: **Large playing field, even number of players, neckerchief or piece of cloth for each player**

Divide boys into two teams. All players tuck their neckerchiefs loosely into their belts in back to signify tails. On a signal, each team rushes toward the other, trying to capture their tails. Once a boy's tail is taken, that boy is out of the game. The capturer ties the tail to the front of his belt. The team that captures the most tails wins. This is a good "stalking game" to play in a place where brush or shrubbery provides cover.

Variation: Set a time limit. If the game is played outdoors, define a specific area that boys must stay in and have a signal for them to return when time is up. Once a tail is taken, the boy who loses it stays in the game to confuse the other players. Boys without tails should still pretend to "hide" their tails by keeping their backs to as many players as possible so others won't know whether they have a tail. The team that captures the most tails within the allotted time wins.

Active Games Without Equipment

ANIMAL GUESSING GAME

Activity Level: **High**

Needed: **Large playing area, even number of players**

Divide the group into two equal teams. Each team chooses an animal and thinks up six riddle clues for that animal (e.g., "I eat flying insects"; "My front teeth are large and I gnaw a lot"; "My eyes are very large"). When both teams are ready, they face each other across a line. Mark a line for each team's home base about 15 feet behind the teams. The teams take turns giving one clue at a time. When one of the teams guesses correctly, they begin to chase the other team toward their home base line. Players who are caught switch teams.

AUTO RACE

Activity Level: **Moderate**

Needed: **Any number of players**

Arrange boys in a circle, with the den chief in the center. He gives each player the name of a car, being sure to use the same name more than once so that several players have the same car. To start play, the den chief calls out the name of a car. The first player with that car name to touch the den chief and return to his place wins the race. The game continues as the den chief calls out another car.

BEAR IN THE PIT

Activity Level: **High**

Needed: **Any number of players**

Boys form a circle. One player inside the circle is the Bear. While the others hold hands tightly, the Bear tries to get through the ring by force or by dodging under their arms. He may not use his hands to break the grip of the players in the ring. When he does break through, the others try to catch him. The first one to tag him is the next Bear.

CROWS AND CRANES

Activity Level: **High**

Needed: **Even number of players**

Divide boys into two teams—the Crows and the Cranes. The teams line up facing each other about a yard apart. Mark off a base line 30 to 50 feet behind each team, or line them up in the center of a room and use the walls for bases. When the leader calls "Crows," the Crows must race to their base without being tagged by the Cranes. When the leader calls "Cranes," they try to get back safely. Players who are tagged become a member of the opposite team. The team with the largest number of people at the end of a given time period wins. The leader can add suspense by prolonging the commands, "Cr-r-r-rows" or "Cr-r-ranes."

FOX AND CHICKENS

Activity Level: **High**

Needed: **Any number of players**

Line up the group in single file. Each boy holds the waist of the player in front of him. The boy at the head of the line is called the Mother Hen and the others are Chicks. Another boy, the Fox, stands in front of the line. On a signal, the Fox starts around the line, trying to catch the last Chick. The Mother Hen flaps her wings and follows the Fox to prevent him from catching the Chick. The others turn away from the Fox as they keep in line with their leader. If the last Chick is caught, he falls in behind the Fox. The game continues until all Chicks are caught.

OWLS AND CROWS

Activity Level: **High**

Needed: **Large playing area, even number of players**

Divide the group into two equal teams—the Owls and the Crows. The teams line up facing each other, about 2 feet apart. About 15 feet behind each team is their home base line. The leader makes a statement that is true or false (it could be related to the monthly theme). If the statement is true, the Owls chase the Crows toward their base line. If it is false, the Crows chase the Owls. Anyone caught must join the other team.

RED LIGHT

Activity Level: High

Needed: Large indoor or outdoor playing area, any number of players

"It" turns his back on the rest of the boys, who are lined up 30 to 50 feet away from him. The object is for the boys to walk or run toward "It" while his back is turned as he counts to 10. At "10," he shouts "Red light!" and turns quickly. Any player who is moving when "It" turns must go back to the starting line. The first to get to "It" and touch him wins the game.

SHERE KHAN (THE TIGER GAME)

Activity Level: High

Needed: Large room or outdoor area, any number of players

One boy is Shere Khan, the tiger, and stands in the center of the playing area. All others line up against a wall. The object of the game is to cross to the opposite wall without being tagged. To start the game, Shere Khan says, "Who's afraid of Shere Khan?" The others answer, "No one," and immediately run across the open space toward the opposite side. All boys tagged help Shere Khan tag the remaining players in the next round. The last one tagged becomes Shere Khan the next time.

Variation: With a big field and a large number of players, half can be Shere Khans and half men. This game is also known as Pom-Pom Pullaway.

Ball Games

BALL OVER

Activity Level: High

Needed: Large playing area, odd number of players, blindfold, whistle, playground ball

Draw a line to divide the area. Divide the group into two teams—one on each side of the line. Players must not cross the line. Blindfold one boy and give him a whistle. When he blows the whistle, the ball is put into play by throwing it from side to side. The object of the game is to keep the ball on the opposing team's side. One point is counted against the team that has the ball each time the whistle is blown. The blindfolded player can blow the whistle whenever he wishes. The lowest score wins.

BALLOON BASKETBALL

Activity Level: Moderate

Needed: Large to medium-sized playing area, any number of players, inflated balloons, empty cardboard box or wastepaper basket

Use an inflated balloon for the ball, batting it around from player to player, and boxes or wastepaper baskets for the goals. Score as in basketball, except that a broken balloon counts five points off for the side that broke the balloon.

BUCKETBALL

Activity Level: High

Needed: Large room or playing area; even number of players; ball; two baskets, boxes, buckets, etc., for goals

50 to 60 feet

30 to 40 feet

This basketball-type game can be played with any type of ball that bounces and a couple of large containers such as laundry baskets, bushel baskets, or large wastepaper baskets. Place the baskets (goals) about 60 feet apart (less if necessary because of space). Divide boys into two teams and play using basketball rules. No points are scored if the ball doesn't remain in the basket or if the basket turns over.

CALL SOCCER

Activity Level: Moderate

Needed: Large playing area, even number of players, soccer ball or volleyball

Divide the players into two teams and line them up facing each other about 30 feet apart. Number the players on each team from opposite ends of the line. Place the ball midway between the two lines. The leader calls a number, and the two players having that number run to the ball, each trying to kick it back to his goal line. The player who kicks it to his goal line scores two points for his team. Then the leader calls another number, and two more players begin. The first team with 10 points wins.

CHAIN DODGE BALL

Activity Level: **High**

Needed: **Large playing area, two teams of five or six players, playground ball**

Arrange one team in a single file, with each player grasping the player in front of him around the waist, forming a chain. The other team forms a circle around the chain and tries to hit the player at the end of the chain with the ball. The players forming the circle may pass the ball around in any manner while those in the chain try to keep the player on the end from being hit. Only the first player in the chain may use his hands to bat the ball away. When the end player is hit, he leaves the game. Continue until all players in the chain are eliminated, and then change sides.

CIRCLE BASEBALL

Activity Level: **High**

Needed: **Large open area with defined boundaries, even number of players, plastic flying disk or a large playground ball or beach ball**

Divide players into two equal teams, with one team up to bat and the other in the field. Batting team members line up single file, one behind the next. Fielding team members scatter in the field. The first batter throws the disk/ball into the field and runs in a circle around his teammates as many times as he can until the other team yells "Stop!" Each time the batter goes around his team is counted as a "run."

In the meantime, the players in the field go after the disk/ball. After a player gets it, all his teammates quickly line up behind him. The player with the disk/ball passes it over his head to the next player as soon as there is someone behind him. This continues until the last player has the disk/ball. He runs to the front of the line, and all members of his team sit down as they yell "Stop!" The batting team can score no more runs now.

The second person in the batting team now throws the disk/ball to the fielding team, and the action is repeated until everyone on the batting team has had a chance "at bat," adding the score for each "inning."

DODGE BALL

Activity Level: **High**

Needed: **Large playing area, any number of players to form two teams, playground ball or volleyball**

Divide the boys into two groups. One group forms a large circle, and the other group scatters inside it. The players in the circle throw the ball at the boys inside, who try to avoid being hit without leaving the circle. Boys who have been hit by the ball join the circle players. The last player in the circle is the winner. When all have been eliminated, the sides change places.

FIVE HUNDRED

Activity Level: **Moderate**

Needed: **Large playing area, any number of players, bat, softball**

A batter tosses a softball up and bats it to the other players, who try to catch it. A fielder scores 100 points for catching a fly ball, 75 points for catching the ball on one bounce, 50 for two bounces, and 25 for fielding a grounder cleanly. When a fielder reaches a score of 500, he exchanges places with the batter. With each new batter, the scoring starts over.

HIT THE BAT

Activity Level: **Moderate**

Needed: **Large paved area or field (the flatter the better), two to 12 players, softball, bat, gloves**

The object of this game is to hit the bat with the ball—rather than hitting the ball with the bat. A player throws the ball up and hits it into the field, where the other players are waiting to catch it. The batter then places his bat on the ground in front of him. The player who catches the ball or retrieves it from the ground then throws or rolls the ball, trying to strike the bat without moving from the spot where the ball fell. If the fielder succeeds in striking the bat, he trades places with the batter. Otherwise, the batter takes another turn.

KICK BALL

Activity Level: **Moderate**

Needed: **Large playing field; enough players for two teams; playground ball, soccer ball, or volleyball; bases**

The play area is similar to a baseball field, with 45 feet between bases and 30 feet from the pitcher's box to home plate. The pitcher rolls the ball to the "batter," who kicks it. Outs are made when a batter kicks three fouls, a fielder catches a fly ball, or the runner fails to circle the bases ahead of the ball. The runner must try for a home run. On a fair ball not caught on the fly, the fielder throws the ball to the pitcher, who throws to either the first or third baseman, who then relays it around the bases. Each baseman must be standing on his base before he can pass the ball to the next base. If the batter succeeds in beating the ball around the bases, he scores a run for his team. Three outs make an inning, and nine innings are a game.

LINE-UP BALL

Activity Level: **Moderate**

Needed: **Large playing area; enough players for two teams; playground ball, soccer ball, or volleyball; bases**

One team takes the field. The pitcher rolls the ball to the first "batter," who kicks it into the field and runs to the far base 80 to 90 feet from home base and then runs back home. The fielder who retrieves the ball holds it over his head, and all other fielders line up behind him in single file. If the runner gets back home before the line is formed, he scores a run for his team. If the line forms before he reaches home base, he is out. Three outs for a team make an inning.

MONKEY IN THE MIDDLE

Activity Level: **Moderate**

Needed: **Medium-sized playing area, three players, playground ball or volleyball**

Three players play this game. Choose one to be the Monkey. The other two players stand about 10 feet apart while the Monkey stands between them. The two end players toss the ball back and forth, trying to keep it high enough or moving fast enough so the Monkey can't catch it. If a player fails to catch the ball, the Monkey can scramble for it, or he can intercept it as it is thrown back and forth. If the Monkey gets the ball, he changes places with the player who threw the ball.

ONE O'CAT

Activity Level: **Moderate**

Needed: **Large playing area, any number of players, bat, softball, bases**

Set up home plate and a first base. One player is the batter; the others are the catcher, the pitcher, and fielders. The batter is out when he makes three strikes or when a fly or foul ball is caught. When he makes a hit, he must run to first base and return home before the ball is returned to the catcher, who must touch home plate to put him out. When the batter is out, all players move up in rotation. The batter moves out to right field. If a player catches a fly ball, he replaces the batter.

ONE-PITCH SOFTBALL

Activity Level: **High**

Needed: **Regular softball diamond, any number of players, bat, softball**

This is a very fast game that any number of boys can play. Play it on a regular softball diamond.

- The team in the field has a catcher, four or five infielders, and any number of outfielders. The pitcher is a member of the team at bat. He tries to pitch in such a way that his teammates hit the ball. He does not field a batted ball.
- Each batter gets only one pitch. The batter runs on a fair ball; anything else (foul ball, strike, ball, or whatever) is an out.
- After the third out, the batting team runs to its fielding positions, running in a counterclockwise direction to get from "up to bat" position to "in the field" position. Players must run around the outside of first and/or third base, and if any player fails to do so, all players must go back and run around the bases.
- Here's the catch: As soon as the pitcher and batter are in position, they may start play *whether or not the fielders are ready.*
- Each team establishes its own batting order.

PASS BALL

Activity Level: **High**

Needed: **Medium-sized playing area, enough players to form two teams, six playground balls (three for each team)**

Two teams form two circles, one inside the other, with boys' backs to one another. Give three balls to each circle. The object is to pass these balls around the circles—one circle passing the balls clockwise and the other counterclockwise—and to keep them going as fast as possible. If a player drops a ball, he is out of the game. The team with the most players at the end of an allotted time wins.

REMOVING COCONUTS

Activity Level: **Moderate**

Needed: **Large room or playing area; four players for each group (you may have more than one group); long piece of rope; four hula hoops; five coconuts, oranges, or balls per group**

This game rarely has a winner; play it for the fun of it.

With the rope, make a large circle in the middle of the playing area. Place the four hula hoops evenly outside of it. Set five coconuts (or balls) in the center of the large circle. One player starts in each of the four outside circles (hula hoops). The object of the game is for each of the four players to try to get three coconuts into his personal hula hoop. He can carry only one coconut at a time. Players can take coconuts from other players. Players cannot guard their coconuts, and they must place—not throw or roll—the coconuts in their circle. By being aware of the other players, boys can work together to keep the game going until everyone decides to stop.

SOAKOUT

Activity Level: **High**

Needed: **Large playing area; enough players for two teams; playground ball, soccer ball, or volleyball; bases**

This is a variation of kick ball. The pitcher, using an underhand pitch, rolls the ball to the "batter," who kicks it and runs all four bases while members of the defensive team try to "soak" him by hitting him with a direct throw. Boys may not relay the ball from player to player.

The batter is out after three strikes, when a fly ball or foul tip is caught, or when he is soaked by a member of the defensive team. After he kicks the ball, he must try a home run but may run the bases in any order. He may halt, dodge, or run any direction on

the playing area but must touch all bases before coming home. If he gets a base on balls, he is not permitted to leave first base until a succeeding batter hits the ball.

SOCCER BOWLING

Activity Level: **Low**

Needed: **Medium-sized playing area; any number of players; 10 2-L. plastic bottles, 10 wooden blocks, or 10 paper milk cartons; soccer ball or basketball**

Set up 10 objects like bowling pins. Players kick the ball at them from a line 25 to 35 feet away. Keep score as in bowling.

THREE-PIN BOWLING

Activity Level: **Low**

Needed: **Large indoor space or level outdoor playing field; three plastic bottles, milk cartons, tin cans, or other items for bowling pins; playground ball**

Set up three "pins" in a triangle with the two rear pins a little farther apart than the width of the ball to be used. Draw a foul line with a stick or chalk 20 to 30 feet from the head pin. It also helps to mark the spots where the pins are placed.

In scoring, credit the player four points for knocking down the head pin and three points for either of the back pins. Strikes, spares, and number of frames played are as in regular 10-pin bowling. All other bowling rules apply. To speed the game along, it helps for one of the players to act as pinsetter.

Variation: Use beanbags rather than balls, particularly when playing indoors. Beanbags don't bounce and don't need to be chased.

Bicycle Games

Note: All boys must wear a bicycle helmet whenever they are riding a bicycle! (Since March 1999, all helmets sold in the United States must be approved by the Consumer Product Safety Commission [CPSC]. If boys are using older helmets, make sure they are certified by either ASTM [American Society for Testing and Materials] or the Snell Memorial Foundation [Snell].)

BIKE RELAY

Activity Level: **Moderate**

Needed: **Large paved area, even number of riders, bike and helmet for each rider**

Establish a starting line and mark off turning lines about 50 feet away in opposite directions. Divide the group into two teams. The teams will ride in opposite directions. The teams should be about 20 feet apart to avoid collisions as the riders return to the start-finish line. On a signal, the first rider on each team races to his turning line and back. The next rider may not start until the first rider's front wheel has crossed the line. Continue until all have raced.

COASTING RACE

Activity Level: **Moderate**

Needed: **Large paved area, any number of riders, bike and helmet for each rider**

The object of this race is to see which rider can coast the longest distance. Each rider pedals as hard as possible for a set distance (at least 15 feet) to a starting line, and then must stop pedaling and coast as far as he can. Mark the spot where a rider's foot touches the ground. The next rider tries to better that mark.

HITTING THE TARGET

Activity Level: **Moderate**

Needed: **Large paved area; any number of riders; bike and helmet for each rider; four to six plastic ice cream containers (or other similarly sized plastic or cardboard containers); marbles, stones, bottle caps, etc.**

This game requires skill, coordination, timing, and marksmanship. Set up the containers about 15 feet apart in a straight line along a 100-foot course. Each rider has a small object (marble, stone, bottle cap) to place in each of the cans. Riders follow each other down the course at an average speed, dropping one object into each container. This game can be played in teams, with the winning team the one with the most hits.

NEWSPAPER RACE

Activity Level: **Moderate**

Needed: **Large paved area, any number of riders, bike and helmet for each rider, six or eight large boxes or baskets, folded newspaper for each rider**

On a 100-yard racecourse, place six or eight large boxes or baskets about 15 feet apart. Put the first basket about 10 feet from the starting line. Each player rides along on a line about 8 feet away from the baskets. As he passes each basket, he tosses in a folded newspaper. The player who gets the most newspapers in the baskets wins.

OBSTACLE SLALOM RACE

Activity Level: **Moderate**

Needed: **Large paved area, any number of riders, bike and helmet for each rider, five markers (empty boxes, cones, or weighted plastic bottles)**

Set up the markers slalom style, with the first marker 20 yards from the starting line and three additional markers about 10 feet apart. Riders must follow a course that zigzags from the right of one marker to the left of the next, and so on. The rider completing the course in the shortest time wins.

POTATO RACE

Activity Level: **Moderate**

Needed: **Enough riders to form two teams, bike and helmet for each rider, two empty boxes, 10 to 12 potatoes or beanbags**

Teams line up with their bikes in relay style. Place a box on the starting line in front of each team. At intervals of 5 yards or more in front of each team, mark four circles and place a potato or beanbag in each before the game begins. On a signal, the first player on each team rides out and picks up the potato in the first circle, returns to the starting line, and places it in the box. He then rides for the second, third, and fourth potatoes, returning each time to put them into the box. When he has finished, he touches off the second player, who rides out carrying one of the potatoes to place it back in the first circle. He returns for the second, third, and fourth in similar fashion, replacing them one at a time. Continue in this way, with one teammate removing the potatoes and the next player replacing the potatoes, until all boys have participated.

SNAIL RACE

Activity Level: **Low**

Needed: **Large paved area with predetermined race course, any number of riders, bike and helmet for each rider**

The object of this race is to see which rider can travel the slowest without putting a foot on the ground—which is quite a feat in cycling! If a player puts his foot down, he is disqualified. The last rider to cross the finish line wins.

Noncompetitive, Cooperative, and Team-Building Games

Children experience a lot of competition in their lives. Many games reinforce that competition either because players are eliminated or because boys lose as individuals or teams, as only one team or player can win.

The games in this section will help promote cooperation and build self-esteem. No one is a "loser"; everyone is a "winner." The only way to accomplish the goal of these games is to play fairly and, often, work together. But everyone will have fun in the process, too, and players will cheer each other on as they help each other.

Most of these games either require no equipment or require equipment that you can find easily around the house or can make from materials on hand. Game equipment does not have to be expensive. Homemade equipment has the further benefit of helping to equalize talent; that is, a "ball" made from newspapers stuffed into a stocking, for instance, is not easy for anyone to throw.

Consider using beanbags in place of balls in many games (and not just the games in this section). Beanbags don't bounce or roll, so you don't have to spend time chasing them. Also, players who might be afraid of catching a ball usually have no trouble catching a beanbag.

Cooperative and noncompetitive games have fewer rules but more directions or possibilities. One of the many advantages of these games and activities is that you can change the rules to fit your group. In many cases, teams are loosely organized; each team need not have the same number of players.

Another advantage to these activities is that age, strength, and speed are not important, which means that the whole family, the whole den, or even the whole pack can enjoy the activities together.

REFLECTING

Review the section on "Reflecting After Games" (page 3–2). As a game leader, you are encouraged to help the group members reflect on what they did, how they determined what to do, and how they felt about it. Some specific questions are suggested below with some of the game descriptions.

P-E-E-P SAFETY CHECKS

The physical and emotional safety of all participants is the most important concern when facilitating team-building and noncompetitive games. You can ensure safety by doing four checks before you begin any team-building activity (or any other type of game). The letters P-E-E-P will help you remember how to implement the checks.

P—Personal: Are participants personally safe? All participants should remove any jewelry or personal items that could injure them or someone else.

E—Emotional: Are participants emotionally safe? Observe participants and check in with them to see how they are feeling emotionally. If someone is preoccupied, angry, depressed, or overly excited, he or she might have a difficult time focusing on the challenge at hand, which therefore might affect his/her personal safety or the safety of the group. All participants should agree to stay focused on the challenge presented.

E—Environmental: Is the group physically safe in the environment? Remove all potential dangers from the area being used for the activity. Groups also need to be aware of everything in their environment that cannot be removed, such as sun, wet or uneven ground, insects, trees, noise, other people, etc.

P—Physical: Do participants have the knowledge needed to be physically safe? That is, all participants must be aware of any injuries, soreness, or allergies (such as to bees) of all other group members. By doing this, participants will be better able to plan their approach to helping group members complete the challenge successfully.

CHECKLIST FOR PRESENTING THE GAMES OR ACTIVITIES

- Choose an activity suited to the ages and physical abilities of group members. All the games in this section are appropriate for Tiger Cubs, Cub Scouts, Webelos Scouts, and adults to play together.
- Choose an area large enough and free from potential hazards to ensure safety.
- Make all ground rules and procedures clear to participants before they try to play the games.
- Present the situation or explain the rules; then step back and allow the group to work through any problems that the game presents or communication it requires. Little good will come from interrupting the problem-solving and communication process by giving hints or indicating to participants a more-efficient or "right" way.
- Stop the group if you see any potentially dangerous situation.
- Stop playing the game while everyone is still having fun. Don't keep it going until they become bored with it.

SPOTTING

Although no games in this section require the use of a spotter, it is important that game leaders know what a spotter is and how spotting is done.

Spotting is important in any activity where a participant is off the ground. The proper use of spotting will reduce the chance of injury. The spotter should keep a balanced stance with knees bent, one foot placed forward and the other foot back for stability. The spotter's hands must be held at chest or shoulder height and be ready to break a fall. The spotter's head must be up, with eyes on the participants. The spotter must be attentive to what participants are doing

and how. It is the spotter's responsibility to *break falls*—not to help the participant try to complete an activity.

ALL-ON-ONE-SIDE VOLLEYBALL (BAT AND SCOOT)

Activity Level: **Moderate**

Needed: **Large room or playing area, six to 10 players, inflated balloons, volleyball net**

In this version of volleyball, both teams begin on the same side of the net. The object is to get your team members to the other side of the net and back as many times as possible. Using the balloon for a ball, each player bats the balloon to another player and then scoots under the net to the other side. The last player to touch the balloon taps it over the net and scoots under. The receiving players try to keep the balloon in play and repeat the process. As the teams get better, try putting two balloons into play at one time.

BACK TO BACK

Activity Level: **Moderate**

Needed: **Large playing area, odd number of players**

Arrange all boys except one ("It") in pairs, standing back to back with their elbows locked. Pairs are scattered randomly over the playing area. When "It" calls "All change!" each boy must find a new partner and hook elbows with him. At the same time, "It" tries to find a partner. The boy left without a partner becomes the next "It."

BATTING DOWN THE LINE

Activity Level: **Low**

Needed: **Large indoor or outdoor playing area, any number of players, inflated balloons**

Two or more groups may play this game simultaneously. Arrange groups in parallel lines with members spaced about 2 feet apart. On a signal, the first player bats the balloon with either hand toward the person next to him, who bats it to the next, and so on until the balloon reaches the end of the line. If the balloon touches the ground, a group member must take it to the starting line, and the group members must begin again. Try varying the spacing between players. Is it more challenging to play the game with people closer together or farther apart?

BLANKET BALL

Activity Level: **Low**

Needed: **Indoor or outdoor area, any number of players, two sheets or blankets, two balls or large soft objects (even rolls of toilet paper work well)**

Form two groups. Group members grab hold of a blanket's edges, with a ball in the center of the blanket. Players practice throwing the ball up and catching it by moving the blanket up and down in unison, trying to get the ball as high as possible. After the groups have developed some skill in catching their own ball, they toss the ball toward the other group to catch on their blanket. Groups continue throwing the balls back and forth. Group members might reflect on how they decided to toss the ball to the other team.

Variation: Try using water balloons outdoors on a hot day.

BODY TAG

Activity Level: **High**

Needed: **Large level playing area, any number of players**

The den leader chooses one of the boys to be "It" by touching him. "It" must then place his right hand on the spot where he has been touched (arms, chest, back, ankle, etc.), and in this position he must tag another boy, who becomes the new "It." Play until all the boys have a chance to be "It."

CHASER AND RUNNER

Activity Level: **High**

Needed: **Large level playing area, even number of players**

Pair off all boys except two—who are the Chaser and the Runner. The pairs stand 8 to 10 feet apart. In each pair, one partner stands behind the other and grabs him around the waist. The Runner tries to get in front of one of the pairs so that the front player can grab him around the waist. If the Runner succeeds, the rear player of the pair becomes the Runner and tries to join another pair. Meanwhile, the Chaser is trying to tag the Runner.

The front player in a pair always tries to help the Runner join on, while the rear player tries to prevent this by swinging his partner out of the way. If the Chaser catches the Runner, they change places.

CAR AND DRIVER

Activity Level: **Low**

Needed: **Large playing area, any number of players**

Each person finds a partner of about the same height. Partners stand one behind the other, both facing the same direction. The front player is the Car; he places his bent arms about chest high in front of him with palms out to act as "bumpers." The Car closes his eyes. The back player is the Driver; he places his hands on the car's shoulders to act as the "steering wheel." No talking is allowed during the game.

Drivers take their Cars for a ride, being careful that there are no "crashes" (bumping anyone else). Drivers should use light pressure on the shoulders to indicate turns and speed. After a short time, ask everyone to freeze and to reverse the roles, with the Cars becoming Drivers and the Drivers becoming Cars. (If you have an odd number of players, have one group of three make a van or truck. The middle player is the Driver.)

For reflecting questions, you might ask boys who were Cars how they felt not to be able to see where they were going. Did they trust their Drivers?

CATCH THE DRAGON'S TAIL

Activity Level: **High**

Needed: **Large clear area without holes in the ground, eight to 10 players, bandanna or neckerchief for each team**

Players line up, one behind the other. Everyone grabs the waist of the person in front of him. The last person in line tucks a neckerchief or bandanna in the back of his belt. To work up steam, the "dragon" might let out a few fearsome roars. On a signal, the dragon begins chasing its own "tail," the person at the head of the line trying to snatch the handkerchief. The tricky part of this struggle is that the people at the front and the people at the end are clearly competing, but those in the middle aren't sure who to cooperate with. When the "head" finally captures the tail, the head dons the handkerchief and becomes the new tail, and the second person from the front becomes the new head.

Variation: Two dragons try to catch each other's tails. The dragon "members" will have to work together as a team to move effectively and quickly.

Reflecting questions might relate to how those in the middle felt when they didn't know which way the "head" was going, and whether or not they had to help keep the "tail" from getting caught.

CHAIN TAG

Activity Level: **High**

Needed: **Large playing area, any number of players**

Boys are scattered over the playing area. One player is "It" and tries to tag another player. The first boy he tags joins hands with him and helps in tagging others. Both may use only their free hand to tag. Each player tagged joins hands with the one tagging him. The line grows longer as more players are tagged, but only the players at the two ends of the chain may do the tagging. Tagging doesn't count if the chain is broken. The game continues until all boys have been tagged.

ELBOW, FRUIT, HOP

Activity Level: **Moderate**

Needed: **Indoor or outdoor playing area, any number of players**

When the leader calls out a phrase such as "nose, clothing, skip," boys must touch (or hold) their nose and skip around calling out the name of an article of clothing. Everyone tries to avoid touching and must make their item heard. Start with "hand, your name, tiptoe," and then try variations such as "foot, farm animal, jump" or "knee, a country, walk." Introduce Scouting items such as "ear, camping item, hop" or "head, Cub Scout motto, hop." Boys stop the action when they see the Cub Scout sign. This is a good game to play with the den when reviewing a list of things to bring to the next meeting or den outing.

ELBOW TAG

Activity Level: **High**

Needed: **Large level playing area and large number of players**

All players get a partner and link elbows. (If you have an odd number of players, make one group of three.) All linked pairs form a circle. One pair is chosen to run first. One person is "It" and begins to chase the other person, the Runner, around the outside of the circle. To be considered "safe," the Runner must link elbows with a person in another pair before being tagged. The person in the new threesome who is not linked with the Runner becomes the new Runner. If the Runner is tagged before linking with one of the pairs, he becomes "It" and the former "It" becomes the Runner.

FIND THE LEADER

Activity Level: **Low**

Needed: **Small playing area and any number of players**

Boys sit in a circle. One boy is "It" and leaves the room. The remaining boys choose a leader. "It" is then called back into the center of the circle and the leader slyly starts a motion, such as waving his hands, clapping, making a face, etc. The others in the circle imitate the leader. "It" keeps a watchful eye on everyone to find out who is starting the motions. The leader should change motions frequently. When "It" discovers who the leader is, the leader becomes "It" and a new leader is chosen.

FOREHEAD SQUEEZE RELAY

Activity Level: **Moderate**

Needed: **Large playing area, even number of players, several tennis balls or oranges**

The object is for two players in each team to carry a ball or orange across the room and back again by holding it between their foreheads. If dropped, start again. When the first pair completes their circuit, the next pair in that team begins. Hand over the ball or orange quickly. There is quite an art in moving in tandem with your partner and gently covering the distance while hurrying.

GIVEAWAY TAG

Activity Level: **High**

Needed: **Large playing area; any number of players; ball, rolled-up newspaper, or beanbag**

One boy is "It." The others are scattered around the playing area. One of the players holds an object such as a ball, rolled newspaper, or beanbag. "It" tries to tag the boy holding the object, who may run with it or pass it to another boy. The player tagged becomes "It."

LAUNDRY GRAB BAG

Activity Level: **Low**

Needed: **Large room; any number of players; whistle; pillowcase or laundry bag; old hats, shirts, shoes, stockings, suspenders, belts, etc.**

Fill a laundry bag with an assortment of old clothing—the more funny looking, the better. Boys stand in a circle, with one holding the bag. On a signal, he passes the bag to the player on his left, he to the next, and so on around the circle. As the bag is being passed around, the den chief blows a whistle. Whoever has the bag in his hand when the whistle sounds must reach inside, take out an article of clothing, and put it on. Play continues until all clothing is being worn.

GROUP JUGGLE

Activity Level: **Low**

Needed: **Large playing area, any number of players, several beanbags or small stuffed animals that can be thrown easily (Have as few as half the number of objects as you have players or up to one per player.)**

The leader arranges boys into a circle and asks everyone to raise one hand. He explains the rules: (1) Throw the beanbag to someone who has his hand raised (but not the person beside you); (2) drop your hand when you catch the beanbag; and (3) if you drop the beanbag, don't try to retrieve it—just continue the game. The leader throws a beanbag to a player, and play continues until everyone has caught the beanbag and no more hands are raised. Play again, but each time with more and more beanbags flying at the same time.

Variation 1: All the items to be tossed might be related, such as an assortment of balls, or fruit, etc. The game leader then might introduce an additional unanticipated, humorous object, such as a rubber chicken. Watch the groups' response as this object goes flying through the air. Expect some missed catches!

Variation 2: The Name Game

The object of this variation is to learn everyone's name. Here are the rules: (1) Call your name when you catch the beanbag and drop your hand; (2) throw the beanbag to someone else (not the person beside you) who has his hand raised; (3) remember the name of the person who threw you the beanbag and to whom you throw the beanbag. The leader throws the beanbag to the first person and continues the pattern until everyone has caught the beanbag. Repeat the game a few more times as boys remember names. Then play again, with everyone calling out the name of the person catching the beanbag.

GROUP STAND-UP

Activity Level: **Low**

Needed: **Indoor room or grassy outdoor area, 10 to 20 players, long thick rope (about an inch thick) tied to form a circle**

Players sit in a circle holding onto the rope, which is on the ground in front of their feet. Everyone grasps the rope and then pulls gently and evenly on it. If everyone pulls together evenly, the entire group should be able to come to a standing position. (Use a shorter rope for a group of six to eight players.)

HARBOR MASTER

Activity Level: **Low**

Needed: **Large room or level playing area, any number of players, blindfold**

One boy is blindfolded and is a Ship; another is the Harbor Master. The rest of the players spread themselves throughout the playing area as Buoys. Buoys may not talk or move, and the Harbor Master must remain at the finish spot ("port"). Using only his voice, the Harbor Master must guide the Ship safely through the harbor to the port. Switch roles and repeat the game.

Reflecting questions might concern how the Ship felt being unable to see; how the Harbor Master felt being able to use only his voice to guide the Ship; or how the Buoys felt being unable to move or speak.

HOT CHOCOLATE RIVER

Activity Level: **Low**

Needed: **Large level playing area, any number of players, several boards (fewer than there are players) long enough to step on**

The object of this game is to get the entire group from one "shore" of the "chocolate river" to the other using only the "marshmallows" (small boards) that are provided.

The leader establishes where the shores of the river are (you might mark them off with pieces of rope). The river should be wide enough to challenge the group. The group begins on one shore of the river. The leader explains that the river is made of hot chocolate. If anyone should fall into the river (step off a board), he must swim back to the original shore for "first aid" before trying to cross the river again.

The leader asks what floats in hot chocolate (anticipating the answer "marshmallows") and shows the players the boards (the marshmallows). The leader points out that for safety, marshmallows must be

placed rather than thrown, and players must *step* from marshmallow to marshmallow rather than jump. The leader places the marshmallows on the shore, and the players decide together how to get the group safely to the other shore. More than one person may occupy a marshmallow at the same time.

There is no one solution to this game. Usually, the first person places a marshmallow in the river and puts his foot on it. A second marshmallow is passed to him, and he places it in the river and puts one foot on it. He then reaches for the second person in the line and helps this person move onto the first marshmallow. A third marshmallow is placed in the river, and players keep moving onto the marshmallows as they are added to the river.

Note to the game leader: If a marshmallow is unoccupied, remove it and say that it has melted. This adds some pressure to the activity but does not jeopardize the accomplishment of the task.

HOT POTATO

Activity Level: **Low**

Needed: **Small playing area, any number of players, a potato or other object for passing**

Boys form a circle, with "It" in the center. One of the players has the potato for passing. When "It" calls "Pass the potato," the player with the potato starts passing it around the circle. When "It" calls "Hot potato," whoever has the potato at that moment becomes "It."

HOT STUFF

Activity Level: **Moderate**

Needed: **Large level playing area, any number of players, ball or potato**

This is a variation of Hot Potato. Boys form a circle. One boy is the Caller and stands outside the circle. As the players in the circle pass the ball from player to player, the Caller counts aloud to a number between 1 and 50 that he chose before play began and then yells "Hot Stuff!" At that point, the person with the ball (or if the ball is between players, the person just about to get the ball) leaves the circle and joins the Caller. As more and more players leave the circle, the Caller group becomes larger and larger and the counting becomes louder and louder. The original Caller tells the new Callers the number to which the group will count. The game ends when there are just two players passing the ball back and forth.

IN THE POND

Activity Level: **Moderate**

Needed: **Large paved area with a chalk line circle, any number of players**

Arrange boys in a circle just outside a chalk line. One boy is "It." If he orders "In the pond!" all boys jump forward. When "It" calls "On the bank!" all boys jump back. If the order "In the pond!" is given when all players are already in the pond, no one should move. Boys should ignore orders such as "On the pond!" or "In the bank!" The first player to make a mistake becomes the new "It."

ISLANDS

Activity Level: **Low**

Needed: **Any number of players, large playing area, several hula hoops (or old T-shirts or open newspapers), portable tape player with marching music if music is desired**

The leader explains that everyone is a swimmer in an ocean, that hula hoops represent islands, and that while the music is playing (or the leader is clapping), swimmers must swim in the ocean. When the music (or clapping) stops, however, or when the leader calls "Shark attack!" swimmers should immediately get onto an island because the sharks are near. (Swimmers should get on an island in a designated period of time.) The object is to save all the swimmers, not to eliminate any of them.

During the next round, the leader removes one of the islands. As play continues, the number of islands gets smaller, so it will be increasingly difficult for swimmers to stand on an island. Boys may have to depend on a friend to hold them up so they don't loose their balance and fall off the island (outside of the hoop). All swimmers need to be out of the water for the group to succeed. Encourage boys to help each other get on and stay on islands, rather than shove each other off to make more room.

Reflecting questions could include: How did you feel as there were fewer and fewer islands? What are some of the things you saw players do during the game to help others stay safely on an island? How did you feel when you helped save others?

KNOTS

Activity Level: **Moderate**

Needed: **Activity room or grassy outdoor area, eight to 12 players**

To form a knot, boys stand in a circle, shoulder to shoulder, extending their hands into the center. Each boy grabs the hand of two different players, taking care that one of the players is not standing adjacent to him. Then the group "untangles" the knot, the object being for the group to find itself in one large circle again, or perhaps two or even interconnected circles. No player may let go of any other player's hand (unless to prevent injury!).

Reflecting questions might be related to who, if anyone, became the "leader" of the group. Did the "leadership" change from person to person? How and why? How did the group decide how to untangle the knot?

LINE UP

Activity Level: **Low**

Needed: **Any number of players, one blindfold per player or "honor blindfolds" (boys close their eyes)**

Players are blindfolded and told that no one may talk during this activity. The leader asks them to line up by height. When they feel that they have accomplished this task, they should stand in place and remove their eye coverings to see how they did. You can substitute other requirements, such as lining up by shoe size.

Variation: Try playing this without blindfolds and with eyes open. Boys still cannot talk but can use sign language to communicate. This time they line up by birthday, middle name, last four digits of their phone number, or any other direction.

MACHINE CHARADES

Activity Level: **Low**

Needed: **Large room, teams of three to eight players**

This is a great game for mixing adults and boys. Try it at a pack meeting. Each den meets in a corner of the room to select a machine that they want to "build" using all the members of the den. They practice privately, acting out the movements of that machine (not the person using it, but the machine itself in action). Bring all the dens back together to act out their machines until someone correctly identifies it.

Variation: Can You Be Things Together?

In this variation, the leader assigns the "thing" the group is to be, asking "Can you be a string of beads [a canoe, a tent, a donut]?" This game is even suitable for Tiger Cubs. You can make this game fit many different monthly themes by the "things" you select.

NUMBER CALL-OUT

Activity Level: **Low**

Needed: **Large activity room, lots of players (the more, the better)**

A leader calls out a number, such as "three," to the group, and everyone scrambles to get into groups of three. Quickly, the leader calls another number to form other sizes of groups, and continues rapidly as players scramble.

Variation 1: The leader tells players that every new combination must not include players from previous combinations.

Variation 2: The leader asks people to find others with similar characteristics, for example:

• Find everyone who has the same kind of pet as you.

• Find everyone with the same color of eyes as you.

• Find everyone with the same birthday month as you.

• Find everyone with the same last digit in their phone number as you.

PASS THE RING

Activity Level: **Low**

Needed: **Indoor or outdoor playing are, any number of players, long rope tied to form a circle, ring or washer slipped onto the rope**

Boys sit in a circle, each holding onto the rope with both hands. "It" stands in the center. On a signal, the boys start to move the ring or washer around the rope, trying to conceal its location from "It." "It" tries to guess the position of the ring. The boy who holds the ring when "It" guesses correctly is "It" for the next game.

PASS THROUGH THE HOOP

Activity Level: **Low**

Needed: **Ten to 20 players, several hula hoops**

Everyone stands in a circle and joins hands, with hula hoops hung over the arms of players at equal intervals around the circle. (Players hold hands through the hoops.) Players do not drop hands at any time. Players who have a hoop on their arm must step through it and pass the hoop to the person next to them. The hoops can go in both directions. The game becomes interesting when one player has to pass two hoops in different directions.

Reflecting questions might concern how boys chose to pass through the hoop (some people go headfirst; others go feetfirst). How much help did others give you? How did you feel when you realized that hoops were coming at you from both directions? How did players help each other?

PERPETUAL MOTION

Activity Level: **Moderate**

Needed: **Large playing area with a smooth surface, any number of players, flying plastic disk or metal pie plate**

Players sit in a circle on the floor and count off so that each person has a number. Place the disk or pie plate on the floor in the center of the circle. The first player gets up, turns the disk on edge, and spins it as you would a coin. As the player sits down, he calls out the number of another player. That player jumps up, gets to the disk before it stops spinning, gives it another spin, and calls out another player's number before sitting down. Players continue calling each other's numbers and keeping the disk spinning. If the disk completely stops spinning, a player starts it again. The object of the game is to cooperate in keeping the disk spinning.

RING CALL BALL

Activity Level: **Moderate**

Needed: **Large playing area, any number of players, volleyball for each group**

Boys form a circle, with "It" in the center. "It" throws the ball in the air while at the same time calling the name of one of the boys in the circle. That boy must catch the ball. If he catches the ball, he returns to the circle; if he misses it, he changes places with "It."

ROPE RING

Activity Level: **Low**

Needed: **Large playing area, any number of players, about 50 feet of clothesline or similar rope**

Tie the ends of the rope together to make a circle. Players stand outside the rope in a circle, holding it with both hands. One player is the Ringmaster and stands in the middle. The Ringmaster tries to tap the hand of a ringside player holding the rope. The players can let go of the rope to avoid being tapped. The Ringmaster may try to trick players by pretending to tap one player and then tap another. When a player is tapped while holding the rope, he becomes the next Ringmaster, and the game continues.

Variation: For large groups, two or three Ringmasters will keep players off guard and the game more exciting.

SHAPES

Activity Level: **Low**

Needed: **Large playing area, any number of players, 50 feet of clothesline or similar rope, one blindfold per player or "honor blindfolds" (boys close their eyes)**

The object of the game is to form a specified shape without being able to see. Players are blindfolded and hold onto the rope with both hands. The leader directs them to form a circle, a square, a triangle, or other shapes.

Reflecting questions might relate to how it felt to be blindfolded. How did you determine that you had the correct shape? Who became the leader? How was this determined?

SPIDER WEB

Activity Level: **Low**

Needed: **Room with chairs arranged in a circle, eight to 10 players, ball of yarn**

Boys sit on the chairs in a tight circle. The den leader holds the ball of yarn and makes a partial statement, such as, "My favorite game is...; I feel scared when...; My favorite Scouting activity is...; When I grow up I want to...," etc. He then gently tosses the ball of yarn to a player across the circle, who catches it and completes the statement (saying, for example, "My favorite game is tic-tac-toe"). That player then tosses the yarn to another player, who also completes the statement. Each person catching the ball holds onto the yarn so that by the time everyone has caught the yarn and completed the statement, an interesting and colorful "spider web" has been created in the center of the circle. The leader may then say a second partial statement and invite the boys to reverse the process, winding up the ball of yarn.

Variation: This is a good introductory game. The leader could say, "My name is Bobby, and I'm tossing the ball to Michael." Michael repeats the pattern of naming himself first and then tossing the ball to a player across the circle.

SPUD

Activity Level: **High**

Needed: **Large playing area, any number of players, foam ball**

All players stand in a circle. One player starts the game by throwing a foam ball high and yelling the name of one of the other players. Everyone scatters quickly except the boy whose name was called. He retrieves the ball, and when he gets it, all the other players must stand still. The boy with the ball throws it and tries to hit another player. If he misses, the boys may run again until he recovers the ball, and then they must freeze and the boy tries to hit someone again with the ball. When a player is hit, the game starts over. *Note:* The ball must be thrown from where it falls.

SQUIRRELS AND FOXES

Activity Level: **High**

Needed: **Large playing area, groups of four players**

Have all except two boys—the Fox and the Homeless Squirrel—form circles of four boys. Each circle counts off, and the No. 1's stand in the center of the circles and become Squirrels. The other boys form "hollow trees" by holding hands. During the game, the Fox tries to catch the Homeless Squirrel. The Homeless Squirrel can take refuge in any tree, thereby forcing the Squirrel inside to leave. The Fox now tries to catch that Squirrel. If caught, the Squirrel becomes a Fox, and the chase continues. After a few minutes, have the No. 2's in each circle become Squirrels.

STIR THE SOUP

Activity Level: **Low**

Needed: **Room with chairs in a circle (a chair for each player, less one), any number of players, cane or broomstick**

Players sit in a circle on chairs, with "It" in the center of the circle holding a cane or stick. The players leave their chairs and walk around "It" in a close circle, saying, "Stir the soup! Stir the soup! "It" goes through the motions of stirring the soup with the cane. Suddenly, when no one is expecting it, "It" taps the cane three times, drops it, and runs for a seat. All players run to find a chair. The player left out is the new "It."

TACTILE COPIER

Activity Level: **Low**

Needed: **Small playing area, any number of players, paper, pencil or pen, index cards or small pieces of paper with simple picture (such as a house, star, fish, etc.) drawn on them**

The object of the game is to copy the picture correctly. Players arrange themselves in a line, all facing one direction. A picture is shown to the last person in line. This person uses his finger to "draw" the picture on the back of the person in front of him. Each player in turn "passes" the picture on to the next person in line by drawing it on his back. The person at the head of the line draws the picture on a piece of paper for the group to compare with the original drawing. Repeat the game after players rotate their positions.

Variations: After passing on the picture, each player draws it on paper, as he perceives it. The group then compares their individual drawings. Or, trace words instead of pictures.

THE SNAIL

Activity Level: **Low**

Needed: **Large playing area, large group of players, 50 to 100 feet of clothesline**

The group stands in a line, each person holding the rope in one hand. Starting at one end, the group makes a large coil, like the shell of a snail. After the coiling is complete, the group moves slowly together 15 or 20 feet in one direction and then uncoils.

TURTLE TAG

Activity Level: **Moderate**

Needed: **Large playing area, any number of players**

One Cub Scout is "It" and the others are Turtles. While "It" counts to 10, Turtles hop up and run at least 10 steps. "It" tries to tag a Turtle but cannot tag when the Turtle is on its back with all four "feet" in the air. Turtles can assume the safe position or keep moving.

Parachute Games

Some children learn to play parachute games in school gym classes. Parachutes come in a variety of sizes, from 12 to 36 feet across. Select the size according to how many players you have. A parachute is an expensive item. Check with your local school or park district to see whether they have one that they can loan to you. Usually, a deposit will be required to ensure its safe return. You may also find a used military parachute at an army-navy surplus store. Clean it thoroughly before using it for games.

When holding a parachute, boys should place one hand on each side of the "rib" of the parachute if enough "ribs" are available. There are three ways to grasp a parachute. The three grips are

- Overhand grip: palms down
- Underhand grip: palms up
- Alternating grip: one palm up and one palm down

Parachute games require a large level area free of hazards. When the weather doesn't permit outdoors play, parachute games can be played indoors in a gym or in a multipurpose room. The more players available, the easier it is to manipulate the parachute. Remember that younger children may find the parachute to be heavy and awkward until they have had the opportunity to play several games and get used to it.

ALLIGATOR

Everyone sits in a circle, feet stretched out straight in front of them with the edge of the parachute pulled up to their laps, covering their legs and feet. The leader may tell a story about people sitting around a pool or swamp in Florida in which there may be alligators. The leader demonstrates how an alligator nibbles on a boy's toes before pulling him into the water (under the parachute). Magically, anyone pulled into the water turns into an alligator as well. Choose a volunteer to be the first alligator and play until everyone is under the parachute. Encourage silliness and screams from boys being nudged by the alligator.

BOUNCE

Bounce a large stuffed animal up and down on the parachute.

EXCHANGES

Players count off up to three, four, or five (depending on how many groups you want to create) so that each player has a number. Holding onto the parachute with both hands, boys raise it over their heads while the leader calls out a number. Players having that number must let go and run under the parachute across to the opposite side and grab on. (Ask boys to run carefully from one side to the other to minimize the risk of collisions.) You can experiment and make the game more exciting by calling out more than one number at a time.

Caution: Players must not bring the parachute down to trap the players underneath while they are running.

Variations: Try different activities while crossing under the parachute, such as hopping, dribbling a ball, etc. See how long boys can jump rope under the parachute. Or the boys with specific numbers run under the parachute to retrieve colored beanbags.

PARACHUTE VOLLEYBALL

Place a small (6- to 10-inch) playground ball in the middle of the parachute. Players distribute themselves evenly around the rim of the chute, with the players along one half being team A and the others, team B. The object is for one team to flip the ball off the parachute on the other team's side to score a point. The high scoring team after a certain time, or the first team to attain a certain score, wins.

Variation: Keep a running tabulation of the scores instead of individual team scores. Play several times to see how low the score can be after a predetermined length of time.

RIM BALL

Place a small (6- to 10-inch) playground ball in the middle of the parachute. Players distribute themselves evenly around the rim of the chute. The object is to get the ball rolling around the rim of the parachute. Players will need to cooperate in producing a wavelike motion to get the ball moving. Some small children will try to bounce the parachute, which is counterproductive to a smooth, wavelike action. Try to discourage them from doing this. After the players get the ball rolling around, you might try keeping score to see how many times they can make it go around without it falling off the parachute.

THE UMBRELLA

Players grasp the parachute waist-high using an overhand grip, making sure the hole of the parachute is on the ground. On the count of "one," everyone flexes his knees to a squatting position. On the count of "two, three, and UP!" everyone stands and raises arms overhead, pulling the parachute up and over their heads. As the chute billows out, the players will be pulled to their tiptoes and their arms will be stretched high in the air. The parachute is allowed to remain aloft and then slowly settle back to the ground. This can be done from a sitting or kneeling position—or even from wheelchairs.

WAGON WHEEL

Everyone holds the parachute with their left hand, walking slowly, then faster, running, slowing down, stopping, reversing hands, and repeating.

Relays and Races

Relays require a large playing area free of hazards. They can be played indoors or outdoors, but keep safety in mind during these action-packed games.

There are four major types of relays in Cub Scout games:

- In **file relays,** boys on each team line up one behind the other. Cub Scout No. 1 goes forward to the goal line and returns to his team, tagging Cub Scout No. 2. This continues until all have had a turn. The team finishing first wins.

- In **partner relays,** each boy has a partner. Teams consist of an equal number of partners. The partners stand side by side in file formation. During the relay, the first set of partners on each team goes forward to the goal line in whatever manner prescribed by the game, returns to its team, and tags off the next set of partners.

• In **shuttle relays,** the boys on each team number off. The even numbers line up in file formation with Cub Scout No. 2 in front. The odd-numbered boys do likewise, with No. 1 in front. Files face each other at opposite ends of the relay course. On a signal, Cub Scout No. 1 runs and hands off the ball, beanbag, or whatever game equipment is necessary to Cub Scout No. 2, and then takes his place at the end of No. 2's line. Cub Scout No. 2 runs and gives No. 3 the game object and takes his place at the end of No. 3's line. This continues until all players are back in their original places.

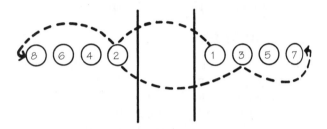

• **Tagging off** is a variation of the file relay. Instead of tagging the next teammate in line, a returning runner goes to the end of the line and "passes the tag" by touching the shoulder of the person in front of him, who in turn taps the next person. When the boy at the front of the line receives his tap on the shoulder, he heads for the goal line.

OVER AND UNDER RELAY

Activity Level: **Low**

Needed: **Even number of players; paper plates**

Each team has a paper plate. The teams form rows with players one behind the other. The team leaders stand at the front of the line and hold the plates above their heads with both hands. On a signal, each leader passes the plate between his/her legs. The second player passes it over his/her head. The third, between the legs again, and so on, over and under. The last player in line runs to the front and starts again.

ANIMAL, BIRD, OR FISH

Activity Level: **Moderate**

Needed: **Even number of players; list of animals, birds, or fish**

Divide players into two teams. Teams position themselves in corners of the room opposite each other. The leader stands in the middle of the room, an equal distance from each team. Each team sends the first player to the leader, who whispers the name of an animal, bird, or fish to him. If the leader says "monkey," for instance, the player runs back to his team and acts like a monkey. When a team member guesses the correct animal, bird, or fish, he runs back and touches the leader, saying "Monkey!" (or whatever the correct animal, bird, or fish is). The leader then gives out another animal, bird, or fish and that player continues the relay race. The first team to get all the animals correct wins.

BAG OF AIR RELAY

Activity Level: **Moderate**

Needed: **Even number of players, enough small paper bags for each player**

At a goal line about 25 feet from each team is a stack of small paper bags. Each boy in turn races to the stack, blows up a paper bag, bursts it with his hand, and races back to touch off the next player.

BAGGAGE CAR RELAY

Activity Level: **High**

Needed: **Even number of people, suitcase for each team, hat, adult trousers, large shirt, jacket or overcoat**

Line up the teams for a file relay. Each team has a suitcase filled with the same amount of clothing. On a signal, the first boy on each team races with the suitcase to the center of the room and dons the clothing. He hurries back with the empty suitcase to the starting point. There, he removes the clothing and repacks it in the suitcase. The second boy repeats these actions, and so on until all have finished.

BALLOON SWEEPING RELAY

Activity Level: **High**

Needed: **Even number of players, balloons, brooms**

Arrange teams in parallel lines. Place an inflated balloon on the floor in front of each team. Give the first boy in each team a broom. On a signal, he sweeps the balloon to a turning line and back and then hands the broom to the second player, who repeats this action.

BALLOON BURST RELAY

Activity Level: **High**

Needed: **Even number of players, balloons, chairs**

Give each boy an uninflated balloon. On a signal, the first boy on each team runs to a chair about 20 feet away, blows up his balloon, ties it, sits on the balloon to burst it, and then returns to the starting line. The other players follow until all balloons are burst.

BALLOON KANGAROO JUMPING

Activity Level: **High**

Needed: **Any number of players, balloons**

Boys line up side by side, each with an inflated balloon between his knees. On a signal, boys hop to the other side of the room and back to the starting line. The one finishing first wins. If a boy breaks his balloon, he is out of the race. If a boy drops his balloon, he must replace it between his knees before he can keep going.

BALLOON KICK RELAY

Activity Level: **High**

Needed: **Even number of players, balloons**

Give the first boy on each team an inflated balloon. On a signal, he kicks it across the room to a line and back to the second player, who repeats the action. The balloon may be touched only with the feet and legs. Continue until one team wins.

BALLOON ON A SPOON RELAY

Activity Level: **Moderate**

Needed: **Even number of players, balloons, teaspoons**

The first boy on each team has an inflated balloon balanced on a teaspoon. He hurries to a goal line about 25 feet away and back, carrying the balloon on the spoon. If the balloon falls off, he must balance it on the teaspoon again before he can continue.

BALLOON STEEPLECHASE

Activity Level: **Moderate**

Needed: **Any number of players, balloons, objects for an obstacle course**

Lay out an obstacle course (indoors or outdoors)—the more obstacles the better. Use fences, trees, chairs, tables, etc. Each boy has an inflated balloon. On a signal, the boys move to the first obstacle and begin to follow the course, batting their balloons in the air with their hands. If a balloon touches the ground, the player must repeat the previous obstacle. If a balloon breaks, the player gets a new one and continues.

BAREFOOT MARBLE RACE

Activity Level: **Moderate**

Needed: **Even number of players, marbles**

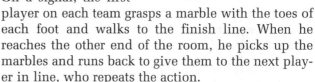

Boys remove their shoes and socks. Place two marbles on the starting line in front of each team. On a signal, the first player on each team grasps a marble with the toes of each foot and walks to the finish line. When he reaches the other end of the room, he picks up the marbles and runs back to give them to the next player in line, who repeats the action.

BEANBAG RELAY

Activity Level: **Moderate**

Needed: **Even number of players, beanbags**

Divide teams in half, putting half of each team on the opposite sides of the room. The first boy on the first side throws a beanbag to his first teammate on the other side, who holds the bag until the thrower has run up and tagged him. Then he in turn throws the bag to the second player on his team on the other side of the room, who holds the bag until he is tagged, etc., until all have had a turn. The thrower moves to the end of the line after he has tagged his teammate. The first team with players in reversed position wins.

BUCKET BRIGADE RELAY

Activity Level: **Moderate**

Needed: **Even number of players, two buckets for each team, water**

Line up two or more teams for a relay. Each team has two buckets—one empty and the other half-filled with water. Place the half-filled buckets at the goal line. On a signal, the first boy runs to the goal line, carrying the empty bucket, pours the water from the half-filled bucket into the empty bucket, leaves the empty bucket there, and carries the half-filled bucket back to his team. The next player does the same, and so on, until all team members have carried both an empty and a half-filled bucket.

BUNDLE RELAY

Activity Level: **Moderate**

Needed: **Even number of players, ball of twine or string**

The first boy on each team has a ball of twine or string. On a signal, he passes it to his neighbor but holds on to the end of the string. The ball is passed from player to player, unrolling as it goes. When it gets to the end of the line, it is passed up the line behind the backs of the players until it reaches the first player again. The first team to "wrap itself into a bundle" is the winner.

A sequel to this relay is unwrapping the bundle by passing the ball back and winding it up as it goes.

CASTING RELAY

Activity Level: **Moderate**

Needed: **Even number of players, fishing rod with plug, target**

Each boy in turn casts a fishing plug at a target. As soon as he scores a hit, he gives the rod to the player behind him and goes to the rear position on his team. The team back in its original order first wins.

CATERPILLAR RACE

Activity Level: **Moderate**

Needed: **Even number of players**

Divide boys into two groups. The first boy in each line places his hands on the ground. Each teammate behind him bends forward and grasps the ankles of the player in front of him. On a signal, the "caterpillars" move forward with everyone holding tight to the ankles. When the last player in the column crosses the finish line, the team has completed the race, provided that their caterpillar is still intact.

CRAB RELAY

Activity Level: **Moderate**

Needed: **Even number of players**

Divide the boys into equal teams. The first boy in each line sits on the floor with his back to the finish line. On a signal, he "walks" backward on his hands and feet with his body parallel to the floor. When he reaches the other end of the room he stands up, runs back, and touches off the next player, who repeats the crab walk action.

DUTCH SHOE RELAY

Activity Level: **Moderate**

Needed: **Even number of players, two shoe boxes per team**

Each team has two shoe boxes. On a signal, boys in turn place their feet in the boxes and shuffle to a goal line and back to the starting point, where the next player repeats the action.

FUMBLE FINGERS RELAY

Activity Level: **Low**

Needed: **Even number of players, pair of large gloves or mittens for each team, fruit jar with lid for each team, five toothpicks for each team**

Each team has a pair of large canvas gloves or mittens. At a goal line is a fruit jar with a lid containing five toothpicks for each team. On a signal, the first boy on each team races to the goal line, puts on the gloves, removes the lid, empties the jar, picks up the toothpicks and puts them back in the jar, and screws on the lid. He takes off the gloves and races back to hand them to the next player, who repeats the action.

Variation: Try using individually wrapped hard candy.

GUM-GLOVE RELAY

Activity Level: **Moderate**

Needed: **Even number of players, paper bag for each team, pair of large work gloves for each team, enough pieces of individually wrapped sticks of gum for each team member**

Divide the group into two teams, which line up facing each other. The first person on each team is given a paper bag that contains individual sticks of wrapped chewing gum and a pair of large work gloves. He must open the bag, put on the gloves, pull out a stick of gum, unwrap it, and put it in his mouth. As he starts chewing the gum, he removes the gloves, places them in the bag, closes the bag, and passes it to the next person, who repeats the action.

IZZY DIZZY RELAY

Activity Level: **High**

Needed: **Even number of players**

Teams line up in relay formation. On a signal, the first boy on each team runs forward to a line, puts one finger on the floor, and circles around the finger seven times. His finger must not leave the floor. When he has made seven turns, he runs back and touches off the next player on his team.

LEG TUNNEL RELAY

Activity Level: **Moderate**

Needed: **Even number of players**

Teams line up single file and stand with their feet apart. The last boy in each line crawls through from one end to the other and stands up with his feet apart. The players follow in rapid succession, each standing up when he has crawled through. The first team to be back in its original order wins.

PAPER CONE DERBY

Activity Level: **Moderate**

Needed: **Even number of players, piece of paper for each team, 30 feet of string, several chairs to use to anchor the string**

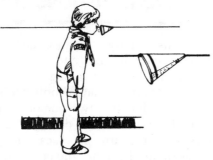

Prepare a paper cone for each team (or use a cone-shaped paper cup). Put a 30-foot string through the cone, tie each end of the string to the back of a chair, and pull it tight. Line up teams for a relay. On a signal, the first boy in each team blows his cone along the string. (For best results, he should keep his head under the string.) When the cone reaches the end, he slides it back for the next teammate.

NOSE-A-PEANUT RACE

Activity Level: **Moderate**

Needed: **Even number of players, peanuts in their shells**

Boys roll a peanut across the floor with their noses for a short distance. They must not touch the peanut with their hands.

Variation: Use a table tennis ball instead of a peanut.

RESCUE

Activity Level: **Moderate**

Needed: **Even number of players, ample supply of newspapers, 50 feet of rope cut in 3-foot pieces**

Divide boys into teams. Each team picks one member as its "victim." The victim sits on a pile of newspapers about 12 feet from the team. On a signal, the rescuers join 3-foot pieces of rope with square knots to make a rope 15 to 20 feet long. One member casts the line to the victim, and the team pulls him to safety. The victim rides on the newspapers, holding the rope with one hand, the newspapers with the other.

SEED-PLANTING RELAY

Activity Level: **Moderate**

Needed: **Even number of players; ample supply of paper cups or jars; ample supply of seeds, popcorn kernels, or candies**

In turn, each boy follows a line drawn on the floor by placing the heel of one foot against the toe of the other. About every 3 feet he must stop and place a seed in a small-mouthed jar set about 1½ feet on each side of the line. When he reaches the end, he runs back and touches off the next person, who plants his seeds in the same manner.

SNOW SHOVEL RELAY

Activity Level: **Moderate**

Needed: **Even number of players, pie tin for each team, spatula for each team, ample supply of cotton balls or plastic foam packing peanuts**

A "snow drift" (a pile of cotton balls or packing peanuts) is placed before each team, and a pie tin for each team is placed at a goal line about 20 feet away. The first boy on each team has a spatula. On a signal, he scoops some of the "snowballs" on his "shovel" and hurries to the goal line, where he deposits the balls in the pie tin and races back to touch off his next teammate, who repeats the action. Players who drop snow along the route aren't required to stop to pick it up; however, the following players must gather it at some point, as the winning team must have all its snow in the tin.

Variation: Relay teams could carry a snowball (cotton ball) in a teaspoon to a goal line.

THREE-LEGGED RACE

Activity Level: **High**

Needed: **Even number of people, fabric strips or neckerchiefs**

Run this contest on either an individual or team basis. Tie a boy's left leg to an adult's right leg. On a signal, they make their way to the turning line and back again.

WAGON TRAIN

Activity Level: **High**

Needed: **Large playing area free of hazards, even number of players, whistle**

Mark a circle 50 feet in diameter. Boys stand at intervals on the circle facing in a clockwise direction. They pretend to be pioneers racing for their lives from outlaws. All run when the whistle blows. When one player is passed by another (always pass on the outside), he is captured and drops out, sitting in the center of the circle. Sharp, unexpected blasts of a whistle signal an "attack," and all players reverse direction.

WASH ON THE LINE

Activity Level: **Moderate**

Needed: **Even number of players, 25 feet of clothesline, five or six clothespins for each team, shopping bag for each team, three or four garments or pieces of cloth for each team**

Stretch a clothesline 20 feet from the starting line. Divide into relay teams. Give the first boy on each team a large shopping bag containing three or four garments or pieces of cloth and five or six clothespins. The first player on each team races to the clothesline, pins up the garments, and runs back to the starting line. The second player races up and takes down the clothes and returns them to the third player, who pins them up again, and so on.

WAY DOWN YONDER RELAY

Activity Level: **Moderate**

Needed: **Even number of players, teaspoon for each player, dish containing popcorn kernels for each team, empty dish for each team**

Boys sit on the floor in two lines that face each other. A dish containing kernels of corn is placed in front and to the right of the players at the head of each line, and an empty dish is at the end of each line. Each player has a teaspoon. On a signal, the first player takes a kernel in his spoon, transfers it to his neighbor's spoon, and so on down the line. The first player may start another kernel down the line right away. As the end player receives the kernel and drops it in an empty dish, he yells, "Way down yonder!" Any kernel that is dropped must be replaced on the spoon by the person who dropped it before it can be passed along.

Physical Fitness Activities

Because many of these contests are tests of strength, coordination, and agility, the older, stronger boys will have an advantage. For this reason, it is a good idea to try to match contestants by size and age, especially for the two-person contests. Consider using these activities as den meeting fillers when the boys need to burn off excess energy. Have several games in mind and ask the boys whether they can do this or that fitness activity. Change the activities as the boys show proficiency. Many of these physical fitness activities meet advancement requirements for Wolf, Bear, and Webelos Scouts.

ANKLE HOP

Boys stand erect and then take a squatting position, grasp the ankles, and hop forward four times without breaking the ankle grip. They turn around and repeat, hopping back to their original places.

ANKLE WALK

Each boy grasps his ankles and walks in a straight line, keeping his knees stiff.

ARM LOCK WRESTLE

Pair off boys according to height and weight. They sit on the floor, back to back, with their legs spread and arms locked at the elbows. On a signal, each tries to pull his opponent over to the side so that his left arm or shoulder touches the floor.

BALANCE WITH CLOSED EYES

Boys stand upright, placing their right foot in front of their left foot, and raise their arms to their sides. With their eyes closed, they see how long they can maintain their balance in this position. Alternate the left and right foot forward.

BICYCLE RIDE

Players lie flat on their backs and raise their feet as high as possible. Then, placing the hands under the hips, they support their body weight on the shoulders and elbows. From this position they pump their feet as if pedaling a bicycle.

BROOMSTICK TWIST

Two boys of equal height and weight grasp a broomstick (held horizontally) with both hands. Each tries to touch the stick to the floor on his right.

BROOMSTICK WRESTLE

Two boys face each other, grasping a broomstick with their hands about 18 inches apart. On a signal, each tries to cause the other to move his feet. The defeated player is the one who first takes a step or releases the stick.

CIRCLE HOP

Draw a circle about 6 feet in diameter and stand two boys inside it. They face each other with their arms folded and one leg extended in front. On a signal, they try to upset or force each other from the circle by using the extended leg. They may hook or lift with the leg but must not touch their opponent with any other part of the body. Kicking or pushing with the uplifted leg is not permitted.

CRAB WALK

From a squatting position, boys reach backward and put their hands on the floor without sitting down. They walk forward, keeping their heads and body in a straight line.

DEEP BOW

Boys place both hands on the floor in front of their left foot and extend their right leg backward. They touch their head to the floor and then stand erect without losing their balance. They reverse their feet and repeat the deep bow.

DIZZY

Boys hold their left ankle in back of their right leg with their right hand. Then they hop, making three turns in place without losing their balance. Then they reverse position and try hopping on the left leg.

FITNESS CIRCLE GAME

Form a circle as large as the room permits, with all boys facing the same direction. Give instructions for various activities as follows:

1. Start walking in a circle, and keep walking between these exercises.
2. Start hopping.
3. Make yourself as small as possible and continue walking.
4. Make yourself as tall as possible and continue walking. Now reach your hands high over your head.
5. Bend your knees slightly, grasp your ankles, and continue walking.

6. Walk as if the heel of one foot and the toes of the other were sore.

7. Walk stiff-legged.

8. Squat down and jump forward from that position.

9. Walk on hands and one foot, with the other leg held high, imitating a lame dog.

10. Walk forward at a rapid pace (don't run) while swinging the arms vigorously.

11. Take giant steps.

12. Walk forward, raising your knees as high as possible with each step.

13. Run, lifting your knees high.

14. Walk on your hands and feet.

FROG HANDSTAND

Boys squat and place their hands flat on the ground between their legs. They lean forward slowly, shifting the weight of their bodies onto their hands and elbows until their feet swing free of the ground. They should keep their heads up and point their toes backward. (This is the first step in learning the handstand).

FROG HOP

Boys take a squatting position, with their feet pointing slightly outward. They place their hands on the floor with the elbows slightly bent, arms between the knees. Then they take short hops by putting their hands just ahead of their feet and bringing their feet up to their hands.

BACK-TO-BACK GET UP

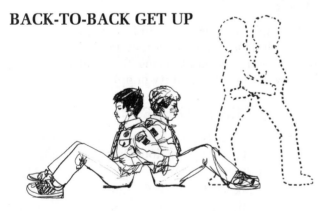

Two boys sit on the floor back to back with their arms locked. Without letting go, they try to stand erect. This is done by bringing the feet close to the body and pushing back against back.

HAND PUSH

Two boys stand facing each other with their toes touching and their palms together at shoulder height. In this position each tries to push the other's hands until one is forced to step back. The player who forces his opponent backward wins.

HAND WRESTLE

Two boys stand facing in opposite directions with the sides of their right feet touching each other. They clasp their right hands directly over the center of their feet. On a signal, the wrestlers try to throw each other off balance by pushing, pulling, or swinging their hands. A player loses if either foot moves.

HAWK DIVE

You need plenty of room for this activity. Boys kneel on one leg with the other leg stretched back, keeping the foot off the floor. They stretch both arms sideways, using them for balance. They bend forward slowly trying to touch their noses to the floor. Then they return to the starting position without letting any part of the body touch the floor except the leg they are kneeling on.

HEEL CLICK

Boys stand with their feet apart. They jump upward, strike their heels together, and land lightly with their feet apart again.

HOP AND TURN

Boys hop in the air, make a half turn to the right, and land lightly on their starting place. They can vary the stunt by making a full turn. Repeat, turning the other direction.

HOPPING—CROSS FEET

Boys hop up on both feet, cross the right foot in front of the left, and land on their toes with heels together. Then they reverse feet.

HUMAN ROCKER

Boys lie face downward, grasp their ankles, and rock their bodies backward and forward on their thighs and chests.

KNEE DIP

Boys stand on one foot and grasp the other foot behind their backs with the opposite hand. They try to touch the bent knee to the floor and return to a standing position without losing balance.

KNEEL STAND

Boys kneel on both knees and return to a standing position with arms folded behind their backs. They must not move their feet or lose balance.

LEG WRESTLE

Two boys lie side by side on their backs with their heads in opposite directions. They hook right elbows. When the leader counts "one," they raise their right legs and touch them together. At count "two," this is repeated. At "three," they hook their right knees and try to turn each other over.

INCHWORM

Each boys supports his body on his hands and feet with his legs extended backward. Keeping his hands in place and his knees stiff, he walks on his toes with short steps until his feet are near his hands. Then, without moving his feet, he walks forward on his hands with short steps until his original position is attained. He continues "walking" alternately with feet and hands.

NO HANDS

Boys fold their arms, lie down on the floor, and try to get up without using their elbows or hands.

NOVELTY WALK

Boys walk by swinging their right foot behind their left leg and then moving it as far forward as possible on the left side. Then they take the same type of step forward with the left foot and continue to walk in this manner.

PEPPER GRINDER

Boys stretch out on the floor and raise themselves on one hand. They then try to pivot in a complete circle around the supporting hand, keeping their bodies in a straight line.

SKIN THE SNAKE

Boys line up single file one behind another. Each stoops over and places his right hand between his legs and with his left hand grasps the right hand of the player in front of him. When all are ready, the last player in line lies on his back while the line moves back over him. The next player then lies down and so on until everyone is lying down. The last one to lie down rises to his feet and walks forward, each following in turn, until all are back in their original places.

SPARROW SPARRING

Establish a 6-foot circle. Standing in the circle, two boys bend forward and grasp their ankles. Each then tries to upset his opponent or shoulder him from the circle.

SQUAT JUMP

The boy does a full squat with his weight on his toes and, from this position, jumps forward several times. Then he stands and walks. Alternate these squatting, jumping, and walking actions.

STORK STAND

The boy stands with his hands on his hips, placing one foot against the inside of the opposite knee while bending the raised knee outward. He then counts to 10 without moving from his place.

STORK WRESTLING

Two boys face each other, standing on one foot and holding their left ankles with their left hands. They then clasp their right hands and try to push or pull their opponent off balance or cause him to let go of his ankle.

THREAD THE NEEDLE

Boys clasp their hands in front of their bodies. They bend forward and step through the loop formed by their arms with the right foot, and then the left foot. They reverse the action by stepping backward with the left foot, then the right, keeping the hands clasped. If the hands are clasped near the floor, the action is easier to perform.

UNDER THE BROOM

Build two stacks of books about 3 feet high and 3 feet apart. Lay a broom across them. Each boy crawls under the broomstick and goes to the end of the line. When all have done that, remove two or three books to lower the broom, and have the players try that. Keep removing more books each round.

Quiet Games With Equipment

STRINGER

Materials: **Chenille stem and buttons or beads for each team**

Each team has a chenille stem and several buttons or wooden beads. On a signal, the first person strings a button or bead on the stem and passes it to the next player, who does the same. Continue until all the buttons or beads are on the stem. The first team to finish holds its stem in the air and yells, "We did our best!"

CLIP IT

Materials: **Small dish with paper clips for each team**

Each team has a small dish filled with paper clips. On a signal, the first person joins two paper clips together and passes the dish and beginning of the chain to the next person. That player adds another clip to the chain and passes it on. After a set time (5–8 minutes), the paper clip chains are held high in the air to see which team has the longest.

This can be a good game to play at a blue and gold banquet, with each table having a dish with paper clips.

ART CONSEQUENCES

Materials: **Pencil, paper**

Each boy gets a pencil and paper and draws the head of a man, woman, or child. After he draws the head, he folds the paper over to the back so nothing shows except two small lines to indicate where the shoulders should start. He passes the paper to the next player, who draws the shoulders, folds the paper back, and passes it on. This continues, with others adding the waist, hips, legs, and feet. When the drawings are finished, open and pass around to see the funny people you've created.

BLOWBALL

Materials: **Small table or large box, table tennis balls**

Boys sit at a table small enough so they are close together. Put a table tennis ball in the center of the table. On a signal, the players, with their chins on the table and their hands behind them, try to blow the ball away from their side of the table. If the ball falls on the floor, return it to the center of the table and continue.

CALENDAR PITCH

Materials: **Large calendar, checkers or bottle caps**

Place one page from a large calendar on the floor as the target. Each player tosses three checkers or bottle caps from a distance of 5 feet and totals his score according to the numbers on which his checkers land. Markers on a line don't count. For added excitement, score double points for holidays, such as 50 points for December 25, or 28 points for February 14.

CARD TOSS

Materials: **Hat, chair, deck of playing cards**

Place a hat on the floor about 6 feet from a chair. Each boy in turn sits in the chair, takes a deck of playing cards, and tosses cards one at a time into the hat. It looks easy, but if a beginner gets more than five cards in the hat on his first try, he's doing well.

CELEBRITIES

Materials: **Old newspapers or magazines, index cards, glue**

From newspapers or magazines, cut pictures of famous athletes, politicians, performers, etc., and paste them on numbered cards for the boys to guess their names. The player who identifies the most wins a prize.

Variation: Use pictures of wildlife, trees, or any category you choose.

CHECKER HOCKEY

Materials: **Checkers, checkerboard, button or other small object**

Each boy's "hockey team" of four checkers is lined up horizontally on a checkerboard, facing the other "team" with an empty row between. One red checker carries the "puck" (a button or other small object that can sit on a checker). A goal is scored by advanc-ing the puck to the opponent's back row. The puck carrier may go one square at a time in any direction, and it may jump any piece. The opponent tries to jump the checker carrying the puck. When he does, he takes over the puck and moves one more space in any direction, but he may not make a jump move. The puck carrier may not move into any of the four corner squares.

COOTIE

Materials: **Small cube covered with white paper, paper and pencils for each player**

Each player gets a pencil and paper. Cover a small cube with plain paper and write one of the following letters on each side: A for *antenna,* B for *body,* T for *tail,* L for *leg,* H for *head,* and E for *eye.* Boys throw the cube and try to draw a complete cootie. (A complete cootie has one body, one head, eight legs, two eyes, and two antennae.) If a boy throws a *B,* he draws a body on his paper. He may continue to throw as long as he can add to the cootie he is drawing. If he shakes a letter for a body part that can't be added yet (that is, you can't add a leg until you have a body) or one he has already drawn, the next player gets to throw the cube. No one may begin drawing until he shakes a *B* first. The first player to draw a complete cootie wins.

CRAZY ARTIST

Materials: **Crayons or marking pens, large pieces of paper or posterboard**

Divide boys into two teams for a relay drawing contest. Each team gets a crayon or marking pen. Place two large pieces of paper or posterboard on a wall or table across the room. The object of the game is for each team to draw a house, with each boy drawing no more than two straight lines. A player from each team runs to the paper, draws his two lines, returns, and hands the crayon to the next player in line. Use sidewalk chalk for an outdoor game.

CRAZY BONE

Materials: **Assortment of objects with various textures, scorecard, pencil**

For this game, boys try to identify objects by touching them only with their elbow. Gather together in advance such things as an eraser, a ring, a penny, a pencil, a piece of sandpaper, a grape, a hairpin, etc. Players should not see these items before the game. Each player rolls up his sleeve, places his arm on the back of his chair, and closes his eyes. Move behind the boys and hold one of the objects against the elbow of each boy, and let him write down what he thinks the object is. See who can identify the most.

UNIFORM GAME

When preparing for a den uniform inspection, have the denner slip in with his uniform rearranged in the following manner and ask the boys to tell what is wrong.

1. Cap on backwards
2. Campaign button on cap
3. Wearing den chief cord
4. Service star on neckerchief
5. Neckerchief twisted into a roll
6. Neckerchief tied around the neck
7. Belt buckle worn to one side
8. One sleeve rolled up
9. Button unbuttoned
10. Pocket turned inside out

FIVE DOTS

Materials: **Paper for each player, pencil for each player**

Each boy gets a paper and pencil and places five dots on the paper wherever he wishes. Players exchange papers and try to draw a person around the dots, with the head at one dot, the hands at two, and the feet at the other two dots.

GRAB IT

Materials: **Clothespins, one for each boy**

Arrange boys in a circle on the floor. In the center, place one less clothespin than the number of boys. One of the boys is the "storyteller." He starts a story, and whenever he says the word "and," all the players grab for a clothespin. Boys get a point for every clothespin they grab. Change storytellers so all have a chance.

JUGGLER TOSS

Materials: **Ball or orange for each player**

Pairs of boys stand about 5 feet apart in two lines facing each other. Each player has a rubber ball or orange. They toss their balls simultaneously. Score one point for the two-boy team when both make the catch. After each catch, they step back one pace and repeat. The pair with the most points after a set time limit wins.

KIM'S GAME

Modeled after the tests of Kim in the Rudyard Kipling book, this game has many variations, each of which helps hone boys' memory and powers of observation.

Kim's Game—Sight

Materials: **Tray, cloth cover or trash bag, 10 to 20 different common objects, scorecard and pencil for each player**

Arrange 10 to 20 common objects in an orderly fashion on a tray or table. Keep the objects covered until the game begins, and then have the players study the objects silently for one minute. Cover the objects again, and each boy writes down the names of as many objects as he can remember. Boys can compete individually or work as teams.

Kim's Game—Touch

Materials: **Large bag, five to six differently textured items**

Place the items in the bag. One-by-one, boys put a hand in the bag without looking and feel the objects, trying to identify each only by touch.

Kim's Game—Smell

Materials: **Five or six 35-mm film canisters, blotting paper or fabric, various smelly substances**

Number each film container and place a piece of blotting paper or fabric in each that is soaked in or wrapped around a smelly substance (try vanilla extract or vanilla bean, lemon peel, orange peel, or spices such as cloves and nutmeg). Boys sniff each container and try to identify the smells. Be careful with your selections, as some boys may be allergic to some odors. (And, of course, don't use any caustic or toxic materials.)

LOG CABIN ON A BOTTLE

Materials: **10 flat toothpicks for each boy, bottle**

Divide boys into two groups. Each boy has 10 flat toothpicks. Alternating between teams, players place a toothpick, one at a time, across the top of the bottle until the stack falls. That player's team must take the toothpicks that were knocked off. The first team to get rid of all its toothpicks wins.

MARBLE CHOP SUEY

Materials: **Supply of marbles or small candies, several pencils or chopsticks, two dishes for each team**

Put six marbles/candies in a small dish. Using two pencils as chopsticks, and using only one hand, boys try to move the marbles/candies into a second dish. Using pencils with eraser tips can make the game a little easier for younger boys. Play this as a skill activity or relay race.

NOAH'S ARK (BARNYARD BABBLE)

Materials: **Index cards**

Write the names of animals on the cards—two cards for each animal. If there is an odd number of boys, write one animal's name on three cards. There should be a card for every player. Shuffle the cards and hand them out. Each player reads his card to himself but keeps his animal identity a secret. Collect the cards. On a signal, each player begins acting out the sounds, shape, and typical movements of his animal, trying to attract his "partner." There might be baying, croaking, screeching, strutting, flapping, and leaping—but no talking! The game ends when each player finds his partner.

CLOTHESPIN RING TOSS

Materials: **Bucket or wastebasket, clothespins, jar rings**

Clamp clothespins around the rim of a bucket or wastebasket. Boys try to toss jar rings over the clothespins from 10 feet away.

SMILE

Materials: **Coin for flipping**

Two teams line up facing each other about 10 feet apart. One team is Heads; the other is Tails. Flip a coin and call it. If "heads" comes up, the Heads team laughs and smiles while the Tails team members try to keep a sober face. Any player who laughs at the wrong time switches teams. Then flip the coin again.

TOOTHPICK PICKUP

Materials: **Saucer for each player, toothpicks, beans**

Boys sit around a table or kneel in a circle on the floor. Each has a saucer with two toothpicks and 12 beans. The contest is to see who can be the first to lift out five beans using only the toothpicks.

WALK THE PLANK

Materials: **Six- to 8-foot-long two-by-four, neckerchief for blindfold**

Lay the board flat on the ground. One by one, blindfold each boy and have him try to walk the length of the "plank." If he steps off at any point, he falls into shark-infested waters and is out of the game.

Variation: Use two or more boards, side by side, and form teams for a relay.

BOYS' LIFE BAGS

Materials: **Small paper bags, various small objects, paper and pencils, prizes**

Print one letter of the words *Boys' Life* on each bag. Place an object that begins with that letter in the appropriate bag. Give each boy paper with the words *Boys' Life* printed vertically so he can write down what he thinks is in each bag after he feels the objects without looking at them. Give prizes to those who get the most correct answers.

WIGGLES

Materials: **Pieces of paper and pencils for each player**

Each boy draws a wavy or zigzag line on a piece of paper. Boys exchange papers and make the line into a picture. Boys share the funny pictures with everyone and tell a story about their picture.

ZOO

Materials: **Unshelled peanuts**

In advance, hide several peanuts around the room. Divide the boys into groups of three or four and give each group the name of an animal. One member of each group is chosen to be the Keeper. The boys start to hunt for the peanuts. When a player finds one, he must not pick it up. Instead, he stands still and makes a noise like the animal his group represents. He continues making the noise until the Keeper for his group comes over and picks up the peanut. The team with the most peanuts at the end of a designated time wins.

Quiet Games Without Equipment

SCOUTING QUIZ

This can be a good game to play during a blue and gold banquet. Make copies for each boy and adult to complete.

How much do you know about Scouting? See how many of the following questions you can answer.

1. How old is Cub Scouting this year?
2. How old is the Boy Scouts of America this year?
3. Who was the founder of the Scouting movement?
4. Who started the Boy Scouts of America?
5. What is the first rank in Cub Scouting?
6. How many achievements are required to earn the Wolf badge?
7. How many electives are required to earn an arrow point?
8. How many Webelos activity badges may be earned?
9. What is your den number?
10. What is our pack number?
11. What chartered organization sponsors our pack?
12. What district are we a part of?
13. What council are we a part of?
14. What is the Cub Scout motto?

Answers: (1) Cub Scouts originated in 1930. To find the answer to this question, subtract 1930 from the current year; (2) The BSA originated in 1910. To find the answer to this question, subtract 1910 from the current year; (3) Lord Robert Baden-Powell; (4) William D. Boyce; (5) Bobcat; (6) 12; (7) 10; (8) 20; (9–13) Check with your pack leadership; (14) Do Your Best.

ABOVE AND BELOW

Boys stand in a circle. One at a time, call out the names of things that are found either above or below the ground. For example, strawberries grow above the ground; potatoes grow below the ground. When you call the name of something that is found above the ground, the players stand; if it is found below the ground, they sit down. A player is eliminated if he responds incorrectly. The last player to remain in the game wins.

Variation: Call out the names of things that fly and crawl.

BIRD, BEAST, OR FISH

Boys stand in a circle with a leader in the center. The leader calls a category—bird, beast, or fish—to anyone in the circle. That player must name a specific species of that category before the leader counts to 10. When one of the players fails to name the required bird, beast, or fish, he becomes the leader. A player may not use a name of a bird, beast, or fish that already has been used by any other person until a new leader begins a new game. For variety, you may call, "fin, fur, or feathers."

BUZZ-FIZZ

Boys are seated in a circle. One boy begins counting, and the rest of the group continues counting one at a time around the circle. When a player comes to 5 or any number with a 5 in it, he says "buzz." When a player comes to 7 or a number with 7 in it, he says "fizz." For example: 1, 2, 3, 4, buzz, 6, fizz, 8, and so on; 55 would be "buzz buzz"; 57 would be "buzz fizz." When a player misses, he drops out and the next player starts over at 1.

DETECTIVES

Two boys are Detectives and are sent out of the room. The others choose an object that the Detectives will try to discover, such as a piece of furniture, a book, or a button on someone's clothing. The Detectives are called back in and try to solve the mystery by asking questions. They can ask each of the other players only three questions. Suggest that they try to find the location first and then identify the object.

DO THIS, DO THAT

Boys line up along a goal line. The den chief or den leader stands in front of the boys and performs certain movements, preceding each by saying "do this" or "do that." Players must immediately copy all movements after the order "do this." They must not move when the leader says "do that." A player who makes a mistake moves backward one step. Continue for a predetermined length of time. The winner is the player nearest the goal line.

ELECTRIC SQUEEZE

Boys form a circle and hold hands, with "It" in the center. One player starts the "shock" by squeezing the hand of one of the boys next to him. That player passes it on. The shock may move in either direction. "It" watches the faces and hands of the players, trying to spot the location of the shock. When he guesses correctly, the player caught becomes "It."

GARDENING

Divide boys into two groups that stand parallel to one another about 10 feet apart. A leader stands in front of the groups and calls out the names of vegetables. When "corn" is called, boys grasp their ears; for "onions," they hold their noses; for "potatoes," they point to their eyes; for "cabbage," they hold their heads. Another leader referees to see which line responds first with the desired action. The first line to have all its members perform the correct action scores a point. The line that scores 10 points first wins.

HA, HA, HA

Boys stand in a circle. The first boy says "ha"; the second, "ha, ha"; the third, "ha, ha, ha"; and so on around the circle. The "ha-ha's" must be said without laughing. Boys who laugh while saying their "ha's" are eliminated.

INITIALS

The den chief or den leader is the questioner and asks a question of each boy in turn. The player must answer in two words that begin with the initials of his name. For example: "What is your favorite snack?" Chuck Parker might answer "cherry pie"; Jimmy Davis might answer "juicy donuts." A player who answers incorrectly or not at all is out of the game. Encourage boys to give funny answers. To make the game easier for younger boys, ask for one-word answers, using the initial of the first name.

LOOK SHARP

Divide the group into two teams that stand in lines facing each other. Boys have one minute to observe their partners on the opposite team. On a signal, they turn their backs to each other, and each player makes three changes in his attire. He may undo a button, alter the position of an activity badge, exchange neckerchief slides with a neighbor, etc. At the next signal, all turn to face their partners again and try to determine what changes have been made. Each change correctly identified counts one point.

PRINCE OF PILSEN

Boys line up facing the leader. They count off consecutively and remember their numbers. The leader says: "The Prince of Pilsen lost his hat. Number _____ has it." The player whose number has been called immediately responds, "No, sir, not I, sir," before the leader can say, "Number _____, to the foot." If the leader beats the player, the player must go to the foot (end) of the line, and the leader calls out another number. If the player beats the leader, the leader says, "Who then, sir?" and the player questioned gives any other number, except the number of the boy at the foot of the line. The game continues as long as desired. If any player calls the number of the player at the foot of the line by mistake, he automatically goes to the foot himself.

REVERSE

The leader calls out instructions to the group, such as, "Hold your left ear with your right hand." All do this. The leader calls out another instruction, such as, "Rub your stomach with your left hand and pat the top of your head with your right hand." In the midst of the instructions, the leader calls out, "Reverse," and the boys must switch hands and reverse their actions.

RHYMING WORDS

Boys sit in a circle. The first player says a one- or two-syllable word. The next boy must say a word that rhymes, and so on around the group. Example: Pan, can, tan, man, fan. When a boy can't think of a rhyming word, one point is scored against him, but he starts the game over with a new word. When any player has three points scored against him, he is out of the game.

THINK FAST

Divide boys into two groups. Ask the following questions, and after each, score a point for the side that gives the correct answer first.

- What letter is a beverage? (T)
- What letter is a bird? (J)
- What letter is a vegetable? (P)
- What letter is a question? (Y)
- What letter is a body of water? (C)

TRAVELERS

The leader tells the boys that they are going on an imaginary trip. Each player can go anywhere he wishes, but in playing the game he must use only words beginning with the first letter of the name of the place he is going. The leader starts the game by asking one of the players where he is going. The reply might be "San Francisco." "What are you going to do there?" asks the leader. Correct answers would include "Sing silly songs" or "Slurp sundaes." A player going to Paris might paint palaces, or one going to Chicago could chase cars. Answers may be two or three words, and players should be given a reasonable amount of time to think of them.

Homemade Games

These homemade game materials should be constructed with adult supervision. Boys should use hand tools for the assembly process; *only adults should use power tools.* Let the boys do the painting with easy-to-clean latex paints.

BOX HOCKEY

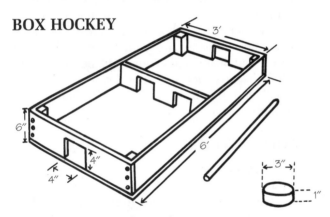

Materials:
    For base: half sheet of ¾-inch plywood cut to 3 by 6 feet
    For sides and midsection: 8-foot pieces of 1-by-6
    For corner pieces: 2 feet of 2-by-2
    For the puck: 1-by-4-inch wood
    Wood screws
    Wood glue
    For hockey sticks: 30-inch broom handle for each stick

This is an all-time Cub Scout favorite. For a good backyard box hockey game, build a box 3 feet wide and 6 feet long. Use 1-by-6-inch lumber for the frame and plywood for the base. Reinforce the corners with 2-by-2-inch blocks glued and fastened with screws. The centerboard takes a terrific pounding and should be fastened securely and braced on both sides. Follow the illustration. Cut the puck from a piece of 1-by-4-inch wood. For hockey or shinny sticks, use a 30-inch length of broom handle.

Two players take part, one on each side of the box. Set the puck in the top notch of the center board and have the players "knock off" as in hockey. They touch their sticks to the bottom of the box, knock them together above the puck three times, and then knock off the puck. Each player tries to bat it into his opponent's section of the box and then out through the hole in the end. If the puck is knocked out of the box, it is returned to the place where it went out and play resumes. Score a point each time a player gets the puck through his opponent's goal. The game is five points.

FISHPOND GAMES

Materials:
    Broom handle or dowel for fishing pole
    String
    Hooks (coat hanger wire, magnets, safety pins, fence staples, eye hooks, or paper clips)
    Fish (cardboard, felt, or thin wood)
    Acrylic paints and brushes
    Cardboard boxes (ocean bottom or stream)

A hook, line, and a fishing pole can make for an infinite variety of games. Make hooks from coat hanger wire, paper clips, open safety pins, or magnets. Attach the hooks to the string, and the string to the pole. Cut the fish from felt, cardboard, or thin wood. Each fish needs some type of fastener for the hook—such as small nails, fence staples, eyehooks, or magnets—so that players can catch the fish by hooking them and lifting them from the "water." Use a cardboard carton as shown or a piece of corrugated cardboard laid flat on the floor for the ocean bottom or trout stream. Boys can paint the fish and the water with water-based paints. Mark fish with different "weights" for points, or assign different colors for different point values.

Variation: Add balloons and mousetraps to the fish pond.

HAND BADMINTON

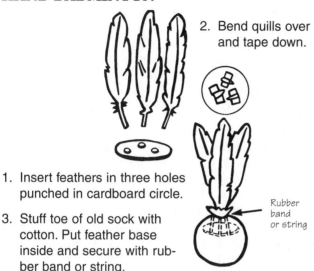

2. Bend quills over and tape down.

1. Insert feathers in three holes punched in cardboard circle.

3. Stuff toe of old sock with cotton. Put feather base inside and secure with rubber band or string.

Rubber band or string

Materials: **Old sock, cotton balls or batting, feathers, cardboard, rubber band**

Make "poputs" as shown using feathers, a cardboard circle, and a stuffed sock. Pack it firmly so that it will travel faster. Stretch a rope across the room for a net. Play as in regular badminton, batting the poputs with the palm of the hand.

MARBLE ROLL GAME

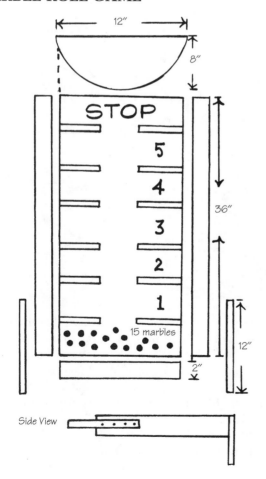

12"

8"

STOP

5
4
3
2
1

36"

15 marbles

12"

2"

Side View

Materials:
¼-inch plywood or Masonite
1-by-4 lumber (8 feet)
1-by-8 lumber (1 foot)
1-by-1 lumber (4 inches)
Wood glue
Wood screws

Build a rocker box as shown (12 by 36 by 4 inches) from wood or fiberboard. Place a rocker on one end and handles on the other end. Divide the box into compartments with strips of 1-by-1 lumber. The object of the game is to get the highest score possible with 15 marbles. As soon as you get a marble in the "stop" section, your turn is over. Total the score by multiplying the number of the section by the number of marbles in it.

MOOSE TOSS

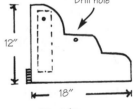

Cut the moose head from Masonite, plywood, plastic signboard, or foam core board. Paint with contrasting colors. Use rubber or plastic rings for tossing.

NINEPINS

Materials: **1-by-12 lumber (3 feet), 2-by-2 lumber (8 feet), two pieces of ½-inch dowel (30 inches long), wood glue**

Cut the two end pieces (12 by 18 inches) as shown. Drill two ½-inch holes in each end piece for the two dowels. For pins, cut nine pieces that are 2 by 2 by 9 inches and drill a ⅝-inch hole 3 inches from the top of each. Slide the pins on a ½-inch dowel rod that is 30 inches long. Insert the dowel rods into the end pieces as shown and fasten in place. Brace the end pieces in

Drill hole

12"

18"

End Piece

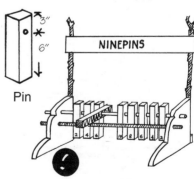

NINEPINS

3"

6"

Pin

the lower back corner with 1-by-2's. Be sure the pins swing freely. To play the game, roll a croquet ball or hardball at the base of the pins. The object is to flip them onto the front dowel bar. Count the numbers turned up to determine the score.

PUTTING GAME

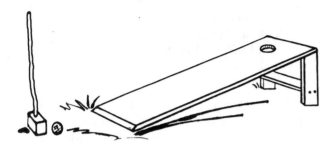

Make a putting "green" from heavy cardboard or plywood. Make the putter from a piece of 2-by-2 lumber and a dowel. Cut a hole for the cup; if desired, insert a tin can to catch the balls.

HOMEMADE RING TOSS

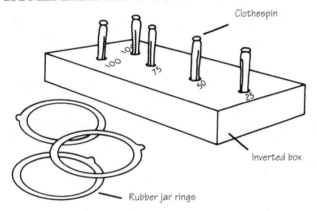

Invert a shallow cardboard box and push old-fashioned clothespins (not the spring-type) through the cardboard. Mark each pin with a number of points. Boys toss rubber, metal, or plastic rings from a distance away.

TARGET LAUNCHER

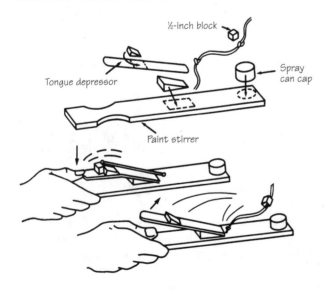

Materials:
   String
   Wood glue
   Wooden paint stirrer
   Tongue depressor or craft stick
   Scrap piece of 1-by-1 lumber cut into wedges and blocks
   Plastic spray can cap

Drill a hole 5 inches from the end of a wooden paint stirrer. Glue a long wedge of wood ¾ inch wide to the stirrer, ½ inch from the hole. Glue a tongue depressor or craft stick to the top of the wedge. Insert a 9-inch piece of string into the hole and knot it on the bottom side of the stirrer 2 inches from the string end. Make a knot on the other side of the stirrer, too. Then knot the string 4 inches from its top end. Drill a hole through the center of a ½-inch square block to pull the string through. Knot the string again to lock the block in position. Stretch the string on the tongue depressor to find the correct place for the short wedge. Glue the short wedge (¾ inch) in place. Tack the plastic spray can cap in position.

To play, place the block on the tongue depressor behind the short wedge. Depress the stick and try to flip the block into the cap.

TEETERBOARD JOUSTING

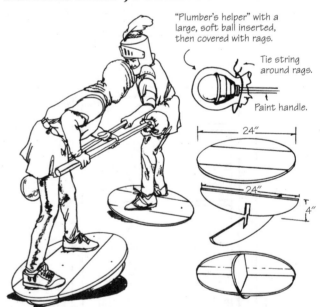

Make two teeterboards as shown (24 inches in diameter with 4-inch-high rockers). Make the padded jousting poles from plumber's suction cups, soft rubber balls, and squares of cloth. Place the boards so that the players are just within reach of each other. Each "knight" tries to push his opponent off his board. When any part of a knight's body touches the floor, he is beaten. *Only pushing is permitted; do not permit swinging or hard thrusting of the poles!*

TIC-TAC-TOE

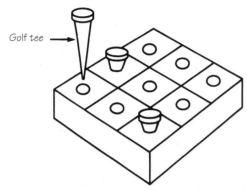

Golf tee

Cut a block of wood so it is 4 by 4 by 1 inch. Mark evenly spaced holes and drill. Paint golf tees—five of one color for "X" and five of another color for "O."

TURTLE RACE

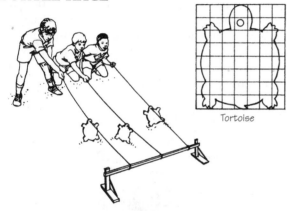

Tortoise

Enlarge the turtle pattern to make the turtles about 8 inches tall. Cut from ¼- or ⅜-inch plywood or heavy cardboard. Make the hole in the turtle slightly larger than the diameter of the cord you will use. Let the boys decorate and paint their names on their turtles.

Attach one end of 15 to 30 feet of twisted cord to a peg driven in the ground, a chair or table brace, or other support the same height as the holes in the turtles. The race begins with the turtles at the far end of the cord and leaning slightly toward the "jockeys." On a signal, boys alternately tighten and relax the cords so that the turtles move toward them in worm-like fashion.

This race can be run as a den relay. When the turtle's nose has crossed the finish line, the first player runs the animal back along the string to the starting line and hands the string to the next player, who begins racing.

If the race is to be indoors, it will help to add rubber bumpers to the rear feet to give traction on smooth floors and to dampen the sound.

Variations: Use other critters, such as tortoise and hare, frog, or crow, or try locomotives and cars, etc.

Tire Games

Old tires are usually easy to find, and garages may be more than happy to donate them to you for tire games. Play these games on enclosed paved areas with plenty of adult supervision. When possible, pair an adult with a boy when playing tire games. Always take the time to carefully examine all tires used for these games or for obstacle courses. Some tires, especially steel-belted ones, may have sharp pieces of metal sticking up through the rubber that can cause cuts and injuries. When you no longer want to use your tires, make sure you dispose of them properly. Ask a garage or check with local solid waste or recycling departments.

MOVING TARGET

Boys take turns rolling a tire parallel to a line of other players 15 to 20 feet away who try to throw beanbags or balls through the rolling tire.

ROLL FOR ACCURACY

Each boy rolls his tire as hard and as fast as he can up to a stopping line, where he must stop while the tire continues to roll to a target of two sticks set 3 to 4 feet apart about 20 feet from the stopping line. Assign boys to stop the moving tires and return them to the starting line.

ROLL FOR DISTANCE

This game is similar to roll for accuracy except there is no target. Each boy rolls his tire as hard and as fast as he can up to a stopping line. The player whose tire rolls the farthest wins.

TIRE OBSTACLE RELAY

Place five tires on their sides in a row, all touching. Divide the boys into two teams and station the teams in relay formation about 20 feet from each end of the row of tires. On a signal, the first player for each team runs over the tires, stepping inside each one. When they get past the last tire, they turn right and run back and touch the next player on their team.

TIRE BOWLING

Use milk cartons, tin cans, or plastic bottles for pins, set up 20 to 30 feet from the "bowler." Roll a tire instead of a ball. Score as in bowling. Assign players to be "ball boys" to stop the rolling tires and return them to the starting line.

TIRE ROLLING RELAY

Form two teams and give the first boy on each team a tire. Place a stake or chair opposite each team on a turning line. On a signal, the first player rolls the tire to the turning line, around the stake or chair, and back to his team to the next player.

TIRE SPRINT

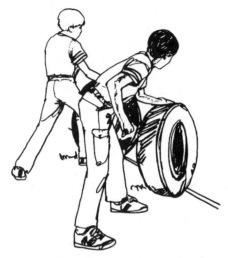

Players line up at a starting line with tires ready to roll. On a signal, they roll tires to the finish line, propelling them by hand.

TIRE TAG

Each boy, including "It," has a tire that he must roll as he runs. A player is safe if he can balance astride his upright tire while resting both feet on it.

Water Games

Safety must be a primary concern when Cub Scouts are in and around water. Always follow Safe Swim Defense, described in the *Cub Scout Leader Book* and *Guide to Safe Scouting*, and follow all requirements for swimming ability groups.

GAMES FOR NONSWIMMERS AND UP

Balloon Race

Swimming Ability Level: **Beginners and up**

Materials: **Inflated balloons**

Line up boys in chest-deep water. On a signal, they propel inflated balloons to shore without using their hands. They can use their heads or blow the balloons.

Frog in the Sea

Swimming Ability Level: **Beginners and up— water no deeper than shoulder height**

This is a good shallow-water pack game. Players form a circle around five "frogs." The players walk close to the frogs and try to tap them on the head as they repeat, "Frog in the sea, can't catch me." The frogs try to tag the players. Any tagged player changes places with the frog.

Minnow and Catfish

Swimming Ability Level: **Nonswimmers and up—water no deeper than 3½ feet**

One boy is the Minnow and tries to keep away from another, the Catfish. The rest of the boys form a circle, holding hands. The game begins with the Minnow inside the circle and the Catfish outside. The Catfish tries to break through the circle to tag the Minnow while its members try to keep him out. The Minnow may dodge in and out of the circle. When the Catfish finally tags him, two others take their places and the game continues.

Table Tennis Ball Race

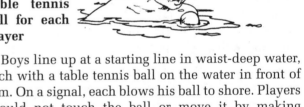

Swimming Ability Level: **Nonswimmers and up—water no deeper than 3½ feet**

Materials: **Table tennis ball for each player**

Boys line up at a starting line in waist-deep water, each with a table tennis ball on the water in front of him. On a signal, each blows his ball to shore. Players should not touch the ball or move it by making waves.

Touch-Bottom Tag

Swimming Ability Level: **Beginners and up**

This is a regular tag game played in knee-deep water, with one boy chosen as "It." If a player is touching the bottom of the pool with his hands, he's safe from being tagged.

Turtle Float

Swimming Ability Level: Beginners and up—water no deeper than shoulder height

Boys pretend to be floating turtles. They start by standing in a circle in waist-deep water. On a signal, they take a deep breath, pull their knees up against their chests, and grasp their arms around their legs so that they are floating facedown with their backs out of the water. See who can float the longest!

Up and Under

Swimming Ability Level: Nonswimmers and up

Materials: Playground ball

Dens line up in relay formation in waist-deep water. The first boy on each team has a large ball. On a signal, he passes the ball overhead to the second player, who passes it between his legs to the third, who passes it overhead, and so on to the end of the line. The last player runs to the head of the line and passes it as before.

Water Dodge Ball

Swimming Ability Level: Nonswimmers and up—water no deeper than 3½ feet

Materials: Beach ball

Divide boys into two teams. One team forms a circle around the other and throws a soft beach ball at those inside the circle until they're all eliminated by being hit. Then the groups switch places.

Water Spud

Swimming Ability Level: Beginners and up—water no deeper than shoulder height

Materials: Playground or foam ball

A starter throws a soft rubber ball high into the air and calls out a player's name. That player recovers the ball while the others scatter about the pool. He tries to hit one of the other players with the ball. A player must stay in the same spot, but he may duck under water to keep from being hit. If a player is hit, he picks up the ball and tries to hit someone else. If the ball goes wild, the thrower has one "spud" counted against him. The player with the fewest spuds wins.

ACTIVITIES FOR SWIMMERS

For these games, all boys should be of the "Swimmer" ability level.

Cork Retrieve

Materials: Ample supply of corks or wooden blocks

Scatter a dozen or more corks or blocks of wood on the far side of the pool. On a signal, boys jump in and try to retrieve the corks, bringing them back to the starting point one at a time. The boy with the most corks wins.

Keep-Away

Materials: Playground ball

Two teams line up in straight lines parallel to each other and about 10 feet apart. The leader tosses a large ball between the teams. The team that gets it tries to keep it by tossing it back and forth. No player may walk or swim with the ball, and he must not hold it more than 5 seconds. Count one point for each successful pass.

Leapfrog

Play in waist-deep water. Divide players into two teams and line them up single file with about 4 feet between team members. Players lean forward and put their hands on their knees with their feet spread apart. On a signal, the last player on each team leapfrogs over the boy ahead and then dives down and swims between the legs of the next. He continues leaping and diving until he reaches the head of the line and raises his hand. This is the signal for the last boy in line to begin leaping and diving.

Live Log

Establish a goal at one end of the pool. One boy is the "log." He floats on his back in the center of the pool. The others swim around him. At any time the "log" may roll over and begin chasing the others, who race for their goal. Any player who is tagged becomes another "log," and the game resumes. Continue until there is only one player left who has not been tagged.

Marco Polo

All boys stand in waist-deep water. One boy, "It," closes his eyes and keeps them shut (honor system). He calls out "Marco!" All other boys respond with "Polo!" "It" then tries to tag one of the responders while they duck under water and/or change locations to avoid being tagged. "It" should call out "Marco!" frequently. When a boy is tagged, he becomes the next "It."

Save Me!

Materials: **Old T-shirt and shorts for each team, rope or clothesline for each team**

Divide players into two teams. In chest-deep water about 20 feet from each team, weight and sink a T-shirt and pair of shorts. On a signal, each team's best swimmer swims to his team's bundle, retrieves it from the bottom, and puts on the clothing. He then calls out, "Save me!" whereupon the others on his team throw one end of their rope to him. He may reach for it but he may not swim or walk to get it. When he grabs the rope, the others pull him to safety. The first team to rescue its "victim" wins.

Water Basketball

Materials: **Beach ball, two inner tubes or swimming rings**

Play in waist-to-chest-deep water. Use a beach ball of basketball size. Moor two inner tubes or swimming rings at opposite ends or sides of the pool to serve as baskets. Divide players into two teams. Use regular basketball rules, except that a player "dribbles" by batting the ball ahead of him in the water.

Winter Games in the Snow

FOX AND GEESE

Needed: **Freshly fallen snow on an open playground**

In a large flat area, make a circle about 30 yards in diameter in the snow. Inside, make crisscrossing paths in any direction. Some may be dead ends. Where the paths cross in the center, make a safe zone. Make more than one circle, depending on the number of players, and make sure the circles are connected.

One player (the Fox) chases the others (the Geese), but all must stay on the snow paths. When the leader says "go," the Fox chases the Geese, trying to tag one of them. A Goose can't be tagged while standing in the safe zone, but if another Goose wants to use the safe zone, the first Goose must give it up. When a Goose gets caught by the Fox, he becomes the new Fox.

FOX HUNTING

Needed: **Plenty of untrodden snow**

Two boys are Foxes and start walking from the middle of an open area. About one or two minutes later, the others follow their trail in the snow and try to catch them. The Foxes are not allowed to follow any existing human tracks (thereby hiding their own tracks), but they may walk along sidewalks or tread in each other's tracks. Boundary limits should be set, with the Foxes trying to avoid capture for a certain period of time.

SNOW EXERCISES

Try cartwheels, skipping, leapfrog, hopping, headstands, forward rolls, and racing in the snow. It's much different than on dry ground. Look in the *Wolf, Bear,* and *Webelos Scout handbooks* for physical fitness requirements and electives that can be done in the snow when weather permits.

SNOW HUNT

Materials: **20 or 25 weatherproof objects (plastic blocks, containers, plastic flying disks, etc.), a scoop for each player**

Hide weatherproof objects around a playground during a snowfall or immediately after. Leave them until they are entirely covered, or cover them up without a trace. Gather players and describe the hidden objects. With their scoops, players dig in the snow to find the objects.

SNOW TUG-OF-WAR

Materials: **Long, heavy rope**

Pile up a big mound of snow and put the tug-of-war rope over this mound. Half the boys grab the rope on one side of the mound and the other half on the other side. Everyone pulls. Guess what happens to the boys on the losing team?

SNOWBALL CONTESTS

To make snowballs, snow should not be too dry or too powdery. On a signal, boys compete to see who can make the biggest snowball in one minute, the most snowballs in three minutes, or the tallest snowball tower in five minutes. Boys can put their heads together to come up with other snowball contests.

SNOWBALL SHARPSHOOTING

Materials: **Old sheet or blanket or piece of cardboard, clothespins, scissors**

Hang an old sheet or blanket on a clothesline with plenty of clothespins. Cut three or four holes in the sheet, each 8 to 12 inches across. Boys stand 12 to 15 feet away and try to throw snowballs through the holes. Each snowball that goes through a hole is worth one point. If boys are real sharpshooters, have them move farther away to throw.

Variation: For Tiger Cubs or younger boys, use a hula hoop as the target. Suspend it from a tree or clothesline. A player could hold the hoop and use it as a moving target, slowly moving up or down as the other boys aim and shoot.

SNOWBALL THROWING RANGE

Needed: **Tin cans, milk jugs, plastic containers, etc.; open playground after a fresh snowfall**

Divide the group into two teams. Set up the throwing range on a table, fence, or wall. Arrange cans and containers in a stack or across the table. Each team makes a pile of snowballs. Teams line up 5 to 10 yards away from the targets. One player is selected to reset the objects. One by one, players take a turn throwing their snowballs (two each). Each time a boy hits an object, his team gets a point. The team with the most points after each player has thrown wins.

SNOWBALL SPUD

Boys form a small circle in the snow. One player stands in the center, armed with a snowball. (Be sure the snowball is not icy.) He drops the snowball and calls the name of another player. All the other players scatter as far and as fast as they can while the one whose name was called runs to pick up the snowball. When he has picked it up he calls, "Stop," and all players must stop where they are. He throws the snowball at one of them. If he hits that player, the player who was hit picks up the snowball and tries to hit someone else. This goes on until someone misses. The player who misses scores one "spud." The play is repeated, with everyone forming a circle again, and continues until one player has three spuds.

SNOWMAN-BUILDING CONTEST

On days when snow can be packed easily, have a snowman-building contest. Have some props available for boys to use: hats, scarves, charcoal for buttons and eyes, carrots for noses, etc. Each boy makes his own snowman (encourage small-sized snow people). Award prizes for biggest, smallest, most lopsided, funniest, and the like. Each builder should get a prize. Treat all the snow sculptors to a special snack.

OUTDOORS

Outdoor activities are an important part of Cub Scouting. Boys learn to appreciate and care for the beautiful environment all around them as they hike, explore, and investigate the world. The Cub Scout outdoor program is a foundation for the outdoor adventure boys will continue to experience when they move on to a Boy Scout troop.

All Cub Scouts and Webelos Scouts should have opportunities to enjoy the outdoors. Remember: You don't need to go far to share the wonder of nature with children. There are many opportunities for everyone to have outdoor experiences—even just in the neighborhood. Also remember that Cub Scouts with special needs can often enjoy outdoor activities with only minor modifications to the activity.

Health and Safety

The health and safety of boys, leaders, and families must be one of the first considerations in planning any outdoor activity. Try to anticipate and eliminate hazards—or at least warn against them. Most accidents can be prevented. See the *Cub Scout Leader Book* for outdoor safety rules, Safe Swim Defense (swimming), and Safety Afloat (boating).

Also, follow these tips when planning and conducting an outdoor activity:

- Always get permission from parents or guardians for activities that are held away from the regular den and pack meeting places. Better yet, take the families with you!

- Be sure to have enough adult leaders for the activity planned. Always follow the policy of two-deep leadership (see page 1–12).

- Check out the site before the activity. Find out about gathering places, restroom facilities, and safe drinking water. Look for hazards such as poison ivy.

- If applicable, get permission from the owner to use the property.

- Use the buddy system to prevent anyone from getting lost. Coach the boys in advance about what they should do if they get lost (see below).

- Carry a first aid kit and know how to use it. Know basic emergency first aid procedures.

- File a Local Tour Permit Application with your local council service center two weeks before any pack trip of fewer than 500 miles. Webelos dens should file a Local Tour Permit Application for Webelos overnight campouts.

- Have adequate and safe transportation.

- When leaving the site, take everything you brought with you. Leave the site in its natural condition.

What to Do if Lost

Have boys learn the following suggestions, which are part of the Hug-a-Tree and Survive Program and are recommended by the National Association for Search and Rescue. They could save a life.

1. **"Hug a tree."** As soon as you realize you are lost, stop walking and "hug" a tree. That is, *stay put*. The closer you are to the place you were last seen, the more quickly you will be found.

2. **Carry shelter.** It's easy to carry along a shelter that folds up and fits into your pocket—that is, a big plastic leaf or trash bag. Cut or tear a hole in the closed end for your head to fit through and slip it on like a poncho. (But be sure to keep your face uncovered so that you can breathe!)

3. **Save body energy.** If the weather starts to cool off, curl up like an animal in the cold, conserving your body heat and energy. Snuggle against your tree or anything else that will shield you from the wind.

4. **Make yourself BIG** so that searchers in helicopters can see you easily. If possible, find your tree to hug near a clearing. If you spot a search plane or helicopter, stretch out on the ground face up and make slow, sweeping motions with your arms as if you are making a snow angel. Also, always carry a whistle when you go hiking so you can make a BIG noise to attract the attention of rescuers. Blow your whistle, shout, or pound rocks together.

5. **Remember that people are searching for you.** The longer you are lost, the more people will join the search. If you hear people, *don't be frightened.* They're exchanging information over wide areas and doing their best to find you. Searchers won't give up. They will find you.

Fun on Hikes

When did you last watch a colony of ants scurrying about as they worked hard? Or investigate a hollow tree? Or travel an unbeaten path? These are just a few things that you and the boys can do when you go hiking. The fun lies in observing everything around you as you hike, and while observing, talking about what you see. Enjoy nature—but *don't remove growing things from their natural habitats.*

You can hike in your own neighborhood or a nearby park, or you can travel to an out-of-the-way location. Or go to a nature center. Many nature centers include wheelchair-accessible trails so all boys can participate.

Your outdoor adventure could be a visit to a nature center.

There are many types of nature hikes, some of which include nature activities. Several nature hikes are described here. See the *Cub Scout Leader Book* for other types of hikes and for hiking safety rules.

Note: Always use the buddy system on hikes for safety and to prevent anyone from getting lost. Buddies should remain together at all times.

SEASONS HIKE

Materials: **Pencils and crayons, notebooks for data collection, field guides**

Choose a hiking area that you can hike in each season of the year. Each season, boys make a list of things they see along the way. Have them draw a particular area along the trail and how it changes. Which things remained the same each season? How many things changed as the seasons changed? (It's a good idea to collect and keep the boys' notebooks between seasons.)

WEB OF LIFE HIKE

Materials: **Pencil, paper**

Animals, plants, and habitats rely on each other and form a "web of life." The soil nourishes the tree; the tree shelters the animal; the animal dies and adds nutrients to the soil. Everything in nature is affected by the many other things living around it.

Boys draw 12 small circles on paper where the numbers would be on a clock face. In each circle they draw or write the name of something they see along the hike. Encourage them to include different types of things: rocks, animals, plants, river, etc. Then have them draw a line from one circle to everything it affects or is affected by it. Continue doing the same with the other 11 circles. They have now created a web of life for this area. Was there anything that didn't have lines and didn't affect anything else? What would happen if you covered up one of the circles and it was gone from your area? How many other things would its absence affect?

TRACKS AND SIGNS HIKE

Be a keen observer whenever you are out in nature. Look for all types of signs of animals and birds. Identify bird and animal tracks. Make plaster casts (see page 2–26 for how to make casts of animal tracks).

MICRO HIKE

Materials: **Strings 3 to 5 feet long**

Lay strings out along an area to study. Boys cover the string trail inch by inch on their stomachs, with their eyes no higher than 1 foot off the ground. They may see such wonders as grass blades bent by dewdrops, colorful beetles sprinkled with flower pollen, powerful-jawed eight-eyed spiders, and more. Ask questions to stimulate their imaginations: "What kind of world are you traveling through?" "Who are your nearest neighbors?" "Are they friendly?" "Do they work hard?" "What would life be like for that beetle—how would it spend its day?"

NATURE SAFARI HIKE

Materials: **Field guides, pencils, paper**

This hike will help boys learn to identify animals. See how many different species each boy can see on this local safari.

SENSE OF TOUCH HIKE

This hike will illustrate the many textures of nature. Make sure that boys are instructed to *examine* the objects they find, not take them. Examples of what the boys may look for:

The hairiest leaf	Something cool
The softest leaf	Something dry
The smoothest rock	Something warm
The roughest rock	Something bumpy
The roughest twig	

Ask questions such as: "What did you find that was dry? Why was it dry?" "How might it be different tonight? Next summer/winter?" "How did it get there?" "Does it belong there?" "Did people have anything to do with it being there?" "Has it always been the way it is?"

NATURE BABIES HIKE

Look for "nature babies"—birds, ferns, leaves, snails, insects, etc. How are the babies protected? How are they fed? Do not touch baby birds or animals. Look only from a little distance. Most babies that seem abandoned by their parents really aren't. Mother or father may be nearby.

HEADS-TAILS HIKE

Materials: **Coin**

Toss a coin each time you reach a crossroads. Turn left if the coin turns up heads, right if the coin is tails.

NATURE NOISES HIKE

This is a great way to help boys notice and enjoy the sounds around them. Stop along the hike at different points. Boys sit or stand very still and listen. As they hear a new sound, they raise their hand as a signal. They can "collect" different sounds on their fingers, holding up a finger for each sound they hear. Can you count to 10 in between sounds? Listen for birds, animals, wind in the trees, falling leaves, or rushing water.

COUNT THE COLORS HIKE

Materials: **Crayons, paper, pencils**

Each boy selects five crayons and colors an area of each on a piece of paper. Take the paper on a hike and write each object found that matches the colors. Write them under the colored area on the paper. Ask boys how many colors they can see without moving from where they are.

INCH HIKE

Materials: **Small rulers**

Find as many objects as possible that are 1 inch high, long, etc. Use the small rulers to measure. This helps boys notice the small things that they might otherwise overlook.

A-B-C HIKE

Materials: **Pencils, paper**

Write the letters of the alphabet vertically on a piece of paper. On the hike, find an object, sound, or smell in nature for each letter and write it down.

STRING-ALONG HIKE

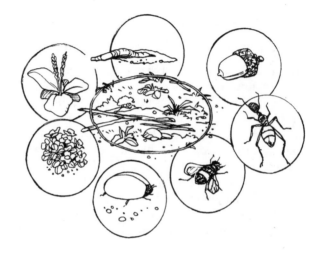

Materials: **36-inch piece of string**

Take the piece of string on your hike. Every now and then, place the string in a circle on the ground. See how many different things you can find enclosed in the circle. Then stretch the string in a line and see how many different things touch it.

SURPRISE BREAKFAST HIKE

Materials: **Breakfast fixings for everyone**

Make arrangements ahead of time with the parents of your boys to go on a "surprise" hike. Pick the boys up at their homes and head out on an early-morning hike, cooking (or providing) breakfast outdoors.

NIGHT HIKE

In areas where it is safe to walk at night, try a hike after dark. See how different things look, smell, and sound at night. Don't use flashlights, as they will lessen your ability to see and reduce your awareness of what is happening in the dark. Carry flashlights for emergency use only.

SILENT HIKE

This hike can be difficult to accomplish but powerful in helping boys appreciate the world around them. Calm the boys by having them sit alone and a few feet apart for a short period of time. On the den leader's signal, the group begins to move along the trail tapping shoulders and pointing to share the sights and sounds of the hike. *No talking!*

Fun With Hiking Games

While out on a hike you might want to stop to have a rest, enjoy lunch, or play a game. Here are some ideas for activities while taking a hiking break.

KNOW YOUR ROCK

Materials: **Tape, pencil, rocks found on your hike**

Each boy finds a fist-sized rock, remembering where he found it so he can return it after the game. All sit in a circle with eyes shut, holding their rocks. Tell them to "get to know" their rocks by its feel, texture, smell, etc. After a few minutes, collect the rocks, mix them up, and redistribute them. The boys pass the rocks around the circle and try to identify their own rock with their eyes still shut. To help prevent any disagreements, affix a small piece of tape to each rock with the owner's initials. Be sure to remember to remove the tape when you leave the rock behind!

KNOW YOUR LEAF

Materials: **Leaves**

This is similar to Know Your Rock. With eyes open, each boy gets to know a leaf by its shape, size, color, veins, etc. Then put all leaves in a pile and let one boy at a time try to find his, explaining to the group how he did it and what he looked for.

GRAB BAG

Materials: **15 nature items, 15 small paper bags**

Collect 15 nature items, such as pinecones, nuts, shells, etc., and place each in small paper bag. Pass the bags around the circle of boys and let them try to identify the object by feeling the outside of the bag.

NATURE PHOTOGRAPHER

Boys work in buddy pairs, with one boy acting as the "camera" and the other as the "photographer." The photographer guides the camera, who has his eyes closed, to an interesting nature picture. When the photographer is ready to "take the picture," he taps on the camera's shoulder to signal him to open and close his eyes. The photographer can "adjust" his camera to take closeups and wide-angle shots and to use interesting angles and perspectives. The camera and photographer should talk as little as possible to enjoy this experience. The photographer should also remember to guide his camera safely. After several pictures have been taken, it will be time for the photographer and camera to switch positions and begin again.

NATURE KIM'S GAME

Materials: **Nature items, towel or jacket**

Gather nature items such as pinecones, leaves, twigs, rocks, etc. Place them in an area for the boys to study. After a few minutes, cover the items with the towel or jacket and have the boys try to remember all the now-hidden items.

CAMOUFLAGE TRAIL

Materials: **15 or 20 human-made objects**

This game can open doors to a discussion about how an animal's color can help protect it. Along an area of trail place 15 or 20 human-made objects. Some objects should stand out and be bright colors. Some should blend in with the surroundings. Keep the number of objects a secret. Boys walk along the section of trail, spotting as many objects as they can. When they reach the end, they whisper to you how many they saw. Invite them to go back and see whether they can spot any that they missed.

NATURE SCAVENGER HUNT

This hunt is intended to test the boys' knowledge of nature in an exciting competition. It is run like any scavenger hunt, with each group of boys having a list of nature objects and finding as many as possible in a time limit (10 to 20 minutes). Set boundaries for the hunt and list 20 to 50 objects from nature that boys can find within the area. They should be common enough that a Cub Scout can identify most of them. Make sure that boys are marking these items off their list and leaving the items themselves undisturbed.

Your list will reflect nature items that can be found in your locale, but here are some common suggestions:

Anthill	Oak leaf	Maple leaf
Dandelion	Insect	Cocoon
Spider web	Animal track	Bird's nest
Needle from an evergreen	Barrel cactus	Acorn

NATURE STATIONS

Materials:
   Station cards for each station
   Scorecard for each group of boys
   Pencils
   Chart to mark groups' scores and winner
   Small prize for winning group
   Treats

Make up your own nature trail using the features available in your area. If it is a wooded site, tree and leaf identification are possible. If the site has a stream, include a station on spotting marine life or water insects. Prepare the trail in advance with five to 10 stations. At each station the group is to find something, identify something, or otherwise show knowledge of nature lore.

This is a competition to test nature skills. It is not a race. Groups of boys start at intervals of about 5 minutes. At each station they find a message that tells them what to do. They have a scorecard on which they write their findings and then move on to the next station. It will help to have an adult at each station to provide help and make sure boys replace the message where they found it.

The sample nature trail below is suitable for a small wooded park.

Station 1: "Look for the biggest tree you can see from here. What direction is it? Write the direction on your scorecard. Go northwest to a picnic table and look under it."

Station 2: "Within 15 paces of this spot, you'll see five different kinds of trees. Write down the names of two of them. Go south 50 paces and find a small mound of pebbles."

Station 3: "Within 20 feet of here, there is a clump of wildflowers. Write down the name of the flower. Go east until you come to a tree with a split trunk. Look around its base."

Station 4: "Somewhere in this tree is a nest with young birds. Spot it, but do not disturb the nest or birds. Try to identify the name of the birds from the shape of the nest and write down what kind of birds you think they are. Go north toward the entrance of the park. Near the gate, look for two rocks, one on top of the other."

Station 5: "Within five paces of this spot is an insect's home. Find it and write down the name of the insect. [Could be an ant colony, beehive, wasps' nest, etc.] Go southeast until you come to a seesaw. Look under one of the seats."

Station 6: "Ten paces due east of this spot is an animal track. What kind of animal made the track?" [If there isn't a real animal track, use a plaster cast of a cat's track.] "Go due east until you come to a weedy patch. Look along its edge."

Station 7: "Pick up a leaf or bit of grass and toss it in the air. What is the wind direction? Write it on your card. Go north 30 paces and look under the pile of rocks."

Station 8: "Look around you. There is a wooded area, a small pond, and a grassy lawn. Remember that animals need different kinds of places to live. Which of the following animals do you think live near here?: Deer, bee, squirrel, rabbit, lion, muskrat, dragonfly, chipmunk, elephant, bear, skunk, frog, mouse, leopard, cricket. Write down the animals that you think live around here. Then go southwest until you come to a drinking fountain. Look around its base."

Station 9: "Within 10 yards of the fountain is a bush whose berries and seeds are important food for some birds. Pace off the distance from the fountain. Write down the number of paces. For an extra point, write down the name of the bush. Then return to Station 1 and turn in your scorecard."

Have judges ready to check scorecards and post each groups ranking on a chart. Give an inexpensive prize to the winning group, with treats for everybody.

Fun With Plants

The wonder of how things grow can be an amazing thing to share with a child. Cub Scouts and Webelos Scouts can enjoy watching fast-growing plants and measuring their progress. They can feel the sense of accomplishment in growing vegetables in their own garden and marvel at the simple sprouting of a seed.

GERMINATING SEEDS

Materials: **Glass or jar; blotting paper or toilet tissue; sawdust; seeds, grains of corn, beans, peas; water**

To watch how seeds germinate and begin to grow, line the glass or jar with the blotting paper or toilet tissue. Fill the glass with sawdust. Put the seeds, grains of corn, beans, peas, etc., between the paper and the glass. Water thoroughly and place the glass in a light place. Through the glass you can observe how the seeds germinate and grow from day to day.

TRAVELING SEEDS

Materials: **Posterboard, marking pen, glue, seeds**

Seeds can be distributed in many ways to start new plants. Make a chart that shows how seeds are spread. Divide posterboard into six sections and label the sections for each method of dispersal below. Collect seed samples and glue down actual seeds as you find them. How do you think each seed came to be in each location?

Helicopters: These winged seeds spiral down from trees such as maples, elms, and ashes.

Hitchhikers: Seeds of this type have burs that can hook on to animals (or your pants leg!) and travel with them. The beggar-tick, cocklebur, and Spanish needle are examples.

Parachutists: On a breezy day you can see these seeds floating through the air. Look for dandelions, milkweeds, and thistles.

Delectables: Birds and animals spread some seeds by eating them; the seeds then go through the animal's digestive tract. Apples, cherries, and berries are examples of this type.

Floaters: Some plants produce pods that when ripe will open and allow the seeds to spread. Some drop to the ground or are blown a short distance. Look for lotus, marigold, and sweet william.

Missiles: This type of seed shoots out of its pod. Exploding pods include impatiens, witch hazel, and wood sorrel.

ARE YOU A SEED SPREADER?

Materials: **Potting soil, tray, kitchen knife, mud from your shoe**

When you are out for a walk, you might be a seed spreader. Scrape the mud from your shoes into a tray of potting soil. Keep it watered and see whether any plants grow. Make a tray from different parts of an outdoor area and see what might be the same or different.

SEED COLLECTIONS

Materials:

Seeds	Egg cartons
Self-stick labels	String tags
Collecting containers (small clear jars or boxes)	Marking pen

Collecting tree, flower, vegetable, and plant seeds can be an interesting hobby. Seeds come in a variety of sizes, shapes, and colors. To add interest to the collection, also gather seed pods, such as pinecones.

Store your seeds in small clear plastic bottles, plastic coin tubes, or square and rectangular plastic boxes. Use egg cartons for larger seeds. Label each jar or box with a self-sticking label. Use tags with strings to label pinecones or other larger items.

Catalogue your collection by categories, such as trees, flowers, vegetables, etc., or group the items by the way they are dispersed, such as winged seed helicopters, burred hitchhikers, etc. (see "Traveling Seeds" above).

ENERGY STORAGE SYSTEMS

Materials:

Carrot with greens	Knife
Cotton	Plate
Water	Onion
Jar or glass	

Plants store food in the roots, stems, and leaves. The plant may use this reserve of food later for a variety of reasons, such as to help the plant survive the winter or to help it form seeds and fruits. You can show how the stored food can be used to start the plant growing again by conducting this experiment.

Cut the top off of a carrot that still has leaves and place it on a plate of wet cotton. Keep the cotton wet. Watch as new roots and leaves form from the food stored in the carrot.

Take an onion and rest it on the top of a jar or glass filled with enough water so that the bottom of the onion in is the water. Soon, roots will grow from the bottom, and a shoot will erupt from the top. At the same time, the layers in the onion will begin to shrivel as the food in them is used up for the new growth.

HOW PLANTS ABSORB WATER

Materials:

Small jar	Water
Food coloring	Spoon
Celery stalk with leaves	Knife

Fill the jar with water. Add about six drops of food coloring and stir. Make a fresh cut on the end of the celery stalk and place the stalk in the jar of colored water. Observe the celery after a few hours, and then cut across the bottom and top of the celery. Observe the cut ends. Compare how the end looked before and after the experiment.

You can also slice the celery lengthwise halfway up the stalk and place each end in water jars with different colors.

OXYGEN MAKERS

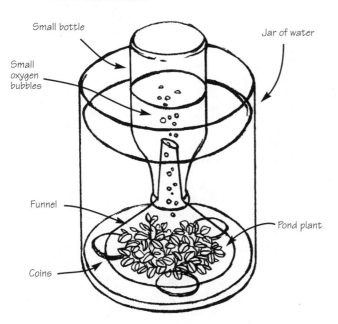

Small bottle

Jar of water

Small oxygen bubbles

Funnel

Coins

Pond plant

Materials: **Small jar of water, funnel, bottle to go over funnel, coins, small pond plant**

Place the pond plant in the jar of water under the funnel, as shown. The funnel should be sitting on the coins so that it is raised off the bottom of the jar. Fill the small bottle completely with water so no air pockets are remaining. (You may want to set up this experiment under water in a sink.) Set the experiment in bright light and watch to see whether bubbles begin forming. The bubbles that are forming are the important gas *oxygen*. All green leaves give off oxygen, which we need to stay alive. This is one of the many reasons plants are so important. If you move the experiment to a shady place, will the bubbles appear more or less quickly?

MUSHROOM SPORE PRINTS

Materials: **Mushroom with a flat cap, white paper, clear glass bowl, hair spray or clear contact paper**

Early autumn is a good time to look for mushrooms in the woods. (*But never eat a mushroom that you find in the woods! Some are very poisonous.*) A mushroom sends out hundreds of tiny, fertile bodies called *spores*. Like flower seeds, spores are the way the mushroom reproduces. You can capture these spores on paper.

Choose a fresh mushroom with a flat cap. Put the mushroom cap, bottom down, on white paper and cover with a clear glass bowl overnight. Tiny spoors will fall onto the paper, making a colorful pattern. Each species of mushroom makes a design of its own. You can set and preserve your print with a fixative, such as hair spray, or cover it with clear contact paper.

TERRARIUM FOR PLANTS

Materials:
- Large wide-mouth glass jar with lid
- Horticultural-grade gravel
- Charcoal
- Soil separator (piece of nylon or other synthetic material)
- Terrarium soil
- Plants (ferns, matted mosses, wild strawberry, violets, evergreen seedlings)
- Spoon

Clean and dry the jar and lay it on its side. Spoon ¾ inch of gravel into the bottom for drainage. Sprinkle in enough charcoal to cover the gravel. This will absorb odors. Cut the soil separator to fit on top of the charcoal. This will keep soil out of the drainage material (the charcoal and the gravel). Spoon 1 inch of soil on top of the separator. Make a hole in the soil and add the largest plant. Scoop some soil around the base to hold it in place. Add the remaining plants in the same manner. Add more soil, so that the soil layer and drainage material fills about a quarter of the container. Tamp down the soil gently with your fingers. Spray the garden with water, but don't get the soil too wet. Put on the lid of the jar and place your terrarium in bright to medium light, but not in direct sunlight.

Check the terrarium the next day to be sure that the moisture balance is correct. It should have a light mist on the inside of the glass, and the soil should be medium dark. Too much water will cause a heavy mist and can be corrected by leaving the cover half open for a day. If there is too little water, there will be no mist at all. In this case, add a teaspoon of water every other day until the terrarium moisture is balanced.

To maintain the terrarium, give it a little fresh air every week or two by removing the top for 15 minutes at a time. Trim the plants when necessary.

MOSS GARDEN

Materials: **Fish tank, gravel, decaying plant matter, soil, moss**

You can create a miniature garden with mosses. Look around for soft, velvety moss. Look in dark corners and remove a small amount, leaving some to reproduce. (Some mosses are protected and should not be taken from their natural environment. You will want to find out which they are; your local library should be able to help you.)

Put clean gravel at the bottom of the fish tank. Then add a layer of decaying plant matter and cover it with a layer of soil. Arrange the gathered moss in the soil. You might add bark, lichen, rocks, or small statues for interest.

Try to re-create the shady conditions in which you found the mosses. Water your garden regularly, or you can cover your moss garden with a lid and let condensation do the trick.

INDOOR GARDEN IN A TRAY

Materials: **Plastic tray, potting soil, vegetable seeds (e.g., radish, cress, lettuce)**

Fill the tray half full with potting soil and dampen. Make lines across the soil for seed rows. Cover the seeds with a thin layer of soil. Leave the tray where it is warm and light. Keep the soil damp, and watch your indoor garden grow. Cut the cress with scissors and add to salads. You may have to thin the young lettuce and radish plants. Pull a few out and place them in a similar tray to finish growing.

NYLON NED

Materials:
- Old nylon pantyhose
- Foam cup
- Sawdust
- Grass seed
- Rubber bands
- Scissors
- Wiggle eyes
- Craft foam
- Waterproof glue
- Small plate

Cut a 12-inch length of nylon pantyhose that includes the toe. Cut the bottom out of the foam cup and slip it inside the nylon, pushing it down to the toe. Fold the excess nylon over the top of the cup. Place about 2 t. grass seed in the bottom of the cup and spread out fairly evenly. Add sawdust on top to fill the cup, being careful not to disturb the grass seed. Unfold the extra ends of the nylon. While pushing down on the top of the sawdust, pull up and remove the foam cup. Gather the ends of the nylon close to the sawdust and close with a rubber band. Cut off and discard the remaining stocking piece.

Turn the grass seed side up, and you are now ready to shape and decorate your Ned. Complete his face by cutting out pieces from craft foam and gluing them in place. Add wiggle eyes. You can create a nose and ears by carefully gathering up a small section of sawdust through the nylon and tying with a rubber band. Let the glue dry.

To grow his hair, soak Nylon Ned in water for a few minutes to dampen and then place him on a small plate. Water him daily to keep him damp. Make sure that you drain any excess water off the plate. Before you know it, Ned will need a haircut! Style with scissors.

THE BOY WITH GREEN HAIR

Materials:

Egg	Pin
Manicure scissors	Soil
Grass seed	Markers
Egg carton cup	Water

Gently puncture the pointed end of an egg with a pin. With manicure scissors, carefully cut away about one-quarter of the pointed end of the shell. Remove the egg contents. Rinse inside the shell and let it dry. Fill the shell with dirt and plant ordinary grass seed. Draw eyes, nose, mouth, and ears on the shell with permanent markers. Set the shell in an egg carton cup. Water every day, and soon the boy's green hair will begin to grow. In about a week, he will need a haircut.

THE GREAT PUMPKIN RACE

Materials: Pumpkin seeds, plant markers, prizes

Who can grow the heaviest, fattest, or most unusual pumpkin? Give each boy the same number of pumpkin seeds. Choose a starting day and a finishing day (pumpkins average 100 to 110 days to harvest). Everyone must plant the seeds on the same day. They can all be planted in one location, with plenty of space between hills, and markers labeled with the boys' names. Or each boy can plant his own at home.

Each boy is responsible for watering, weeding, and caring for his plant. As small pumpkins appear, they should be picked off the vines to allow all the growing energy to go into the biggest pumpkins.

On the ending date, boys display their best pumpkin. Give prizes for the heaviest, fattest, tallest, most unusually shaped, etc. Make sure all boys get a prize for their efforts.

Fun With Trees

Trees are one of the world's most important types of plants. Whether your Cub Scouts are identifying trees, leaves, and pinecones or just enjoying the wind rustling through the leaves, trees can be the source of an interesting outing.

THE SHAPE OF THINGS

Materials: Chart paper, pencils

Trees have distinctive silhouettes. Many times, you can identify a tree by its shape. In this simple classification game, you can find trees that have similar shapes. Some guidebooks include a tiny silhouette that may be helpful. You can use trees with or without leaves for this activity. It isn't necessary to know the names of many trees to participate.

Divide the chart paper into sections and draw a simple shape, such as a circle, oval, rectangle, or pyramid, in each section. Leave a few blank sections for the boys to create additional shapes as needed.

While on your outing, have boys look for trees that match the basic shapes. Write down their names or draw a picture of them in the coinciding section.

You can make this a cooperative activity by seeing whether the whole group can find a certain number of each shape. Or make it competitive by having teams compete to find the most.

TREE'S JOB DESCRIPTION

Materials: Paper, pencil

We use trees for many things in our lives, but what about the different roles trees play in nature? Write a "Want Ad" for a tree including all the things that a tree does in the natural world.

Look around at different trees for clues. Roots help hold the soil together and prevent erosion. They also help shelter burrowing animals. Look for other animal homes in trees, such as nests for birds and holes that squirrels and birds have made. You might find small holes made by insects. Leaves can also be homes for insects.

Many animals get their food from trees; nuts, fruits, twigs, bark, and leaves are all food sources. Leaves give off oxygen and add moisture to the air. When leaves fall and decompose, they enrich the soil, as does the entire tree when it dies and rots. Fallen trees have great jobs of providing homes and food. Look for new plants and fungi growing on fallen logs or stumps. Trees have a big job to fill.

COUNTING TREE RINGS

Materials: **Tree stump, paper, crayon**

Find the stump of a tree that has just been cut down. Count the rings to see how old the tree is. Each ring represents a growth season of one year. A wide ring shows a good year of growth for the tree, with lots of rain and plenty of sunshine. A narrow ring shows the opposite: not enough rain and a poor growing season. When a tree is hurt by forest fire, its growth may be slowed down for several years.

To be able to count these rings at home, make a stump rubbing. Place the paper over the top of the stump and rub the crayon carefully across it. Try not to move the paper and you will be able to clearly see the annual growth rings of the tree.

HISTORY STUMP

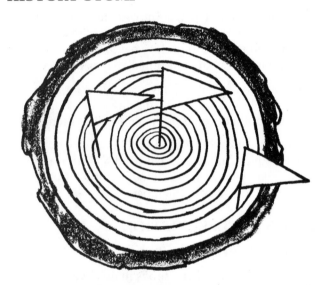

Materials: **Slice of a tree trunk, pins or nails, small strips of paper, pens**

Have a large slice of a tree trunk that shows the rings (sanding the slice can help bring the rings out). Count the rings and calculate what year each ring represents. Boys write down important events and the date they happened on small strips of paper. Attach them to the corresponding rings on the stump with pins or small nails. You might like to mark the boys' birthdays or some dates from Scouting's history or the history of your pack along with other historical events.

LISTENING TO A TREE

Materials: **Deciduous tree that is at least 6 inches in diameter and has thin bark, stethoscope**

A tree is a living, growing thing. It eats, rests, and has circulation just as we do, as water comes in through the roots, moves through the trunk, and then goes out the leaves. The heartbeat of a tree—the water and sap moving through it—is a wonderful sound. The best time to hear it is in early spring when the tree sends the first sap upward to its branches, preparing them for another season of growth. Some species of trees have a louder heartbeat than others. Press the stethoscope firmly against the tree, keeping it motionless so you won't hear any interfering noises. You may need to try several different places on the tree trunk before you find a good listening spot.

BREATHING TREES

Materials: **Plastic bag, string, tree with big leaves**

Place a plastic bag over one of the green leaves on a tree and tie it firmly around the stem. As water enters the tree through the roots and moves through the trunk, it heads down the branches and into the tree's leaves. Water then passes out through the leaf and appears as droplets of condensation inside the bag. This process is called *transpiration.* Up to 25 gallons of water can move through a medium-sized tree!

DO LEAVES NEED SUNLIGHT?

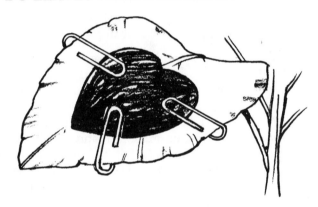

Materials: **Tree with green leaves, heavy black construction paper, paper clips, scissors**

Chlorophyll is the pigment that gives leaves their green color. Plants need it to produce food. Most of this food production happens in the leaves when sunlight shines on them. Without light, the plant won't be able to produce food.

Cut two hearts the same size from black construction paper. Place them on the top and bottom of a tree leaf that will be in full sun most of the day. Paper clip the hearts to the leaves such that no light will peek through.

After a week of sunny weather, remove the paper hearts and find out whether sunlight is needed to produce chlorophyll in leaves.

GET TO KNOW A TREE

Materials: **Trees, blindfolds**

Have boys work with a buddy. One partner is blindfolded, and the other partner "introduces" him to a tree. Carefully, the guide leads his buddy to any tree. The blindfolded boy tries to get to know every detail of the tree by feeling it. Can he reach around the tree? Feel for lumps and bumps and special textures. When the blindfolded buddy feels that he knows his tree, he can be led back to the starting place to remove his blindfold. Now he can see whether he can find the same tree again by feeling, this time with his eyes open. Take turns and have the guide become the blindfolded buddy ready to get to know a tree.

BARK RUBBING IDENTIFICATION

Materials: **Rice paper or other thin paper, tape, crayons**

Divide boys into two teams. Each team takes turns making three or four bark rubbings of different trees. (Smooth-bark trees work best, such as birch, slippery elm, butternut, or wild cherry.) To make a bark rubbing, tape the paper to the tree and, using the side of a crayon, gently rub back and forth. Remind each team to keep track of which tree each rubbing is from. Have the two teams work out of sight of the other. When the rubbings are complete, the teams switch drawings and see whether the other team can guess which trees they came from.

TREE TAGGING

Materials: **40 pieces of 1-inch gauze bandage, 12 inches long; two marking pens of different colors; paper and pencils**

Divide the boys into two teams. Give each team 20 pieces of gauze bandage. Using a different color marking pen for each team, mark the numbers 1 to 20 on each of the pieces of gauze. The object is to tie the gauze bandages on as many different types of trees as possible within 100 feet of a starting point. One team member keeps a list of the trees tagged. The team tagging the most trees correctly within a time limit wins. Remember to remove the gauze before you leave!

MUSIC IN THE TREES

If you stop and listen, you can hear music in the trees. Begin by listening to all the sounds. Listen to the leaves of a tree fluttering in the wind. Next, concentrate on the sound made by all the leaves and branches. Try to focus on the sounds coming from just one branch. Then try to hear the music of just one leaf. Can you pick out your tree's song from all the other trees?

ID GAME

Materials: **Seven to 10 samples of tree leaves or cones from different trees**

This game will help boys learn the names of trees. In advance, collect seven to 10 small samples of leaves or cones from different trees. Form two equal teams and line them up facing each other about 30 feet apart. Put the samples in a row on the ground between the two teams. The teams count off individually so each player has a number. The leader calls out the name of a tree and then calls a number. The player on each team whose number is called races to the samples and tries to identify the sample from the name of the tree called. Each player who is successful earns two points for his team. Choosing the wrong sample deducts two points from the team's score.

LEAF COLLECTION

Materials:
    Leaves
    Newspapers
    A board the same size as the newspapers
    Books or rocks for weight
    Glue mounting paper
    Clear adhesive paper

By drying and mounting leaves, boys can begin a leaf collection. Select a leaf that is full-grown and has not been damaged by insects. Lay the leaf between a folded sheet of newspaper. Add several more layers of newspaper underneath and on top. Cover with the board and weight down the newspaper pad with books or rocks. Leave to dry for about 10 days, changing the inside layers of newspaper every few days.

To mount the dried leaves, glue the leaf to mounting paper, such as cardboard, large index cards, construction paper, or a scrapbook page. Label with the name and location of the tree and the date. Cover with transparent adhesive paper.

MAKING A LEAF SKELETON

Materials:
Fresh green leaf with sturdy veins
Felt, soft cloth, or old piece of carpet
Hairbrush or shoe brush
Newspapers
Books for weight
Mounting paper or two pieces of glass
Tape

You can see the delicate veins of a leaf by removing the fleshy part. You'll be able to clearly see the network of veins through which the leaf got the raw materials (minerals and water) needed to make food that was then carried through the veins to the rest of the tree.

Place a leaf on an old piece of carpet or a pad made from several thicknesses of felt or soft cloth. Tap the leaf with the brush, periodically turning the leaf over to tap the other side. Continue tapping until only the veins are left. Dry the leaf skeleton between layers of weighted newspaper. Then mount on paper or between two pieces of glass held together with tape.

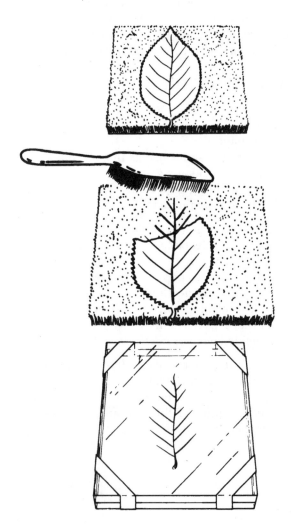

Fun With Soil

To some people it's just dirt that needs to be cleaned out of the clothes of active boys, but the soil of the earth can provide a lot of fun while boys discover interesting facts about it.

SOIL HORIZONS

Materials: **Clear jar with a lid, spoon or scoop**

You can observe the beautiful layers of soil, called *soil horizons*, many places where areas have been cut away. You can also reproduce them in a jar. At the bottom of a clear jar, place small rocks about one-eighth of the way up the jar. These represent the deepest layers of soil, which are rocky because they aren't exposed to wind or much water. Find suitable rocks along a stream bed or other rocky area.

For the next layer, dig down several feet to the subsoil. This subsoil layer is broken down rock. It is usually dry and hard. Place a layer of the subsoil next in your jar on top of the rock. This layer should reach about halfway way up your jar.

Topsoil is the layer produced by leaf litter that is broken down by micro-organisms. This layer produces the nutrients necessary for plant life. Brush away any leaf litter on the ground and you will find this soil layer easily. Add this in the next quarter of the jar.

The last layer on the very top is leaf litter and the remnants of dead plants and animals. Once this hits the ground, it begins the process of decaying to make topsoil. Gather a bit of crumbly leaf litter and add it to the top of your jar. Add the lid and you will have your completed jar of soil horizons.

NATURE'S LAYER CAKE

Materials: **Jar with tight-fitting lid, scoop of soil, water**

Many layers and different-sized particles make up our soil. You can separate them to see what soil is made of. Fill a jar halfway with soil and add water to the top. Screw the lid on tightly, shake the jar well, and let the contents settle. Soon, you will see leaf litter floating on the top. You'll also see the sand and clay that provide structure to the soil. Stones, which will settle on the bottom, help the water drain away so that the soil doesn't become waterlogged.

Try taking samples from different areas and see how the layers differ.

COMPOSTING IN THE WOODS

Materials: **Leaf litter, magnifying glass**

As trees lose their leaves and plants and animals die, they eventually decompose and add nutrients to the soil. Investigate how this happens. Find a thick layer of leaf litter. What things are happening to this layer? Look to see whether it is dry on the top and moist on the bottom. Some plants and animals feed on decaying matter. Can you see evidence of this? Worms break down this dead matter and mix it through the top layers of soil. Can you find any worms? Fungi don't make their own food like many plants. Instead, they absorb nutrients from dead things through their roots. Look carefully and you might see these soil helpers.

ROCKS INTO SOIL

Materials: **Two sandstone rocks, paper**

To demonstrate how subsoil is formed, rub two pieces of sandstone rock together. Collect the particles on a piece of paper. How long does it take to make a teaspoon of soil?

NATURE'S CLEANERS

Materials:
> **Grape powdered drink mix**
> **Large container**
> **Three foam cups**
> **Pencil**
> **1 C. each of soil, pebbles, and sand**
> **Tape**
> **Four glasses**

In a large container, mix the powdered drink without adding sugar. Poke a hole in the bottom of each foam cup with a pencil. Fill one cup with soil, one with sand, and one with pebbles. Label each cup with its contents. Using tape, mark three glasses with the same labels, and mark the fourth glass "grape drink." Run a glass of water through the cups and into a sink to remove any particles that may cloud your experiment. Let them drain completely.

Place each cup over the glass with the matching label and pour the grape drink in, letting it drip through the cup into the glass. Stop before the glass is full. Repeat with all three cups. Fill the fourth glass with grape drink. Wait several days to let the particles settle to the bottom of the glass. Then compare the colors of the filtered grape drink.

Which glass has the lightest liquid? Which has the darkest? How fast did the grape drink travel through each cup? The grape drink that went through the soil should be the clearest. This is actually how water gets cleaned: It drains into soil, and as it drips down through the layers of soil to lakes and rivers underground, the soil acts as a filter to clean the water.

SOAK IT UP

Materials:
> **Clay soil**   **Sandy soil**
> **Two clean jars**   **Masking tape**
> **Marking pen**   **Small paper cup**
> **Water**   **Stopwatch**
> **Pencil and paper**

Fill one jar half full with clay soil and the other with sandy soil; label. Pack down the soil with your hands. Pour a cupful of water on the soil in each jar. Record how long it takes for the water to soak into the soil. Add cupfuls of water to each jar until the soil can't soak up any more. Record how many cupfuls each soil holds. Which soil soaks up water faster? Which soil soaks up the most water? Which soil would have the least amount of runoff during a heavy rain? Why? Which kind of soil would have the biggest mud puddles after a heavy rain? Why?

EROSION EXPERIMENT

Materials:
> **Two cardboard boxes**   **Scissors**
> **Screening**   **Soil**
> **A square of turf**   **Two watering cans**
> **Two collection buckets**

Vegetation that covers the ground reduces water runoff and prevents erosion by water. Keeping this topsoil layer that holds the nutrients for growth is important.

Cut the end out of two cardboard boxes and make funnels as shown by stapling the cardboard pieces onto the cut ends. Put screening across the ends. Fill the boxes with soil. In one box, cover the soil with a square of turf that has been carefully cut so that you can put it back where it came from when the experiment is finished. Sprinkle the same amout of water simultaneously over both boxes and collect the runoff from each box in collection buckets. Which jar fills faster? Which has the clearer water running off it? What does this tell you about the value of plants in controlling erosion?

ROCK AND MINERAL COLLECTIONS

Materials:

Rocks and minerals	Newspaper
Small cards	Marking pen
Hammer and chisel	Safety glasses
Collection bottles,	White paint
boxes, or egg cartons	

Many boys like collecting rocks and minerals. A good place to find rock specimens is in roadbeds, in riverbeds, and around construction sites and building excavations. Be sure to ask permission before entering the property of others. In some areas, mineral collecting may be prohibited, so always check the regulations in your area first.

- Wrap each specimen in a piece of newspaper with a card to show where you found it.

- Rocks can be chiseled to a standard size, such as 2 by 3 inches, with a geologist's hammer or a regular hammer and a chisel. *Be sure to wear protective glasses when chiseling.*

- Label rocks by attaching a small label to the underside with transparent tape or by painting a small white spot on which you can write an identification number. Your identification should include the type of rock, where you found it, and the date.

- Keep small rocks in small bottles such as pill bottles. Keep larger rocks in sectioned boxes or egg cartons.

Fun With Water and Aquatic Life

Our oceans, ponds, and rivers are full of wonders to explore with boys. *Always be careful when water is involved with any Scouting activity, and follow all water safety rules.*

WATERSCOPE

Materials: **Two or three small fruit juice cans, small plastic or glass jar, 1-inch-wide waterproof adhesive tape, wire**

With this device, boys can see the world that lives underwater.

1. Remove both ends from the cans. Punch holes near the ends of the cans so they can be wired together.

2. Align the seams of the cans, placing them end to end, and fasten with wire and waterproof tape.

3. Insert this tin cylinder into a jar and make the joint watertight by covering with waterproof tape.

Tin can wired together and taped

Waterproof tape

Plastic or glass jar

Boys can watch the movements of fish or study underwater rocks or plants from the water's edge or a boat. The waterscope eliminates surface reflection and allows them to see directly under water.

POND DIPPING

Materials: **Kitchen strainer, broomstick, waterproof tape, glass or jar**

Tape the kitchen strainer handle to the broomstick. Skim a pond for water creatures. Put small water animals and fish in a glass or jar for observation. Be sure to add pond water to the container and handle carefully so you can return them to the pond after observation.

SEALED WORLD

Materials: **Large, wide-mouthed jar, 1-gallon minimum; sand or sandy soil; water plants; water from a pond**

This project illustrates how everything in nature depends on something else. You will be making a self-sufficient world of plants and small animals.

1. Place about 1½ inches of sand or sandy soil in the bottom of the jar.

2. Plant five or six water plants in the sand, such as eelgrass and elodea, which you can get from a tropical fish dealer.

3. Fill the jar with water from a pond to where the neck narrows. The water may look lifeless, but it contains *plankton*—tiny plants and animals. By the next den meeting, the water will have cleared, and you will see tiny animals swimming about.

4. Add a snail and two minnows not more than 1 inch long.

5. Put a screw lid on the jar, and seal it with tape.

6. Keep the jar where it will get indirect sunlight. With no further attention, the sealed world will sustain itself. Be sure to return your specimens to the pond in a few weeks so that they will not die.

What happens? The green plants use light, minerals from the soil, and carbon dioxide exhaled by the plankton, fish, and snail. The fish eat the plankton, but the tiny plankton keep multiplying so the food supply will last a long time. The snail eats plankton, too, but it is a scavenger that also feeds on the tiny plants that grow on the glass and on larger plants. This is an excellent demonstration of the "web of nature."

WHAT'S IN THE WATER?

Materials: **Jar; water from a lake, pond, river, or sea; magnifying glass; microscope (optional)**

Fill a jar with water collected from a lake, pond, river, or sea. Place the jar in the sun for a few days. As the water evaporates, add more collected water. In most cases, small algae and plankton develop. Study them with the aid of a microscope or magnifying glass. Note the color and shape.

Algae and plankton are the basic food in the food chain of many animals that depend on a water environment for their lives—fish, turtles, crabs, clams, ospreys, herons, etc.

ABOUT FISHING

You don't have to have fancy tackle to have fun fishing. You can use a fly rod, but cane poles and hand lines are also effective when catching fish. Probably more fish have been caught with an inexpensive cane pole than with all the more expensive rods made. The real secret is knowing where and when to fish. Water temperature varies in lakes, ponds, and streams. Fish are sensitive to water temperature. If the water is too warm or cold, they won't be very active or eager to eat your bait. As the weather changes, you will find the fish at different depths of water. It pays to do some experimenting to find out where to fish.

Another important consideration is the type of bait to choose. Worms are the best all-around bait for most fish. Minnows, crayfish, and insects are also used. The type of bait depends on the kind of fish you want to attract.

Many kinds of hooks are available, and some are constructed so as to enable you to release fish easily. Some hooks will dissolve and fall out if they remain in the fish's mouth. Catch-and-release is popular among people who fish and can offer many hours of enjoyment for boys and adults.

PRINT A FISH

Materials:
Whole flat fish (one you've caught or one from the market)
Soap
Water
Cotton
Rice paper or other thin paper
Water-soluble printers' ink
Pane of glass
Brayer (printing ink roller)

For many centuries, the Japanese have used rice paper to make fish prints. Some are so beautiful, they are in museums. If you've caught a fish for dinner, you might try making a fish print before you eat it.

1. Wash the fish in mild, soapy solution to remove any surface slime. Dry the fish thoroughly.

2. Study the parts of the fish you want to print. Look at its shape, placement of fins, and patterns of scales. Plug up the gills or any other openings with cotton so they won't leak.

3. Squeeze some ink onto the pane of glass. Roll the brayer over the ink until it sounds "sticky." Then roll the ink across the surface of the fish, from head to tail, so the scales won't be disturbed. Be sure that the head, fins, and tail are inked completely.

4. Lay a piece of rice paper over the fish and run your fingers around the head, over the scales, and along each fin. Lift the print and examine it. You may be surprised by its detail.

Continue making prints, using more or less ink and more or less rubbing until you get the results that please you. If the scales become clogged with ink, wash the fish off, pat it dry, and try again.

Before cooking your fish, be sure to wash it well with soap and water and remove the skin.

OBSERVING UNDERWATER NIGHT LIFE

Materials: **Two-cell flashlight, watertight plastic bag, strong twine or light rope**

If a stream or lake is nearby, take the boys out to see what fish do at night. A pier would be ideal. Seal the flashlight in a watertight plastic bag. Tie strong twine or a light rope around the center of the flashlight so it hangs level. After dark, slowly lower the light into 6 to 8 feet of water. Turn the light slowly. It will attract many fish, crabs, and crayfish. See how many the boys can identify.

FROG RAFT

Materials: **Candle, 1-foot length of 1-inch board, rope or twine, nail, hammer**

Fasten a candle to the middle of a 1-foot length of 1-inch board with candle drippings. Pound a nail in one end of the board, and tie a rope or twine to the board so you can retrieve it. After dark, light the candle and float the raft into the water and watch for passengers who might get on board.

COLLECTING SHELLS

Materials:
    Soap, water, and old toothbrush for cleaning
       shells
    Cardboard or shallow box
    Glue
    Cotton
    Paper
    Pen
    Field guide for shells

As you walk along the beach, sooner or later you'll find yourself picking up shells. These beautiful natural objects make great collections. Make sure shells are empty before you bring them home. Look for small creatures that sometimes draw their bodies tightly up into the ends to hide. Leave these homes where you find them.

Clean the empty shells and then mount them on a piece of cardboard or the bottom of a shallow box. Glue them in place. Use a cotton ball under large or fragile specimens to help keep them from breaking. You can also keep shells in a box subdivided into small compartments.

Label each specimen. Record the date, location where you found it, and type of shell. A field guide will help you identify your shells.

CAN YOU CLEAN THE WATER?

Materials:

Spoon	Water
Cheesecloth	Strainer
"Pollution": Dirt, twigs,	Tongs
plastic bag or wrap,	5-gallon bucket
olive oil, pebbles,	Stick
food coloring	

To understand what happens when humans pollute water, try this activity and see just how hard it is to clean up water. Fill the 5-gallon bucket with water. Drop some dirt, twigs, plastic bag or wrap, olive oil, pebbles, and food coloring into the water. Stir with a stick. Using the strainer, spoon, tongs, and cheesecloth, try to take the "pollution" out of the water. Can you remove any of the pollution? Some of it? All of it? Which tools worked best?

Fun With Insects

Who needs insects, anyway? We do! Although sometimes it's hard to live with them, we can't live without them. Insects sting and bite, they invade our food, devour our crops, and carry disease. But they are also a food source for many animals—and even for people. They pollinate crops and plants and are used to treat diseases and help scientists make new discoveries. Insects also produce honey, wax, shellac, and silk and help to clean up dead animals and plants.

Insects are attracted by food. They have a very strong sense of smell, usually through their antennae. Some can even sense food miles away. Insects are also attracted by light.

COLLECTING INSECTS

Hunting for insects depends partly on what kind of insect you want to find.

- You can find crawling bugs almost anyplace— even in your home. Outdoors, look under rocks, where it is moist and dark and where they like to hide.

- Catch bugs that live in tall grass by sweeping a net back and forth near the top of the grass as you walk forward.

- Hold an umbrella, sheet, or cloth under a bush or shrub. Gently shake the branches. The insects will fall onto the umbrella and can easily be collected.

- At night, many insects may fall to the ground under street lights.

After you observe your insect visitors, always return them to where you found them.

BUG PIT

Materials:
> **Container (margarine tub, glass jar, tin can, etc.)**
> **Stones about ½ inch wide**
> **Piece of wood or cardboard a little larger than the container**
> **Trowel**
> **Food scraps**
> **Leaf litter and dirt**

Dig a hole in the ground just a little larger than the container. Sink the container in the ground, making sure the edges don't stick up. Place a few scraps of food such as fruit, lettuce, cheese, or cereal in the container. Add some leaf litter and earth with the food scraps for the creatures to shelter in. Place stones around the edge of the container and cover with wood. The cover will keep your catch from drowning if it rains. The stones allow a small space between the wood and the edge of the container for the insects to enter.

Check your container in a day or two. How many insects have been attracted to the food in your pit? Be sure to free the insects, remove the container, and refill the hole you dug after you are finished.

BUG TRAP

Materials:
> **Three small bottle tops (about ½ inch high)**
> **Quart-sized glass jar**
> **Cap from a 1-gallon plastic milk jug**
> **Disposable dinner plate**
> **½ t. honey**
> **Double-sided tape**

Arrange the three bottle tops upside down on the plate in a triangle so that they will support the inverted glass jar. Use the double-sided tape to stick the bottle tops to the plate. Tape the milk cap upside down in the center of the bottle tops, and place a dollop of honey on the milk cap. Set the plate in a place where it will not be disturbed, and place the jar upside down onto the bottle tops. Insects will be attracted to the honey and fly up inside the jar, becoming trapped. Check the jar frequently, and free the trapped insects after you have observed them for awhile.

ATTRACTING INSECTS AT NIGHT

Materials: **White sheet, bright light**

Tie a white sheet between two trees. Shine a bright light on it. Many insects will be attracted to the light. Move the light around and see what happens. The insects will probably follow the light.

MIDNIGHT SNACK FOR MOTHS

Materials: **Fruit pulp, sugar, tennis ball, string**

Many beautiful moths can be attracted with a nightly treat. Mix together fruit pulp and sugar. Tie a tennis ball to a length of string and dip the ball into the sticky, sweet mixture. Hang it from the top of an open window or outdoors. Soon, you should have attracted some lovely, hungry visitors. Try hanging balls in different locations. Are the same types of moths attracted at all locations?

INSECT HOUSE

Materials:
   **Two 6-oz. tuna or cat
     food cans
   6-by-12-inch metal
     screen mesh or plastic
     canvas
   Pop bottle cap
   Three round-head
     brass paper fasteners
   Stick or branch
   Plaster
   Paint**

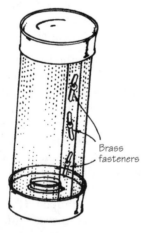

Brass fasteners

Remove one end from each can and paint the cans as desired. Roll the wire or plastic canvas into a tube 12 inches long and as big around as the inside of a can. Fasten the screen together with the paper fasteners. Mix enough plaster to fill a can to within ¼ inch from the top. Set the screen down into the wet plaster. While the plaster is wet, push in a small stick or branch (for the insect to climb on) and the bottle cap, open side up, as a "watering hole." The second can acts as the top.

Remind the boys that when they capture an insect alive and keep it for observation, they must keep it alive by adding water and food. Encourage them to find out what type of food the insect prefers. A few days later the insect should be released.

INSECT AQUARIUM

Brooks, ponds, lakes, and swamps are alive with insects. The water strider walks and runs on spider-like legs across the water's surface. A beetle called the back swimmer clings to the underside of the surface while his hind legs propel him along. Whirligig beetles skate over the surface of the water chasing one another in a crazy patch of circles. A scuba diver called the water boatman keeps the air supply in a bubble between his front legs and moves through the water with his oarlike hind legs. Nymphs and naiads swim through the water, catching and eating smaller insects, and then finally crawl onto a log or rock above the surface and turn into dragonflies and damselflies. All of these aquatic insects are common and can be easily caught.

Take along jars to bring insects home to your aquarium. Put sand, rocks, and plants on the bottom of the aquarium as you would for fish. Cover the aquarium with wire screening. Feed the aquatic insects flies, mosquitoes, mosquito wrigglers, ants, or grasshoppers by dropping them on the surface of the water. After enjoying your aquarium, return the insects to their natural environment.

MAKE AN ANT FARM

Materials:

Quart canning jar	**Canning jar ring**
Skinny olive jar	**Rubber band**
Square nylon net	**Ants**
or screen	**Crumbs of food**
Black construction	**Soil**
paper	

To make an ant farm, place a small skinny olive jar in the center of a quart canning jar. Fill in all around it with moist soil. Wrap black construction paper around the jar and secure it with a rubber band. Look for a group of ants. *Be careful when choosing your ants. Watch out for ants that sting!* Remember not to disturb any anthill that you find.

Place your ants in the soil and screw the jar ring down over the net or screen square and set somewhere out of the sun. When you peek under the black paper in a few days, you can see the ants busy building their tunnels. Feed the ants by putting different kinds of food on top of the soil. Try bread, bits of meat, honey, small pieces of vegetables. Always remove unused food before adding any more. After a short period of time, return the ants to their original habitat.

WATCHING WOOD LICE

Materials:
Wood lice (sow bugs or pill bugs)
Paper cup
Sand
Peat moss
Plastic container
Cardboard
Plastic or cardboard container about 12
  inches deep
Moist sponge
Raw potato
Three large jar tops
Black construction paper

You can find wood lice in damp places. Look under stones, logs, and leaves where they feed on decaying plants. Collect some wood lice in a paper cup. Keep them in a plastic container in which you have placed a mixture of sand and damp peat moss. Add a moist sponge to the container, and put a cardboard cover over it. About once a week, add a piece of raw potato.

To find out what kind of environment that wood lice prefer, cover the bottom of a plastic or cardboard container with sand. Push three large jar tops into the sand with their open sides up. The open tops should be level with the sand, but empty. Place dry peat moss in one jar top, moist peat moss in the second jar top, and wet peat moss in the third. Cover half of each jar top with black construction paper. Place about 20 wood lice on the sand, and put the container in a lighted but not hot place. A day later, look for the wood lice. Are they on the sand, or have they chosen one of the three peat moss environments? Do they prefer light or darkness?

WATCH A BUTTERFLY GROW

Watching a cocoon turn into a butterfly is one of nature's greatest shows. It begins with moth or butterfly eggs, which hatch into a caterpillar, which becomes a cocoon or chrysalis. The caterpillar emerges and becomes a moth or butterfly, which lays eggs and starts the whole process again.

Look for cocoons/chrysalises before trees and shrubs leaf out. They can be easily spotted hanging from branches and twigs. Cut away part of the twig to which the cocoon is attached, taking note of the kind of tree or shrub. Once the butterfly or moth emerges, it will need food—leaves from the same plant on which you found it. Shake the cocoon gently. If you hear a rattling sound, discard it. The pupa inside is probably dead.

Keep the cocoon in a clean can or jar with a tight cover. Punch a few holes in the cover to provide ventilation. Put it in a cool place. When the trees are fully clothed with leaves, make a suitable home for the cocoon. A half-gallon jar with a 1-inch layer of dirt or moss and a couple of sticks inserted is good. The emerged adult will need a place to crawl to dry and spread its wings. Sprinkle the cocoon and dirt with water about once a week to keep them from drying out. Once the butterfly has emerged, release it.

MAKE A BEE FEEDER

Materials:
Glass jar with lid
Small nail
Hammer
Tape
String
Honey or sugar and water

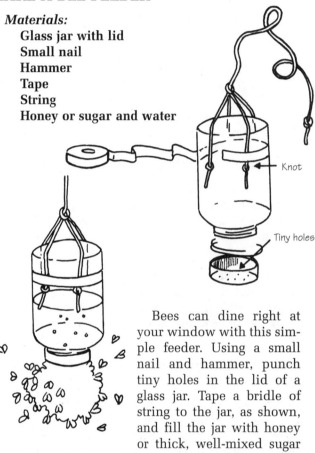

Bees can dine right at your window with this simple feeder. Using a small nail and hammer, punch tiny holes in the lid of a glass jar. Tape a bridle of string to the jar, as shown, and fill the jar with honey or thick, well-mixed sugar water. Hang the jar upside down in front of a second-story window, and watch who comes to eat.

OBSERVING FRUIT FLIES

Materials: **Ripe fruit, small glass jar, paper, cotton**

Because they multiply rapidly, fruit flies make a good exhibit for boys to watch. A new generation will be born every few days. To catch fruit flies, place a piece of ripe fruit in the bottom of a small glass jar. Fit a paper funnel to the top to make it harder for the flies to escape. Put the jar out in the open.

When six to 10 flies have entered, remove the funnel and plug the opening with loose cotton. There should be both males and females; the males are smaller and have black-tipped abdomens. Soon, some eggs will be deposited. Within two or three days, larvae will hatch, which will soon pupate. The adult insects will come from the pupae. Take the young, adult insects out and start a new colony in another jar. After a few days, release them outside.

Fun With Birds

Birds are one of the most interesting of all wild creatures in nature. Whether you are identifying species, listening to their cheerful songs, or just watching them fluttering at your feeder, birds can be a great source of enjoyment.

BE A BIRD DETECTIVE

Materials: **Notebook, pencil, bird guidebook**

You can answer many questions about birds through observation. Observe birds in the woods, in a park, or in your own backyard. Even city bird-watchers can learn many things about the birds they see.

Choose a spot near your home. It can be a bird feeder in your yard or a quiet spot in a park. Visit that spot every day at the same time. Leave birdseed or suet, and then sit down a little distance away where you can watch without disturbing your visitors.

Keep a pad of paper or notebook handy so you can write short descriptions of the birds you see. Write down how big they are, what colors they are, and the shapes of their heads, tails, beaks, and wings.

In a bird guidebook, find the birds that fit your descriptions. Read about them to find out their nesting habits, their migration patterns, and their diets.

After you identify all the birds, keep track of when you see them. If you live in a cold climate, which birds stay around all year? Which are the first to return after a long winter?

Here are some good things to find out about:

• What are the differences in appearance between males and females?
• Do they both build the nest?
• What is the nest made of?
• Does the male or female hunt for food?
• How much of the day does the birds spend looking for food?
• What kind of food do they like best?
• How many eggs does the species lay?
• When do the young birds leave the nest?
• What sounds does the bird make?
• How much time does the bird spend preening?

• How often does the bird drink?
• How does the bird react to animals?
• Which animals does it fear?

FEEDING BIRDS

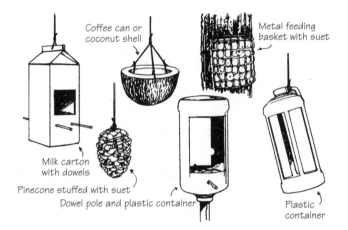

Coffee can or coconut shell

Metal feeding basket with suet

Milk carton with dowels

Pinecone stuffed with suet

Dowel pole and plastic container

Plastic container

• Once you start feeding birds, continue. They will get used to coming and finding food in your feeders. Don't disappoint them.

• Birds need water, too. If you don't have a regular bird bath, us an old hubcap, disk, or shallow pan on top of an overturned trash can. If the temperature is freezing, boil water every morning and pour it over the pan, melting any ice. The remaining water will cool quickly for the birds to use.

• Feed the birds early every day. This is when they eat.

• Cracked corn is a good all-purpose bird food. Ask for "fine" or "chick cracked corn" at a poultry supply store or garden center. Sunflower seeds are popular with cardinals, finches, grosbeaks, woodpeckers, and other seed- and grain-eating birds.

• Birds like nuts, in or out of the shell, but only birds with strong bills, such as blue jays and titmice, can crack the shells. For other birds, shell the nuts and chop them.

• Beef suet gives energy that helps birds stay warm in winter and is a good substitute for the insects they can no longer find. Ask a butcher for beef suet for birds. Use it only during cold weather and in a special container so other animals can't eat it.

• Some birds like fruit, such as cut-up apple, banana, or pear.

Keep Your Feeder Safe

• Cover anything sharp on any bird feeder you might make. This protects the person handling the food as well as the bird. Cover wire ends and sharp edges of plastic and metal with tape. Sand smooth all rough edges of wood.

- Never use thread anywhere on a feeder. Birds can easily become entangled in it.
- Never give birds moldy bread or any other moldy or spoiled foods. Use only fresh, clean grain and seeds. A deadly fungus sometimes grows in moldy food.
- Be sure the container used to make the bird feeder has never held anything poisonous. Even a tiny amount of a harmful substance can affect a bird.
- Leave the feeder unpainted, or if you must paint, use exterior latex paint.
- Do not use plain peanut butter or raw rice to feed birds.

BIRD CAKE

Materials:
> Wild birdseed
> Piece of mesh vegetable sack (such as potatoes or onions come in)
> 12-oz. juice can
> ½ pound suet
> Double boiler
> Long piece of wire

1. Cut the vegetable sack to fit inside the can, with the extra sticking up above the can top.
2. Cut the suet into small pieces and heat in the double boiler (so it won't burn). Let it cool and harden. Remove any pieces of meat.
3. Reheat the suet and mix in 1 C. birdseed. Pour the mixture into the can. Set in the refrigerator to harden.
4. Set the can in warm water and carefully run a knife around the inside to loosen the sack. Pull out the sack.
5. Tie the ends of the sack with wire, leaving enough to tie it to a tree limb.

This same mixture can be molded in a cut-down cardboard milk carton, small foil dishes, or half a grapefruit shell and the cakes set on a fence post or in a feeder.

BIRD'S DELIGHT

Ingredients:

1 C. melted suet	3 T. cornmeal
1¼ C. peanut butter	3 T. butter
¼ C. cracked corn	¼ C. raisins

Melt the suet as described for the Bird Cake, adding the peanut butter during the second heating. After the suet has cooled the second time, add the other ingredients. Pour into containers and set in the refrigerator to harden.

BIRD TREAT TOWER

Materials:

Two mesh bags from fruit or onions	Maize
	Plastic lid
Shelled peanuts	Scissors
Sunflower seeds	
Plastic wire or string	

Place one mesh bag inside of the other to reduce the size of the holes. Place sunflower seeds in the bag about a third of the way up and tie together. Next, add a layer of maize in the middle third of the bag and tie together. Add the final layer of peanuts and tie the bag closed. Punch a hole in the center of the plastic lid and pull the end of the bag through it. The lid will protect the food from the weather. Make a hanger from the wire or string, attach it to the end of the mesh bag, and hang it in a suitable place.

PINECONE TREATS

Materials: Peanut butter, cornmeal, pinecone, wire

Mix together equal amounts of peanut butter and cornmeal, about 2 T. of each. The cornmeal keeps the peanut butter from being sticky and is safer for birds to eat. Tie a piece of wire around a large pinecone for hanging from a tree. Spoon the mixture in between the pinecone petals. The birds will love it.

BIRD BRUSH

Materials: Old scrub brush, bacon rind or lard, birdseed mixture

Melt the bacon rind or lard in a pot and dip the brush into the fat. Sprinkle the seed mixture onto it and as the fat congeals, the seeds will be fixed to it. Tie the brush to a tree in a safe spot.

SUET LOG BIRD FEEDER

Materials:

16-inch-long log about 4 inches in diameter (or use 4-by-4-inch lumber)	Sandpaper
	Varnish
	Suet
Drill	Knife or ax
Heavy screw eye	

1. Drill six to 10 1-inch holes halfway through the log.
2. Have an adult taper the top of the log with an ax or knife and apply varnish to prevent the wood from cracking.
3. Insert the screw eye at the point and attach a wire for hanging to a low branch.
4. Force suet into the holes and hang the feeder from a tree in the yard where it can be observed from the house. Hang it low enough for easy refilling but out of reach of dogs and cats. Woodpeckers, chickadees, titmice, and other suet-feeding birds will enjoy your creation.

MILK CARTON BIRD FEEDER

Materials:
   **Half-gallon milk
      carton (card-
      board or plastic)
   Paper clip
   Two brass paper
      fasteners
   Wire coat hanger
   Marker
   Scissors**

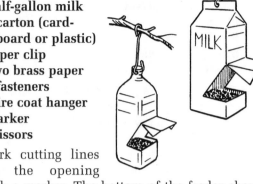

1. Mark cutting lines for the opening with a marker. The bottom of the feeder should be 1¼ inch deep. Cut out the opening, leaving the top to be folded back for a roof.

2. Straighten the paper clip and push it through the carton about 1¼ inch from the gable. Bend the clip inside the carton to secure it. Insert the other end of the clip through the feeder roof and bend back to hold.

3. Push the paper fasteners through the peak to seal the top of the feeder. Punch a hole in the peak to hold the coat hanger hook.

4. Punch a few small holes in the bottom of the feeder to let out moisture. Hang your feeder from a branch.

DECORATED TREE HOTEL

Materials:
   **Small evergreen tree in the yard
   Bird Cakes, stale donuts, stale bread
   Strings of popcorn, cranberries, or raisins
   Orange or grapefruit shells
   Bread
   Cookie cutters
   Shortening or butter
   Seeds**

A small evergreen tree in your yard makes a good shelter and feeder for birds. It will provide protection during the coldest part of the winter. Trim the tree with Bird Cakes (see above), stale donuts, or very stale bread tied on with a string of popcorn, cranberries, or raisins. Fill orange or grapefruit shells with Bird's Delight (see 4–21). You can cut bread shapes out with cookie cutters and then spread them with shortening or butter and sprinkle with seeds.

BIRD FEEDER SNOWMAN

Materials:
   **Snowman
   Pinecone with suet and birdseed mixture
   Dates, raisins, apple pieces
   String of cranberries
   Straw beach hat with wide brim
   Birdseed, sunflower seed
   Two thick branches
   Pail of water**

Make a snowman. For a nose, give it a pinecone stuffed with suet and birdseed mixture. Use dates for eyes, a line of raisins for the mouth, and apple pieces for buttons. String cranberries on strong string to make a belt. Add the beach hat and sprinkle birdseed and sunflower seeds on the brim. Make arms for the snowman from thick branches so the birds will have a place to perch while they are eating. Set a pail of water nearby to give them something to drink.

EXAMINE A BIRD FEATHER

As you hike through the woods and across fields in late summer and early fall, you may find quite a few bird feathers on the path or in the grass. This is the time when birds *molt,* or lose their old feathers and grow new ones.

When you take a good look at a bird feather, you'll see that it has a stiff shaft in the middle. The lower part of this shaft, the *quill,* is hollow. On each side of the shaft is a flat vane. When you look at this vane through a magnifying glass, you'll discover that it has hundreds of separate barbs held together by tiny hooks.

Most birds have three types of feathers. The *flight feather* of the wings has a curved shaft, and the vane along one side is narrower than the vane on the other side. The *steering feathers* of the tail have an almost straight shaft, and the vanes on each side are about the same width. The *contour feathers* that cover the bird's body are much smaller than the others and are usually curved.

The color of the feathers will give a clue to the type of bird. A bright red feather might have come from a scarlet tanager or cardinal. A banded light-blue feather may have come from a blue jay. A solid black feather may come from a crow.

Don't collect feathers. Only the feathers of gregarious birds (ducks, geese, chickens, etc.), English sparrows, starlings, and pigeons may be in the possession of non-native Americans. All other birds are classified as migratory and are protected under the Migratory Bird Treaty Act, and it is against federal law to be in possession of their feathers.

NESTING MATERIALS BASKET

Materials: **Mesh bags; scrap lumber; fine mesh hardware cloth; short lengths of yarn, string, and raffia; string hanger**

In the spring, help birds collect nesting material by providing an assortment for them to use. Fill a mesh bag of the sort that onions and potatoes are sold in with yarn, string, or rope fibers cut to about 6 to 10 inches. Or, build a simple frame from scrap wood and overlay with fine mesh hardware cloth. Make a string hanger and place your nesting materials in a tree. Look around your neighborhood to see whether you can notice any nests with your special materials woven through them.

CALLING BIRDS

You can do a birdcall easily with no other equipment than your mouth. It attracts many smaller species: sparrows, warblers, jays, chickadees, nuthatches, wrens, and others. The call consists of a series of rhythmically repeated "psssh" sounds. Different rhythms work with different birds.

Try these rhythms:

Pssh...pssh...pssh...

Pssh...pssh...pssh-pssh...pssh...pssh

Each of these series should last about three seconds. Experiment to find the rhythms that work best for the birds in your area. For the best results when you use this call, wait until you hear birds nearby, and then stay motionless by shrubs or trees that will partially hide you and give the birds something to land on. Begin calling in a series, pausing after three or four rounds to listen for the incoming birds.

BIRD CALLER

Materials: **2-by-1-inch hardwood, drill, screw eye, resin powder**

Drill a hole in the end of the hardwood slightly smaller than the screw eye. You can also use a piece of an old hammer or ax handle for this project. Turn the screw eye into the hole and then unscrew it and take it out. Put a little resin powder in the hole and screw the eye back in the hole. As you twist the screw eye back and forth in the hole, it will make a squeaky sound that will attract birds. With practice, you can make several different bird noises.

Fun With Animals

On one of your hikes, you may be lucky enough to see some animals. In an open field, a rabbit may jump in front of you and scurry off with its fluffy tail bobbing. A woodchuck may sit up for a quick look around and then scurry back into its borrow. As you walk in the woods, a deer may bound past you and then quickly disappear into the brush. You may spot some squirrels playing in the leaves. When they see you, they will probably rush to the nearest tree, run up the trunk, and hide among the branches. They might even scold you for bothering them!

Even if you don't see any of these animals, you can look for their homes and hiding places. Look up. You may see squirrel nests or raccoon or opossum dens in hollow trees. Look around. You may discover a muskrat house made of reeds and twigs or a beaver den of branches and mud. Look down. You may see where rabbits bed down or spot the entrance to a fox's den or a skunk's hiding place. *Stay a safe distance from these animal homes and the animals themselves; do not disturb their habitats.*

Chewed-off twigs may indicate where deer have been feeding. You may see shells of nuts left behind after a mouse party. Look for the remains of pinecones where squirrels have bitten off the petals to get to the seeds.

Animal tracks show where they have walked slowly to their feeding places or have hurried off at full speed to get away from an enemy.

Keep your eyes open and you will learn a lot about animals.

ANIMAL SCRAMBLE

Materials: **One index card per player, pencil or pictures of animals, tape or pins**

Write the names of common animals on index cards or place a picture of the animal on each card. Pictures will allow younger children to give more accurate answers. Pin or tape a card on the back of each player's shirt. Players ask questions of other players to get clues to their own identities. They should ask only one question of each person and have that person ask one question of them so they can mingle with the other players. Answers are limited to "yes," "no," "maybe," and "I don't know." Players continue to ask questions to discover characteristics about their animal until they are able to guess who they are. A player might ask questions such as: "Am I a predator?" "Do I have a tail?" "Do I have four legs?" "Am I active at night?" "Do I live in the forest?"

WHO'S GONE THERE?

Materials: **Paper; ink pads; stamps of animal tracks make from erasers, craft foam and wood blocks, or cut potatoes; mammal guidebooks**

Make animal track stamps using your favorite craft method and a guidebook for patterns. Boys study a bit about the animals and their tracks before the game. Divide the group into teams. Using the ink pads and half of the animal print stamps, each team prints a set of animal tracks for each animal on a separate sheet of paper. Then the other team tries to guess which prints belong to which animal. On your next hike, look for these animals' real prints in the wild.

PREDATOR

Materials: **Two blindfolds**

This game helps boys think about food chains in nature. Boys form a circle about 15 feet across. Two blindfolded boys stand in the center of the circle. One is the Predator, and he calls out the kind of predator he is. The other is the Prey and calls out the kind of animal that is the Predator's prey. The Predator tries to catch his Prey by listening for him and tracking him down and tagging him. If either "animal"

goes too near the edge of the circle, the boys that form the circle tap him twice. Stress the need for silence while the game is in progress. Boys can imitate the animals they've chosen to be. You can experiment with different numbers of predators and prey or put bells on some of the animals, thereby making them modify their strategies.

SQUIRREL FEEDER

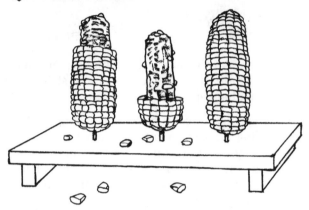

Materials: **Three or four 3- or 4-inch nails, 1-by-4-by-12-inch board, two 1-by-4-by-2-inch boards, 2-inch nails, corncobs**

Using the 2-inch nails, nail the short boards onto the 12-inch board toward the ends for "feet." Nail three or four longer nails up from the bottom to spear corncobs. Along with squirrels, birds might also come to dine at this feeder.

SNIFF OUT A NUT

Materials: **Three small cups; potting soil; two peanuts, walnuts, or other nuts**

Squirrels bury nuts in the ground to store for a later meal. Many people think that squirrels remember where they left their nuts, but actually, they find them again using their keen sense of smell. To see whether you would make a good squirrel, place potting soil in three small cups. Bury a nut with the shell on in the first cup. In the second, bury a nut without the shell. Leave the third cup with just plain potting soil. After several days, see whether you can tell which cups the nuts are in by sniffing.

EAT LIKE A SQUIRREL

Materials: **Masking tape, peanuts in the shell**

To find out how squirrels eat without thumbs, tape your thumbs to your palms with masking tape. Try to crack open some unshelled peanuts for a snack. It won't be long before you'll find yourself doing it the squirrel way—with your teeth!

HATCH A BATCH OF EGGS

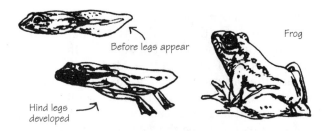

Before legs appear

Hind legs developed

Frog

Materials: **Bucket, aquarium with sloping rock or floating log, aquarium cover**

Eggs of amphibians, such as frogs and toads, are ready to view in the spring. Look for frogs' eggs bunched together in a clump; toads' eggs are generally arranged in long strings. You might even find salamander eggs, which are larger that frogs' eggs but found in smaller bunches. If you have permission, bring a few home in a pail, along with plenty of pond water and some algae and pond plants for the tadpoles to eat. Don't mix eggs from different species. They develop at different rates and may feed on each other.

Frogs' eggs will grow and change into tiny tadpoles within a week or so. Keep only one or two tadpoles, returning the others and any unhatched eggs to the pond. Tadpoles will eat algae and plants in the bucket, but soon they will need more nutrients. When they are big enough, hang a piece of raw meat in the bucket for them to eat. A tadpole soon develops hind legs and then tiny front legs where the gills were. Lungs also replace the gills at this stage, although you can't see this. Gradually, the tail disappears, during which time the tadpole doesn't eat. Transfer your frog to an aquarium now, one with a sloping rock or a floating log, and cover. Frogs are great jumpers. Adult frogs require live food and lots of it, so soon it will be time to return your frog friend to its natural habitat.

WONDERFUL WORMERY

Materials:

2 C. dark-colored soil	Large bowl
10 to 12 earthworms	Spoon
Quart-sized wide-mouth jar	1 T. oats
	Rubber bands
Cheesecloth or piece of nylon stocking	Sand
	Water
Dark-colored construction paper	

Pour the soil into a bowl. Slowly add water while stirring until the soil is slightly moist. Pour half of the moistened soil into the jar. Pour the sand over the soil and then add the remaining soil. Sprinkle the oats over the soil.

Put the worms in the jar and cover it with cheesecloth or a piece of nylon, securing it with a rubber band. Wrap the dark paper around the jar and secure it with a rubber band also. Place the jar in a cool place. Every day for a week, remove the paper and observe the jar for a few minutes. Then, put the paper back over the jar and put the jar away. At the end of the week, release the worms where you found them.

Your worms will wiggle and burrow into the soil, and after a few days you'll be able to see their tunnels. Soon, the light sand and dark soil become mixed. The worm gets nourishment from the remains of plants in the soil. The worm's movements loosen the soil so that the water and air plants need can more easily pass through it.

Fun With the Night Sky

On a clear night when the stars are out, the sky is transformed into a twinkling show—one of nature's most beautiful displays. Whether you are following the moon's path or locating the Big Dipper, the time you spend gazing upward can be a peaceful outdoor experience.

STARGAZING

Billions of stars shine in the sky. Although they are millions of miles away, we can see many of them. Check out your library for guides on stargazing.

Choose a clear night. A night with no moon is best for beginners because constellations are easier to see. Find a place that is dark, away from street and house lights. City lights, as well as moonlight, will obscure the fainter stars. Take a flashlight covered with red cellophane to help you read your star guide. (Red light won't blind your eyes as white light will.)

Lie on your back on a blanket and enjoy the entire display of stars before looking for specific ones. If it is very dark, you'll easily see the Milky Way, our galaxy, stretching across the sky.

Start with a star group you already recognize, such as the Big Dipper, and use it to star-hop. Move to the Little Dipper, nearby. The star at the very end of the curved handle is Polaris, the North Star. It is almost directly above the north geographic pole of the earth. Sailors and travelers have used it for centuries to tell which way is north.

Cassiopeia is easy to find and remember because of its shape: a **W** formed by five bright stars. To find Cassiopeia, draw an imaginary line from the star where the handle joins the Big Dipper's bowl through the North Star and beyond. Cassiopeia and the Big Dipper are on opposite sides of the North Star and rotate around it. In the northern hemisphere, they are always above the horizon and can be seen any time of the year.

In winter months (in the northern hemisphere), look for Orion, the mighty hunter. You will recognize him by his belt—a row of three bright stars. Try to locate the bright star Betelgeuse that marks Orion's right shoulder. Follow the belt stars upward and you'll find the constellation Taurus.

With these as a beginning, continue to locate other constellations. Work your way around the night sky, using a star guide to help you find and identify stars, planets, and constellations. You'll probably be able to see Venus. Except for the sun and the moon, it is the brightest object in the sky. Mars has a steady, reddish light. Jupiter is steady and whiter than stars. Saturn has a yellowish light.

If you see a "star" moving, it's probably a satellite or plane instead of a star.

CONSTELLATION PICTURES

Materials:

Black construction paper	Tagboard
Glow-in-the-dark star stickers or glow-in-the-dark paint and brushes	Pencil
	White chalk
	Star guidebook
	Scissors

Make this glowing project to help your Cub Scouts and Webelos Scouts remember star placements and constellation shapes. Using a star guidebook, make patterns of the constellation you would like to use for this project. Poke holes in the pattern to represent the stars, and draw lines to connect them properly. Boys place the pattern over the black construction paper and mark the star placement. Remove the pattern and complete the stars by placing the glow-in-the-dark star stickers over the star markings or painting a small dot with the glow-in-the-dark paint. Boys connect the stars by drawing the lines with white chalk. Write the name of each constellation on the papers. Boys can hang these on their bedroom ceiling. Before they go to sleep, they can enjoy their own star show and prepare to identify the constellation patterns in the night sky.

STAR COLOR

Materials: Telescope

To the naked eye, stars don't look like they have much color, but they actually range in hue from red to bluish white. You can detect these differences with a telescope. Some stars appear red or orange, others are definitely yellow, and some are yellowish white and bluish white.

These colors correspond to the temperatures of the stars. As the size of the star increases, usually so does its temperature. The small red stars are the coolest. Orange stars are the next in line. Medium in size and heat are the yellow stars (like our sun). And then come the larger white stars. The blue-white ones are the hottest and largest. If you look at logs burning in a fireplace, you can see the same color variations in the flames.

See whether you can detect the colors of the stars with your telescope. No matter what their color, they generate their own light and shine all night and all day long. We just can't see them during the day because the light from the sun is too bright.

MOON WATCH

Materials: Binoculars or a telescope

Use binoculars or a telescope to look at the moon. Can you see the pockmarks where meteoroids have hit the surface? Try to observe the moon when it is not full. Look at the part of the moon that is close to the line dividing the light part of the moon from the dark part. The shadows there are long. Shadows on the earth are long when the sun is rising or setting. The shadows along the dividing line on the moon are long for the same reason. If you were standing on that dividing line, you would see the sun setting or rising on the moon's horizon.

Watch the moon with binoculars or a telescope during all of its phases. Watch it as it *waxes* (gets bigger) from new crescent to first quarter to full. Then watch it as it *wanes* (gets smaller) from full to third quarter to old crescent.

If you looked at the moon month after month, you would find that it always looks the same. We see only one side of the moon. This means that the moon rotates at the same rate that it revolves about the earth.

MOON FLIP BOOK

Materials: 30 index cards, quarter, pencil, stapler

Track the changing phases of the moon, which completes a cycle every 29½ days. The moon doesn't generate its own light so we see only the portion that is lit by the sun. When there is a full moon, the sun is shining directly on the moon; at the other times, Earth gets in the way, shadowing the moon so that only part of it is visible.

Make a flip book of the moon's phases. On the right-hand side of the index cards, trace around a quarter. Make sure the tracing is on the identical place on each card. Number the cards from 1 to 30. For the next 30 nights, check the moon and draw what you see on the corresponding card. Keep the cards in order. When you have completed the last card, staple them all together on the left-hand side. Flip the pages for a fast-forward look at the moon's changing face for the previous month.

KITCHEN SOLAR SYSTEM

Materials:
27-inch beach ball (the sun)
One tiny ³/₃₂-inch pea (Mercury)
Two ⅛-inch peas (Pluto and Mars)
Two ¼-inch peas (Earth and Venus)
Two 1-inch walnuts (Uranus and Neptune)
One 2¼-inch tangerine (Saturn)
One 2¾-inch orange (Jupiter)
Sheet
Book about the planets

It's fun to learn about the nine planets that circle our sun. Here's a way to make a planet display and estimate the relative sizes using items from your kitchen.

Place a sheet on the ground or a table. Tell your boys a few fun facts about each planet as you place their corresponding models on the sheet around the sun. Have the boys study this model for a short time. Then mix up the items, and either as a cooperative group or by teams, have them try to place them back in the proper planet order.

You can color the smaller planets different colors to make them easier to remember. You can also roll small bits of colored clay into balls that match the sizes shown.

Fun With Weather

The weather can provide Cub Scouts with an ever-changing show. From blue skies with puffy clouds that look like animals to the excitement of a menacing storm, our changing weather provides much to see, experience, and learn. Whether your weather fun is for advancement or just plain fun, you'll discover many great weather-related activities to enjoy with boys.

PREDICTING THE WEATHER

People have been watching the skies for millennia to help them predict the weather. Check the following folklore predictions with your own observations to see how many might be true.

- Red sky at sunset is a sign of a fair tomorrow. (The sky you see at sunset is air that will reach you tomorrow. Dry air produces a red glow, whereas wet air produces a yellow-gray sky color.)
- Dull moon and stars foretell a rainy tomorrow.
- Lightning from the westerly sky is from a storm that is on its way toward you.
- Towering, ragged clouds predict a rain squall and wind.
- A sky full of webby cirrus clouds foretells a rainy spell on its way.
- A halo around the sun or moon means a warm front is on its way, with rain.
- Dark clouds against a lighter ceiling foretell a windy rainstorm.
- The higher the clouds, the finer the weather. Lowering clouds foretell rain.
- When swallows fly high, it will be dry.
- If the cows are lying down, it will rain.
- A good fall for fruit means a hard winter to come.

Wind direction also helps forecast the weather:
- The west wind generally brings clear weather, except when it blows off the ocean.
- The north wind brings clear, cold weather.
- The south wind brings heat and sometimes showers.
- The east wind brings rain east of the Rockies.

When rain is near, nature gets excited. Look for these signals:
- Tree frogs cry.
- Fish swim near the surface.
- Flies sting.
- Low clouds move swiftly.
- Gone-to-seed dandelions close up like an umbrella.
- Cloverleaves fold together.

RAIN GAUGE

Materials: **Plastic pop bottle, colored tape, scissors, ruler, pencil**

1. Cut off the top of the bottle where the curved top meets the straight sides.

2. Turn the top upside down and fit it into the base. This will stop the water inside the bottle from evaporating.

3. Cut thin strips of tape and use them to mark ¼-inch divisions along the straight part of the base. Write the level on the tape. Pour water up to the lowest division.

4. Place your rain gauge outside, away from any buildings and trees. Record the amount of rain each day for a week, and remember to pour out the water down to the lowest division each morning.

WEATHER VANE

Materials:
Wooden block
Sewing spool
Glue
Plastic straw
Plastic bottle
Tape
Coat hanger wire

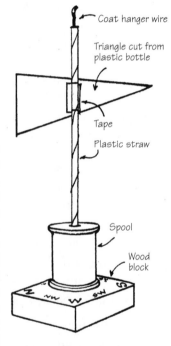

Coat hanger wire

Triangle cut from plastic bottle

Tape

Plastic straw

Spool

Wood block

A weather vane can tell you which direction the wind is blowing. Use the wooden block for a base marked with compass directions. Glue the spool in the center of the block. Cut a triangle out of the flat area on the plastic bottle and tape it to the middle of the straw. Place the straw in the hole in the spool. Place a straight piece of coat hanger wire in the center of the straw. The wire should be long enough to stick out of the top of the straw. Place the vane outdoors with the "North" mark facing north. Record wind direction at the same time every day. Remember that the wind direction is where wind is blowing *from*.

WIND ROSE

Materials: **Paper, colored pencils**

This is a good way to keep track of the wind's direction and weather conditions over a month. Draw a wind rose like the illustration. On each leg of the chart, keep track of the date and weather condi-

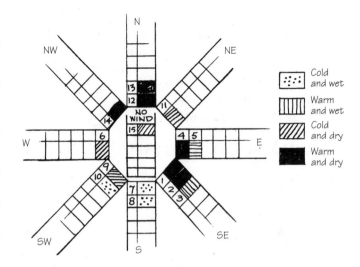

Cold and wet

Warm and wet

Cold and dry

Warm and dry

tions for that day. Use patterned boxes as shown to indicate weather conditions, or color the squares beside the dates different colors to show weather conditions each day: yellow for sun, blue for cold and dry, red for warm and dry, etc.

ANEMOMETER

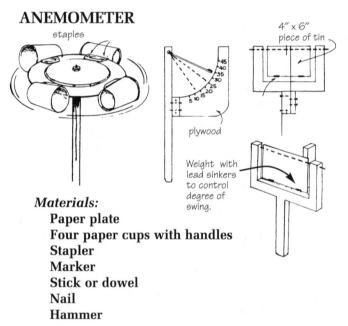

staples

4" x 6" piece of tin

plywood

Weight with lead sinkers to control degree of swing.

Materials:
Paper plate
Four paper cups with handles
Stapler
Marker
Stick or dowel
Nail
Hammer

This device measures wind velocity. Staple the cup handles to the rim of the plate. Drive a small nail into the end of a stick or dowel and punch through the center of the plate so that the plate turns freely. Use a marker to make a stripe on one of the cups; this will make it easier to count the number of revolutions and thus estimate the wind's speed.

LIQUID BAROMETER

Materials: **Glass or clear plastic quart bottle, saucer, water, marker**

This device shows atmospheric pressure. Fill the quart bottle with water. Put the saucer over the top, and turn it over quickly. Allow a little water to escape into the saucer. With the marker, draw eight or 10 scale marks ⅛ inch apart. The middle mark should be even with the water level. Check your barometer each day. If the water level has risen, the atmospheric pressure is higher and fair weather is coming. If the level is lower, look for unsettled weather.

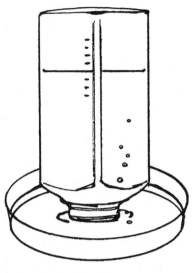

HUMIDITY CONE

Materials: **Pinecone**

A pinecone is a good tester to find out how much water vapor is in the air. When the air is dry, the cone's scales open wide. When the air has high humidity and rain is probably on the way, the scales close up.

MAKE A RAINBOW

Materials: **Clear glass of water, white paper, sunshine**

On a sunny day, falling rain or fog may split the sun's rays into a rainbow. You can make a rainbow if the sun is shining on a windowsill. Fill a glass with water and put it on the sill with a piece of white paper behind it. The water *refracts*, or bends, the light, and the sunlight will show on the paper as a spectrum of colors.

SUN DAPPLES

Materials: **Sunny day, leafy tree, two file cards, pin, pegboard**

On a sunny day, find a leafy tree that provides shade. If you look under the tree, you will see many small circles. These circles are called *sun dapples*. To see what causes sun dapples, use a pin to make a small hole through the center of one of the file cards. Hold both cards in the sunlight. The card with the pinhole should be between the sun and the other file card. Look at the lower card carefully. It serves as a screen on which you can see an image of the sun. What happens to the size of the image if you move the screen farther from the pinhole? What about closer to the pinhole?

Use the pin to make a second pinhole in the upper card. How many images of the sun do you see on the screen now? If you add more pinholes what will you see?

Hold a piece of pegboard in sunlight. Look at the shadow of the pegboard. What do you think causes all the bright circles you see?

Note: Never look directly at the sun. It can damage your eyes!

SHADOW CLOCK

Materials:

Hammer	Scissors
Paper	Tape
Pencil	Watch
12-inch-square board	
2- or 3-inch finishing nail	

Tape a sheet of paper over the board. Drive the nail a short distance into the board near the middle of one end of the board about 2 inches from the edge. Place it in a sunny, level place outdoors early in the morning. Be sure that the nail is on the south side of the paper.

Use a pencil to mark the position of the nail's shadow on the paper at one-hour intervals throughout the day. Label each line you draw with the time you read on a watch.

Mark the position of the board so you can put it in exactly the same place several days, weeks, or months later. Compare the times on the shadow clock with times on your watch during a day several days after you make the shadow clock. Do the same thing a week later. Do it again a month later. Do the times on your shadow clock still agree with the times on your watch after several days?

CAPTURE A SNOWFLAKE

Materials: **Sheet of black construction paper, magnifying glass, pane of glass, hair spray or artist's fixative**

Because snowflakes melt so quickly when they land on a warm surface, catching them requires some planning. Chill a sheet of black construction paper outdoors or in the freezer. Examine snowflakes with a magnifying glass as they land on the paper before they melt.

You can make a permanent impression of snowflakes by catching falling flakes on a chilled pane of glass that has been sprayed with chilled hair spray or artist's fixative. Store supplies in the freezer until you are ready to use them. Keeping the sprayed glass as cold as possible, take it outdoors and allow some flakes to settle on it. When you have collected enough, take the glass indoors and let it dry at room temperature for about 15 minutes. You'll have a permanent record of some of nature's most amazing designs.

TAKING THE SNOW'S TEMPERATURE

Materials: **Outdoor thermometer, yardstick, tape**

Tape an old outdoor thermometer to the end of a yardstick. Don't tape over the bulb. Gently push the thermometer end into a snowdrift. It will take a little time for the thermometer to adjust to the snow's temperature, so leave it there for a few minutes. Measure the temperature in deep snow and shallow snow, in shady spots and in sunny spots. What is the difference? Is snow always colder than air? To find out, hold the thermometer in the air for a few minutes and then read it.

MEASURING A SNOWDRIFT

Materials: **Yardstick**

Push a yardstick into a snowdrift until the end touches the ground. Measure the drift next to trees, up against buildings, next to fences, on driveways, and in other spots. Find the deepest drift. Is it in a shady, sunny, or windy spot?

MAKE A SNOW GAUGE

Materials: **3-pound coffee can, ruler, permanent marker**

Use a snow gauge to measure how much snow falls in your yard. With a ruler and permanent marker, mark lines on the inside of a coffee can. Make a line for each inch and label from the bottom up. When it starts to snow, put the can on the ground in an open spot away from trees and buildings. Check to see how many inches have fallen when the snow stops falling.

Does 1 inch of snow make 1 inch of water? To find out, let the snow melt in the can. Does the water measure to the same mark as the snow? Different kinds of snow contain different amounts of water. Loose snow has less water than wet, tightly packed snow.

WHO MELTS FIRST?

Make five snowballs that are about the same size. Place each in a different location—one on a snowy rock, one on the ground, one under a bush, one on the hood of a car, etc. Try to guess which will melt first and why. Keep checking until one of them has melted. Were you right?

Family Camping

Cub Scout family camping is an overnight camping experience other than a resident camp program. A family camping trip can be rewarding for boys and every member of the family. There are three categories of Cub Scout family camping:

- **Council-organized Cub Scout family camping** is an overnight camping event involving more than one pack. The council usually provides food service, staff, and an activity program based on a theme.

- **Pack-organized Cub Scout family camping** is an overnight event involving more than one family. Pack members plan an enjoyable and safe outing for all pack family members. Adults giving leadership to a pack campout must complete Basic Adult Leader Outdoor Orientation (BALOO). Only Webelos dens may schedule den campouts. All camping for Cub Scouts and Tiger Cubs should be pack-organized family camping.

- **Family-organized recreational camping** is an opportunity for a family to camp together. Whether you camp in your own backyard or at the top of a mountain, family camping experiences will provide great fun and memories.

WHERE TO CAMP

Cub Scout pack-organized camping should be conducted only at sites approved by the local council. Approved sites might include federal, state, or local parks in addition to BSA property. Check with your council service center for locally approved sites before planning your trip.

Selecting a Campsite

Look for the following when selecting a campsite:

- Try to camp with a south or southeast exposure.
- Your campsite should be protected from wind.
- Camp on level and reasonably smooth ground (even a shallow depression can collect water in a heavy rain).
- Avoid nearby gullies and ravines; they can be dangerous during flash flooding.
- Avoid camping near trees with dead or dying branches.
- Make sure you have a water supply nearby.
- Don't camp near swamps, tall grasses, or watery meadows.

SETTING UP CAMP

- Pitch a tent on smooth and level ground with the tent back to prevailing winds. The slope of the stakes will depend on the condition and texture of the ground. Usually, stakes driven at an angle toward the line of pull will hold in either hard or soft ground. Use a tautline hitch on guy lines.
- A door mat of plywood or heavy cardboard will help keep the inside of the tent clean. When possible, leave shoes outside the tent.
- Many campers take along a large tarp or dining fly and set it up as a shelter to provide a covered area for cooking, eating, and other activities outside the tent.
- Keep an adequate supply of drinking water on hand. It's a good idea to keep several bottles full of water in the tent at night, especially for children.
- Always gather firewood during daylight and stack it under shelter. Don't count on firewood being available. Bring wood, charcoal, or stoves. *Many state parks do not allow the gathering of wood for fires.* Check local regulations about fires as you are planning your trip.
- Before turning in for the night, be sure everything is secure and covered for protection from rain and animals. Be sure food is well-covered or hung out of reach. Don't leave open containers of food in the car. The food may be safe, but animals may scratch the car. *Don't store food in tents.*

TENTS

Living in a tent is enjoyable if you prepare for it, have the right tent, and follow safety precautions. Here are some pointers.

- Allow about 20 square feet per person for tent living. Straight-walled tents provide more living area. All-cotton or cotton/polyester canvas and ducks are durable and water-resistant but are prone to mildew. Synthetics are strong, lightweight, and mildew-resistant.
- Many states have mandated the use of flame-resistant tents. Remember, however, that a flame-resistant tent is not *flameproof,* so use fire safety precautions. Keep all flames away from the tent. *Never use liquid fuel stoves, heaters, charcoal, lanterns, lighted candles, matches, or other flame sources in or near tents.*
- Some tent features that are helpful are a floor of plastic-coated fabric, heavy-duty zippers, reinforced stitching at stress points, double-stitched seams, and screened windows with inner-zipper flaps.
- Tent ropes should be clean, strong, and securely attached to the tent. Keep extra ropes available for quick storm rigging.
- Canvas and rope shrink when wet. Tight ropes can rip your tent in a storm. If it rains, loosen the tent ropes a little.
- Never pile dirt and leaves against the lower walls of a tent.
- Never use flammable chemicals, charcoal lighter, spray paint, or insect repellent near tents. These may remove the waterproofing.
- Clean and dry the tent thoroughly before storing it. Carry and store the tent in a bag, if possible.

SLEEPING BAGS

Sleeping outdoors is half the fun of camping. Sleeping bags make it easy, and air mattresses add to comfort. Foam pads keep you warmer and don't deflate. Some campers use a sleeping bag on a cot.

Choose a sleeping bag that suits the season and area. Down bags are the warmest and lightest but the most expensive, and they do not insulate when wet. Several other types are available. Be sure the fabric covering the bag is sturdy.

OTHER EQUIPMENT

If you are not an experienced camper, someone who is can give you helpful hints on what to take and how to use it. In addition to a tent and sleeping bags, your camping list will include cooking and eating equipment, food and food containers, some tools, and personal equipment. Nearby Boy Scout troops will be glad to help with advice and suggestions. Some families borrow or rent larger equipment until they know what purchases they need to make.

- Using paper plates and cups can solve the dishwashing problem, leaving only the cooking utensils to be cleaned. *Do not burn disposable tableware.* If a trash receptacle isn't available, carry the used dinnerware home for disposal.
- Always bring plastic garbage bags. They serve many useful purposes, in addition to holding trash.
- Don't forget to include a first aid kit.

FIRES

- Always be careful when building a fire. Build fires only in designated fire rings provided by the landowner or with permission in off-the-ground fire pits, such as a metal barrel cut down to one-third its size with legs welded on. (You can also try the Fire in a Lid, 4–34.)
- Always break burnt matches before throwing them away, and be sure the matches are *cold out.*
- Never leave a fire unattended. A breeze may come up while you're gone and spread the fire. Keep a bucket of water, dirt, or sand handy for emergency use. An unattended campfire or sparks from a fire can cause an entire forest to burn.
- Be sure fires are out—*dead out*—before breaking camp. Spread the coals and ashes and drench the fire and ground around it with plenty of water. Or mix soil and sand with the embers so the fire will go out. Continue adding and stirring until all material is cold enough to feel with your bare hand. Don't just bury the fire; it may smolder and break out again.

DISPOSING OF TRASH

- Dispose of trash, including food scraps and paper products, properly in a trash receptacle. Do not burn it.
- Don't put plastic or plastic foam in a fire; burning plastic can release toxic gases into the air.
- Don't bury leftovers or scatter them in the woods. Animals will find them, and it is not healthy for them to eat leftover food from humans.
- If there are garbage disposal facilities at the campsite, use them. Otherwise, pack your garbage out—that is, take it home with you and dispose of it there.
- Recycle whenever possible. Wash bottles and flatten tin cans for recycling.

Outdoor Cooking

Cub Scouts and Webelos Scouts love a cookout. No matter which kind of cooking method you use or which recipes you try, boys will enjoy this outdoor experience. Remember to have safety equipment handy: a bucket of water and shovel or a fire extinguisher. Also nearby should be your cleanup station for washing hands before cooking and eating, doing the dishes, and disposing of your garbage. And, of course, extinguish all fires when you leave the area.

WATERPROOF MATCH HOLDER

Materials: **Plastic film canister, stick matches, scissors**

A plastic film canister makes a useful match holder. Cut the ends of the matches so that they fit in the film canister. If you are not using strike-anywhere matches, cut a piece of the striker off a kitchen matchbox and roll it up to fit into the canister.

TRENCH CANDLE FIRE STARTER

Materials: **Newspaper, string, paraffin, double boiler, tongs**

These fire starters are also called paraffin logs or fire bugs and are useful in building fires in wet weather. Tear several thickness of newspaper into 2-inch strips. Roll to make a log about 1 inch thick and tie with a string. Melt paraffin in a double boiler. Holding the newspaper roll with tongs, dip it into the melted paraffin. The saturated string becomes a wick. Trench candles produce a high, steady flame to help get a fire going.

Another way to make a fire bug is to roll up four newspaper sheets, beginning at the short side. Tie strings 2 inches apart. Cut between the strings to make 2-inch "bugs." Soak in paraffin as directed above.

To provide a little more burning area, create a candle effect with the fire bug by using your finger to push out some of the middle. When completed, you can use the string for a wick and also light the small "top" end of the candle.

EGG CUP FIRE STARTER

Materials: **¾ C. sawdust, melted paraffin, 3-oz. paper cup or cup from a cardboard egg carton, string**

Mix the sawdust with enough melted paraffin to saturate it. Put in the 3-oz. cup or the cup cut from a cardboard egg carton. Insert a string in the center for a wick.

MATCH BUNDLE FIRE STARTER

Materials: **Kitchen matches, melted paraffin, string**

Tie six to eight kitchen matches together with a string, and dip the whole bundle into melted paraffin while holding on to one end of the string. Let it dry on a bit of newspaper or wax paper. Put the bundle at the bottom of your fire and light the string.

BUDDY BURNER

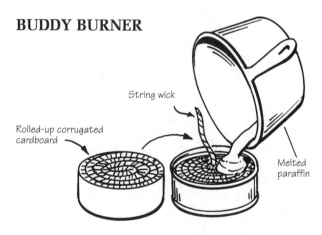

Rolled-up corrugated cardboard

String wick

Melted paraffin

Materials:

6-oz. tuna can	Paraffin
String	Pan of water
Can for melting paraffin	
Strip of corrugated cardboard	

This fire starter can be used with a Tin Can Stove (this page) or as an emergency road flare.

Cut a long strip of corrugated cardboard. The width should be slightly less than the height of the tuna can. Remove the paper from one side. Roll the cardboard in a tight coil and place on edge in the tuna can. The tighter the cardboard is rolled, the longer it will burn. Insert a piece of string in the cen-

ter for the wick. Melt the paraffin in a clean can set in a pan of water. Pour the melted paraffin over the cardboard in the can until the can is three-quarters full. Let the wax harden.

TIN CAN STOVE

Cut

Materials: **No. 10 can, can opener, tin shears**

Cut one end out of the tin can. Use tin shears to cut a hinged opening at the bottom end of the can. This door can be folded up or to one side. It allows a way to light the Buddy Burner and provides airflow. Smooth all sharp edges. Use a can opener to punch out triangular openings around the side of the can near the closed end. Before using the stove, spray the stop with non-stick cooking spray. Set your stove over a Buddy Burner, light the wick, and you're in business!

CHARCOAL CHIMNEY

Materials: **2-pound coffee can, beverage can opener, screwdriver or other hard implement, heavy gloves**

Use this handy tin can gadget to help get all the pieces of charcoal in a charcoal fire equally hot at the same time. It's great for a backyard cookout.

Remove one end from the coffee can. Use a beverage can opener to punch rows of triangular holes all around the sides of the can (as in the Tin Can Stove, above). Protect your hands with heavy gloves. Use a screwdriver to flatten down the metal inside the can. Cut out the other end of the can, and the chimney is ready to use. Put crumpled newspaper in the bottom of the chimney. Add pieces of charcoal and light the newspaper at the bottom. The chimney helps the charcoal start with an even heat and more quickly than it would otherwise.

Once your fire has started, remove the charcoal chimney with tongs and spread your coals to cook.

COOKING FIRES

The first and most important requirement for outdoor cooking is fire safety. Follow fire safety rules and heed the flammability warning found in the *Cub Scout Leader Book.* Careless use of fire can cause a disaster.

Start with crumpled paper, shavings, or small dry sticks. In wet weather, split a log and cut slivers from the dry, inside part. Or, use one of the fire starters described above. Use dry hardwoods, oak, maple, walnut, or birch for the fire rather than evergreen branches. Keep the cooking fire small. A good bed of coals with a low flame, surrounded by rocks, gives plenty of heat for cooking. Tamp the coals flat with a stick if you want to make it level. Make the fire only large enough to serve its purpose.

Be sure to build the fire out of the wind. And remember to start the fire early because it will take a while to burn down to coals.

In some areas, wood for cooking fires is not plentiful, so use packaged briquettes to make fairly fast coals. Find out whether fires are allowed at your outing destination and use established fire rings. Cooking fires can char the ground, and vegetation can have a hard time growing again where a fire has been.

Fire in a Lid

Materials: Metal garbage can lid, bricks, charcoal briquettes

To protect the ground from having a fire built directly on it, you can use a metal garbage can lid for a fire pit. Turn the lid upside down and steady it by balancing it on bricks placed on the ground along the outer edges of the lid. Light briquettes in your new fireplace. You can also place a grill across the top for grilling.

Grill on the Ground

Materials: Heavy-duty foil, briquettes, bricks or rocks, grid from kitchen range or barbecue grill

Lay foil on the ground in the cooking area. Set up bricks or rock on ends so that the cooking grid will be supported and level. Place briquettes on the foil and light. When coals are ready, place the grid on the bricks for cooking. When briquettes are completely cool, you can gather up the ends of the foil for easy cleanup and disposal.

OUTDOOR COOKING UTENSILS

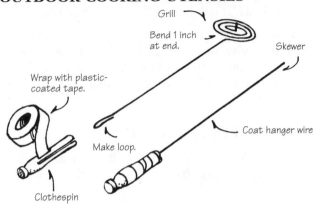

Materials: Coat hangers, pliers, clothespins (not the spring-type), plastic-coated tape

You can use coat hangers to make some simple cooking utensils. Bend the coat hangers with pliers to make a grill and a skewer as shown. Sand or burn off any paint. On the grill, bend up a 1-inch point in the center to help hold the meat. For handles, make a narrow loop at the end of your utensil, slip a clothespin over the loop, and wrap with plastic-coated tape.

To make a fork for roasting, twist two wires together so that you have two fork points. Add a handle, and again, sand or burn the paint off the wire.

ALUMINUM FOIL COOKING

Aluminum foil cooking is simple and fast, and the food retains its juices. Preparation is easy because you can do it at home. Foil cooking also helps cut down on dishwashing because the meal is cooked in the foil and eaten from it.

Always do foil cooking over a bed of hot coals, never a flaming fire. Start the fire well ahead of the scheduled eating time and allow it to die down to glowing embers.

Tasty Stew

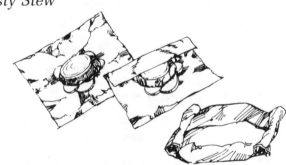

Materials: Heavy-duty foil; potatoes, carrots, onion, celery, stew meat, or hamburger patty; 1 to 2 T. tomato juice or other liquid; seasonings; bed of hot coals

Cook a tasty stew in foil. Cut up potatoes, carrots, onion, and celery. Add stew meat, a thin hamburger patty, or crumbled hamburger. Sprinkle with tomato juice or other liquid. Season as desired. Use heavy-duty foil or a double thickness of lightweight foil and fold the food in a "drugstore wrap." Place the food in the center of the foil and fold up both sides to make a "tent" over the food. Fold the edges together down over the food, and then fold in each side about three times to make an airtight container. Place the packet on the coals and cook about 15 minutes on each side. Because different fires cook at different speeds, timing the meat can be a little tricky until you have experience.

Use the drugstore wrap with foil to cook a fresh fish fillet, chicken, baked potatoes, corn on the cob, and many other types of foods.

THE HANDY PLASTIC BAG

Heavy-duty resealable plastic bags will save dishwashing time. Use them as substitutes for mixing bowls when you make cakes, biscuits, or instant pudding. Carry the mixed dry ingredients in the bags. When you're ready to mix, add the necessary liquids and press down on the bag to expel excess air. Reseal the bag and "mix" by squeezing the bag firmly.

You can also use these bags to carry prepared salads or other dishes. When you're ready to serve, simply place the bag in an appropriately sized empty can, open the bag, pull the top over the outside edges of the can, and serve from your simple "bowl."

OUTDOOR CLEANUP

Materials: **Squeeze bottle, plastic milk jug, golf tee**

For easy cleanup while cooking outdoors, bring a squeeze bottle filled with water and a few drops of liquid detergent. Use to clean hands before, during, and after food preparation.

For easy access to a flow of water, poke a hole in the side of a milk jug near the bottom. Place a golf tee in the whole as a stopper. Fill the jug with water and set on a table or stump. To wash hands, remove the golf tee and allow the small stream of water to pour over your hands. Replace the golf tee when you're finished.

DISHWASHING

Materials: **Three pots, heat source, dishwashing soap, bleach, tongs**

Whether you're using an open fire or a stove, put on a pot of water to heat before you serve a meal. That way, you'll have hot dishwater by the time you finish eating.

To begin cleanup, set out three pots. To the first pot, add hot water with a few drops of soap for the wash pot. In the second, place cold water with a few drops of bleach to kill bacteria for a cold-rinse pot. To the third, add just hot water for a hot-rinse pot.

Scrape dishes and wash them in the wash pot. Dip them in the cold-rinse pot and then using tongs dip them in the hot rinse. Place dishes on a plastic ground cloth to air-dry.

FOOD PACKING TIPS

Materials: **Cardboard box, newspapers, resealable plastic bags, milk cartons**

Keeping hot food hot and cold food cold can be a problem on a trip, but it's important to do to prevent spoilage. Commercial insulated thermal bottle containers, plastic foam containers, and hot boxes come in handy.

- Before packing your cooler, chill it in the refrigerator.

- If you don't have a thermal container to keep foods warm, make a "hot box." Use a Dutch oven or heavy aluminum pan to bring a one-pot meal to a boil. Cook to a point just short of the last 10 to 20 minutes of the recommended cooking time. Remove from the heat and place in a large cardboard box lined with 2 to 3 inches of newspapers. Pack newspapers around the Dutch oven or pan on all sides and the top and bottom of the box to prevent heat loss. The food will continue to cook in the box and stay hot for hours.

- Commercial coolers will keep drinks and salad cool for a longer time if you use a large block of ice rather than ice cubes. Freeze water in half-gallon or gallon cardboard or plastic milk cartons.

- For meats to be cooked later, freeze them in resealable plastic bags and carry them in a cooler. They will keep other foods cold and will thaw without leaking.

- You can also carry well-sealed hot or cold foods wrapped in a sleeping bag to keep a constant temperature longer.

PLANNING A COOKOUT

- Plan menus carefully and write them down.
- Make a list of the foods and equipment you need for the number of people you are serving.
- Pack the food carefully so it won't spoil or spill.
- Store food properly before and after cooking.
- Keep food preparation simple.
- Be safety conscious at all times when working around fire. Have a container of water handy to use in case of an emergency, and extinguish any fires completely when you are through.

Outdoor Cooking Recipes

HEARTY HOT DOG SPECIAL

Materials: **Thermal bottle, soup, string, hot dog, hot dog bun, condiments**

Fill a thermal bottle three-quarters full with your favorite hot soup. Tie a string around a heated hot dog and drop it in the soup, leaving the end of the string outside the bottle. Cap the bottle. For a quick meal on the road, open the bottle, pull out the hot dog, place it on a bun, and spread with your favorite fixings. Serve it with the hot soup, a drink, and cookies or cupcakes.

INSTANT TACOS

Ingredients: **Taco mixture in a thermal container, small bag of corn or taco chips, grated cheese**

Put your favorite taco mixture in a thermal container. At mealtime, open the chips and pour the taco mixture into the bag to mix. Sprinkle with grated cheese and eat from the bag.

SUBMARINES IN FOIL

Ingredients:
Hard rolls
Canned luncheon meat, corned beef, or minced ham
Pickle relish
Diced boiled egg
Grated cheddar cheese
Salad dressing or undiluted cream of chicken soup

Scoop out a "bowl" in the center of the hard rolls. Mix together the meat, diced boiled egg, and grated cheese. Moisten with salad dressing or undiluted cream of chicken soup. Fill the rolls with the mixture and wrap each individually in a double thickness of foil. Cook 20 to 25 minutes over hot coals.

KABOBS

Ingredients: **Skewer or stick, cubed pieces of meat (luncheon meat, precooked ham, quartered wieners, or beef chunks), cut vegetables (onion, potatoes, green peppers, mushrooms, or cherry tomatoes), melted butter, barbecue sauce**

On a skewer or stick, place bite-sized pieces of meat and vegetables, alternating them. Brush the skewered food with melted butter and barbecue sauce. Broil over hot coals. Turn the kabobs occasionally as they cook.

PIZZA BOMBS

Ingredients: **Can of flaky biscuits, pizza sauce, sliced pepperoni, grated cheese**

Fold up a square of foil into a bowl shape. Separate flaky biscuits into four or five layers. Spread the layers onto the foil and pat together. Layer pizza sauce, sliced pepperoni, and cheese on the biscuits. Place over hot coals and cook.

GRILLED CORN ON THE COB

Ingredients: **Corn on the cob, cold salted water, butter**

Strip the husks back over the end of the cob but don't tear them off. Remove all silk and soak the corn in cold salted water for 15 minutes. Then smooth on some butter. Bring the husks back over the corn, wrap each ear in a piece of foil, and twist the ends tightly. Lay on hot coals and cook for 15 to 20 minutes, turning once.

HUNTER'S STEW

Ingredients:

½ lb. beef, veal, or lamb	1 T. cooking oil
1 C. water	Carrots
Celery	Onions
Potatoes	Salt and pepper

Cut the meat in 1-inch chunks. Place the oil in a pan (a skillet or Dutch oven) and brown the meat. Add the water and diced vegetables. Simmer for 30 minutes over hot coals. Season with salt and pepper.

WALKING SALAD

Ingredients: **Apple, peanut butter, raisins**

Cut the top off an apple and remove the core. Take care not to cut all the way through to the bottom of the apple. Fill the cavity with peanut butter mixed with raisins. Replace the top of the apple and wrap in plastic wrap. Take along for a quick snack on a hike. Create your own filling using your favorites, such as cheese, nuts, marshmallows, dried fruit, etc.

ANTS ON A LOG

Ingredients: **Celery, peanut butter, raisins**

Spread 4-inch-long celery sticks with peanut butter. Dot raisins along the peanut butter for your "ants."

PIGS IN A BLANKET

Ingredients: **Biscuit mix, water or milk, wiener**

Add water or milk to biscuit mix until you have a stiff dough. Mold the dough around a wiener that is on a clean roasting stick. Pinch the ends of the dough to hold. Roast over coals.

TWIXER BISCUITS

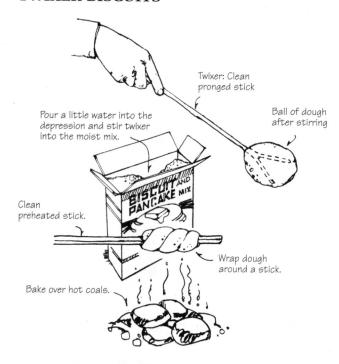

Twixer: Clean pronged stick

Ball of dough after stirring

Pour a little water into the depression and stir twixer into the moist mix.

Clean preheated stick.

BISCUIT AND PANCAKE MIX

Wrap dough around a stick.

Bake over hot coals.

Ingredients: **Biscuit mix, water**

Optional: **Jam, jelly, or cheese**

For pizza: **Tomato sauce, oregano, cheese, and pepperoni**

Open a box of biscuit mix and make a depression in the contents so you can pour a little water into the hole. Stir it gently with a clean, pronged stick (your "twixer") until it forms an egg-sized ball on the stick. Remove the ball from the stick, flatten it, and wrap it around a clean, preheated stick to bake as twisted over coals. Or, form it into a biscuit shape and bake in aluminum foil, leaving space for the biscuit to rise.

For extra flavor, make a depression in the dough and fill with jam, jelly, or cheese.

For pizza, flatten the dough. Spread on some tomato sauce and a sprinkle of oregano. Add thin slices of cheese and pepperoni. Wrap in foil and bake in hot coals.

FOIL-CUP EGG

Ingredients: **Egg, 7-inch square of foil, 16-oz. can**

For each egg, make a cup by molding the square of foil around the bottom of the can. Slide the cup off the can and break an egg into it. Place the cup on a grill and cook 10 minutes, or place directly on coals and cook 2 to 3 minutes.

EGGS ON A RAFT

Ingredients: **Oil, slice of bread, egg, seasonings**

Grease the cooking surface of a Tin Can Stove (see page 4–33). Cut a hole 2 to 2½ inches in diameter in the center of a slice of bread. Place the bread on the stove and break an egg into the hole. Season as desired. Turn over once and cook to your satisfaction.

OMELET IN A BAG

Ingredients: **Eggs, milk, cubed cheese, cubed ham, chopped onions, seasonings**

Materials: **1-quart heavy-duty resealable freezer bags, marker, pot of boiling water**

Crack one or two eggs into a bag and add a splash of milk and other ingredients as desired. Carefully press the air out of the bag and seal. Gently knead the mixture to combine ingredients. Write the boy's name on the bag with a marker. Place the bag in boiling water and cook until done. Eat right out of the bag.

BREAKFAST IN AN ORANGE

Ingredients: **Orange, egg, muffin batter**

Cut an orange in half and carefully remove the pulp without tearing the cup-shaped peeling. Break an egg into one orange cup and fill the other with your favorite muffin batter mixed in a resealable plastic bag. Place each cup on its own square of double-thickness foil, and then bring the four corners of the foil to the top and twist securely to seal. Be sure to leave enough room for the muffin to rise. Set the foil-enclosed cups on hot coals for 10 to 15 minutes, and then enjoy your delicious breakfast.

POPCORN ON A STRING

Ingredients: **1 t. cooking oil, 1 T. popcorn, butter, salt**

In the center of a piece of 6-inch-square foil, place the oil and popcorn. Bring the foil corners together to make a pouch. Seal the edges by folding, but leave room for the corn to pop. Tie each pouch to a long stick with a string and hold the pouch over hot coals. Shake constantly until all the corn has popped. Season with butter and salt. Make one for each person.

BANANA BOATS

Ingredients: **Banana, chocolate chips, miniature marshmallows, nuts**

Optional tropical treat: **Crushed pineapple, coconut, brown sugar, butter**

Strip back one section of a banana peel but don't remove it. Cut lengthwise a triangle-shaped wedge from the banana to make a cavity running the length of the banana. Fill the cavity with a mixture of chocolate chips, miniature marshmallows, and nuts. Replace the banana peeling. Wrap the banana securely in foil and place it in hot coals for about 10 minutes so the chocolate melts and the marshmallows puff up. Unwrap and enjoy!

Variations: Try butterscotch, butter brickle, or peanut butter chips. For a tropical treat, fill the banana cavity with crushed pineapple, coconut, a little brown sugar, and a dab of butter. Bake 5 to 10 minutes on hot coals.

SHAGGY DOGS

Ingredients: **Chocolate syrup, marshmallows, coconut or chopped pecans**

Open a can of chocolate syrup and heat it over coals until the syrup is runny. Toast a marshmallow on a stick until just golden. Dip the marshmallow in the syrup and roll it in coconut or chopped pecans.

BAKED APPLE

Ingredients: **Apple, raisins, brown sugar, cinnamon, butter**

Core an apple and place it on a square of foil. Fill the core with raisins, brown sugar, a dash of cinnamon, and a pat of butter. Seal with a drugstore wrap and place on hot coals. Cook until the apple is soft.

FRUIT KABOBS

Ingredients: **Banana, pineapple, cherries, marshmallows**

Follow the instructions for regular kabobs above (page 4–36), using chunks of banana, pineapple, cherries, etc., alternating with large marshmallows. Toast over hot coals using a skewer or stick until the marshmallows are golden brown.

HIKER'S GORP

Ingredients:

Salted nuts	Chopped dates
Raisins	Semisweet chocolate bits
Dried fruit pieces	Cubes of hard cheese
Cocktail-sized miniature crackers	

Mix all the ingredients together and divide into individual bags to send along with hikers.

HIKER'S BIRDSEED

Ingredients: **Two individual packages of sugared breakfast cereals, two small bags of coated chocolate candies, handful of raisins, half handful of dry roasted peanuts**

Mix all the ingredients together to provide energy on hikes.

TIN CAN ICE CREAM

Ingredients: **3¾-oz. package instant pudding mix, 13-oz. can evaporated milk, regular milk**

Materials: **1-pound coffee can with lid, 3-pound coffee can with lid, duct tape, crushed ice, rock salt**

1. Place the package of instant pudding mix and the evaporated milk in a clean 1-pound coffee can. Add enough regular milk to fill the can three-quarters full. Mix well. Cover with a plastic lid. Tape the lid on securely with duct tape so the can is airtight.

2. Place the 1-pound can inside the 3-pound can. Add layers of crushed ice and rock salt around the smaller can until the ice and salt surround it on all sides. Put the lid on the larger can. Tape with duct tape.

3. Roll the can back and forth on a table or the ground for 20 to 25 minutes. The boys can form two lines or sit in a circle to do this, rolling it back and forth to each other.

4. Carefully untape the large can and remove the smaller one to check the ice cream. Wipe off all salt before removing the lid from the smaller can. Scrape the ice cream from the insides of the can. Put the lid back on and tape securely.

5. Place the smaller can back in the larger can and add more ice and salt. Tape the lid on the large can and continue to roll for about 10 more minutes. By then, the ice cream should be ready to eat.

ICE CREAM IN A BAG

Ingredients: ½ C. milk or cream, 3 T. sugar, 1 t. vanilla

Materials: **Quart-sized resealable freezer bag, gallon-sized resealable freezer bag, crushed ice, rock salt**

Mix the milk, sugar, and vanilla in the quart-sized bag. Carefully push the air out of the bag and seal. Place this bag into the gallon-sized bag. Add crushed ice and several spoons of rock salt to the gallon-sized freezer bag. Remove any excess air and seal. While holding the sealed edge, shake and roll the bag for 10 or 15 minutes. Once the ice cream freezes, open the large bag and remove the ice cream bag. Enjoy your treat right from the bag.

Fun With Campfires

Campfire magic! You've experienced it. You chose the songs, practiced skits, and organized everything into a program. Then people came together and you began. Everything went without a hitch. Participants sang songs enthusiastically and laughed uproariously (or groaned painfully) at skits. Then the tone and pace of the program slowed to the calming closing thought. As the dying campfire embers crumbled into ashes, boys reluctantly drifted off to bed with their new memories. You stood before the glowing embers, soaking in their fading warmth and knowing that everything was just right. You've been touched by campfire magic.

Campfires like this are special, but you may think they are rare. They need not be! With careful thought and preparation, the campfire described above can become the rule rather than the exception. What follows are some hints and ideas to help you plan a campfire program, deliver it smoothly, and bring that special campfire magic to it and to everyone attending.

PLANNING

Start with the BSA Campfire Program Planner. This helpful resource sheet prompts you to include all of the elements necessary for a successful campfire. Think of your campfire as flowing along a curve. The campfire has a serious start, working upward along the curve to peak excitement, and then slowing down as the fire dies and the evening ends with an inspirational closing.

BUILDING THE FIRE

Council Fire Lay

Have your fire site ready before you begin. Make sure you are using a designated fire ring with permission of the landowner. Have plenty of tinder, kindling, and the fuelwood that you will need.

Begin with a small tepee fire lay. Place big, loose handfuls of tinder in the middle of your fire site. (Dry pine needles, grasses, and shredded bark work well for tinder.) Mound plenty of small kindling over the tinder. Arrange small and medium-sized sticks of fuelwood around the kindling as if they were the poles of a tepee. Leave an opening in the tepee on the side the wind is blowing against so that air can reach the middle of the fire. This foundation fire must be a sure thing; the trick is to have plenty of tinder and small kindling and a place to insert the first light. For campfires, it is better to use extra tinder than to have the fire lighting not go as planned. Crisscross larger fuelwood log cabin style around the tepee foundation fire. Place wood across the top of the log cabin to form a roof. Form another smaller tepee fire lay on top of this roof.

Backlog Fire

For a smaller group, use a backlog fire lay. Begin with a big, seasoned log for the back. Mound your tinder in front of the large log. Lean the kindling up against the seasoned log and add fuelwood as needed.

THE NINE S'S FOR A SUCCESSFUL CAMPFIRE

Safety

Health and safety are always the first consideration when working with Cub Scouts and Webelos Scouts.

- Be aware of and avoid roots and overhanging branches near your fire lay.
- Build your campfire in an approved campfire pit.
- Maintain a safe distance from the fire at all times.
- The fire should never be higher than your knee.
- Designate one person to feed and extinguish the fire. All others should follow that person's directions. Since the fire should crescendo and fade along with the program, be careful not to add too much wood to the fire.
- Never use unapproved petroleum products, such as kerosene or gasoline, to start your fire.
- Have fire-extinguishing materials and a first aid kit readily available at ALL times.
- Consider lighting the path to and from the campfire. Remember that it is generally darker when the campfire is over, and participants' eyes are adjusted to gazing at the light. Participants can carry flashlights, or adults only, or flashlights could be held along the path by designated "trail lighters." You could also light the path with Tin Can Lanterns (see page 2–28) or plastic luminaria. Use plastic milk jugs. Add about 2 inches of sand and

place a votive candle in the center of the sand. Cut designs in the sides of the containers for the light to shine through. Use your imagination!

Start

The actual start of the campfire is the time when the participants approach and assemble at the campfire location. You may have asked participants to enter together in silence, or you may have announced a start time and have guests enter at will. If participants don't enter all at once, the master of ceremonies and crew should be prepared for preopening ideas and song practice. Don't let this go on too long, however. *Start on time!*

- Have a plan in hand! (And don't forget a small flashlight.)
- Plan for safe, dry seating. If the campfire setting doesn't have seating, tell participants to bring something to sit on (plastic bags are easy to bring and work well).
- Often, it is appropriate to have the fire already started. If you prefer to light the fire after participants have gathered, be certain to have the fire built well ahead of time.
- Set the tone for appropriate behavior from the start. Insist on respect, and set a good example.

Showmanship

The perfect campfire is a show. It needs a master of ceremonies to keep things moving and a stage crew to help participants to and from the campfire circle with appropriate props.

- Be sure that those who take part in the show will know what the lighting conditions will be at show time.
- Participants in the show should stand behind the fire so that the audience members can see them.
- Speak loudly enough for everyone to hear.

Songs

In the upward part of the campfire curve, choose action songs. In the downward part, choose songs that are softer and more inspirational in nature. Mostly choose songs that are familiar to the participants, but it's always fun to learn a new one. See the "Razzle Dazzle" chapter of this book or the *Cub Scout Songbook* for ideas, and use favorites that you have learned at roundtable and from campfires you have attended.

Stunts

Stunts and applauses are for fillers and fun. Use them between songs, skits, and ceremonies to keep things moving. Applauses not only fill time but also give you an opportunity to recognize the efforts of those participating in the program. Make sure the cheers you choose are appropriate and positive. See the "Razzle Dazzle" chapter of this book for ideas.

Skits

Kids love skits. Help your boys practice so that they can be heard and understood. Refer to the "Razzle Dazzle" chapter of this book for some enjoyable and creative skits. It is essential that you help boys choose skits that are appropriate. Any skit that involves "put-downs" or joking at the expense of others is unacceptable. *Never joke about physical characteristics, nationalities, disabilities, or religious beliefs—or anything else about another person that might be "different."* If it isn't fun for everyone, it isn't fun.

Settling

When you're on the downward curve of the campfire, it's time to change the mood. Soften your voice and choose quiet songs. Avoid getting the crowd excited again, but don't let things get dull. Even though you are on the downward curve, it's still important to keep things moving.

"S"eremonies

Ceremonies are your opportunity to provide inspiration and recognition. They can be especially meaningful when they take place in a campfire setting. See *Cub Scout Ceremonies for Dens and Packs* for ceremony ideas.

Stopping

Ideally, a campfire should last about one hour. The size of the group will determine the amount of individual and den participation. Campfires that drag on cause boys to fidget and adults to check their watches. Leave everyone eager to return and create more memories at the next campfire.

5

RAZZLE DAZZLE

Razzle dazzle? This chapter of the *Cub Scout Leader How-To Book* presents activities that will impress, astonish, surprise, and entertain your den or pack. Dip into each section to discover ways to add razzle dazzle to your meetings: from audience participation stories to skits, jokes, and tricks. Never worked with puppets or told a story? Now is the time to try something new!

THE IMPORTANCE OF GROUP PARTICIPATION (A POEM)

The pack meeting seemed to drag that night,
And people were tiring fast;
The Cubmaster sensed the sleepy feeling
And hoped through the meeting he'd last.

Then came a lull in the evening's action;
The Cubmaster wiped his brow;
If only he could perk things up—
He sure wished that he knew how!

Then suddenly quite like some kind of magic,
His assistant appeared on the stage;
She held up a book called *Group Meeting Sparklers*,
And opened it to a page.

Eagerly she made the announcement
That the audience would help out.
She divided them into several groups
And tested each one for their shout.

Before they knew what had happened to them,
They had all joined in the fun;
Each group was doing its very best
To out-do the other one!

Right then and there the meeting perked up;
Things moved along in style,
And the Cubmaster heard the people say,
"Best meeting we've had in a while!"

So remember the words "group participation"—
A very special key,
And all your meetings will be filled with fun,
The way they ought to be!

Audience Participation Stories

Audience participation stories add variety, action, and fun to den and pack meetings. Some get people on their feet, going through motions under the directions of a leader. For others, the audience is divided into groups that respond to a key word in a story read by a leader. Here are several examples. The key words are listed first, with the appropriate words or actions defined. It's a good idea to let groups practice their motions or phrases first. This also might help "loosen" everyone up a little before the story is read.

THE THREE TREES

BIG TREE: Plunk! *(in a deep voice)*

MIDDLE-SIZED TREE: Plank!

BABY TREE: Plink! *(in high voice)*

BABBLING BROOK: Gurgle gurgle

RABBIT: Clippety-clip, clippety-clop

HUNTERS: *(Make a bugle call)*

GUN: Bang!

NARRATOR: Once upon a time in the deep, dark woods, there stood three trees—the BIG TREE, the MIDDLE-SIZED TREE, and the wee BABY TREE. And through the trees ran the BABBLING BROOK and hopped the little RABBIT.

One day, a group of HUNTERS came into the forest in which stood the three trees—the BIG TREE, the MIDDLE-SIZED TREE, and the little BABY TREE—and through the trees ran the BABBLING BROOK and hopped the little RABBIT. As the HUNTERS wandered through the forest, one of the HUNTERS spied the little RABBIT. He raised his GUN and shot at the little RABBIT—and sadness reigned in the forest, in which stood the three trees—the BIG TREE, the MIDDLE-SIZED TREE, and the little BABY TREE—and through which ran the BABBLING BROOK, but no longer hopped the little RABBIT.

The BIG TREE, the MIDDLE-SIZED TREE, and the little BABY TREE were all very sad. Even the BABBLING BROOK was sad. But all of a sudden, out from the thicket hopped the little RABBIT! The HUNTER'S GUN had missed! And once again happiness reigned in the forest in which lived the three trees—the BIG TREE, the MIDDLE-SIZED TREE, and the little BABY TREE—and through which ran the BABBLING BROOK . . . *and* hopped the little RABBIT.

BOBBY WANTS TO BE A CUB SCOUT

TIGER: Ro-arrrr!

BOBCAT: Mee-ooooow

WOLF: Ahhhh-ooooo!

BEAR: Grrrrrrr!

WEBELOS: We'll be loyal Scouts!

ARROW OF LIGHT: *(Everyone clap)*

Bobby was out for a walk one day near his home. As he walked along, he met a TIGER who, along with a partner, seemed to be searching for something. Bobby asked the TIGER what they were doing. "We are in search of the BOBCAT trail," the TIGER replied. "I need to find the way so that I can become a BOBCAT."

That's odd, thought Bobby. A TIGER becoming a BOBCAT? What an imagination the TIGER had! Bobby continued on his walk. In a few minutes, he came upon a BOBCAT. The BOBCAT appeared to be reading a book. Bobby asked the BOBCAT what he was doing. The BOBCAT said that he was trying to become a WOLF.

Bobby laughed. Who ever heard of a BOBCAT changing into a WOLF? He continued on along the way. Soon he met a WOLF. The WOLF was working on a woodworking project. "What are you trying to become?" laughed Bobby. "I'm going to become a BEAR," the WOLF said.

How strange, thought Bobby. A TIGER who wants to be a BOBCAT, a BOBCAT who wants to be a WOLF, and a WOLF who wants to be a BEAR. Maybe I can find a BEAR who wants to be something else, too!

Sure enough, soon he met a BEAR who was busy packing for a camping trip with his family. "And what are *you* trying to become, big BEAR?" The BEAR said, "I'm going to be a WEBELOS."

"What's a WEBELOS?" Bobby asked. So the BEAR explained to Bobby how he could become a Cub Scout. First, he could be a TIGER Cub, then a BOBCAT, then a WOLF, then a BEAR, and then a WEBELOS Scout. He might be able to earn the ARROW OF LIGHT, the highest award in Cub Scouting.

Bobby said, "Thank you" to the BEAR. Then he ran back past the WOLF, past the BOBCAT, and past the TIGER and his partner. He ran right out of the woods and straight home. He wanted to tell his parents that he wanted to join Cub Scouting so he could become a TIGER Cub, a BOBCAT, then a WOLF, then a BEAR, and then a WEBELOS Scout—and maybe even earn the ARROW OF LIGHT!

CAR TROUBLE

For a small group, write several of the items below on 3-by-5 cards and give each person one or more cards. For a large group, write only one item on each card, so more people can participate. The narrator reads the story, pausing at the blanks. In turn, players read one item on their cards to fill in the blank words.

A loose tooth	Three boiled eggs
A tall pine tree	A fat onion
A green tomato	Two snowballs
A can of tar	A telephone
A bald eagle	A limping dinosaur
A bar of soap	A purple crayon
A cat's meow	A butterfly net
A rattlesnake	Four hot rocks
Three raisins	A bike horn
A short pencil	Four sour pickles
A juicy watermelon	A swarm of bees
A can of dog food	An ice cream bar
Six plump skeletons	A can of worms
A ferocious lion	A dog's footprint
Seven pounds of feathers	A used firecracker
A red kite	

NARRATOR: One fine day, two elderly women—Alice and Maud—decided to drive out of town for a picnic. Alice loaded a basket with _____, _____, and _____, and other tasty things. They took their lunch and drove off in Maud's old car. The radiator cap was decorated with _____, and the holes in the roof had been patched with _____ and _____.

As they drove along, Alice pointed to the side of the road and said, "Oh, look at that bush with the _____ growing on it." "Let's stop here," Maud said.

They carried their picnic basket to some shade cast by _____ and spread out _____ to sit on. Nearby, _____ sang gaily in a tree.

They went to the low bushes they had noticed and picked the _____ that was growing on them. The two friends had a wonderful picnic.

"There's nothing as delicious as _____ with mustard and pickles," Maud said, as she brushed the crumbs off her lap with _____. "Yes," Alice sighed. "But it's getting late. We'd better start for home."

Unfortunately, the car refused to start. The motor made a noise like _____ and then stopped altogether. "Oh dear!" Maud said, looking under the hood. "I think I see _____ and _____ caught in the fan belt." "Impossible!" Alice said. "Could the gas tank be empty? Are you sure you put enough _____ in it before we left home?"

"Of course, I did!" Maud said. "It must be the wheels. We'll jack them up with _____ and then replace them with _____." She covered her clothes with _____ and took _____ to loosen the bolts.

Just then Farmer Jones drove up and asked whether he could help. "Looks like _____ in the engine," he said, tightening a bolt with _____. He turned the key and the car started. "I just connected the _____ to _____, which had come loose." Alice and Maud looked in their picnic basket and gave Farmer Jones the rest of their _____ to thank him. Then they drove happily home.

JOHNNY MIX-UP

Prepare a set of 3-by-5 cards with each of the three-phrase sets below written on them; you should have 54 cards in all. Deal all of the cards to the boys and adults, who keep them facedown. (Each person may get more than one card.) Then read the story. When you come to a space, pause and let each player in turn read one of the lines on his or her top card. The crazier the better, although sometimes it's just as much fun when one of the objects on the card happens to fit perfectly.

Some dirty dishwater
A rusty nail
A jar of jam

A pig's tail
A wild donkey
An old horn

A banana skin
A bad dream
Some axle grease

Pink lemonade
A bundle of shingles
A bag of rags

A toadstool
A pumpkin vine
A skyscraper

A camel's hump
A rubber chicken
A black cat

A streetcar
A loud noise
A swarm of bees

A hunk of cheese
A heap of pancakes
A high-toned hobo

A bathtub
A tiny speck
A beautiful sunset

A wise old owl
A bobtailed bunny
A wet kitten

A toothbrush
Some hot pepper
A loud sneeze

A black mustache
A wall-eyed fish
A sinking tea kettle

An old radio
An old shoe
A bug bite on the nose

Some pattering rain
An old hay rack
A red necktie

A pushcart
A rattlesnake
A rhinoceros

A secondhand sponge
A young earthquake
A glass eye

A sourpuss
A battleship
A roaring lion

A bent hairpin
An exclamation point
A runaway kitty cat

A shovel full of coal
A black cloud
A can of red paint

A trolley car
A snapping turtle
A rusty horseshoe

A broken umbrella
A cake of soap
A silly giggle

A bunch of posies
A litter of puppies
An inquisitive ostrich

A puff of smoke
A monkey-faced baboon
A bucket of slop

A bucking horse
A purple cow
A red barn

A crazy bedbug
A carload of fish
A leaky pail

A barrel of tar
Three blind mice
Somebody's Scout shorts

A squeaky wheel
An old egg
A cross-eyed cat

My polka dot belt
A yellow parrot
A pile of peach fuzz

A blue hen
An elderly porcupine
A freezing farmer

A green pair of stockings
A keg of nails
A barrel stove

A pink ghost
A three-legged stove
A dish of beans

A green-eyed monster
A hot dog
A set of false teeth

A tall hat
A stuffed apple
An energetic turtle

A ton of bricks
A merry widow
Mary's little lamb

A frowzy bird
A green snake
A pan of milk

A bean shooter
A prickly thistle
Your old shirt

A flashlight
A prickly cactus
Some red ants

A derby hat
A country bumpkin
A crying baby

A Model T Ford
A buggy bumper
A gas stove

A piece of ribbon
A rainy day
A race horse

An ear of corn
A chunk of wood
A spare tire

A tin can
The hot sun
A Border collie

A skittish kitten
A ripped road map
Some ink spots

A broken umbrella
A pair of suspenders
A spinning wheel

A scrub brush
A head of old cabbage
A corncob pipe

A cross-eyed peanut
A bow-legged horse
Some Limburger cheese

A cross-eyed potato
A stick of dynamite
A big fat worm

Two fat skeletons
A peanut roaster
A Spanish onion

A military haircut
A brass monkey
A second-hand car

A juicy watermelon
A flat can
A blow-out

A crowing rooster
A laughing pony
Your red nose

A rip in your pants
A slice of cold ham
A pain in the neck

A crawling lizard
A polka-dot frog
An old crab

A windy day
Mickey Mouse
A pair of bee's knees

NARRATOR: Once upon a time there was a little boy named Johnny who lived in Mix-Up Town. His home was indeed very strange, for it had _____ on the roof and _____ on each window sill and _____ with _____ on it planted on each side of the front door to make the house beautiful. The house was painted so that it looked like _____. Instead of having flowers and vegetables growing in the garden, Johnny's family planted _____ and _____, and over in a corner was a tree with _____ growing on it.

Johnny's father had a pet that was _____, and he would go for long walks with it, leading it with a chain while it hopped about merrily like _____. Johnny went with his father on these walks, but he always had to dress up nicely like all the other boys in Mix-Up Town whenever he went out. This is how he dressed: On his head he wore _____, on one foot he had _____, and on the other was _____. Instead of a necktie, he wore _____.

One morning Johnny's father told him they were going to the zoo to see _____ and the other things there. So Johnny dressed quickly and washed himself with _____ and dried himself on _____, which was hanging on the towel rack. He brushed his teeth with _____ and

combed his hair with _____, and he was ready for breakfast. He was very hungry that morning, so he took _____ and _____ and put it on his plate and mixed them with _____ and ate it all up.

At the zoo Johnny's father had to buy tickets, so he reached into his pocket and pulled out _____ and gave it to the ticket seller, who gave Johnny's father his tickets and his change, which was _____. They went inside, and the first thing they saw was _____, which was pacing to and fro and roaring loudly at _____, which was standing on _____ and making faces at Johnny and his father.

That morning the monkeys were very playful. One of them was hanging by its feet on the trapeze and holding _____ with its hands and tickling another monkey with it. Another monkey with _____ on its head was throwing _____ up like a ball and letting it bounce. A little monkey close by saw _____ buzzing around in the cage and tried to catch it, but it made a noise like _____ and frightened the little monkey, which ran away like _____ was after him.

Then they went to see the elephants, which were walking around in a pen just large enough for _____. Johnny reached into a paper bag he was carrying and pulled out _____ and gave it to the biggest elephant. The elephant was so pleased that it shot water through its trunk and then reached out and gave Johnny _____.

When Johnny tired of seeing the zoo, he and his father went to the aquarium, where they saw _____ swimming around like _____ and singing as happily as _____. Now, across the street was a sideshow where a band was playing music that sounded like _____ running after _____. High up on a platform was a very strange-looking man. His head was shaped like _____ and his body was shaped like _____. And one ear was as long as _____. As the man puffed on his pipe, great clouds of smoke came out of his ear. Just as he took an extra deep puff on his pipe, a man slapped him with _____ and out of his ear jumped _____.

By this time it was time for Johnny and his father to go home, so they went to the corner and climbed on top of _____ and rode home feeling as tired as _____.

The next day Johnny, who was an unusual sort of a Cub Scout, went to his den meeting. First of all, the Cub Scouts had to sign their names on the back of

_____. Instead of a pencil they used _____. Their uniforms were indeed strange ones. They were the color of _____. They had _____ wrapped around each leg. And on their heads they each had _____, and their neckerchiefs looked like _____. When they went into their den, they were each given a puzzle that was _____ cut up into several pieces, and they all tried to put it together with _____.

They sang a song about _____; then they worked on crafts. One Cub Scout was hammering on _____. Their den chief was helping the denner to earn his knots achievement. This is what they were doing: The den chief was holding _____ on the table while the denner was trying to tie it up with _____. When they had finished, he showed him how to jump over _____. Then they all played a game in which each Cub Scout threw _____ as far as he could while he carried _____ in his left hand.

As the meeting came to a close, the den chief lit _____ and told the Cub Scouts that it resembled _____ and that all good Cub Scouts should grow up to be like that, too. Then they all went home as happy as _____, throwing _____ at each other as they sang a beautiful song about _____, which sounded like _____ that had fallen into a washing machine.

FIRE SAFETY STORY

Setting: This story is full of mistakes often made in fire safety. Two adults should lead it. One will read the story, and the other will hold up a sign that says "Oh, no—not that." The person with the sign should hold it up when a mistake is read so that the audience can shout "Oh, no—not that!" The sign holder should then correct the story reader with the correct information. If the story reader and the sign holder have a little ad lib give-and-take, the message will have more of an effect.

NARRATOR: Once upon a time a group of boys and some adults went camping. The boys were excited because they would be spending the whole weekend outdoors. They would get to set up tents, play games, eat food outdoors, have a campfire program, and return home tired but happy campers.

As soon as they got to their campsite, two of them set up their tent next to where the fire would be because they wanted to be close to the cooking and warm at night. *("Oh, no—not that!" You can't do that. Sparks from the fire might catch the tent on fire.)*

The next two boys set up their tent a little bit away from where the cooking fire would be; they had learned their lesson from the first group. They began gathering sticks and piling them inside their tent, because they wanted to be warm all night, too. *("Oh, no—not that!" You can't do that. Never have an open flame inside of a tent.)*

Two more boys set up their tent and hung their liquid fuel lantern in the center of it. They knew how dark it could be inside a tent at night, and they wanted to read in bed. *("Oh, no—not that!" You can't do that. NO open flames inside a tent, even if it is a lantern. Only flashlights.)*

Finally, everyone got the idea and set up their tents in a semicircle well away from the fire with all the lanterns outside and the kindling laid neatly by the designated fire area. The area was in an established fire ring well away from overhanging branches. It was time to begin the cooking fire. All the boys helped collect firewood. One of the adults told them to arrange the wood by size, but the boys thought that was stupid so they just dumped it by the fire. *("Oh, no—not that!" You can't do that. It is best to arrange firewood by size so that the correct pieces are close at hand and easy to get to when building the fire.)*

After rearranging all the firewood, the boys were told they could build the fire. They did it exactly like they had been taught. And it was a beautiful fire lay. They started to light the fire... *("Oh, no—not that!" You can't do that. Don't light the fire until a shovel and a bucket of water are close by in case the fire gets out of hand or for when you are ready to put it out.)*

After they had the bucket and shovel nearby, they lit the fire. But after a while, it started to go out. They were reaching toward the lantern fuel to pour it on the fire... *("Oh, no—not that!" You can't do that. Never use liquid flammable substances around a fire. It might make the fire flame up and burn somebody.)*

Finally, the fire was burning correctly, but it would be some time before the coals were ready for cooking. One of the boys grabbed a stick from the fire and began writing his name in smoke in the air. *("Oh, no—not that!" You can't do that. What goes in the fire, stays in the fire.)*

As the fire burned down, one of the boys decided to see whether he could jump over it. *("Oh, no—not that!" You can't do that. No running or playing near the fire.)*

The fire burned down, the boys cooked and ate their foil dinners, and things quieted down. The adults breathed a sigh of relief. It looked like everything was going to be OK and that the boys had learned their lessons.

After dinner, the adults stoked up the fire again and had a wonderful campfire—singing songs and telling stories and, as the flames grew low again, giving the boys something to think about. When it was time for bed, the boys wanted to put the fire out. They poured the bucket of water on the fire and turned to go to bed... *("Oh, no—not that!" You can't do that. You must stir the fire and be sure that all the embers are out and cold to the touch.)*

With the fire out, completely out, the day was done and sleeping bags unrolled. Now the adults were sure that the boys knew that even though a fire is a wonderful thing with many uses, it must be treated carefully or it can become harmful.

CLANCY TO THE RESCUE

CLANCY: Feel your muscles, like a strong man.

HORSES: Slap thighs.

YELL: Shout "Hey, Guys!" with hands cupped around your mouth.

FIRE ENGINE: High-pitched siren sound.

BELL: Swing arm like a clapper, saying, "Clang-clang, clang."

HOSE: Shh-sh-sh sound like water from a hose.

STEAM: Hissing *s-s-s-s* sound.

NARRATOR: If you like HORSES, you would have enjoyed living back in the 1800s when HORSES pulled old-fashioned steam-type FIRE ENGINES. One of these FIRE ENGINES was driven by the a great hero, CLANCY. Yes sir! CLANCY was a real hero! Every day when there was no fire, he would take the HORSES out for exercise, trotting them up and down the streets. If children were playing along the way, CLANCY would always stop and let them pet the HORSES.

Sometimes, the fire alarms happened during the daytime, but sometimes they happened at night. When the alarm sounded at night, one person would YELL up to the firefighters above, and they would wake up and slide down the pole as fast as they could. Then they would run to the FIRE ENGINE where the STEAM was up, and away they would go to the fire, clanging the BELL, with CLANCY driving the HORSES.

One night most of the firefighters were in bed and the others were playing checkers when the alarm sounded. Where was the fire? At the mayor's big two-story house! Quick as a flash they were there. CLANCY stopped the HORSES and YELLED, "Keep the STEAM up, men!" They started the fire HOSE and began to squirt water on the fire.

CLANCY strained to see upstairs where the mayor and his wife were trapped. Flames were everywhere! CLANCY YELLED, "You'll have to jump!" The firefighters held a net out to cushion their fall. The mayor and his wife were afraid, but CLANCY encouraged them, and as the flames licked their heels, they jumped and came right down into the middle of the net.

The firefighters kept battling the fire. They put the HOSE on it and kept up the STEAM in the FIRE ENGINE. Before long, the fire was out, so they turned off the HOSE, got back on the FIRE ENGINE, and returned to the firehouse, clanging the BELL all the way. To CLANCY and the other firefighters, it was all in a day's work—but to the mayor and his wife, they were heroes.

THE HOUSE WHERE SANTA CLAUS LIVES

HOUSE: Hands over head in an inverted V.

SHED: Hands in front of chest in an inverted V.

SLED: Hands together in a waving motion from left to right.

REINDEER: Hands on sides of head, palms out.

PACK: Both hands over a shoulder as if carrying a pack.

LITTLE GIRLS: Females, young and old, stand.

LITTLE BOYS: Males, young and old, stand.

DOLL: Hands with palms together on cheek, with head slightly bent.

BOX: Both hands outline the three dimensions of a box.

LION: Extend both hands and give a deep growl.

SOLDIER: Stand at attention; give the Cub Scout salute.

TRAIN: Make a figure 8 with a hand.

SANTA CLAUS: Pat stomach with both hands and say "Ho, ho, ho."

NARRATOR: This is the HOUSE where SANTA CLAUS lives. This is the SHED behind the HOUSE where SANTA CLAUS lives.

This is the SLED that is kept in the SHED behind the HOUSE where SANTA CLAUS lives.

These are the REINDEER that pull the SLED that is kept in the SHED behind the HOUSE where SANTA CLAUS lives.

This is SANTA CLAUS who guides the REINDEER that pull the SLED that's kept in the SHED behind the HOUSE where SANTA CLAUS lives.

This is the PACK all filled with toys for good LITTLE GIRLS and good LITTLE BOYS that is carried by old SANTA CLAUS who guides the REINDEER that pull the SLED that is kept in the SHED behind the HOUSE where SANTA CLAUS lives.

This is the BOX that is kept in the PACK all filled with toys for good LITTLE GIRLS and good LITTLE BOYS that is carried by SANTA CLAUS who guides the REINDEER that pull the SLED that is kept in the SHED behind the HOUSE where SANTA CLAUS lives.

This is the DOLL that is in the BOX that is in the PACK all filled with toys for good LITTLE GIRLS and good LITTLE BOYS that is carried by SANTA CLAUS who guides the REINDEER that pull the SLED that is kept in the SHED behind the HOUSE where SANTA CLAUS lives.

This is the LION that frightened the DOLL that is in the BOX that is in the PACK all filled with toys for good LITTLE GIRLS and good LITTLE BOYS that is carried by SANTA CLAUS who guides the REINDEER that pull the SLED that is kept in the SHED behind the HOUSE where SANTA CLAUS lives.

This is the SOLDIER that captured the LION that frightened the DOLL that is in the BOX that is in the PACK all filled with toys for good LITTLE GIRLS and good LITTLE BOYS that is carried by SANTA CLAUS who guides the REINDEER that pull the SLED that is kept in the SHED behind the HOUSE where SANTA CLAUS lives.

This is the TRAIN that runs on the track and carries the SOLDIER forward and back, who captured the LION that frightened the DOLL that is in the BOX that is in the PACK all filled with toys for good LITTLE GIRLS and good LITTLE BOYS that is carried by SANTA CLAUS who guides the REINDEER that pull the SLED that is kept in the SHED behind the HOUSE where SANTA CLAUS lives.

THE BIG TURKEY HUNT

PILGRIM: *(Whistle)*

TURKEY: Gobble, gobble

FISH: Bubble, bubble

BEAR: Growl, growl

SQUIRREL: Chatter, chatter

BEE: Buzz, buzz

DUCK: Quack, quack

HUNT: *(All sounds at once)*

Once upon a time, there was a PILGRIM who decided to go out and HUNT for a TURKEY. As he walked along through the forest, he met a DUCK. The PILGRIM asked the DUCK, "Have you seen the TURKEY? I'm on a big HUNT for him." "No," the DUCK said, with a sly wink. So the PILGRIM marched along until he spied a SQUIRREL playing in the tree tops. "Good day, SQUIRREL," the PILGRIM said. "Have you seen the TURKEY? I'm on a big HUNT for him." "No, no," the SQUIRREL said, smiling behind his paw.

As the PILGRIM crossed the brook, he bent toward the water and saw a FISH swimming near the surface. "Oh, FISH," said he, "has the TURKEY been down to the water for a drink today?" "No, not for a long time," the FISH said, diving deep to hide his laughter. The poor PILGRIM continued down the shady path and suddenly came face to face with a big, brown BEAR. "Hello, B-B-BEAR," said the PILGRIM. "H-h-have you s-s-s-een the TURKEY? I'm on a big HUNT for him." "No," the BEAR said. "I don't even know what a TURKEY is." But he gave a rumbling laugh.

The PILGRIM was feeling quite depressed by now, for he thought that he would never find the TURKEY. Finally, he saw a BEE buzzing by. "Stop a minute, BEE," he said. "You fly just about everywhere. Is the TURKEY near? I'm on a big HUNT for him." "No," buzzed the BEE. "Nowhere around here," and he flew away, buzzing hard to hide his chuckles.

Soon the PILGRIM saw ahead of him a clump of bushes and small trees. As he neared it, there suddenly rang out of them the most deafening noise you ever heard! It was the most ferocious growl of the BEAR, the loudest buzz of the BEE, the biggest bubbles of the FISH, and the deepest gobble of the TURKEY. Mr. TURKEY had hidden himself In the midst or the thicket, and all of his animal friends had gathered together to try to scare the PILGRIM out of his boots and away from the TURKEY.

But the joke was on them, because guess what? All the PILGRIM had wanted to do was invite the TURKEY to help him eat his bountiful Thanksgiving harvest! As the poor misunderstood PILGRIM let out a loud yell and took off for home, all heard him exclaim as he went out of sight, "That's the last HUNT I'll go on—so good night, good night!"

Mixers, Icebreakers, and Pack Meeting Games

Getting a meeting off to a good start often depends on little things—the greeting at the door, the activity involving people as they arrive, or the opening song or icebreaker. These little things add sparkle and punch to meetings—and add to everyone's enjoyment. If you allow "ice" to form at the beginning of a meeting, you'll have to spend valuable time and effort thawing it out. Icebreakers help solve this problem.

Also important are mixers—activities that help visitors get acquainted with others and feel at ease in the meeting. Icebreakers and mixers are used for this purpose, and also for a change of pace during a meeting to prevent audience members from becoming restless or bored.

If your mixers have winners, you can recognize them early in the meeting with simple, inexpensive, humorous prizes or with applause stunts. Several examples of mixers and icebreakers follow.

Occasionally, you will want to lighten up a pack meeting with a game. This chapter also presents several that will help you do that.

NAME ACROSTICS

As people arrive, hand them a pencil and 4-by-6-inch card. Ask them to print their full name in capitals vertically at the left of the card. They move about, trying to find people whose last names begin with those letters. For variation, use the monthly theme or other word along the left of the card.

PAPER HEADS

As people arrive, give them a numbered slip, pin, pencil, card, and large paper bag. Each person pins the numbered slip on his/her chest, tears eye holes in the bag, slips it over his/her head, and moves about the room trying to recognize other people. Write the numbers and names on the card.

WHO ARE YOU?

This is a good icebreaker for a den meeting. Hang a sign on the door that reads, "Who are You?" The lower part of the sign, which can be changed, has the subject or theme for that meeting, such as planets, cars, birds, etc. As each boy arrives, he must say, "Today, I am Mars" (or a Ford, or a bluebird, depending on the subject).

WHAT'S MY NAME?

As people arrive at a pack meeting, pin the name of a person or object on their backs. For a circus theme, it could be a circus performer or animal (clown, tall man, lion, etc.). For a citizenship theme, it could be the name of a president or politician (George Washington, the name of your mayor, etc.). People move around the room, asking other people questions about themselves to try to find out who they are. Answers must be "yes" or "no" only. When a person guesses his/her name, the card from the back is pinned on the lapel.

LAUGHING TUNES

Everyone in the audience laughs to a familiar tune, such as "Yankee Doodle" or "Row, Row, Row Your Boat." Use the same rhythm and tune; just sing "ha, ha" instead of the words.

YOU NEVER SAW IT

Tell the group, "I have something in my pocket that you never saw before, and you will never see again." Then take a peanut out of your pocket, crack the shell, show it to the audience—and then eat it. Say, "You never saw it before, and you'll never see it again!"

DARK, ISN'T IT?

Tell the audience that this is a test of intelligence, coordination, and the ability to follow directions. Have each person raise his/her left hand and point the left index finger to the right, parallel to the floor. Then have them raise the right hand and hold the right index finger on a level with the left finger, pointing in the opposite direction. Then raise the left hand 2 inches and lower the right hand 2 inches. Now ask them to close their eyes. After a moment, remark innocently, "Dark, isn't it?"

WHO'S WHO?

As people arrive at the meeting, hand them a sheet of paper with the following descriptions printed on it. They are to move around the room and find someone who fits each of the descriptions. That person writes his/her name beside the description. You may want to give a prize to the person who has the most blanks filled in.

- Someone who wears size 8½ shoes
- Someone with blue eyes
- Someone who has a birthday in January

- Someone who plays a musical instrument
- Someone with red hair
- Someone with a younger sister
- Someone who likes to eat liver
- Someone who speaks a foreign language
- Someone who was born in another country
- Someone who was a Cub Scout as a boy

By necessity, some of the descriptions must be answered by an adult, which will encourage boys and adults to interact.

SPELLING MIXER

Print a large letter on 5-by-8 cards—one letter for a card. Do not use the letters *J, K, Q, V, X* or *Z*. Make several cards with vowels on them. Have a card for each person in the group. Three adults act as judges.

On a signal, people hold up their cards and rush around to find two letters that will make a three-letter word when added to the card they are holding. The three people lock arms and race to the judge, who writes the word on the back of their cards. Then they separate and rush back to find two more letters. Continue the activity for 5 or 10 minutes. The person with the most words on his/her card wins.

GIANT SNEEZE

Divide the audience into three groups. Explain that some people believe that a good sneeze clears the mind. Each group rehearses one of the sounds:

"O-Hishie!"

"O-Hashie!"

"O-Hooshie!"

On a signal, everyone combines their sounds into one giant sneeze. The leader responds, "God bless you!"

STAND BY SIXES

Audience members—boys and adults—stand in a large open area. They respond as the leader shouts instructions: "Stand by sixes!" "Stand by threes!" "Stand by fours!" Everyone quickly forms groups of sixes, threes, fours, etc., and stand together with arms around each other's waist. People who can't find a group to join are eliminated from the game. The action is fast and exciting. Just as soon as groups are formed, the leader shouts another command. Eventually, most of the players will be eliminated. When there is only one group of six left, the command "Stand by fours!" will eliminate two more players, and so on.

PRISONER'S ESCAPE

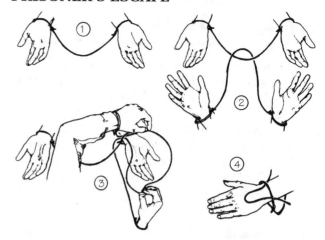

This is a good icebreaker for a den or pack meeting. As people arrive, tie a piece of string around the wrists of one person; loop another piece of string over that person's string and tie the ends to another person's wrists. They are now tied together. Challenge them to get away without breaking a string or untying any knots. The solution is to push the center of one string through the loop on the inside of the other person's wrist, bring this new loop back over that person's hand, and draw it back through the wrist loop. (See the illustrations.)

THE MOON IS BIG AND ROUND

This is a good campfire icebreaker. The leader says: "The moon is big and round. It has two eyes, a nose, and a mouth." As he/she says these words, he/she makes a sweeping circle with the left hand to indicate that the moon is big and round, makes dots in the air with the forefinger for the eyes and nose, and makes a small semicircular motion for the mouth. Then the leader invites the audience to do *exactly* the same thing. Most everyone will fail and wonder why. The secret is that the motions are made with the left hand. Most people will use their right.

LUCKY HANDSHAKE

Three or four people are secretly given pennies before the meeting. As people arrive, they are encouraged to shake hands with everyone else. The tenth person to shake hands with someone holding a penny receives the penny. This goes on for a predetermined time; then those holding pennies get to keep them.

POCKETS

Ask people to compare the contents of their pockets, discovering who has pocket items in common. Try to determine what the most common pocket item is.

Cheers and Applause Stunts

Applause stunts are short, snappy, and lots of fun for both boys and adults. They are a good way to involve the audience and are often used to recognize a person or den for an accomplishment. A den or pack may have its favorite applauses and cheers that they use frequently. Many cheers and applauses fit monthly themes. Boys can also create their own cheers and applauses. (Always emphasize the importance of keeping them positive.) Following are some examples.

Applaud and Cheer: Announce to the group that when you raise your right hand, everyone is to applaud. When you raise your left hand, everyone is to cheer. When you raise both hands, they are to applaud and cheer. You can vary this by telling them that the higher you raise your hand, the louder they should applaud and/or cheer. As you lower your hand, the volume goes down.

Baseball Applause: Get out your pretend bat, take a couple of practice swings, pretend to throw a ball up into the air, swing at the ball, and yell, "It's a home run!"

Bravissimo Applause:

Bravo, bravo, bravo, bravissimo,
Bravo, bravo, jolly well done!
Bravo, bravissimo, bravo, bravissimo,
Bravo, bravissimo, jolly well done!

A Big Hand: The leader says, "Let's give them a big hand!" Everyone holds up one hand with the palm open. But they say nothing!

Bow and Arrow Applause: Pretend you have a bow and quiver of arrows. Take an arrow from the quiver, place it in the bow, pretend to draw back the bowstring, aim, and let the bowstring go. Watch as the arrow flies through the air, and then yell, "A bull's-eye!"

Champion Applause: To the count of four, do the following: stomp, stomp, clap, pause. To the beat say, "We do, we do, thank you!"

Cheese Grater Applause: Pick up your cheese grater and a chunk of cheese. Pretend to pass the cheese over the grater, each time yelling, "Grate, grate, grate!"

Compass Applause: Take your compass out of your pocket. Hold it in front of you to get your bearings. With your other hand, point to the person/group you are recognizing and shout, "Way to go!"

Cookie Applause: Hold your pretend cookie and then take a bite. Rub your tummy in a circular motion while saying, "Yum, yum!"

Cow Chorus Cheer (for a humorous song/skit): "Very a-MOOOOO-sing!"

Coyote Applause: The group stands, cups their hands around their mouths, and says, "Yip, yip, yippeeee!"

Flapjack Applause: Pretend to push a spatula under a pancake. Then throw it up in the air and nod three times as if watching the flapjack flip in the air; catch it on the spatula as you bring your other hand down with a loud clap.

Frankfurter Applause: Hold up a frankfurter on a bun, squeeze on ketchup, take a big bite. Then say: "Hot dog! That was good!"

Giant Beehive Cheer: The group buzzes like a hive of bees. When the leader raises a hand, the volume increases. When the hand is lowered, the volume decreases.

Giraffe Applause: Stand on tiptoes and yell, "Outta sight!"

Good Turn Applause: Stand up and turn around in circles as you applaud.

Grand Salute Applause: Stamp your feet four counts, slap your knees four counts, clap your hands four counts, and then stand and give a salute.

Handkerchief Applause: Throw a handkerchief into the air, telling the audience to applaud until you catch it or it falls to the floor. Vary the length of applause—long throw, short, no throw at all. You can also do this with a ball, a neckerchief, or other item.

Ice Cube Applause: Pick up an ice cube and say, "C-O-O-O-O-L!"

Ice Water Applause: Pretend to wipe sweat from your brow with a bandanna. Pick up a pitcher and pour yourself a glass of ice water. Throw your head back as you drink the water and then say, "Ahh…that was cool!"

Knee Slapping Applause: Slap your knees.

Lion Applause: "A R-O-A-R-R-R-R-I-N-G success!"

Motorcycle Applause: Raise your foot and kick down three times. Make a noise like a sputtering motor. Hold your hands out as if gripping handlebars. On the third try, the engine starts. Say, "Varr-oo-omm!"

Owl Applause (for a humorous skit or song): Open your eyes as wide as possible, flap your arms as if they were wings, and say, "What a hoot, hoot, hoot!"

Paper Bag Applause: Make motions to simulate opening a paper bag, forming a neck, and blowing it up; then pop it, saying, "Pop!"

Popcorn Applause: Close one hand and cover it with the other hand. Let the closed hand "grow" larger as the other hand moves up. Then spring your fingers open and say, "Pop! Pop! Pop!" quickly.

Rainstorm Applause: Extend one hand palm up. Using your other hand, start by tapping one finger at a time, then adding the number of fingers you tap, increasing the sound to simulate a rainstorm starting and building to all hands clapping. Then decrease the storm by slowing down the action one finger at a time.

Roller Coaster Applause: Lean back in your chair, holding onto an imaginary bar, making an "Achh-chh-chh" sound. As the roller coaster reaches the top of the hill, throw your arms up into the air and yell, "Wheeee!"

Round of Applause: Audience members clap while moving their hands in a large circular, clockwise motion.

Rudolph Applause: Put your thumbs to your head with the fingers pointing up to form "antlers." Wrinkle your nose and say, "Blink, blink, blink!"

Seal of Approval Applause: Put your elbows together, open and close your forearms and hands, and bark a high-pitched "Arf, Arf, Arf!"

Soda Cheer: Pretend to pull the tab from a soda can, gulp it down, and then say, "Give me more, more, more!"

Soup Applause: Pick up a spoon and slurp a spoonful of soup. Rub your tummy and say, "Mmmmm, Mmmmmm, good!"

Stamp of Approval 1: Pound your left fist on your right palm several times rapidly.

Stamp of Approval 2: Throw a handkerchief into the air. Audience members stamp their feet until it hits the ground.

Stirring Round of Applause: Clap your hands in a BIG circle, waist level, as if you were stirring or mixing a big pot.

Tank Applause: Put your hand over your eyes as if looking off into the distance and say, "Tanks, tanks, tanks a lot!"

The Wave Applause: For a SWELL job! People on the end of each row stand up, raise their arms, and promptly sit back down. As the first person stands, the person next to him/her follows suit with the same action, and so on down the line. When "the wave" reaches the last person, it can come back the other way, beginning with the person next to him/her.

Thumbs Up Applause: Hold your hand in front of you. Make a fist, hold your thumb up, and say, "Great job!"

Tiger Applause: "That was G-R-R-R-R-R-E-A-T!"

Whittling Stick Applause: Pick a tall stick up off the ground, take out your pocket knife, and start making notches in the stick, going higher and higher. When you get as far as you can reach, say "Top notch!"

Zebra Applause: "Zee-bra, zee-bra, ZEEEEEEE-BEST!"

DEN YELLS

Den yells help build den spirit and enthusiasm and also can help boys let off steam at den and pack meetings.

Den yells are usually simple and rhythmic and often end on a word or phrase that the boys can shout. You can adapt many high school and college cheers for den yells. When the boys help develop the den yell, they feel it is "theirs" and will enjoy using it even more. Here are some sample den yells:

Den 1! Den 1!
Is there a better den? None!
What den has the most fun? One!
Den 1! Den 1!

We'll do our best for the gold and blue!
We ARE the best! Den 2! Den 2!

We're the Cub Scouts from Den 3,
and no Cubs could be prouder!
If you can't hear us now, we'll yell a little louder!
(Repeat twice, louder each time.)

One, two, three, four,
Which den do you cheer for?

Which den can you hear more?
Den 4! Den 4! Den 4!

Which den is really alive?
Which den has all the drive?
Den 5! Den 5!

We're the den that is alive!
We're the den that has the drive!
Den 5! Den 5!

T-H-R-E-E—
The den that's best for you and me!
Watch us go and you will see!
It's T-H-R-E-E!
Den 3! Den 3!

Puppets

Puppetry is an ancient art that appeals to boys of all ages, perhaps more to boys of Cub Scout age than any other. No one knows when or where puppets first appeared. They have been found in Egyptian tombs, in China, and in India in very early history. They were used widely during the Middle Ages for teaching Bible stories. Puppets have acted before royalty. They have been made and enjoyed by scholars, poets, and artists.

You can use puppets in connection with several achievements and electives and with many of the monthly themes. Webelos Scouts may expand their knowledge of puppetry while earning the Showman activity badge.

WHY PUPPETS?

Puppetry can help Cub Scouts to

- Improve enunciation and voice projection.
- Develop coordination and a sense of timing.
- Gain self-confidence and personal satisfaction.
- Release fears and frustrations in an acceptable way.
- Recognize the importance of teamwork and cooperation.
- Develop creativity.
- Improve listening habits.
- Learn lessons of everyday living, such as getting along with others and good sportsmanship.
- Learn and appreciate the effects of light, sound, and movement.
- Experience the enjoyment of entertaining others.

In addition, teachers and leaders of boys with special needs find puppets useful in helping boys to overcome stuttering and emotional inhibitions, relieve tensions, strengthen weak muscles, and develop coordination.

TIPS FOR PUPPETEERS

Let the boys decide on the play they wish to present and the type of puppets they will use. They can plan the dialogue themselves and say their lines informally, even if it comes out a little differently each time. It is difficult for some boys to manipulate a puppet and recite memorized lines at the same time. An alternative is to have a reader backstage so the boys only have to operate the puppets.

- Keep the theater and the puppets in proper scale. Small puppets on a big stage lose their appeal.
- Be sure that all puppeteers have plenty of room behind the scenes.

- Plan frequent exits and entrances of puppets to hold interest and to avoid having too many puppets on the stage at one time.
- Keep actions clear, simple, and exaggerated. An excited puppet should be *wildly* excited, whereas a tired puppet should groan and sag so wearily that the audience knows immediately how tired it is.
- The puppet should speak and act according to the kind of person, animal, or object it represents.
- Sometimes it's good for puppets to speak aloud to themselves as they go about their actions. For example, a puppet might say while looking for something, "I'll look under this tree for the treasure."
- Avoid hiding one puppet behind another.
- Hold the puppets vertically.
- Let the puppets walk off the stage, not sink out of sight.
- Remember to wait for laughs to die down so that the audience doesn't miss any lines.
- Use music during the production, if possible.
- *Keep It Simple, Make It Fun (KISMIF).*

PUPPET PLAYWRITING

It is usually best to decide on a story or situation to act out and let the boys develop their own lines, rather than having a written script with dialogue. They may run into difficulty if they try to read a script or remember lines while they are operating puppets.

- A simple comic story is best for Cub Scout–age boys. Consider adapting a familiar children's story for a puppet play.
- Exaggerated actions and slapstick comedy are fun for both the audience and the puppeteers. A few misplaced lines or mistaken actions may help rather than hinder the play.
- Lots of grunting, groaning, sniffing, wheezing, and coughing adds to the value of a funny play.
- Music adds much to a play. It sets the mood for the characters and adds a professional touch. A CD player or tape recorder will come in handy.

When making assignments for your puppet play, select someone to act as stage manager to be responsible for the props, scenery, music, and lighting. This could be the den chief, one of the Cub Scouts, or a parent.

Follow these simple steps in developing your puppet play:

1. Read the play or story carefully. Pick out the important parts—or develop your own story.
2. With the boys' help, develop an outline.

3. Keep the play short—3 to 5 minutes at the most.

4. Keep the puppets in mind. How many will there be? Where do they fit into each scene? What will they be doing and saying?

5. Plan entrances and exits carefully, so the puppeteers won't be climbing over each other.

6. Keep dialogue short and simple, or use a reader offstage.

7. In adapting a play, change the number of characters to fit the number of boys in the den by giving some boys more or fewer lines.

Choose scenes that

• Sustain action and further the plot.

• Build up an important character.

• Have comedic possibilities.

• Add suspense.

• Offer unusual effects, such as with scenery or lighting.

• Have fast action and good dialogue.

HAND PUPPET STAGES AND THEATERS

Hand puppet theaters may be as simple or complex as desired, but for Cub Scout–age boys, a simple stage is best. The simplest stage consists of a table set on edge. A cardboard carton with a window cut in one side works well also. A large piece of foam board with an opening for the puppets is an excellent stage.

You can use many things as temporary puppet stages so the boys can practice during den meetings. Several hand-puppet stages are described and illustrated here.

Box Theater

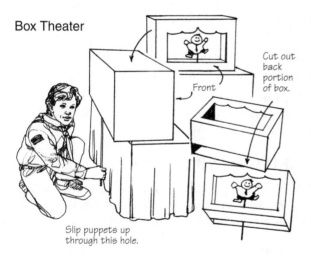

Cut out back portion of box.

Front

Slip puppets up through this hole.

Table Stage

Blanket Theater

• A doorway can serve as a temporary puppet stage. Hang a twin-sized bed sheet from a curtain tension rod, adjusting its height so boys can stand behind the sheet and operate the puppets above their heads.

• Make a simple portable stage by putting together several pieces of display posterboard (three panels like the ones used in science fairs). You can place this stage on a table or the floor, and boys can use their imaginations to decorate the front.

SCENERY FOR PUPPET PLAYS

Scenery not only makes a puppet play more believable, it also helps set the time and place of the story. It can be as simple as a single flower, or as complex as a jungle. It is best, however, to use only enough scenery to *suggest* the setting, letting the audience imagine the details. Elaborate scenery may detract from the puppets.

Backdrops are recommended, and often a solid-color backdrop is all you need. Scenes can also be painted on backdrops, or scenery pieces cut out and pinned on them. Cloth or paper backdrops are easily rolled up for storing or transporting.

When making a backdrop, it is best to first draw a miniature sketch. Then make an enlarged pattern of the desired size and transfer it to the backdrop. When using color on backdrops, keep in mind the mood of the play, the color of the puppet costumes, and the lighting.

The simplest way to add scenery to your play is to cut small scenery pieces—such as trees, bushes, fences, boats, houses, tables, chairs, or even bathtubs—out of cardboard and attach them to a dowel or stick. Boys can hold a piece of scenery with one hand and their puppet with the other.

Prop Board

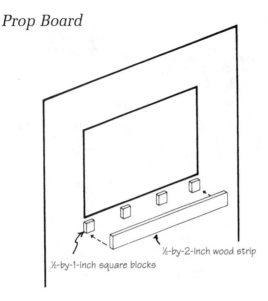

½-by-1-inch square blocks

½-by-2-inch wood strip

This device holds furniture, scenery, and other props on the stage without a platform. Glue and nail four ½-by-1-inch square blocks to the inside of the crosspiece at the bottom of your stage opening. To these, attach a ½-by-2-inch wood strip the length of the opening. This makes a channel the entire width of the stage opening. The props will slide into and out of place quickly for scenery changes, or the puppets can pick up, carry, and set down a variety of objects on the prop board.

LIGHTING FOR PUPPET PLAYS

Darkening a room and illuminating the puppets with spotlights or stage lights helps the audience see the show and adds a theatrical atmosphere. Let boys experiment with lighting in different ways and from different angles—above, below, in front, and to the sides of the puppet stage opening—to find out which type of lighting throws unwanted shadows and which kind gives the desired illumination. The best way to learn how to use lighting properly is by trial and error, during practice, before the actual show. Strong flashlights, goose-necked lamps, light sockets with clamps, electric lanterns, shaded bulbs, light bars, and small spotlights can all be good sources of lighting for puppet plays.

You can obtain special lighting effects by using black lights, colored cellophane over lights, dimmer switches, flickering Christmas lights, etc. Make housings for lights from tin cans.

Remember that the lights must be on the front of the stage and directed toward the puppets. Too much light will wipe out the puppets' features. They will lose their shape and look flat. Also remember that lights should not be set so they shine in the eyes of the audience members.

Make sure that all light cords are located where no one will trip over them. If cords are on the floor, tape them down.

SPECIAL EFFECTS FOR PUPPET PLAYS

Sound effects and other special effects make a puppet production more lively and vivid. The audience always remembers the scene where something unusual happened, such as when the soup burned and smoke billowed everywhere.

Boys will enjoy inventing ways to make special effects for puppet plays. Use a cassette recorder to record needed sounds such as street noises and animal sounds. In addition to the suggestions that follow, see the sound effects described in "Skits and Costumes" below.

Smoke, Steam, Fog, Magic Dust: Blow excess powder off a powder puff.

Snow: Throw white confetti.

Mist, Rain: Spray water from an atomizer bottle.

Wind: Blow a fan on the set.

Lightning: Flick lights off and on quickly, or use a camera flash.

Door Slam: Slam two books together.

Crickets Chirping: Run a fingernail over a small piece of fine-toothed comb (near a microphone, if available).

Rustling in Underbrush: Crush broom straws (near a microphone, if available).

Gurgling Stream or Boiling Liquid: Put a straw in a cup of water and blow hard (near a microphone, if available).

Fire: Create dancing shadows by placing something that moves in front of a red light.

Wilting Flower: Make a flower stem from a curtain spring; insert a rod and then, when wilting is to happen, pull the rod out.

MAKING HAND PUPPETS

Most of the puppets Cub Scout–age boys will use will be *hand puppets*, which are worn on the hand and manipulated by one finger that guides the head and two other fingers that guide the puppet's hands. Boys will enjoy making their own hand puppets.

Materials

Before starting to construct puppets or build scenery or props, it helps to be familiar with a wide range of possible construction materials. Have a place for organizing and storing odds and ends. The list below is just a beginning of items that you might collect.

- Old bottle brushes, scouring pads, steel wool, fly swatters, wooden and plastic spoons, hair curlers.
- Broom handles, dowels, wooden craft sticks, coat hangers, umbrella parts, bicycle spokes, chopsticks.
- Plastic containers, small boxes such as egg cartons, plastic and wood baskets and trays, rubber balls, table tennis balls, tennis balls.
- Buttons, beads, sequins, glitter, costume jewelry, bits of glass.
- Corks, sponges, lids and caps, spools, weights, fishing floats.
- Socks, stockings, gloves and mittens, felt and other fabric scraps, cotton, materials for stuffing, such as old nylon stockings.
- Lace, fringe, pom-poms, trimmings, fur pieces, feathers, raffia, ribbon, string, shoelaces, yarn, rope.
- Pipe cleaners, chenille, toothpicks, wire, tinsel.
- Plastic foam balls and pieces, wood scraps, sponges, leather scraps.
- Doll clothes, dollhouse furnishings, stuffed toys.
- Construction paper, crepe paper, cardboard, cellophane, paper plates, bags and cups, cardboard and plastic tubes.

Heads

More than any other part of the puppet, the head must express personality. Because the audience won't notice small details, this should be done simply. It is usually best to keep the facial expression neutral and let the voice and movements of the puppet show emotions. If you use removable features, however, you can change the facial expression as often as desired.

The puppet head should be no smaller than one-sixth the body size. Try puppet heads made from paper plates, paper cups, fly swatters, blocks of wood, boxes, craft sticks, and plastic containers. Here are some other ideas for puppet heads:

- **Ball or Egg:** Use a plastic foam ball, rubber ball, or plastic egg shape.
- **Papier-Mâché:** Cover a crinkled-up newspaper ball, plastic foam ball, balloon, or a clay model with papier-mâché.
- **Sock:** Stuff a sock and decorate it, or pull it over another shape such as a ball or plastic bottle.
- **Sponge:** Shape sponges with scissors.

- **Polyfoam:** Cut and form ½- or ¾-inch sheets into any shape; use heavy-duty glue or contact cement to join.
- **Cloth:** Use felt, muslin, and fake fur. Stuff to shape.

Consider how the puppet's head will be attached to its body. In some cases a rod or finger hole can be poked into the head; in others, a sturdy cardboard tube neck band should be attached to permit good control of the puppet's head.

Some puppet heads must be painted; others, because of the material from which they are made, can be used as is. To make skin tones, vary the amount of white, red, brown, black, and yellow paint to get the desired results. After the base coat dries, touch up the cheeks and lips with pink. Use gray or blue for eye shadow. Some paint will need an overcoat of shellac, varnish, or clear nail polish for protection.

Hair and Eyes

The most effective puppets have simple, clearly defined, and exaggerated features. The size and position of the features will help develop the character of the puppet. Look at the sample eyes and facial hair in the illustration and imagine the different characters each might express.

Hair in the form of wigs, beards, mustaches, and eyebrows can be pinned, taped, glued, stapled, or sewn onto a puppet head. Narrow streamers of crepe paper, strips of scrub pads and steel wool, fur pieces, wood shavings, feathers, string, and yarn can all be used for hair, depending on the effect you want.

Nothing helps a puppet's face and character more than sparkling eyes. Use a touch of glitter, the head of a pin or tack, a sequin, or a shiny button for the puppet's pupils. Also make eyes from stick-on dots available in various sizes and colors at office supply stores, or cut them from paper or felt. You can use a black felt-tip pen to make a dot for the pupil.

For some puppets, loosely attached moveable plastic eyes will be effective. These are available at hobby and craft stores. Eyes made from buttons and table tennis balls can be attached so they will move when the puppet moves.

Pinned-on eyes, eyebrows, and mouths can be changed during a puppet performance to show different expressions.

Hands/Paws

Hands or paws add to the versatility of the puppet if they allow the puppet to pick up items. Make hands from leather, wood, heavy cardboard, felt, or other fabric. They can be an extension of the costume sleeve or made separately and attached. Some puppet hands are stuffed, others aren't. Above all, like the facial features, the hands or paws should be exaggerated.

Costumes and Bodies

You can make puppets of everything—people, animals, a musical instrument, a tool, or even a tooth! The simplest hand puppets have a handkerchief, piece of shirtsleeve, or other piece of cloth for a costume. You can also use baby or doll clothes. You can use one basic costume along with interchangeable heads and removable accessories.

Remember these important points about puppet costumes:

- Make the costume long enough to extend to the end of the puppeteer's forearm.
- Use a material that hangs well when the puppet is still and that moves easily without restricting the puppeteer's hands.
- Select a texture and color that suits the puppet's personality.
- Hats, vests, sashes, scarves, bandannas, and eyeglasses can be added and removed.

OPERATING HAND PUPPETS

Operating puppets is called *manipulation*. The basic movements are simple. Puppets can nod, shake or scratch their heads, clap, bow, twist, sit down, walk, jump, limp, climb, dance, and perform many other actions.

Hand Positions

Two basic ways of holding your hand inside a puppet are shown here. The first position gives the puppet arms a longer reach and better grip on props, but it tends to tilt the puppet to one side. The second position results in better balance, but the little finger may restrict the arm movement and make it more difficult to hold props. The first position is usually best for small hands.

Puppet Actions

It is important to move puppets every time they speak or react to what another puppet says and keep them still the rest of the time. If you move your puppet too much or at the wrong time, the movements will detract from other puppets and make your puppet's own movements less effective.

The best way to learn how to manipulate a puppet is by going through the various movements in front of a mirror. Try some of the following:

Walking: Puppets shouldn't pop out of thin air but should enter at the side of the stage or come upstairs or downstairs in view of the audience. Raise and lower the entire arm slightly, and at the same time, turn the wrist from left to right. Make your wrist motion slower or faster depending on how fast you want your puppet to walk. Try to avoid jerky movements.

Talking: If the mouth is moveable, it is simple to indicate talking. Otherwise, move the head up and down rhythmically when the puppet is talking. Like people, puppets should look at whomever they are speaking to.

Listening: Puppets should have good listening manners, again like people, and face the puppet that is speaking.

Sitting: Bend the wrist forward and drop your arm a little. This pushes the back of the puppet out and looks as if he or she is about to sit down.

Climbing: Slowly lower whatever the puppet is climbing—tree, beanstalk, fence, ladder—while the puppet remains at stage level. Its only movement would be grasping the tree branches or beanstalk at intervals.

Piano Playing: Use a toy piano that has been muffled so that it doesn't make any sound. The puppet pretends to play the piano as a tape recording plays offstage.

Dancing: Two puppets can dance together or make kicking movements by using the index finger of the opposite hand to make kicks underneath a full costume.

Clapping Hands: Bring the thumb and second finger together. Practice touching the puppet's mouth, ears, and forehead with its hand.

Kneeling: Drop your arm down and allow the legs or skirt of the costume to fold under the puppet.

Standing: Let the puppet place its hands on a nearby table or chair and pull itself erect.

Lying Down: Drop the puppet to a kneeling position and place the puppet hand on stage, as if bracing itself. Turn your wrist slowly around until the puppet is on its back. Move your entire hand as if the puppet is settling itself in bed or on the floor.

Yawning: Place the puppet's hand over its mouth.

Picking Up: Grasp the object firmly between the fingers operating the puppet's hands. To pick up an object, first look at it, then touch it, and finally pick it up.

A puppet can show feelings and personality by the tone of voice you use or through its actions. Here are some emotions and the actions that might show the emotions:

- **Excited:** Clasping hands and jumping up and down
- **Sad:** Putting hand to the face and drooping the head
- **Angry:** Banging hands or clenching them together; beating the head with a hand
- **Afraid:** Trembling and clasping the hands to the body
- **Tired:** Making slow, languid movements
- **Old:** Making shaky, slow movements

Just for fun, let the boys try these actions with their puppets:

- Marching to music
- Leading an orchestra
- Sweeping or scrubbing a floor
- Stacking blocks
- Washing dishes
- Hopping like a rabbit
- Coughing, hiccuping, sneezing
- Walking with a limp

TYPES OF HAND PUPPETS

Several types of hand puppets are suitable for Cub Scout–age boys, including those made from paper bags, socks, cardboard cylinders, and boxes. Jointed puppets, or *marionettes,* require more detailed construction and operation and are not covered here.

Talking Paper Bag Puppet

Paper bag puppets are the easiest, least expensive, and fastest type of puppets for Cub Scouts to make. Use small paper bags (lunch bag size). You'll need crayons, felt-tip pens or paint, scissors, and a pencil to make faces and decorate them. You can also use additional materials, such as felt, construction paper, yarn, buttons, etc.

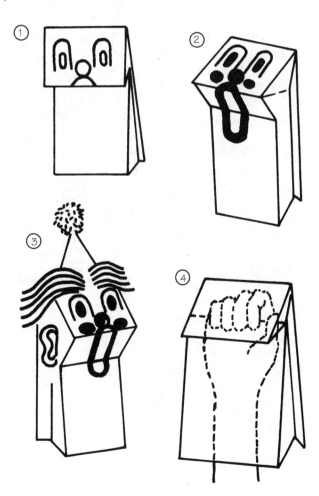

Leave the bag folded (with the fold on top) and mark lightly where the features will go. The eyes, nose, and top of the mouth should be on the bottom of the bag; the bottom of mouth, on the front of the bag, as shown. Glue on or decorate with hair, ears, clothing, etc. Manipulate the puppet by placing your hand in the bag with your fingers over the fold in the bottom. Open and close your hand to make the puppet talk or sing.

You can use this same technique to make a puppet that opens and closes its eyes.

Flap down   Flap up

Stuffed Bag Puppet

1. Stuff a small paper bag with newspaper to form the head. Tie the head to a small dowel or rod. Add features as desired—eyes, nose, mouth, ears, hair, etc.

2. Make a costume from a square of fabric. Make a hole in the center so you can slide the dowel with the head into the fabric. Tie or glue the fabric just under the puppet's head.

3. Hold the puppet dowel in your hand to find the proper places to make slits in the fabric for your thumb and index finger to slip through.

4. Manipulate the puppet by holding the dowel with three fingers and slipping your thumb and index finger through the slits to act as the puppets hands.

Sock Puppets

Two types of sock puppets are shown here—the first where the entire sock is used to form an elongated animal head, and the second where only the heel or toe of a sock is stuffed to form a round puppet head. Any old sock will do, but a fleecy or wool one will work best.

Use the Entire Sock

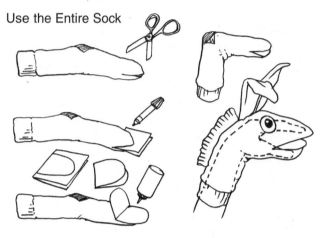

1. Spread the sock out flat so the heel is facing up. Cut around the edge of the toe and back, about 2 inches, as shown.

2. Use a small piece of red, pink, or orange felt or cloth, folded in half, for the inside of the mouth. Insert the cloth in the open part of the sock toe so that the folded edge fits all the way back against the edge of the opening. Mark the cloth to fit, and then cut it to the proper shape. Turn the sock wrong side out and sew or glue the red cloth inside the opening. When the glue is dry, turn the sock right side out.

3. Glue or sew on features. Glue a pad of cotton on the inside heel of the sock to give shape to the animal's head.

4. Operate the puppet with the thumb in the lower lip and all the fingers in the upper lip.

Use the Heel or Toe

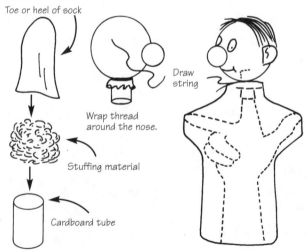

Toe or heel of sock

Wrap thread around the nose.

Draw string

Stuffing material

Cardboard tube

1. Make a cardboard tube ¾ inch across and 2 inches long. Fasten with tape.

2. Cut the heel or toe from an old sock (white or tan is usually the best color). Place a ball of stuffing material (cotton, piece of nylon stocking, or tissue paper) over the end of the cardboard tube and slip the sock toe or heel over the stuffing. Pull it down and tie securely near the bottom end of the tube.

3. Make a nose by pulling out a small piece of the sock and stuffing and tying it with a strong thread. Or you can glue on buttons or beads for the nose, eyes, and ears.

4. Make a puppet costume out of fabric and attach it to the head with a draw string. Put your finger in the cardboard tube to manipulate the head, and make arms as shown with your fingers.

Cardboard Box Puppets

Boxes are a good material for making puppets. For small puppets, use gelatin boxes; for large ones, cereal boxes work well. But any box can be a puppet.

Draw your features on with felt-tip pens, paint them on, or glue on felt or paper cutouts. If boxes have a waxy surface, add a small amount of liquid soap to tempera before painting them. Scratch the surface lightly before gluing on trim. Or cover the boxes with construction paper or adhesive-backed paper.

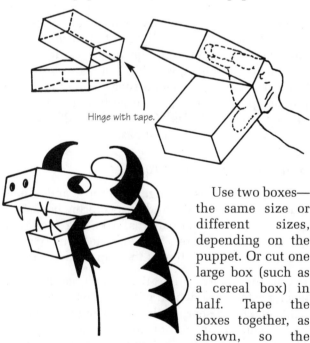

Hinge with tape.

Use two boxes—the same size or different sizes, depending on the puppet. Or cut one large box (such as a cereal box) in half. Tape the boxes together, as shown, so the backside of the puppet is open and hinged. Add features and decorate as desired. Operate by inserting the thumb in the lower box and fingers in the upper box. You can add a fabric skirt to cover the puppeteer's hand.

Cardboard Cylinder Puppets

Cotton   Stick   Cardboard   Yarn   Hand puppet position

These small puppets, made from toilet tissue cores, are best suited to a small tabletop theater. Cut the cardboard core to the desired length. Cover the top with construction paper or crepe paper and decorate or paint as desired. Glue on a fabric skirt or costume to cover the puppeteer's hand. To operate, insert two fingers in the bottom of the core, or tape a stick on the back of the puppet for the operator to hold.

Plastic Foam Cup Puppets

Use a whole cup to make the puppet's head, cutting the cup lengthwise to make the upper and lower parts of the head. (The upper section should be a little bigger than the lower section.) Cut mouth linings to fit from cardboard and glue them in place, as

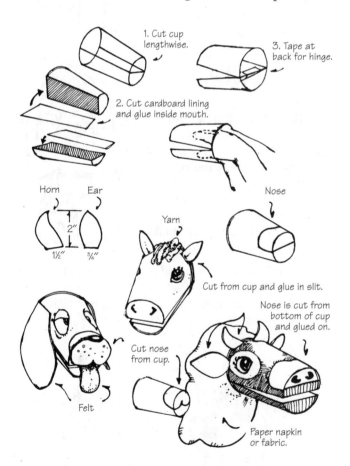

1. Cut cup lengthwise.
2. Cut cardboard lining and glue inside mouth.
3. Tape at back for hinge.
Horn   Ear   2"   1½"   ¾"
Yarn   Nose
Cut from cup and glue in slit.
Nose is cut from bottom of cup and glued on.
Cut nose from cup.
Felt
Paper napkin or fabric.

shown. (Tape will hold these in place until the glue dries.) Tape the upper and lower parts together at the back, making a hinge. Paint and decorate as desired.

For the body, cut a hole in the center of a paper napkin or square of fabric. Slip the napkin or fabric over the hand and forearm, and then put the puppet head on the hand. To operate, insert your fingers in the top of the head and your thumb in the bottom part.

Glove and Mitten Puppets

Making puppets out of worn-out or outgrown gloves and mittens is a good way to put them to use.

Mitten Mutt. Sew or glue button eyes and felt ears on an old mitten as shown. When you are wearing the mitten, your thumb is the lower jaw and the rest of your fingers the upper jaw of your mitten mutt. Move your fingers to make your mutt talk or bark.

Mitten Duck Puppet. Stuff a mitten with stuffing material. Turn the mitten so the thumb becomes a beak. Glue on button eyes. Tie a string or ribbon around the duck's neck. To manipulate, put your index finger into the head and make a fist with your other fingers.

Glove Bunny. Turn an old glove inside out. Cut off the index and smallest finger (but save to use as feet) and sew up the openings. Turn the glove right side out, except for the thumb. Leave it turned inside for

the bunny's mouth. Glue on button eyes and a felt nose and pipe cleaners or broom straws for whiskers. A second glove is the bunny's body. Stuff the two fingers cut from the first glove and sew them onto the bottom of this glove for the bunny's feet. To manipulate your glove bunny, put the body glove on your hand and put three fingers in the bunny's head.

Shadow Puppets

Shadow puppets are easy to make, fun to use, and lend themselves to the telling of tall stories. Figures and scenery are cut from lightweight cardboard and held next to a screen, which is lighted from the rear. The story can be narrated offstage while the shadow puppets perform, or they can perform to a song that the boys sing, such as "Old MacDonald's Farm" or "The Twelve Days of Christmas."

Shadow Puppet Figures

Choose patterns for figures, props, and scenery that will fit the story. Children's coloring books are a good source for such patterns. About 12 inches is a good height for figures. You don't need many details because only the outline of the puppet will show.

Cut the figures from lightweight cardboard or black posterboard, which will eliminate all reflected light, making a sharper shadow. Mount each cutout on the end of a pencil or dowel with a thumbtack. The shadow puppet is a rigid figure, held straight up against the screen by the handle at its base.

Shadow puppet figures grow large or small as they move toward and away from the screen. They can vanish quickly or make an instantaneous appearance on the screen. They can be transformed from humans to animals or the reverse by pulling one puppet back out of the light while another is put in its place. You can use various types of hinges at body joints to enable them to move independently. Attach another dowel or rod to each limb to control its movement.

Scenery can be changed quickly and easily. A car, bicycle, wagon, or other prop can be pushed or pulled across the screen. Scenery that won't be moved during the show can be attached to the screen with cellophane tape or fitted between the frame and screen.

Shadow Puppet Screen

The screen material can be white cotton sheeting, glazed chintz, or oiled paper (butcher paper or newsprint oiled with linseed oil or vegetable oil, which makes the screen translucent). Attach the material to a light wood frame made from 1-by-2-inch lumber or to a large cardboard carton with a window cut in one side. For 12-inch puppets, the screen should measure about 24 by 26 inches. Hang a curtain below to conceal the puppeteers, or lash the frame to a card table on its side, as shown.

Whatever type of frame you use, it's a good idea to include footing for the figures. This can be a ledge 1 to 2 inches wide fastened across the bottom of the screen on the inside. This provides something for the shadow puppets' feet to touch so they won't seem to be floating in air.

Shadow Puppet Lighting

The lighting in a shadow puppet play is very important. Place a light source behind and slightly above the puppet screen about 3 to 4 feet away. The source may be a 150-watt unshaded bulb, a 300- to 400-watt reflector spotlight, or special stage lights. These lights can be placed on a dimmer and the illumination varied for special effects.

The room should be as dark as possible during a shadow puppet show, and the puppeteers should be cautioned to keep their heads below the screen so their shadows won't show. Two or three rehearsals before the performance will ensure that the lighting is properly situated.

FINGER PUPPETS

Even the youngest and most inexperienced puppeteers can easily manipulate finger puppets. The index and middle fingers serve as the legs and feet of the puppet, so the body is small. Because these puppets are so small, they are not suitable for a production at a large pack meeting; however, they are ideal for use in den meetings, at home, or during hikes or for entertaining in a children's hospital or long-term care facility. They are easy to transport, require little equipment, and can even be used without a stage.

Follow these easy steps to make a simple finger puppet:

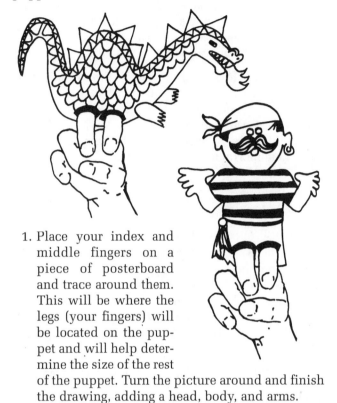

1. Place your index and middle fingers on a piece of posterboard and trace around them. This will be where the legs (your fingers) will be located on the puppet and will help determine the size of the rest of the puppet. Turn the picture around and finish the drawing, adding a head, body, and arms.

2. Color or paint the figure. Cut holes near the base of the puppet's body for your fingers to fit through. Add yarn hair, if desired.

3. Cut out the puppet, insert two fingers, and practice walking forward and backward, kneeling, jumping, and kicking.

4. Make shoes or boots if appropriate from small cylinders of cardboard to fit over your fingertips.

Glove Finger Puppets

Cut the fingers off an old glove; glue on button or bead eyes and a nose; cut ears, mouths, tails, etc., from felt and glue on; glue on yarn or fur for hair—and you have a handful of easy puppets!

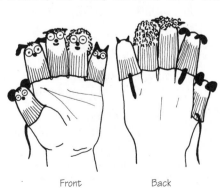

Front   Back

SAMPLE PUPPET PLAYS

YOU WERE THERE

Characters: Three Pilgrim puppets and two American Indian puppets. Narrator and sponsor offstage.

NARRATOR (offstage): Good evening, ladies and gentlemen of the television audience. Den [number] of Pack [number] presents, "You Were There." Now, here's a word from our sponsor.

SPONSOR (offstage): Friends, this program is being brought to you by Mother Fletcher, who is famous for such products as Rattlesnake Oil Shampoo, Corn Pone Corn Sticks Mix, and Dainty Doggie Biscuits. Be sure to look for these products in your neighborhood store. And now, back to "You Were There."

Scene 1: Early New England coast with a ship and trees in the background.

NARRATOR: We'd like to take you back to the year 1621 and the first Thanksgiving. Several events of great importance have led up to this momentous day. Last year, in 1620, the Pilgrims landed at Plymouth Rock. Let's look in on this scene and talk to some of the people who were there. *(Three Pilgrims come on stage.)* Sir! You look like the leader of the group. What is your name?

FIRST PILGRIM: William Bradford, your servant, sir!

NARRATOR: And how was your voyage, Mr. Bradford?

FIRST PILGRIM: Rough, very rough!

NARRATOR (turning to another Pilgrim): And you, sir. Did you find the *Mayflower* comfortable?

SECOND PILGRIM: Are you kidding? It wasn't exactly the *Queen Mary,* you know!

NARRATOR: And how was your first year in the New World?

FIRST PILGRIM: Very hard! Our crops failed and many of us got sick. *(The other two Pilgrims lie down as if sick.)* The snows came early and stayed late. *(Throw confetti for snow.)*

(First Act curtain)

NARRATOR: What's going to happen in this sad scene? Sorry, but we have to interrupt the show to bring you a word from our sponsor.

SPONSOR: Friends, are you bothered with bad teeth that are falling out of your mouth? Try Mother Fletcher's Guaranteed Gum Glue for the tightest teeth in town. It's on sale right now at your neighborhood pet shop! And now, back to our program.

Scene 2: Background with cabins and trees. Pilgrims are onstage as the curtain opens.

NARRATOR: The harsh winter passed and things looked brighter for our little band of Pilgrims. How did they do it? *(American Indians enter.)*

FIRST AMERICAN INDIAN: I'm Squanto. I helped teach my new Pilgrim friends to fish and plant corn so that they didn't starve.

SECOND AMERICAN INDIAN: I'm Chief Massasoit. I signed a treaty with these new people that established peace.

FIRST PILGRIM (stepping forward): Friends! Friends! Let us celebrate our survival, our harvest, and our peace with a feast! Hurry! Let us prepare! *(Everyone begins rushing around in preparation.)*

(Second Act curtain)

NARRATOR: Before we the last act of our show, here's a word from next week's sponsor, the Boy Scouts of America.

SPONSOR: Cub Scouting is a family program, designed to get boys and their families working and playing together. Just try it! You'll like it! Back now to the final act.

Scene 3: American Indians and Pilgrims seated at a table.

NARRATOR: With the help of the American Indians, the Pilgrims survived. To celebrate their first harvest and to thank God for their good fortune, they had a feast—the first Thanksgiving. And they invited those who had helped them so much. Let's listen to their prayer of thanks.

THIRD PILGRIM: Dear God, we are grateful for these good things. Help us to be worthy in the years to come. Amen.

NARRATOR: What kind of a day was it? A day, like all days, filled with those events that alter the course of human destiny...and you were there! *(Curtain)*

LITTERBUGS BEWARE

Puppets: Any number of Litterbug and Tidy Bug bag puppets

Setting: Park or countryside backdrop. Litterbug puppets come onstage and begin littering the stage area with pieces of paper, candy wrappers, etc.

NARRATOR:

We are Litterbugs, it is true,
And oh, what we Litterbugs can do!

We clutter the country with papers and trash.
At making a mess, we're really a smash.

The roadsides and parks are scenes of our folly.
We really enjoy it and think it's quite jolly

To leave behind garbage, bottles, and paper
As little mementos of our daily labor.

(Litterbug puppets exit and Tidy Bug puppets enter and begin to clean up the litter.)

NARRATOR:

We are Tidy Bugs of the Tidy Bug clan.
We work to keep everything spic-and-span.

We pick up the litter wherever we are
And always carry litter bags in our car.

We'll squash the Litterbugs as fast as we can
And make America a beautiful land,

Free of litter, clutter, and trash.
If you will help us, we'll be a smash! *(Curtain)*

KNIGHTS OF YORE

Puppets: Sir Galahad, Sir Trueblood, Servant, the Black Night, and any number of Friendly Knights carrying swords

Setting: Inside a medieval castle. The Servant is onstage. A knock at the door is heard. The Servant goes to one side of the stage to answer the door.

SIR TRUEBLOOD: Kind sir, pray let me spend the night. I am weary and long for rest. *(Droops wearily.)*

SERVANT (motions Trueblood to come in): Enter and rest thyself. Pray tell me, sir, why do you travel so late at night?

SIR TRUEBLOOD: I am the King's messenger and I must take a message to Sir Galahad in a far country.

SERVANT: You are in luck, sir. Sir Galahad is at this very moment resting in this castle!

SIR TRUEBLOOD: Will you please call him? I must speak with him right away. *(Servant exits to get Sir Galahad.)*

SIR GALAHAD (coming onstage with Servant): You wish to speak to me, sir?

SIR TRUEBLOOD: I have a message from the King, sir. You have an enemy who is trying to do you harm.

SIR GALAHAD (surprised): Impossible! I have no enemies.

SIR TRUEBLOOD: But you do! and he is looking for you right now. He plans to slay you! *(A knock is heard at the door.)*

SIR GALAHAD (urgently): Arise! Arise, Knights of Galahad! Make ready to do battle! *(Friendly Knights come onstage in armor, ready to fight.)*

SERVANT (from side of stage): No! You may not enter! *(Black Knight rushes onstage with sword drawn.)*

SIR TRUEBLOOD (fearfully): It's the Black Knight! *(The knights fight. The Black Knight is knocked down.)*

SIR GALAHAD: We have fought a good fight. Before we go our separate ways, let us promise to use our swords to fight only the battle for truth and honor. *(All Friendly Knights point swords upward.)*

ALL: For truth and honor! *(Curtain)*

THE PIRATES' BIG DECISION

Puppets: Any number of pirates, one Cub Scout

Setting: A pirate ship. Pirates are onstage when the curtain opens.

NARRATOR:

Here are some pirates, brave and bold.
Many times you've heard their story told.
They sail the seas on their homemade raft.
Listen now, and you'll hear them laugh.
(Pirates laugh heartily.)

Let's sneak in closer,
And what do we see?
They seem to be happy—
Listen to their glee.
(Pirates laugh again and say "ho-ho-ho" in pirate fashion. Cub Scout comes onstage and stands in the center of the pirates.)

Oh dear, a Cub Scout.
I can't see his rank.
What if those Pirates
Make him walk the plank?
(Pirates draw closer to Cub Scout.)

Wait just a minute:
Something's not right.
Look at that Cub Scout—
There's no sign of fright!
(Cub Scout begins shaking hands with pirates and talking to them.)

What we see here leaves us no doubts.
Our Cub Scout is asking
The pirates to become Scouts.
(Cub Scout motions to pirates and leads them offstage.)

So with this happy ending,
We'll drift out of sight.
For our brave Cub Scout
This was a happy night! *(Curtain)*

WONDERFUL WILFRED, THE WOODY WOODPECKER

This is a narrated play with lots of special effects. Use two boys for the sounds and actions. A microphone will be helpful.

Puppets: Woody Woodpecker family: Mother Woodpecker and four young woodpeckers, one with a huge beak

Setting: Forest backdrop; big nest in the foreground with loose strips of newspaper hanging that will blow in the wind. The young woodpeckers are in the nest.

NARRATOR: Once upon a time many years ago, there lived in the deep forest a very famous family of Woody Woodpeckers. Down through the ages, this family increased in numbers, in strength, and in wisdom...until we come to the day when we find the hero of our story—Wonderful Wilfred! *(Fanfare sounds offstage. Wilfred takes a bow from the nest.)*

Now, Wonderful Wilfred was no ordinary woodpecker. *(Sound-effects boys shout, "No!")* He was smart—in fact, he was the wisest of all the woodpeckers. While the soft breezes blew outside...*(blowing or fanning movement offstage causes nest and trees to rustle)*...you could hear Wilfred's brothers and sisters tapping away. *(Offstage two wooden blocks are tapped to together. Three woodpeckers make tapping motions on a nearby tree.)* But not Wilred! He just sat there and rubbed his beak back and forth. *(Rubbing sound made offstage by rubbing blocks together as Wilfred rubs his beak on a nearby tree.)*

And when the winds blew...*(blowing or fanning movement again)*...and the rains rained...*(gentle hand-clapping offstage)*...and the owls hooted...*(hooting noise offstage)*...you could hear the brothers and sisters tapping *(same as above)*. But not Wilfred. *(Boys offstage shout, "No!")* He'd just sit there and rub his beak back and forth. *(Same as above.)*

When their mother would bring them food, you could hear Wonderful Wilfred's brothers and sisters close their beaks hard on the food. *(Mother Woodpecker comes onstage pretending to give food to her young. Offstage, hands are clapped together sharply as young woodpeckers close their beaks.)* But not Wilfred. *(Offstage, "No!")* He would close his beak quietly...*(offstage, "Shhh")*...and then sit there and rub his beak back and forth. *(Same as above.)*

At last came the day for them to leave their nest, and you could hear Wilfred's brothers and sisters take their last peck at the tree before they left home. *(Sharp tap with woodblock offstage as each brother*

and sister makes a final tap on the tree and exits. Wilfred remains in the nest.) Wilfred looked around and picked the biggest tree in the forest and flew directly to it. He didn't waste any time. Once more, he rubbed his beak back and forth—until it shone so it could be seen for miles around. *(Rubbing sound offstage.)* He reared back, and with one mighty swipe of his beautiful beak, he cut the huge tree in two! *(Boys offstage yell, "Timber!" as tree collapses. Wilfred takes a final bow and exits. Curtain.)*

THE ANIMALS' CHRISTMAS STORY

This is a shadow puppet play. Cut out the 25 figures listed in the play and attach them to rods. As the Narrator mentions each, a boy holds it up to the screen.

NARRATOR: Everyone has Christmas wishes. We all dream about the packages we find under the tree. Did you know that animals dream too? Den [number] will show you what I mean.

"I want a CANTALOUPE," said the ANTELOPE.

"I want a FISHING LINE," said the PORCUPINE.

"I want a WAGON," said the DRAGON,

"Underneath the CHRISTMAS TREE."

"I want an OVERCOAT," said the BILLY GOAT.

"I want a NEW FRONT DOOR," said the DINOSAUR.

"I want a VIDEO GAME," said the GREAT DANE,

"Oh, how happy I would be!"

"I want a BARBECUE," said the KANGAROO.

"I want a PHONOGRAPH," said the BIG GIRAFFE.

"I want a ROCKING CHAIR," said the GRIZZLY BEAR,

"To rock all winter long."

"I want a PRETTY HAT," said the KITTY CAT.

"I want some MISTLETOE," said the BUFFALO.

"I want a HAPPY TUNE," said the BIG BABOON,

"To sing all winter long."

As you can see, each animal has its own special wish—just like you do. Merry Christmas to all, and to all a good night!

Puzzles

The den leader or den chief will want to have a new trick or puzzle to show boys at almost every den meeting. These are good preopening activities that boys enjoy. They should be simple enough for boys to perform, however, because boys will want to show them to family members and friends.

The puzzles below are mystifying at first but are easy to learn and fun to do. You can find the necessary materials around the house.

TANGRAM PUZZLE

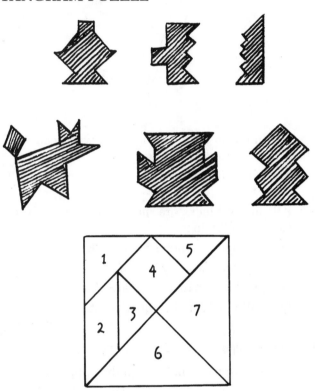

Materials: **Cardboard, scissors**

In this ancient puzzle from China, you cut seven shapes from one square of cardboard, as shown. Then using the pieces, you can make silhouettes of hundreds of animals, people, and geometric figures.

STRAP AND BUTTON PUZZLE

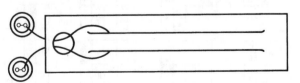

Materials: **Strip of pliable leather or vinyl, knife or scissors, heavy string, two large buttons**

Make two parallel cuts in the center of a strip of flexible leather or vinyl, as shown. Just below this, cut a hole the same width. Pass a heavy string under the slit and through the hole. Tie the buttons to the loose ends of the string.

Puzzle: Remove the string without taking off the buttons.

Solution: This can be easily done by bending the leather and drawing the narrow leather strip through the hole.

BLOCK PUZZLES

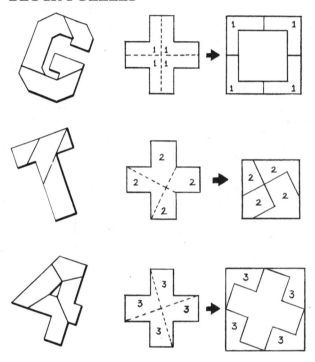

Boys can draw a puzzle design on light cardboard and separate into pieces, as shown. Mix up the pieces of each individual puzzle and see who can be the first to put one together.

HOLIDAY JIGSAW

Cut up several old greeting cards into jigsaw pieces. Put each in a separate envelope. Boys can work these individually, or divide the den into teams to see who can finish a puzzle first.

YOKE PUZZLE

Materials: **1-by-6-inch piece of thin board (a tongue depressor or craft stick is excellent), string, two washers**

Puzzle: Challenge boys to get the washers together, hanging from the same loop, without untying any knots, breaking the stick, or pulling the knots through the holes.

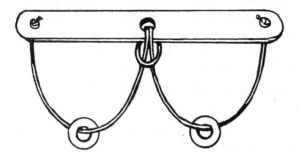

Solution: Loosen the string slightly and pull the loop at the center hole straight out about 2 inches. Slide the left washer up the string and through the center loop. Then pull the rest of the center loop through the center hole. Slide the washer along the string through the center loop onto the opposite side. Pull the center loop back through the hole to its original position. The washer is now hanging on the opposite loop. Reverse this procedure to separate the washers again.

HEART PUZZLE

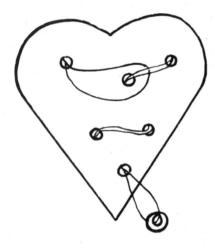

Materials: **Board, string, washer or bead**

Make a heart-shaped board 3½ inches high and 3½ inches wide. Bore six holes in it, as shown. Lace a 30-inch string to the heart in this manner:

1. Fold the string in the center and thread the loop from the back through the upper left hole. Hold it in place with your thumb while you thread the two free ends through the upper right hole and then across the front and through the loop and the upper center hole.

2. Next, thread the two free ends from the back through the lower right hole, across the front to the lower right hole, and from the back through the lower center hole.

3. Tie a washer or bead that is too large to slip through the holes at least 6 inches below the bottom hole.

Puzzle: Remove the string from the heart without untying the washer.

Solution: Draw in all the free string from the washer end up to the loop end at the upper center hole. Now, thread the loop back through the center top hole to the lower right hole, lower left hole, and lower center hole. Don't twist the string. Then slip the washer through the loop, thread the loop back again through the hole, and it will come off.

SLIDING BLOCK PUZZLE

An adult who likes to work with wood can make these puzzles for boys.

1. Make a box with inside measurements of 3⅝ inches.

2. All puzzle blocks are made from ⅜-inch wood. Cut the following:
   - Four blocks ⅞ inch square (D, E, F, G)
   - Three blocks 1¾ by ⅞ inch (B, C, H)
   - One block 1¾ inches square (A)

3. Sand all blocks and stain or paint.

Puzzle: Slide the blocks and move the largest one (A) to the diagonally opposite corner and back.

Solution: To move block A to the opposite corner:

1. A right	7. A right, DE up, H left, FG left
2. B up	8. F right and down
3. C left	9. A down
4. DE left	10. D right, E up and right, H up
5. H Left	11. G left and up, F left, A down
6. FG down	

Skits

WHY WE USE SKITS

Skits appeal to Cub Scout–age boys. Acting comes naturally to many boys, and often they make little distinction between make-believe and the world of reality. Skits help channel a boy's imagination. He doesn't just *pretend* he's a pirate; he *is* one, sailing the high seas. Or he *is* an astronaut, flying into space. Play-acting is important in the growth of a boy because it

- Gives him an outlet for the "let's pretend" part of his character.
- Gives him a chance for creative expression rather than imitation.
- Develops his powers of observation, coordination, and timing.
- Helps him gain self-confidence and personal satisfaction.
- Allows him to play the parts he has always dreamed of.
- Shows the importance of teamwork and cooperation.
- Improves speech and voice projection.
- Helps him develop an appreciation for other people and their abilities.

You may come across a shy boy who would prefer not to take part in skits. Sometimes, a costume or mask will help him with his shyness; or try giving him other important responsibilities, such as handling sound effects or lighting offstage. Each boy should be recognized as an important member of the group, and everyone should take part in some way.

To get boys interested in dramatics, try these things:

- Describe a situation that a boy might find himself in and let the boys take turns acting it out. Lead a discussion, asking questions such as: Which was the best solution? Are there other solutions?
- Suggest that the boys watch people during the week and come to the next den meeting with an idea to role-play (see below).
- With the boys' help, make up a short story, weaving together the characters the boys act out.
- Ask the boys to act out the story in pantomime (see below).
- With the boys' help, add words to the story. Decide how the characters would look and behave in that situation.
- Ask the boys to act out the story using their own words to fit the situation.

Role-playing, pantomime, and charades help boys gain self-confidence and build enthusiasm for dramatics. These are a good foundation for planning and presenting den skits at pack meetings.

ROLE-PLAYING

Role-playing is the spontaneous, unrehearsed acting out of a situation with words and gestures. It is putting one's self in another person's place to try to understand that person better.

Role-playing lets a boy *show* how he would handle a situation rather than just *telling* how it should be done. It can help him develop an appreciation for other people and how they make decisions.

Avoid these things:
- Role-playing undesirable characters
- Allowing a boy to role-play a character that is too difficult for him, causing him to be discouraged
- Unfair criticism of people or events, with no attempt to show a better way or to recognize improvement

PANTOMIME

Pantomime is acting without using words. Facial expressions, hand gestures, and body movements tell the story. Long, memorized dialogue is discouraged in Cub Scout skits, so pantomime is an especially good method to use. To show the boys how to pantomime effectively, let them try some of the following:

How would you act if
- You had a nail in your shoe?
- You were scared?
- You slipped on ice?
- Someone pinched you?

How would you lift
- A baby?
- Something very fragile?
- Something very hot?
- Something heavy?
- Something big and bulky?

How would you look if
- You saw a ferocious lion?
- Someone gave you a surprise?
- Your report card was all A's?
- You smelled something bad?
- You heard a strange sound?
- You were watching an exciting game?
- You tasted bitter medicine?
- You heard a sudden crash?

Another way to use pantomime in the den is to fill a Cub Scout cap with slips of paper that have written instructions. Each boy draws a slip and pantomimes the instructions. Here are some suggestions:

- Crawl through a jungle full of hanging vines and branches.
- Walk a tightrope in the air.
- Follow a buzzing fly around the room and finally swat it.
- Pretend you are a cat, waking up from a nap.
- Pretend you are a dog, sitting up and begging.

Or, put several things into a paper bag, one for each boy—a pencil, a clothespin, an eraser, an empty chewing gum wrapper, a paint brush, etc. One by one, the boys remove something from the bag and pantomime a short scene using the item as a prop. The others try to guess what he is doing.

CHARADES

Boys enjoy both the acting and the guessing of charades. The game can provide them with an opportunity to use their imaginations.

To play charades, divide the group into two teams. Give one team a piece of paper that has a word or title (of a movie, book, TV show, etc.) written on it. They leave the room and plan their action. After a quick rehearsal, they return and put on their act for the second team, in pantomime.

Each word or each syllable can be acted out separately. Two-syllable words are good for Cub Scout–age boys. Try the following list, and let them suggest others:

Billboard	Cattail
Birdcall	Checkbook
Basketball	Fullback
Football	Garter snake
Mousetrap	Bookend
Downpour	

WRITING YOUR OWN SKIT

Sometimes it's hard to find a written skit that fits the monthly theme and your den of boys. If that's the case, the best thing to do is to adapt a skit to fit your needs, or to write one of your own. You already know two of the most important things: (1) the facilities available, and (2) the number of boys in your den. Now, jot down the following information:

- The subject of the plot
- The title (It can be serious or funny.)
- The number of actors
- The kind of actors (boys or puppets?)

- The amount of time allowed (Write a skit timed for 20 minutes, and then boil it down to 5 minutes, saving only the best lines.)
- Your stage (Is it an open floor, a platform at one end of the room, or a real stage?)

Remember: The audience must like your skit, too, so write it to "fit" them. Keep the action moving, so keep scene-changing to a minimum.

Start by making an outline of your skit. Follow these simple steps:

- Boy wants something (friendship, a gold mine, a prize, to find a lost planet, etc.).
- Boy starts to get it (by canoe, plane, horseback, foot, etc.).
- Obstacles stop boy (a secret enemy, a crocodile, false friend, weather, etc.).
- Boy achieves goal (through an act of kindness, bravery, wisdom, magic, unexpected help, etc.).

Things to Remember

- Keep it simple.
- Keep it short (3 to 5 minutes at the most).
- Avoid long memorized dialogue. Pantomimes are good for Cub Scouts. (If more explanation is necessary, the den chief may be narrator while the boys pantomime the action.)
- Scenery, props, and costumes should be simple, if used at all.
- Let every boy take part.
- Use stage directions liberally—tell who goes where and does what.
- Stimulate interest and surprises as you go along. A "walk-on" (someone hunting a rabbit or bird, blowing up a balloon, or engaging in some other nonsense) in each scene sparks interest.
- Be sure the audience can hear. Boys should be coached to speak slowly, clearly, and loudly. If the audience laughs or claps, actors should pause before continuing their lines.
- Let the boys help write the skit. They will have some great ideas, and that's part of the fun.
- Avoid skits that ridicule anybody or anything. They are in bad taste.

MAKING YOUR OWN SCENERY

Making scenery for skits can be a good den project. Scenery can add to the mood of the skit and make it more believable. It doesn't have to be detailed or complicated; it only has to provide an idea or suggestion of what it represents. Scenery isn't necessary for every skit. Use it only if you and the boys think it will add to the interest.

You can make scenery from large pieces of corrugated cardboard. Check with furniture stores, appliance stores, grocery stores, or warehouses for large furniture and appliance cartons. You can use cardboard for mountain ranges, bushes, trees, lampposts, forest outlines, picket fences, houses, tents, cabins, or even a sun, moon, or stars that you can suspend overhead. Wooden laths nailed to the back of the scenery will make it more sturdy and keep painted cardboard from curling.

Here are some tips to help you make simple but effective scenery:

- An adult should cut heavy cardboard.
- Boys can do the painting after guidelines are drawn with heavy pencil to show what colors go where.
- Latex wall paint or tempera is good for painting scenery. Use tempera to tint latex paint to a different color.
- When painting large areas, use a roller.
- Paint on the blank side so any printing on the cardboard won't bleed through.
- Boys can use felt-tip marking pens to emphasize details or to outline a design on the painted cardboard.
- Create moods with color. Paint scenery in grays if the skit is spooky or sad; use bright colors if the skit is happy or funny.
- Children's coloring books are a good source for patterns for simple cutout scenery. Just enlarge them to the desired size, using the instructions for enlarging patterns found in the "Crafts" chapter of this book.
- Always keep in mind that the audience will see the scenery from a distance, so they won't be able to see fine lines or details.
- To give the appearance of distance, make scenery small.

SOUND EFFECTS

A flash of lightning, a loud crash, a train chugging down the track—boys can create all of these and many other special effects for their den skits with a few simple preparations. Bells, drums, gongs, cymbals, castanets, whistles, horns, rattles, coconut shells, and even pots and pans can create unusual and comical sounds.

Sound effects can add to the appeal of some Cub Scout skits. One of the Cub Scouts or the den chief could be the person in charge of sound effects and stand offstage to make the sounds at the appropriate time. Another alternative is to prerecord sounds on a cassette recorder.

Knock at the Door: Hit a half-gallon plastic bottle sharply on the end with a rubber spatula.

Thunder: Grasp a metal cookie sheet at one end, placing your thumb on the underside. Shake the sheet so that it vibrates. Bang it against the knee for an occasional loud thunderclap.

Lightning: Flash a white light off and on, or use a camera flash, along with the sound of thunder.

Hail: Pour rice on a pane of glass (near a microphone if you have one).

Rain: Fill a tin can full of dry peas or beans. Rotate the can slowly (in front of a microphone, if you have one).

Train: Place small wire nails inside a small flat box, such as a bandage box. Move it back and forth in rhythm...chug, chug, chug...chug.

Creaking Door or Animal Roar: Use a coffee can or two foil pans taped together. Tie a string in the center of a pencil and rub the string with resin. Punch a hole in the container, place the pencil inside, and pull the string out through the hole. Drag fingernails along the string to produce noise into a microphone.

Hoof Beats: Clap two coconut half-shells on a wooden board to produce the sound of horses walking or galloping on a hard road.

Auto Brakes: Slide a drinking glass across a pane of glass (in front of a microphone, if possible).

Sword Fight: Hold an aluminum cookie sheet in one hand and hit it with a metal spoon for each clash of swords.

Fire: Crumple and twist cellophane into a ball and then release it (near a microphone, if possible).

Campfire: Cover a flashlight with red cellophane or tissue paper, with wood piled on top to create a red glow, and use the fire sound above.

See other special effects described in the "Puppets" section above.

COSTUMES

Costumes can help set the theme or mood for the skit. They also have an almost magical ability to help transform a boy into a creature from outer space, an astronaut, a magician, a Pilgrim, an exotic animal—or anything else his imagination suggests.

Keep costumes for Cub Scout skits simple and inexpensive. More than likely, you will use them only once. Sometimes, a sign to identify a character is all you might need. A sign can turn a boy into anything—a tree, a lamppost, an animal. Simple props, such as a cardboard mustache, an eye patch, a bandanna, and a cardboard sword for a pirate, will be sufficient to set your mood.

Pipe cleaners

Glue on paper cups.

Silver jacket

Ice cream container with face area cut out and piece of plastic glued in place.

Ski pants

Oversized boots

You can find most of the materials for simple costumes around the house.

Old Clothes: Discarded clothing items are probably the most important thing for making easy costumes: old tights, T-shirts, robes, pajamas, hats, and jackets. Use them as-is, or cut them up and use them as parts of costumes.

Old soft hat with crown pushed out, creased in front, dimples on the sides

Cub Scout neckerchief

Make chaps from vinyl scraps or heavy cloth. Fasten behind the leg with string. Add buttons with hanging fringe for decoration.

Cut cuffs from light cardboard or construction paper; decorate with paper fringe.

Old rope for lariat

For spurs, cut straps from vinyl or leather scraps. Cover with aluminum foil. Flatten a bottle cap for the wheel and glue on.

T-Shirt Costumes: You can decorate T-shirts with fabric paint, material, ribbon, and many other items to set the mood for any song or skit. They are easy to store and can be adapted for use again and again. And best of all—one size fits all! (Make sure you use extra large sizes that will fit over a boy's uniform.)

For example, if your skit has cows in it, use black T-shirts and cut out white felt circles. Velcro or glue the circles randomly over the T-shirt. Make a tail for the cow with white clothesline, and pin it on the T-shirt. (For the cow's head, use paper bag masks or an inexpensive animal nose available at most toy stores.)

Cardboard Boxes: With a simple box, you can be a clown, an animal, a vegetable, a robot, or a musical instrument! Cut holes for the head and arms, and then let the boys paint boxes with latex paint, using felt-tip marking pens for highlights.

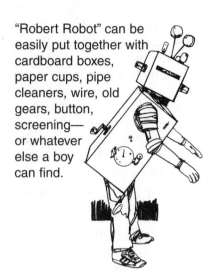

"Robert Robot" can be easily put together with cardboard boxes, paper cups, pipe cleaners, wire, old gears, button, screening— or whatever else a boy can find.

Plastic Trash Bags: Large plastic garbage bags can be an excellent basis for quick costumes. Cut holes for head and arms and decorate as desired:

- Staple cardboard or construction paper wings or legs onto the bag.
- Stick colored masking tape on the bag to create designs.
- Thread ribbons or streamers through small holes punched into the back of the bag.
- Cut adhesive-backed paper into shapes and stick them to the bag.

After placing the costume on a boy, you can "plump up" the costume by stuffing the bag with loosely crumpled newspaper. Tape or staple the bag around the bottom to hold the stuffing in place.

Note: Take an opportunity to instruct boys on the dangers of plastic bags and the potential for suffocation.

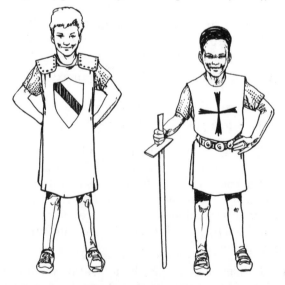

For the basic garb of a knight of King Arthur's Round Table, use old pajamas (without designs) or thermal underwear. Cut tunics from crepe paper or use an old pillowcase with slits cut for the arms and head. Paint on emblems. Cover an old belt with aluminum foil.

Paper Bags: Use grocery bags and brown wrapping paper for both costumes and masks. Paint them with latex paint (to add strength) or tempera. For a leather-like appearance, crush and recrush brown paper bags or brown wrapping paper until it is soft and wrinkled. Then press with a lukewarm iron.

STAGE MAKEUP

The skit is written, the parts assigned, some simple scenery and costumes are made, and the boys have been busy practicing. What's left? How about makeup?

Makeup can help show the audience what a character is like. It also makes the character more real to the other actors, and as a result, everyone plays their roles better. It can hide an actor's features, make him larger or smaller, younger or older, or change his appearance completely.

Theatrical makeup is expensive, and most Cub Scout leaders work on a limited budget. Following are some inexpensive substitutes and some tricks for using makeup to its best advantage.

Makeup Bases

A base for makeup that can color large areas is easy to make. Combine equal parts of liquid cleansing cream and sifted confectioner's sugar. Mix well. This results in a white base, which you can use for clown white. Tint it with a few drops of green food coloring or tempera paint for monster makeup, or tint with a mixture of red and blue for a purple Martian.

Here's another base that gives a soft skinlike texture and is easily removed: Mix together 2 t. white vegetable shortening, 5 t. cornstarch, 1 t. flour, a few drops of glycerin, and any food coloring desired. For brown, add 2 T. unsweetened cocoa.

You can also use tempera paint as a makeup base, without fear of allergy problems. It can be washed off.

Added Touches and Suggestions

- Use lipstick for both lip and cheek color.
- Use eyebrow pencil to darken or change the shape of eyebrows, to line the eyes, and to make freckles, mustaches, sideburns, and wrinkles.
- Cornstarch powdered into the hair helps age characters. Hair usually begins to gray at the temples first, and in streaks.
- The more light on stage, the more makeup you'll need.
- Apply makeup after the character is in costume, using a makeup cape or towel to protect the costume. This way, the makeup won't get smeared while boys are putting on the costume.
- Keep plenty of tissues and cleansing cream handy for makeup removal.

How to Age a Character

Have the actor frown and wrinkle his forehead. Use gray eyebrow pencil to mark in the creases of the wrinkles. More lines add more years. (You can also have the actor smile and fill wrinkles in at the cheeks and eyes.) Powder the hair with cornstarch, or use a wig. For a bald head, use an old swimming cap to cover the hair. Glue on pieces of yarn hair for a fringe just above the ears.

Classic Clown

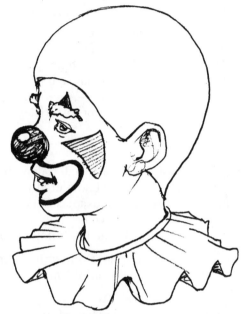

Apply clown white base all over the face from the hairline to the neck. If you want to attach artificial eyebrows, clean off the white makeup from the eyebrows. Spirit gum will hold the eyebrows in place. Use an old white swimming cap with holes cut for the ears to cover the head for a bald clown, or use a wild wig (see below). Use bright red lipstick to paint long triangles or circles on the cheeks. Apply red lipstick around the mouth, about 1 inch wide. Then use a black eyebrow pencil to outline an oval mouth shape. Cut a red rubber ball to fit the nose, and attach a rubber band that slips around the head to hold it in place.

Wigs

White Hair: Pull an old nylon stocking over the hair and ears. Tie it off at the top and cut off the excess. Use cellophane tape or glue to fasten white cotton balls all over the stocking.

Curls: Cut pieces of paper in strips. Curl each strip by holding one end between your thumb and a long pencil. Press lightly with the thumb and pull the strip over the pencil with the other hand. Repeat several times for a stiff curl. Glue curls to a stocking cap base.

Braids: Stretch about three strips of ¾-inch-wide crepe paper. Twist each strip around and around and then braid the three strips together.

Scarecrow's Wig: Glue uneven lengths of heavy cotton rug yarn or crepe paper to a stocking cap base, or glue to the inside of an old hat.

Also try using untwisted wool or rope for wigs, or use an old mop dyed any color.

MASKS

You can make masks from almost any container and any type of material. Let your imagination be your guide. Try cardboard cartons, paper bags, foil pie pans, posterboard, and plastic bottles. Use masks for many Cub Scout themes—American Indian, circus, space, holiday, nature, or historic.

Decorating Masks

You can paint most mask materials with tempera paint and draw features with colored marking pens. Use heavy, bold lines and splashes of color. The brighter and funnier the colors are, the better. You can also make features from the following materials:

Hair: String, yarn, rope, fabric strips, paper curls, kinky wire, cotton balls, an old mop, or even soda straws

Noses: Rubber balls, cardboard, paper cups, plastic containers, egg carton cups, spools

Ears: Paper cups, plastic containers, spools, cardboard

Cardboard Cylinder Masks

Use a rolled-up section of posterboard or cardboard for a simple and effective mask.

1. Wrap a rectangular piece of cardboard around the boy's head to determine the size of the cylinder. Cut out curved slots in the bottom so the cylinder will fit on the boy's shoulders.

2. Sketch and paint the details of the masks while the cardboard is laid out flat. Sketch your designs with pencil and then decorate with tempera paint, colored

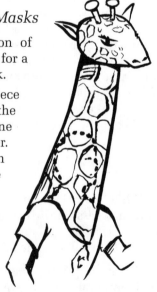

With a very long cardboard cylinder and a stuffed paper bag on top, you can be a giraffe!

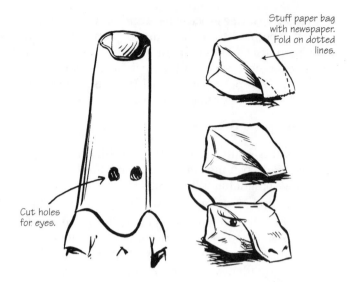

Cut holes for eyes.

Stuff paper bag with newspaper. Fold on dotted lines.

marking pens, or crayon. Cut out eye and mouth holes as needed.

3. Glue on noses, antlers, ears, horns, false eyebrows, eyelashes, lips, etc. made from colored paper, felt, or other materials.

4. Roll the cardboard into a cylinder and fasten with staples, glue, or tape. Add rope or yarn hair to cover the seam and give the mask more depth.

Paper Bag Masks

Paper bag masks are fun and inexpensive to make. Use grocery-sized paper bags large enough to fit over a boy's head. Add construction paper or felt ears, noses, eyebrows, or horns and hair made from yarn, paper, or even soda straws. Experiment with markers, paint, and crayons.

Craft Foam Masks

Craft foam is an excellent material for boys to use in creating masks. This material cuts easily with a pair of scissors yet is much more durable than paper bags and cardboard. It comes in a variety of colors, which can be enhanced with permanent markers. Cut pieces can be easily glued together.

SAMPLE SKITS

ROBOT INVENTORS

Scene: A table covered with an old sheet or other cover reaching to the floor at the front. A fishbowl or other glass bowl, test tubes, flasks, and a black top hat are on the table.

Characters: Six boys posing as scientists.

Setting: The six scientists in lab jackets (men's shirts, collars turned inside, put on backwards) stand at both ends and behind the table. Scientist 2 is reading a large book, plainly titled *How to Invent a Robot.* Scientist 3 is looking over his shoulder. Scientist 4 is stirring liquid in a bowl with a wooden spoon. Another boy, a robot with a bunny tail, is hidden behind the table.

(*Note:* If seven boys aren't available, some could take more lines.)

SCIENTIST 1: It doesn't seem to be working.

SCIENTIST 2: I can't understand it!

SCIENTIST 3: We'll have to change the formula.

(*Scientist 4 adds soda to vinegar water in the bowl The mixture fizzes.*)

SCIENTIST 4: Wait a minute. What did you say your friend's name was?

SCIENTIST 5: Magisto the Magician. He says he's pulled a robot out of a hat lots of times.

SCIENTIST 4: That's rabbit, not robot!

(*Scientist 2 raises his book; Scientist 4 raises his spoon; Scientists 1, 2, 3, and 4 chase Scientist 5 offstage left. Scientist 6 starts to follow, stops, and looks at the hat.*)

SCIENTIST 6 (shrugging his shoulders): It might work! Abracadabra 1-2-3! (*Takes hold of the hat with his left hand, tips it toward himself at the edge of the table, reaches "in" behind the table—grabs and pulls the robot out of the hat*).

SCIENTIST 6: Hey! It worked! Now I'll just push this button. (*Pushes button on robot. Robot drops to all fours, hops offstage, showing bunny tail bobbing at the back*).

THE BIG CATCH

Characters and Setting: Four boys at a movie, eating popcorn or other movie treats

CUB SCOUT 1: Too bad Joe isn't with us.

CUB SCOUT 2: Yeah.

CUB SCOUT 3: Bummer.

CUB SCOUT 4: Why isn't he here anyway?

CUB SCOUT 2: You didn't hear about that?

CUB SCOUT 4: Hear what?

CUB SCOUT 1: Remember that new fishing pole he got for his birthday?

CUB SCOUT 4: Yeah, so?

CUB SCOUT 1: Well, he got some lures for bass, too.

CUB SCOUT 4: Yeah?

CUB SCOUT 2: Yeah. And he got some lures for catfish, too.

CUB SCOUT 4: Sounds good.

CUB SCOUT 1: Well, he decided to take a big fishing trip. He went down to the stream behind the house and was planning to fish until he caught a big mess of fish. He didn't care what kind.

CUB SCOUT 4: Did he catch anything?

CUB SCOUT 2: He caught something all right!

CUB SCOUT 3: He fell in the stream and caught a cold!

"AH" SKIT

An "ah" skit is a great one to use because of the limited dialogue; the only word spoken during the entire skit is "ah." Pantomime, facial expression, and tone of voice convey all the meanings. The repetition of the word "ah" adds humor to the skit. It's important to really "ham it up."

Actors: Announcer, a parent or two, Cub Scout, thief, police officer, and friends of Cub Scout (optional)

Setting: The announcer comes onstage and says that a Cub Scout is working in his room on a robot that is 12 inches high.

A Cub Scout is in his room busily creating a robot. He adds something to the robot and tests it; it doesn't work and, with disgust, he says, "Ah!" He tries again and this time is successful. He says "Ah!" with satisfaction.

He gets his parents to show them his robot with pride. Pointing toward his room, he excitedly says "Ah" to encourage them to follow him. They question him to ask whether he is finished by saying, "Ah?" and then follow him to his room.

There he proudly shows his robot and, pointing to it, exclaims, "Ah!" In return, they proudly say "Ah" and show delight over the boy and his robot.

(If you are short on actors, this part can be deleted.) He goes to get some of his friends. He tells them that he has accomplished his goal by excitedly saying, "Ah! Ah!" Some of them eagerly and some of them skeptically say "Ah" and follow him back to his room. Again, the Cub Scout points to his robot and proudly says "Ah." The other boys express amazement at the completed robot by exclaiming "Ah!" The boys go home waving and calling "Ah" as they leave.

His parents remind him that it is bedtime by pointing to their watch, pantomiming sleep, and saying "Ah." The boy agrees to go to bed, saying reluctantly, "Ah." His parents leave; the boy opens his window, leans out and breaths in and says, "Ah." Then, with pride, he takes his robot and puts it on the open windowsill and says "Ah." The boy goes to bed near the open window.

During the night a thief comes to the window and steals the robot. The boy wakes up as this is happening and shouts with alarm, "Ah!" His parents come in, shouting "Ah?" to ask what is wrong. The boy points at the windowsill and shouts, "Ah!" The parents dial 9-1-1, saying "Ah! Ah!" to report the crime and then soothe their son with gentle "Ah's".

A police officer catches the thief, saying a firm "Ah!" The thief disgustedly says "Ah" and hands over the robot. The two then come to the house, and the officer hands over the robot with a satisfied "Ah!" The thief expresses his disappointment, saying "Ah," and is taken off to jail. The Cub Scout expresses his joy at having his robot returned, saying "Ah!"

The announcer comes onstage, wipes his brow, and says "Ah," as if to say that all is now done. All bow.

FITNESS CHAMPS

Characters: Six Cub Scouts in uniform, holding props as described below

ALL: We all excel in fitness. We're champs as you can see. Just listen to our stories, and I'm sure that you'll agree.

CUB SCOUT 1: I hold the title of the strongest in our den. Do you suppose that it's because of my friend? *(Holds up toy skunk, while others hold their noses.)*

CUB SCOUT 2: I'm known as the den's muscle man of the year. But most of my muscles are between my ears. *(Pulls out a too-small hat and tries desperately to put it on his head.)*

CUB SCOUT 3: I hold the title of the fastest one of all. I'm always first in line for the refreshment call. *(Pulls out a bag of cookies and begins eating them.)*

CUB SCOUT 4: I'm known as the champion of the high jump. One time I missed and got a big lump. *(Rubs his head with a painful expression on his face.)*

CUB SCOUT 5: To keep in good shape, I exercise each day. I wonder why my muscles turned out this way. *(Removes his shirt to show colorful padding on his arms.)*

CUB SCOUT 6: I'm the champion at making things disappear, you see. Watch us all disappear as I count to three. *(Slowly counts 1—2—3...as the curtain closes.)*

BASIC INGREDIENTS

Characters: Five boys and a narrator

Setting: The narrator (den leader or den chief) reads the script while the boys act out the parts.

NARRATOR: Cub Scout packs are made up of 6-, 7-, 8-, 9-, and 10-year-old boys. *(Enter five Cub Scouts, each stating their age.)*

Some are solemn and wide-eyed. *(One Cub Scout says, "I'm solemn"; another says, "I'm wide-eyed.")*

Some are wiggly and giggly. *(Two Cub Scouts say "I'm wiggly" and "I'm giggly.")*

They come in three varieties: Tiger Cubs, Cub Scouts, and Webelos Scouts. *(I'm a...)*

Cub Scouts like making noise *(all boys howl)*, competition *(boys pair up and arm wrestle)*, getting awards *(boys proudly point to the badges on their uniforms)*, and singing silly songs *(sing one line of a favorite song)*.

Cub Scouts like to play games *(do a crab race)*, to make things *(pretend to hammer and saw)*, and just to get together *(boys huddle around each other)*.

Cub Scouts are fastest at voting for field trips *(boys jump up and down, raising their hands)*, eating refreshments *(boys pretend to eat)*, and getting to the head of the line *(boys all try to get in line first)*.

Cub Scouts are quietest at a flag ceremony *(boys turn and salute)* and during a prayer *(they bow their heads)*.

Cub Scouts are most helpful while doing good deeds *(show Scouting for Food bags)* and community service *(show a poster of the latest project)*.

Cub Scouts are the basic ingredient for two important things: The time a volunteer leader gives and...Boy Scouts!

BACKYARD PICNIC

Characters: Six to eight Cub Scouts (Adapt parts for the number of boys in the den.)

Equipment: Paper bags

Setting: Skit opens with boys standing together in a backyard.

CUB SCOUT 1: Gee, there's nothing to do.

CUB SCOUT 2: Yeah, I know. I'm bored.

CUB SCOUT 3: Me too. Hey! Let's have a backyard picnic!

ALL: Yeah!

CUB SCOUT 1: I'll bring the potato chips.

CUB SCOUT 2: I'll bring the hot dogs.

CUB SCOUT 3: I'll bring the hot dog buns.

CUB SCOUT 4: I'll bring the drinks.

CUB SCOUT 5: I'll bring cookies.

CUB SCOUT 6: I'll bring something special. *(All walk offstage and return carrying bags.)*

CUB SCOUT 1: Here are the chips. *(Other boys announce similarly what they have.)*

CUB SCOUT 6: Oh no!

CUB SCOUT 4: What's the matter?

CUB SCOUT 6: I brought the ants! *(All run offstage.)*

ENERGY SAVERS

Characters: Six Cub Scouts in uniform; one den leader in uniform

Setting: Den meeting place, decorated as desired. The den leader sits at a table. As the skit opens, all Cub Scouts arrive together and sit down.

DEN LEADER: Today, let's take turns and tell how we can help to conserve energy in our homes.

CUB SCOUT 1: I know a good way. My mom doesn't use her clothes dryer as much as she used to. She uses a new solar energy device called a clothesline and hangs her laundry outside to dry in the sunshine.

CUB SCOUT 2: Did you know that if you take a shower, you use a lot less water than if you take a bath?

CUB SCOUT 3: My Mom even uses a timer, and we have learned to take 3-minute showers at our house.

CUB SCOUT 4: We keep the drapes closed on summer days to keep the hot sun out of the house and then keep them open for light and warmth in the winter.

CUB SCOUT 5: We keep the damper in our fireplace closed whenever we aren't using it. If it's left open in the winter, the warm air in the house escapes up the chimney, and that's a waste.

DEN LEADER (to the last Cub Scout): Johnny, do you have anything to add about saving energy? *(The den leader turns to see that Johnny is fast asleep.)* I guess Johnny is the best energy saver of us all! *(Curtain)*

THE OPERATION

Characters: Narrator, one boy in Cub Scout uniform, a boy in a white lab coat, two leaders in uniform, two other adults in ordinary clothes. Additional boys could be dressed in lab coats and assist in surgery.

Setting: This is a pantomime skit that involves leaders and parents. The uniformed Cub Scout lies on a large table, covered with a sheet. The props indicated below are taped to the back of the table out of sight. The doctor holds a large cardboard knife and stands behind the table. His assistants stand at both ends and behind the table.

NARRATOR: We're going to show you how to make a new Cub Scout in one easy operation. To do this, we need a boy...*(doctor points to the boy on the table)*...a den leader...*(uniformed den leader enters and stands near the table)*...a Cubmaster...*(other uniformed leader enters)*...and a family *(two adults in ordinary clothes enter).*

First, the boy needs to be covered with fun and good times. *(The doctor and assistant raise the sheet, taking care not to reveal the boy on the table. In large letters on the sheet is written "FUN AND GOOD TIMES.")* We use laughing gas for anesthetic. *(One of the assistants uses a tire pump or suction cup labeled "Laughing Gas.")* We take out bad feelings and put in love. *(The doctor removes a big rock from under the sheet and puts in a big red paper heart labeled "LOVE," which an assistant hands him.)* We take out selfishness and put in cooperation. *(The doctor removes a sign marked "ME" and puts in a sign marked "WE.")* We put in some good citizenship. *(The doctor puts in a cutout of the U.S. flag.)* And we add some reverence. *(The doctor adds a cutout of a church.)*

Our operation has been a great success! Just look at the results! *(The uniformed Cub Scout throws off the sheet, gets off the table, stands at attention, and gives the Cub Scout salute. The Cubmaster holds up a sign labeled "SUCCESS.")* *(Curtain)*

LAMPPOST

Characters: Any number of uniformed Cub Scouts; one boy playing the part of a lamppost

Setting: A boy stands onstage holding a lighted flashlight. He wears a sign marked "Lamppost." The stage lights are dimmed. As the skit opens, the first Cub Scout comes onstage and begins to look for something near the lamppost.

CUB SCOUT 2 (entering): What are you looking for?

CUB SCOUT 1: I've lost a dollar and have to find it. *(Cub Scout 2 helps look, as Cub Scout 3 enters).*

CUB SCOUT 3: What are you looking for?

CUB SCOUT 1: I've lost a dollar and I have to find it. *(Cub Scout 3 begins to look as the next boy enters. Continue this procedure until the last boy enters.)*

LAST CUB SCOUT: What are you looking for?

CUB SCOUT 1: I've lost a dollar and have to find it.

LAST CUB SCOUT: Where did you lose it?

CUB SCOUT 1: Down the street.

ALL (looking disgusted): Then why are we looking here?

CUB SCOUT 1: Because this is where the light is! *(Others chase Cub Scout 1 offstage.) (Curtain)*

SHIP AHOY

Characters: Narrator plus two Cub Scouts

Setting: The narrator stands in the middle with the two Cub Scouts facing each other at opposite sides of the room.

NARRATOR: Through the pitch-black night, the captain sees a light straight ahead on a collision course with his ship. He sends a signal—

CUB SCOUT 1: Change your course 10 degrees east!

NARRATOR: The light signals back—

CUB SCOUT 2: Change yours, 10 degrees west.

NARRATOR: Angry, the captain sends—

CUB SCOUT 1: I'm a navy captain! Change your course, sir!

NARRATOR: Comes the reply—

CUB SCOUT 2: I'm a seaman, second class, Change your course sir!

NARRATOR: Now the captain is furious and he signals—

CUB SCOUT 1: I'm a battleship! I'm not changing course!

NARRATOR: To which there's one last reply—

CUB SCOUT 2: I'm a lighthouse. Your call.

SHOP, SHOP

Characters: Shopkeeper, one boy as a duck, as many others as are in the den

Setting: The shopkeeper is dusting the counter, and a duck walks in.

DUCK: Quack! Got any duck food?

SHOPKEEPER (annoyed): Get out of here. We don't have any duck food. *(One or two boys enter shopping for [anything that fits the theme]; the shopkeeper smiles and sells them what they want.)*

DUCK (walking in again): Quack! Got any duck food?

SHOPKEEPER (more annoyed): Get out! I told you—we don't have duck food, and if you come back I'm gonna nail your tail to the counter! *(One boy buys nails; the shopkeeper smiles and sells them to him.)*

DUCK (sneaking in again): Quack! Got any nails?

SHOPKEEPER: Nope—just sold the last of 'em.

DUCK: Quack! Got any duck food? *(The shopkeeper pulls at his hair and runs off, screaming.)*

SHERLOCK AND DR. WATSON

Characters: Two Cub Scouts as Dr. Watson and Sherlock Holmes

Setting: The setting can be theme-related, and the skit can be done in a series, with any number of things missing.

DR. WATSON: Isn't it great—sleeping here in the great outdoors?

SHERLOCK: Yes, but don't you notice something?

DR. WATSON: Why, yes—it's a fine night with the stars above.

SHERLOCK: But isn't there something more?

DR. WATSON: Well, there's the shining moon and the sound of the wind.

SHERLOCK: Nothing more?

DR. WATSON: What, Sherlock, what?

SHERLOCK: Watson, someone has stolen our tent!

THE MUSIC MAKERS

Characters: A violin, cello, drum, cymbals, clarinet, and flute. Cub Scouts can wear costumes made from boxes, with instruments painted on the front—or they can hold up simple signs identifying themselves.

Setting: A cluttered room with chairs, sheet music, and music stands scattered around. The instruments walk onstage, mumbling and grumbling to each other. (This skit can also be performed with hand puppets.)

VIOLIN: Well, everyone knows the importance of strings! As first violin, my lovely tone rings.

CELLO: Really, my friend! Your strings are a riddle! You call yourself a violin, but to us you're just a fiddle!

DRUM: Now, now, all you strings—just go take a seat. For without my rhythm, you'd not have a beat!

CYMBALS: As a kettledrum, you're more kettle than not. And what's a kettle but an empty pot?

DRUM: If I were you, Cymbals, I think I'd keep hid, or else we'll replace you with garbage can lids.

CLARINET Honestly, Drum, I'd really rather that all of us just learned to play together!

FLUTE: Well, what about flutes? Or don't we matter? I've never heard such endless chatter!

DRUM: You know, I've been thinking…

CYMBALS (interrupting): Where would you get a thought? We know you're as hollow as when you were bought.

VIOLIN: Cymbals, Cymbals, I do declare! For ugly manners, there's none to compare!

CELLO: Now listen to me…and maybe you'll see that we're all important and necessary.

CLARINET: It's true that we all are necessary. But without players, not a tune could we carry!

ALL: He's right! It's true! Without the boys, we wouldn't know what to do!

DRUM: Let's all learn a lesson from this little fuss. The boys are what's important…and *then* comes us! (*If additional boys are available, two or three uniformed Cub Scouts could enter and pretend to play the instruments as the curtain closes.*)

Songs

For many boys, singing is as natural as talking. Most boys and adults have a sense of basic rhythm—they will often respond to a lively song or the beating of a drum by tapping a foot, humming to themselves, or even gently swaying. Singing helps people relax, improves attitudes, and sets the tone for what is to come.

Most den and pack meetings will include at least one song. The secret to good singing in the den and pack is fun: If the songs are ones the boys enjoy and can sing with a smile, singing can become one of the important regular elements of a den or pack meeting.

The *Cub Scout Songbook* contains a variety of songs and good tips for song leaders, and many packs have enough copies of it to pass out at den and pack meetings. Anyone can lead songs, but the proven methods found in that book and in the *Cub Scout Leader Book* will guarantee your success.

SONGS IN DEN OR PACK MEETINGS

A lively song can provide a change of pace in den or pack meeting activities and helps boys release stored-up energy. A quiet or patriotic song helps to set the mood for more serious activities.

The den leader, assistant den leader, or den chief might be the regular song leader, but don't overlook the possibility of a potential song leader among the boys. The song leader at pack meetings should be someone who can start a song on the right pitch and with a proper tempo. This person needs enough contagious enthusiasm to get the adults to sing along with the boys. A guitar will help enhance singing so find out whether anyone in the den or pack can play one.

The boys may know some of the old familiar songs such as "Old MacDonald Had a Farm," "Row, Row, Row Your Boat," and "She'll Be Comin' 'Round the Mountain." The *Cub Scout Songbook* contains many other songs that the boys can easily learn.

The choice of songs depends on the mood and theme of the meeting. A patriotic song is good at the beginning or end. During the meeting, use lively action songs to lift spirits and build enthusiasm.

When teaching new songs, it will help if the boys practice during den meetings. Then, at the pack meeting, have the words written large on a blackboard or big sheet of paper, or use an overhead projector if available, so everyone can see. This will encourage adults to join in.

USING SONGS CREATIVELY

You can use songs in various ways. Try some of these ideas at pack meetings:

- Divide the pack into two groups and have one group sing the first line, the other group the second, and so on. Or have one group sing while the other group claps or hums.

- Leave some words out and use hand claps instead. For example, when singing "The More We Get Together," have the audience clap hands each time the word "together" would be sung. Or ask them to stand on a certain word in the song.

- Add musical instruments or rhythm instruments.

- Sing "contra songs," where two or more different songs are sung together with a pleasing effect. For example, "Row, Row, Row Your Boat" with "Frère Jacques," or "Little Tommy Tucker" with "Three Blind Mice."

- Make up your own songs to fit the theme or special occasion, using familiar melodies such as "Yankee Doodle" or "Clementine."

- Check out *Cub Scout Program Helps* for songs. New songs may also be introduced at your district roundtable and the annual pow wow.

WRITING YOUR OWN SONGS AND THE PUBLIC DOMAIN

It isn't necessary to be a professional songwriter to write your own songs. Just fit your own words to the tune and rhythm of a familiar song. *But be careful when printing songbooks because copyright laws may apply.* If you want to print a songbook, you should familiarize yourself with copyright law and the public domain. A good place to start is on the World Wide Web at www.pdinfo.com.

Here are two basic guidelines about public domain music:

- Works written and published in the United States in 1904 or earlier are *probably* in the public domain throughout the world.

- Works written and published in the United States 1904 to 1922 are *probably* in the public domain in the United States.

Here are some familiar songs in the public domain (although be aware that some *arrangements* of these songs may still be under copyright protection).

"A-Hunting We Will Go"—Traditional

"Battle Hymn of the Republic"—copyright 1862

"Down By the Riverside"—copyright 1865

"For He's a Jolly Good Fellow"—1783

"Give My Regards to Broadway"—copyright 1904

"Home on the Range"—copyright 1873

"I've Been Working on the Railroad"—copyright 1894

"Rock-a-Bye Baby"—1765

"Skip to My Lou"—copyright 1844

"Yankee Doodle Boy"—copyright 1904

ECHO SONGS/CHANTS

Echo songs/chants are the best to start a group singing. The group will "echo" what you sing or say first, making the art of teaching a new song much easier. Here's an example of a rousing chant.

"BOOM CHICKA BOOM"

(Leader says a line, and everyone repeats.)
I said boom!
I said boom chicka-boom!
I said booma-chicka-rocka-chicka-rocka-chicka-boom!
Uh huh!
Oh yeah!
One more time…

Some extra ideas:

- Underwater: Chant with fingers dribbling against your lips.
- Loud: Chant as loud as you can.
- Slow: Chant as slowly and drawn out as possible.
- Monster style: Chant like Frankenstein's monster.
- Janitor style:
  I said a broom.
  I said a broom-pusha-broom.
  I said a broom-pusha-mopa-pusha-mopa-pusha-broom.
- Barnyard style:
  I said a moo.
  I said a moo-chicka-moo.
  I said a moo chicka-bocka-chicka-bocka-chicka-moo.
- Flower style:
  I said a bloom.
  I said a bloom-chica-bloom.
  I said a bloom-chica-blossom-chica-blossom-chica-bloom.
- Race car style:
  I said a vroom.
  I said a vroom-shifta-vroom.
  I said a vroom-shifta-grind-a-shifta-grind-a-shifta-vroom.

ACTION SONGS

Songs with movement are fun for boys and adults. They are harder to learn and the leader must know the song well to teach others—but don't let that stop you from all the fun to be had! If you find a song that everyone enjoys, repeat it at all your meetings, and soon everyone will catch on to the words and actions. These are great songs to do at the beginning of a meeting to get everyone ready for the activities.

"Dino Drama"
Tune: "Frère Jacques"

Stegosaurus, stegosaurus *(open hand at the back of the neck)*
Triceratops, triceratops *(thumb, index, and middle finger pointing forward; back of hand on the bridge of the nose)*
Flying pterodactyl, flying pterodactyl (flap your arms)
Tyrannosaurus rex, tyrannosaurus rex (curve the fingers and move the arms in front like snapping jaws)

"Stop, Drop, and Roll"
Tune: "John Brown's Body"

Actions:

- Stop: Hold hands out in front, palms forward.
- Drop: Bend the knees.
- Roll: Rotate the hands around each other in a rolling motion.

If your coattails catch on fire you should stop, drop, and roll.
If your coattails catch on fire you should stop, drop, and roll.
If your coattails catch on fire you should stop, drop, and roll.
It might just save your life!

"A Ram Sam Sam"

Actions:

- Ram sam sam: Make fists with both hands. Place one on top of the other on "ram," and then reverse the position on "sam," and then reverse back to the original position.
- Gooli gooli: Hands open, facing out. On each "gooli," clinch the fingers down toward the palm—like a lion flexing its claws!
- A rafi: Wave arms in the air.

A ram sam sam, a ram sam sam
Gooli gooli gooli gooli ram sam sam
A ram sam sam, a ram sam sam
Gooli gooli gooli gooli ram sam sam

A rafi a rafi
Gooli gooli gooli gooli ram sam sam
A rafi a rafi
Gooli gooli gooli gooli ram sam sam

(Repeat the chant a number of times, getting faster and faster. Or alternatively, do the chant as a four-part round.)

"Frog Chant"

Actions:

- Frog: *Mmmm*—make a big deliberate blink; *la-dee-da-dee-da*—hands in front of you, one palm up, one down; wiggle fingers, then switch.
- Bear: *Grrr!*—claws like a bear in front of you; *huggy-huggy*—hug your neighbors (first the right and then the left).
- Fish: *splish-splash*—hold your nose like you're diving into water; *na-nee-na-nee-na*—twirl around to the left and then to the right.

Mmmm, mmmm, went the little green frog one day,
Mmmm, mmmm, went the little green frog.
Mmmm, mmmm, went the little green frog one day,
So we all went mmmm, mmmm, ahh!
But we all know frogs go la-dee-da-dee-da, la-dee-da-dee-da, la-dee-da-dee-da,
We all know frogs go la-dee-da-dee-da,
They don't go mmmm, mmmm, ahh!

Grrr! Grrr! Went the big brown bear one day,
Grrr! Grrr! Went the big brown bear.
Grrr! Grrr! Went the big brown bear one day,
So we all went Grrr! Grrr! Grrr!
But we all know bears go huggy-huggy-huggy, huggy-huggy-huggy, huggy-huggy-huggy,
We all know bears go huggy-huggy-huggy,
They don't go Grrr! Grrr! Grrr!

Splish, splash, went the little blue fish one day,
Splish, splash, went the little blue fish.
Splish, splash, went the little blue fish one day,
So we all went splish, splash, splash!
But we all know fish go na-nee-na-nee-na! na-nee-na-nee-na! na-nee-na-nee-na!
We all know fish go na-nee-na-nee-na!
They don't go splish, splash, splash!

CAMPFIRE SONGS

Echo and action songs can be fun around the campfire, but traditional songs around every campfire can be uplifting and have special meaning. Don't forget those familiar folk songs and spirituals, such as "Michael Row the Boat Ashore," "Puff the Magic Dragon," and "He's Got the Whole World in His Hands."

"Make New Friends"

Here's a new twist to an old round. Sing the original, if you know the tune, or sing to the tune of "Twinkle, Twinkle Little Star." This is a good example of how you can "mix and match" tunes and words!

Make new friends, but keep the old,
One is silver and the other gold.
A circle is round, it has no end,
That's how long I want to be your friend.
The fire burns bright, it warms the heart,
We've been friends from the very start.

"CLEMENTINE" VARIATIONS

Often, a group enjoys singing, knows the tune, but can't remember all the words. One solution is to sing the same words to several different tunes. That adds some challenge and humor to the singing.

For instance, the words to "Clementine" can be sung to numerous tunes. Here are the traditional words to "Clementine" with a listing of a few tunes that you can mix and match with the words. This list is by no means complete—you'll have fun trying out some of your own!

In a canyon, in a cavern,
Excavating for a mine,
Lived a miner, forty-niner,
And his daughter Clementine.
Oh my darling, oh my darling,
Oh my darling Clementine.
You are lost and gone forever,
Dreadful sorry, Clementine.

Alternative tunes: "The Marine Hymn," "Take Me Out to the Ball Game," "Yellow Rose of Texas," "Yankee Doodle," "Ghost Riders in the Sky," "La Cucaracha."

"FIVE DAYS OF CAMP"
Tune: "12 Days of Christmas"

On the first day of day camp my mommie sent with me
A brand-new Cub Scout T-shirt.

On the second day of day camp my mommie sent
  with me
Two kinds of sunscreen,
And a brand new Cub Scout T-shirt.

On the third day of day camp my mommie sent with me
Three squirts of bug spray,
Two kinds of sunscreen,
And a brand-new Cub Scout T-shirt.

On the fourth day of day camp my mommie sent with me
Four sack lunches,
Three squirts of bug spray,
Two kinds of sunscreen,
And a brand-new Cub Scout T-shirt.

On the fifth day of day camp my mommie sent with me
Five water guns,
Four sack lunches,
Three squirts of bug spray,
Two kinds of sunscreen,
And a brand-new Cub Scout T-shirt.

"FUN IN SCOUTING"
Tune: "Alouette"

Chorus:
Fun in Scouting,
Lots of fun in Scouting.
Fun in Scouting,
Changing boys to men.

First verse:
Tiger Cubs are first in line,
Bobcat, Wolf, and Bears are fine.
So come have fun,
Come have fun,
OHHHH...

Chorus

Second verse:
Webelos is Cub to Scout,
Finding out what it's all about.
To advance,
What a chance.
OHHHH...

Chorus

Third verse:
Scout to Life, a mighty test,
Makes an Eagle, very best!
For a Scout,
So let's shout!
OHHHH...

Chorus

"OH, GIVE ME A PACK"
Tune: "Home on the Range"

Oh, give me a pack
Full of Webelos tracks,
That will lead on to Boy Scouts someday.
Where we all tie our knots
And pitch tents for our cots,
And then eat everything that we cooked!
Scouts, Scouts all are we,
Where we play while we learn constantly.
Obey the Scout Law; a friend to one and all,
And we all like to do a Good Turn!

Musical Instruments

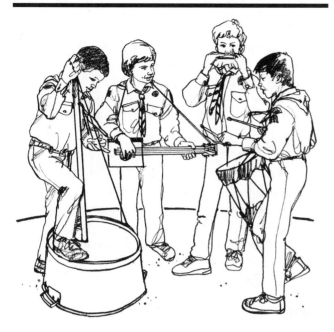

Boys have fun making musical instruments that really work. Your den might like to form its own band and learn to play a simple tune on homemade instruments. The instruments will come in handy at a Cub Scout circus or fair, a pack or den entertainment night, or just for fun in den meetings.

You can find most of the materials required for these instruments around the house.

ONE-STRING BASS

Materials: **Old washtub or paper barrel; broomstick; wire; nail, washers, nut, eye bolt**

1. Use sandpaper on the broomstick so the player won't pick up a splinter as he runs his hand up and down the stick while playing the bass.

2. Cut or file a notch about ½ inch deep in the bottom of the broomstick so it will fit over the rim of the tub

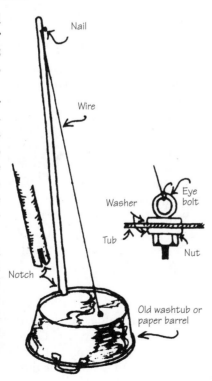

bottom. Wrap the broomstick just above the notch with heavy wire to prevent the stick from splitting.

3. Hammer a nail in the top of the broomstick so that the top end of the wire can be fastened to it.

4. Drill a hole for the eye bolt in the center of the tub bottom. Thread on a washer, insert the bolt in the tub, add the other washer and the nut, and tighten, as shown.

5. Fasten one end of the wire to the eye bolt on the tub. Fit the notched stick over the tub rim, holding the stick straight up, and stretch the wire tight. Fasten the other end of the wire to the nail at the top of the broomstick. Cut off any excess wire.

6. To play the bass, stand and rest the tub against the legs. Hold the stick at the top with one hand and pluck the wire with the other hand.

MUSICAL POGO STICK

Materials: **5-foot dowel or broomstick; homemade drum and other noisemakers; two tin pie plates; screw; rubber foot**

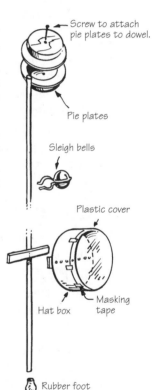

1. Fasten the various noisemakers to the dowel or broomstick. (You can make a drum out of a hat box, as shown.)

2. Using a screw, fasten the two pie plates loosely to the top.

3. The player uses one hand to thump the stick on the floor for rhythm, and with his other hand he beats the drum and sounds the noisemakers.

SAND BLOCKS

Materials: **Two 1-by-2-by-4-inch pieces of wood, sandpaper, thumbtacks**

1. Cut pieces of sandpaper the same width as the wood blocks and about 4 inches longer.

2. Turn the sandpaper over the block ends, with the rough sides out, and tack in place.

3. To play, brush the two sandpaper surfaces together briskly for a pleasant shuffling rhythm.

CYMBALS

Materials: **Two tin (not foil!) pie plates, two spools, 15 inches of heavy cord**

1. Punch two holes near the center of each pie plate.
2. Run the cord through the holes, tying a spool tightly to the bottom of each pan for a handle.

KAZOO

Materials: **Comb, tissue paper or waxed paper**

Hold a piece of tissue paper or waxed paper against a comb. Place your mouth against the paper and hum a tune through the paper and comb.

COCONUT CLAPPERS

Materials: **Coconut, sharp saw, paint or shellac**

1. Cut a coconut in half with a sharp saw. Drain the milk, pry out the meat, and clean the inside out.
2. Sand the edges of the coconut. Paint or shellac inside and out.
3. Experiment with different sounds and rhythms by clapping the shells together, tapping them on a board, or rubbing them together with a paper between them.

MUSICAL BOTTLES

Materials: **Assortment of variously sized and shaped bottles, water**

Line up the bottles and blow gently across the top of each to hear its tone. By adding a little water to a bottle, you can change the tone. The more water, the higher the tone.

Use a straw to add and take out a little water at a time to tune the bottles. Insert a straw in water, place a finger over the open end of the straw, and lift the water out of the glass in the straw.

For more accurate tones, use eight 10-oz. bottles. Fill them to the following depths in inches: 1⅜, 2, 2⅜, 3, 3⅜, 4, 4⅜. Leave one empty. This should produce a fairly accurate musical scale, and with some practice, you can play a tune.

SODA STRAW PIPE ORGAN

Materials: **Corrugated cardboard (with large corrugations), 1½ by 8 inches; eight straws**

1. Cut the straws in the following lengths in inches: 8½, 7¾, 7, 6¾, 6, 5¼, 4½, 4¼.

2. Push the straws between the corrugations of the cardboard, beginning about 1½ inches from one end and leaving four empty corrugations between each straw.
3. Flatten the top ends of the straws and cut off the corners. Blow into the instrument with your lips lightly around the straws—like a harmonica. Slide the instrument across your lips as you blow and hear the unique sounds you can make!

PADDLE RATTLE

Materials: **Wooden paddle, 12 bottle caps, nails**

1. Remove the liners from 12 bottle caps and hammer the caps flat. Punch a hole in the circle of each cap.
2. Nail the caps loosely to the wooden paddle, using three caps per nail.
3. Shake the paddle for a clattering rhythm.

SOUP CAN MARACAS

Materials: **Two soup cans; pebbles, dried beans, or rice (or an assortment of nails, screws, and washers); adhesive or strapping tape; paint**

1. Open the soup cans just enough to empty and wash them.
2. Put a few pebbles or dried beans in each can, or use an assortment of nails and screws. Reclose each can and seal with tape.
3. Fasten the two cans together at the ends that were opened using adhesive or strapping tape. Paint or cover with colorful adhesive-backed paper.

PAPIER-MÂCHÉ MARACAS

Materials: **Small round balloon; newspaper strips; wallpaper paste; pebbles, dried beans, rice, etc.; ½-inch dowel about 12 inches long**

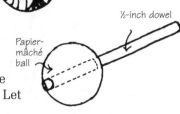
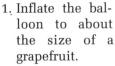

½-inch dowel

Papier-mâché ball

1. Inflate the balloon to about the size of a grapefruit.
2. Cover with strip papier-mâché as described in the "Crafts" chapter. Let it dry.
3. Punch two ½-inch holes in the papier-mâché on opposite sides of the ball. Insert a few pebbles, beans, or some rice. Glue a ½-inch dowel handle through the holes. Let the glue dry, and then paint and decorate as desired.

Stories

Of all the tools a Cub Scout leader can use, none can compare with the art of storytelling. Stories are a lead-in to many other parts of the program. You can tell a story

- To introduce the monthly theme.
- To explain a game.
- To introduce a craft session.
- While on a hike.
- To explain advancement requirements.
- To emphasize a point.
- For a change of pace in activities.
- For enjoyment and fun.

Stories may help boys develop a love of reading. Scouting's founder, Lord Baden-Powell, said, "If you can hand on something of the love of books to your Scouts, you will be giving them friends which will never fail them."

Cub Scout–age boys are curious. They have been introduced to books and reading in school, but not always as a source of entertainment or pure enjoyment. A leader can take a book in hand, read a few well-chosen sentences, put the book down, and then *tell* the story so it will come alive for the boys.

TYPES OF STORIES

- **Fun stories** can be enjoyed by both the teller and the listener. Nonsensical stories lend themselves to the use of actions and sounds. They help everyone relax and enjoy themselves.
- **Adventure stories** always appeal to boys. They include such things as science fiction, fantasy, and true-life adventure.
- **Teaching stories** can describe a moment in history, an invention or discovery, or a character-building attribute. Stories with a moral can help discipline boys without actually pointing fingers.
- **Animated stories** can be used to help boys learn pantomime. The leader tells the story while the boys act it out.
- **"What Would You Do?" stories** are action tales where the leader describes a dilemma and the boys provide solutions.
- **Mystery stories** appeal to boys and challenge them to solve the mystery before the story ends. (But avoid things that are gruesome or gory.)

Be sure to use only stories that are in good taste and appropriate for Cub Scout–age boys and families.

STORYTELLING HINTS

In addition to the tips on storytelling found in the *Cub Scout Leader Book*, these suggestions will help you be a good storyteller:

- Know the story.
- Be completely at ease.
- Help put the listeners at ease. Make sure they are comfortable.
- Arouse interest by having a catchy or exciting beginning.
- Create a setting or mood through descriptions.
- Make the story move. Maintain suspense.
- Match the speed and pitch of your voice to the action in the story.
- Keep the listeners' attention by varying the speed and tone of your voice and by using gestures where appropriate.
- Don't prolong a story unnecessarily. Decide beforehand how and when to end the story. A good ending is essential.
- Make the story short and to the point.

SAMPLE STORIES

THE ORIGIN OF THE PLEIADES: A CHEROKEE LEGEND

Long, long ago seven boys who lived in a village belonging to the Cherokee became famous because they were more interested in bowling stone hoops on the ground than in tending the cornfields. These boys were very skilled at bowling the hoops. But their mothers thought hoop bowling was a useless pastime and forgot that by bowling hoops the boys learned many useful things.

In fact, the mothers were so sure that it was a useless pastime that they decided to cure their boys of laziness. They collected several stones, like those the boys used as hoops, and boiled them for their sons' supper instead of the usual corn. Then when mealtime came, the mothers said, "Since you like bowling stone hoops better than working the cornfields, you may eat stones or go hungry!"

The boys didn't like this treatment at all, so instead of being sorry and promising to spend more time working in the fields, they decided they would play all the time. They got together and began to dance around the village. They danced and danced and danced until their mothers noticed that the boys' feet were whirling through space in a circle. As their mothers watched in desperate fear, the boys rose higher and higher. Up, up they went until they reached the sky.

Now, when you look at the sky on a clear night, you will see those seven boys. We know them as a constellation called the Pleiades. But the Cherokee call them "Ani'tsutā," which means "the boys." *(Show a chart of the sky and stars and point out the constellation, or if telling the story outdoors on a clear night, point it out in the sky.)*

BENNY THE FROG

Benny was a big bullfrog who lived in a swamp. This swamp was just an ordinary swamp, with nice big lily pads, nice houses for the frogs to live in, running water, televisions, and a rowboat parked in front of every house. It was just like any other swamp.

One day Benny decided he needed to have something special that would make all the other swamp creatures envy him. He thought and thought and finally decided he would like to have a beautiful, long, white beard. He wished so hard that one day the Fairy Frogmother appeared and said: "Benny, I will grant your wish. But if I give you a beard, you must promise never, never to shave it off. For if you do, I will turn you into an urn!"

Benny promised he would never shave it off, so the Fairy Frogmother waved her magic wand, and...Poof!...a big, long, beautiful white beard appeared on Benny's chin.

After a while, Benny's neighbors heard about the beard and came to see it. Everyone came: the alligators, the muskrats, the snakes, the raccoons, the turtles, and even the dragonflies. Benny was very proud of his beard. For days and days the creatures came from everywhere in the swamp. And then after a while, fewer and fewer came to see his beard, until finally, no one came at all. Benny wasn't as proud of his beard now as he had been at first. He was always tripping over it.

Finally, Benny just couldn't stand it any longer. He shaved! Suddenly, the Fairy Frogmother appeared and said: "Benny, I warned you about what would happen if you shaved your beard. Now I'm going to turn you into an urn!" So she waved her magic wand and...Poof!...Benny was turned into an urn.

And that just goes to show you that a Benny shaved is a Benny urned!

THE GIFT OF TREES

The American Indians believe that the secret of happiness comes from giving to others. Many, many moons ago, the Great Spirit first put people on the earth and they were frightened. "Where will we find food and water?" they asked. The trees laughed softly. "We are your brothers," they said. "We will help you."

The maple tree spoke: "I will give you sweet water to drink and make into sugar." The elm tree said, "Use my soft bark to make your baskets and tie them together with my tough muscles." The hickory tree said, "My cousins and I will fill your baskets with sweet nuts." And the hickory called the chestnut, beech, and walnut to help. The great pine tree whispered softly: "When you get tired, brothers and sisters, I will make you a bed. My cousins the balsam and cedar will help me."

The people's hearts were filled with sunshine as they set out to explore this new world. But soon they came to a deep, wide river. "How will we ever cross the river?" they asked. The trees laughed and laughed. "Take my white skin," the birch said. "Sew it together with the muscles of the elm tree, and you can make a boat that will carry you across the widest river."

When the sun crossed the sky to the lodge in the west, the people felt cold. Then the balsam fir tree whispered to them: "Little brothers and sisters, there is much sunfire in my heart. Rub my branches together and you will make a fire." So the people made fire. And that night they slept soundly on the branches of the great pine tree. The north wind blew cold, but the people's hearts were filled with sunshine.

Now when American Indian children ask how they can repay their friends the trees, wise people answer: "They do not ask for payment. But you can give them care and attention. You can give love and care to every plant and flower that makes your life beautiful."

THE ADVENTURES OF ICKY CRANE

(Long rhyming poems make especially good stories, as listeners enjoy the rhythms and rhymes.)

'Twas a dark and gloomy Halloween in Sleepy
    Hollow Land.
The moon cast eerie shadows that fell across the
    sand.
This Cub Scout's name is Icky Crane, and he is not
    afraid
Of witches, ghosts, and goblins, whether alive or dead.

Wait! What's that I hear? Hoofbeats drawing near—
Surely it is just a friend; there's not a thing to fear.
But since he's not so sure of what it might or might
    not be,
Icky decides to wait behind the most convenient tree.

The thing is coming closer now, the hoofbeats louder
    still,
And Icky trembles in the dark, as even Cub Scouts
    will.

Then the horseman comes in view, a figure all in
  black,
And Icky wishes he were home, tucked safely in the
  sack.

But there is one thing very wrong; what kind of man
  is he?
For there is nothing on his neck where his head
  ought to be!
The mighty stallion rears up high; the horseman
  gives a shout,
"Who is the crook who stole my head? Where is that
  thieving lout?"

The rider spots our brave Cub Scout, crouching in the
  night,
And Icky knows he must stand tall; he tries with all
  his might.
He rises up on shaking legs to meet this gruesome
  foe,
With a heart so full of courage, a Cub Scout head to
  toe.

The horseman points a finger at him, shouts, "Are
  you the rotten heel?"
And Icky answers strong and true, "A Cub Scout
  would never steal!"
The rider stomps and shakes his fist, acts like a
  spoiled kid;
Our Cub Scout cannot help but laugh at this nut
  who's lost his lid.

"Could it be it was your temper, sir? Good manners
  aren't a bother,
And if some patience you could learn, perhaps you'd
  grow another."
The rider climbed back on his steed, rode quickly
  through the night,
And Icky sighed with great relief that he was still all
  right.

So all you Cub Scouts far and wide, remember what
  I've said:
Be patient and have good manners—or you just
  might lose your head!

THE SKUNK MONKEY

(This is a good story to tell around a campfire.)

Joey, a brave Webelos Scout, had heard many stories around the campfire about the mysterious creature that lived in the Cascade mountain range. The
Skunk Monkey was a large, hairy creature believed to
be related to Bigfoot, but it was mostly renowned for
its fierce temper and foul smell. Many people had
claimed to have seen it, and others told of the many
people who had disappeared after encounters with
the creature. Yes, Joey had heard the stories, but he
knew they were only tall tales and legends. So it was
that one day, Joey decided to prove to his den that the
Skunk Monkey was just a story.

Joey left the campsite shortly after lights out,
under the bright light of a full moon. He traveled by
foot for a while until he reached the horse stables.
Joey picked a large, strong horse to ride. Soon he was
on his way, riding through snow-covered Cascades.

It didn't take long before Joey came upon a lake.
He noticed a canoe to his left. Joey dismounted the
horse and tied it securely to a small tree. He got into
the canoe and paddled across the lake. When he
reached the opposite shore, he walked farther into
Sasquatch territory.

As he walked, Joey noticed that the trees were
closer together and larger on this side of the lake. It
was hard to see where he was going, and he walked
carefully with his walking stick toward the area
renowned for Skunk Monkey sightings. Then it happened! *(Pause for effect.)*

(In a whisper) Joey heard a sound to his right and
froze in midstep. The sound was getting closer and
closer. The trees were packed so tightly together, Joey
couldn't see what was coming toward him. Perhaps
it was a wild pig...perhaps it was a harmless
deer...perhaps... *(Pause)*

(Loudly) Then he smelled it. It was the worst smell
that he had ever smelled. It was stronger than 20
smelly skunks. It was worse than the smell at the
garbage landfill. It was putrid and foul and rotten.
The noise got closer and closer, and before Joey could
turn and run away, two great trees were torn down in
front of him and he found himself face to face with—
the Skunk Monkey!

The creature gave a loud howl and banged its mas-
sive chest with powerful arms. Joey scrambled away
and ran as quickly as he could. *(Pick up the pace of
the story.)*

He ran through the close trees as hard as he could,
but he heard the creature only steps behind him, its
foul breath huffing. He wasted no time when he got
to the lake, scrambling into the canoe and paddling
swiftly away from the shore with all the strength he
could muster. He then heard another loud howl, followed by KERSPLASH!...The creature had jumped
into the lake and was swimming hard behind him!

Joey paddled with all his might and reached the other side of the lake in no time at all. He looked behind him, only to see the fangs of the Skunk Monkey as it got closer and closer! He jumped on the horse, striking it hard with his feet as he urged it to run for all it was worth.

The horse was powerful and galloped away in a flash. But all the while, Joey could hear the gruntings and howlings of the Skunk Monkey as it followed behind. Joey then saw the lights of a ranger's cabin and headed straight to it. He jumped off the horse and ran in the front door, banging the door shut behind him. He dashed up the stairs into the bedroom, but the ranger was nowhere to be seen. He slammed the bedroom door and wondered what to do next.

Joey heard a loud crash as the Skunk Monkey broke through the cabin's door. Joey heard the creature puffing up the stairs. He ran into the closet and shut the door behind him, crouching low in the clothes. But then he heard the bedroom door being smashed…and then a horrifying howl as the creature tore open the closet door, looked straight into Joey's eyes, and said…"Tag, you're it!"

I REMEMBER DAVY

(Sometimes stories can be enhanced with a few simple props or costumes. This story might be told by an old-timer dressed in frontier clothing, speaking slowly with a drawl.)

I was a friend of ol' Davy Crockett. He was quite a man. Why, I remember Davy when he was knee-high to a milk cow. 'Course, that was Davy when he was a baby—lyin' down! His cradle was 14 feet long. His ma had to put it up in a tree so the wind would rock little Davy to sleep.

I remember the day I was tryin' to drive some fence posts. Ground was frozen. Young Davy, he jumped along the tops of the posts, poundin' 'em with his feet. He kept goin' in one direction, 'cause if he jumped on 'em comin' back, those fence posts woulda gone clean under the frozen ground!

I remember Davy's tame bear, Ol' Death Hug. That was some bear! One day he and Davy were ridin' in a log Davy had whittled out, racing a steamboat up the river. Davy was paddlin' and Ol' Death Hug was sittin' in the back, steerin' with his tail. Shame about that bear! Davy taught him to close doors and churn butter and the like. Blamed thing got so civilized that he caught the whoopin' cough and died.

One day Miz Crockett said Davy couldn't go huntin' 'til he finished grindin' a hun'red bushels of corn. Davy saw a hurricane comin' so he grabbed holda that hurricane and hitched it up to his grindin' mill in nothin' flat. Why that cornmeal was so fine, Miz Crockett had to nail the corncakes to the table so they wouldn't float away!

I remember Davy the mornin' daybreak was frozen. Everything was frozen! That mornin' was dark as midnight. Davy climbed to the top of Daybreak Mountain and he saw that the whole world was frozen on its axis. Just wouldn't turn. Now Davy just happened to be carryin' a ton o' bear grease along, and he blew on that bear grease and melted it. Then he poured it on the earth's axis, and sure enough, the world started turnin' again and we got daybreak!

Then there was the time Davy ran fer Congress. We were all fixin' to vote fer him. Even the four-legged critters hoped he would go to Washin'ton. When we counted the votes, Davy was elected unanimously— plus 463 votes!

Yeah, I sure remember ol' Davy. He stood mighty tall for a man!

MEMORIES

A long time ago was a small, peaceful kingdom that had been ruled for many years by a beloved king. Everyone in the kingdom had always had enough food to eat, and the people worked together to make life comfortable. All the people worked hard, but they took pleasure in their work. The children played, dreaming of the day when they, too, would be old enough to contribute to the happiness and prosperity of the kingdom.

The time came when the old king knew he should pass the crown on to a younger person. He gathered his people together and told them that he could no longer rule them in the manner in which he felt they should be guided. It was time for a new monarch. But the king had no children, so the succession could not move automatically to a worthy prince or princess.

And so the old king asked the people whether there were any among them who considered themselves worthy of this honor. Such people were asked to stand before the king and before the people of the kingdom.

Now, you might think that everyone would rush forward at such a chance. But the people in the kingdom knew what a responsibility this was, and they knew how special a new monarch had to be. So only three young people ventured forward. All were upstanding, well-respected citizens. All were strong, hard workers and were eager to guide the kingdom in the years to come.

The king was proud of these young people and knew and respected each one. But he admitted that he could not choose among them. And so he gave them this challenge: "Travel to the mountains in the north and bring back to the kingdom the most precious thing that you can find. When you have all returned, I will decide which one of you is the worthiest by how you measure what is most precious for the people of the kingdom."

The first young person knew immediately what he wanted to do. He ran to his home, grabbed some provisions, and strode confidently into the wilderness toward the mountains.

The second young person was a bit slower. He went to his home, reflected carefully a few moments, and then gathered some belongings. He didn't know how long he might be, so he took food and blankets for a camp.

The third young person was even slower. She went to her home, built a warm fire, and looked deeply into the flames as she reflected on the challenge. When morning came, she also gathered provisions and set out for a long journey.

Soon the first young man returned. The king called the people together, and the young man presented him with a perfect red rose. "This is the most precious thing I found on the mountain," he told the king. "It is a perfect red and a perfect bloom. It will remind the people to strive for perfection and beauty and do only their best."

The old king took the rose and nodded slowly. He laid it beside him and waited for the other young seekers.

He didn't have long to wait for the second young man's return, who sought out the king early the next morning. He presented the king with a beautiful blue stone, saying that not only was it precious because it was beautiful, but it was also useful. "It can help grind the cornmeal so that the people of this kingdom will never go hungry," he told the king. The old king nodded and laid the stone beside the flower. He then settled back to wait for the return of the young woman.

A day passed. And two. Then a third. It was not until the fourth day that the young woman returned to the kingdom. She walked slowly, with her head down, as she came before the king and the people. For in her hands was nothing.

Then she spoke: "My king, I have returned empty handed. For four days and nights I have sat in the mountains, searching for the most precious thing.

And I saw many things that I thought were beautiful, but I thought they were beautiful *only* in the mountains. If I were to bring them back to you, they would lose their beauty. I saw a perfect bird building a nest in a mountain ash to start her gentle family. I saw a perfect butterfly of many colors, floating on the mountain breezes. And I sat awake all night, hoping that a thought would come to me—a thought of what I might bring home to this precious kingdom. And as I sat, I saw a huge, perfect red ball of fire rise above the horizon. It shone with colors more beautiful than I have ever seen. The yellows and golds and shades of red told me that a new day had begun. The rising of the sun was the most beautiful and precious thing I saw in the mountains, but I could not bring it back with me. I have only the memories of these things."

The old king nodded slowly and spent the night pondering over what he had heard, wondering who would make the best ruler for the people. Finally, at the end of the fifth day, he stood before the people with his decision. He called the three young seekers to stand before him and spoke.

To the first young man he said: "Your flower was indeed beautiful when you first brought it to me, but look: It has withered and died and is no longer precious or beautiful. It is a temporal thing. Inspiration is often like that, withering without the hard work and good decisions needed to help one reach the goal."

To the second young man he said: "Your stone is a beautiful stone, and it is useful, too. But what happens when we grind the cornmeal and the stone wears down and disappears over time? The stone is then gone forever, and is no longer precious. Hard work alone is like that. It takes a wise person to plan for many possibilities over many years."

To the young woman he said: "You should not be ashamed that you had nothing to bring back. For in fact you brought back the most precious thing anyone can have. You brought back the memories that touched you deeply, and you shall carry your precious memories with you always. Memories keep us warm through long nights, but they are more than that. When you share your memories, all who listen, learn. The happiness of the people depends on wise leaders who make good decisions. A good decision comes from our memories of what we have already seen and learned. It is your memories that will give you wisdom to be a fair and just queen to the people."

With that, he passed his crown to the young woman, who guided the people wisely as their queen for many years.

Jokes

Jokes help achieve one of Cub Scouting's important purposes—fun! Use them to add sparkle to meetings and put the group in a happy, lively frame of mind. Or use them as icebreakers or to help change the pace during a meeting.

RUN-ONS

Run-ons are similar to skits but are much shorter and require only one or two people. Run-ons are good for a change of pace during a pack meeting—something to make everyone laugh and relax. They come in handy during pack shows and circuses as fill-ins between acts. Also use them at campfires to fill dead time or to enliven the program.

Stiff Neck: The first person enters the room, looking up. Another person enters, looks at the first, and also looks up in the air. Repeat with as many others as desired. Finally, the last person enters and asks, "What are you looking at?" Each person down the line asks the next person the same question, until the first person answers, "I don't know about you, but I have a stiff neck!"

Wrong Feet: One person enters the room with shoes on the wrong feet. Another person enters, looks at the first, who is groaning, and says, "What's wrong?" "My feet are killing me!" the first replies. "Do you have bunions?" "No." "Oh, I see. You have your shoes on the wrong feet!" The first person replies, "But they're the only feet I have!"

It's All Around Me: The first person runs into the room yelling, "It's all around me! It's all around me!" Someone asks, "What's all around you?" The reply: "My belt!"

Loose Rope: A person enters the room pulling a rope. The leader asks, "Why are you pulling that rope?" The person replies, "Did you ever try pushing one?" (The stunt can end here, or later in the meeting the same person can come back, pushing a rope to the delight of the audience. Just push a wire through the rope so it will be stiff and straight and can be pushed.)

You Don't Say! The first person pretends to pick up a ringing telephone. He says, "You don't say...you don't say...you don't say!" (with more emphasis each time). Another person says, "Who was that?" The first person replies: "I don't know. He didn't say!"

It's in the Bag: A person comes into the room carrying an inflated paper bag that he holds tightly by the top. Another person says, "What are you carrying in that bag?" "Milk," he replies. "You can't carry milk in a bag!" "A cow does!"

The Redcoats Are Coming: Several people run into the room during the meeting at different times, with frightened expressions. Each shouts, "The redcoats are coming! The redcoats are coming!" Later, toward the end of the meeting, two or three adults enter wearing red Scout jackets and say calmly, "We're the redcoats."

I've Got a Cold: Several people enter the room tiptoeing cautiously. The first one in line whispers, "That's where I saw the ghost!" and points. This message is passed down the line in loud stage whispers. The last person says, "Where?" This is passed back up the line in whispers. The first one whispers back, "About 20 feet away." (Message goes down line.) "How big was he?" (Message comes back up line and so on, with each additional statement.) "About 10 feet tall." "When did you see it?" "About two months ago." "Then why are we whispering?" The first person says loudly, "I've got a cold!"

There's a Fly in My Soup: The customer says to the waiter, "Waiter, what's this fly doing in my soup?" The waiter comes to the table, looks in the bowl, and answers, "I believe it's doing the backstroke, sir!"

An Appealing Stunt: A person enters the room carrying a suitcase and states, "I'm taking my case to court!" A little later he enters again carrying a ladder and says, "I'm taking my case to a higher court!" A stranger runs through carrying a suit on a hanger. The first person enters, saying, "I lost my suit." He carries a banana or orange that he begins to peel as he makes his last statement, "I'm appealing my case!"

Wrap at the Door: One person says, "Say, wasn't that a rap at the door?" Another person says, "No, I don't think so." First person: "Yes, I'm sure I heard a rap at the door!" "I don't think so." The first one goes to the door and brings back a coat or jacket, saying, "I just knew there was a wrap at the door!"

The Viper: Periodically during the meeting, people run in the room with frightened expressions, shouting, "The viper is coming! The viper is coming!" Each time, the audience becomes more curious until finally, toward the end of the meeting, someone walks in carrying a pail and wiping cloths and announces: "I am de viper. I come to vipe de vindows."

Rock Concert: Several boys walk onstage clacking rocks together. Another person enters and asks, "What are you boys doing?" They reply, "Having a rock concert!"

Sun Fishing: One boy, wearing sunglasses, walks out with a fishing pole. He keeps tossing his fishing line into the air. Another person enters and asks:

"What are you doing with that fishing pole? There's no water around here." The first person tosses the line into the air again and says: "That's OK. I'm trying to catch a sun fish."

Spelling Champ: Two boys enter. The first says he just won the school spelling bee. The second says, "Then I guess you can tell me how many i's are in Mississippi." The first boy replies, "That's easy—four." The second boy says, "I can spell Mississippi with only one eye." When the first boy asks him how, the second boy covers one eye with his hand and begins to spell.

The Painter: A person wearing two coats enters the room with a bucket of paint and a paintbrush. He pretends to "paint" the walls of the room. When asked why he is dressed for winter, he replies that he was told to paint the room with two coats.

KNOCK-KNOCK JOKES

This series of knock-knock jokes can be done all at once or called out from the audience at various times.

Knock, knock
Who's there?
Repeat.
Repeat, who?
Who, who, who.

Knock, knock
Who's there?
Fascinate.
Fascinate, who?
Fascinating, isn't it?

Knock, knock.
Who's there?
Ima.
Ima, who?
Ima still hungry—when do we get s'mores?

Knock, knock.
Who's there?
Issue.
Issue, who?
Issue through yet?

Tricks and Magic

Magic and mystery are two surefire ways to capture a boy's imagination. Almost everyone enjoys magic, and no one more than a Cub Scout–age boy.

Along with puzzles (see 5–25 and 5–26), the den leader or den chief will want to have a new trick to demonstrate at almost every den meeting. You can also use tricks during pack meetings, where the boys and their families can enjoy them together.

One of the most important secrets to doing a trick is to practice until you can do it perfectly several times in a row. It is boring and a little embarrassing to watch someone try to do a trick and barely fumble through it. The tricks included here are mystifying at first but are easy to learn and fun to do. You can find the necessary materials around the house.

TRICKS WITH COINS

The Expanding Hole

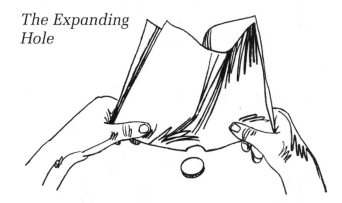

Materials: **Sheet of paper, scissors, a quarter**

In the center of a piece of paper, cut a round hole about the size of a dime. Hand the paper and quarter to a friend and ask him whether he can pass the quarter through the hole without tearing the paper or touching the coin. He won't be able to do it.

Solution: Fold the paper in half so the fold bisects the hole. Slip the quarter between the folds. Hold the extreme ends of the paper where the fold is. Raise them upward and toward each other. Shake the paper gently and the quarter will slip through the hole.

Stack of Coins

Materials: **Six or more pennies, smooth table, one dime**

Make a neat stack of five or more pennies on a smooth table. With a finger and thumb, flick a dime along the table so that it hits the bottom penny of the stack. It will fly out, leaving the rest of the pennies in the stack. You can repeat this, removing the bottom pennies one at a time.

Explain what is happening to the boys. The momentum of the moving dime is transferred to the bottom penny only because that is the only coin it hits. The rest of the pennies tend to stay in place because of the principle of *inertia*, and the stack just drops down. Notice that the dime bounces back a little. Also notice that if you push the bottom penny slowly with the dime, the whole stack will slide along. The bottom coin must be hit sharply.

Turntable

Materials: **Two coins, table**

Take a coin in each hand and stretch out your arms far as possible. Tell everyone that you will make both coins pass into one hand without throwing the coin or bringing your arms together.

With your arms still outstretched, turn your body and place one coin on a table. Then turn your body around again until the hand with the other coin comes to where the first coin lies. You can easily pick up the coin, and both will be in one hand while your arms are still wide apart.

The Disappearing Coin

1. Pretend to drop a coin in a glass. "Plink" the glass with your ring.

"Plink"

2. The coin is really under the glass in your hand.

3. Cover the glass with a handkerchief and hide the coin.

4. The coin will be gone!

Materials: **Two identical coins, a clear drinking glass with a flat bottom**

Tell your audience that you will make a coin disappear. You will drop a coin into a glass you are holding and show them the coin in the bottom of the glass. Cover the glass with a handkerchief and say some magic words. Then hand the covered glass to someone else to uncover. When the glass is uncovered, the coin will be gone.

Trick: Use a clear drinking glass with a flat bottom. When you "drop" the coin in the glass, you only pretend, "plinking" the glass with a ring you have on your finger. When you show the audience the coin in the glass, it is really under the glass in your hand. While the audience is looking at the empty glass in amazement, you can secretly hide the coin.

Coin Through the Head

Materials: **A dime**

Show a dime in your right hand. Bend your left arm and put the left hand near your left ear. Put the coin on your left elbow and rub it with a circular motion of your right hand, keeping up a patter about making the coin grow smaller and smaller until it disappears. "Accidentally" drop the coin and pick it up with your left hand. Now pretend to transfer it back to the right hand, but actually keep the coin in your left hand.

Go back to the original position with your left hand near your right ear. Resume rubbing the left elbow and keep talking about the coin growing smaller while you put it in your left ear. Now you are ready to show that the coin has disappeared by showing your empty hands. Then say that although it has disappeared, you can make it pass right through your head. Stick the phantom dime in your right ear, and presto! The real dime comes out the left ear.

Snap the Card

Materials: **Playing card, one coin, a drinking glass**

Lay a playing card on a glass and place a coin on top of the card. Ask whether anyone can put the coin in the glass without picking up the card.

Trick: It's easy! Snap your finger against the card's edge, sending it flying parallel off the rim of the glass. The coin will drop into the glass.

TRICKS WITH TOOTHPICKS

Remove Five Trick

Lay toothpicks in the arrangement shown. Rearrange them to make only three squares by removing only five toothpicks.

Remove Three Trick

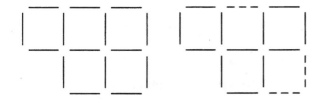

Lay toothpicks in the arrangement shown. Rearrange them to make three squares by removing only three toothpicks.

Remove Eight Trick

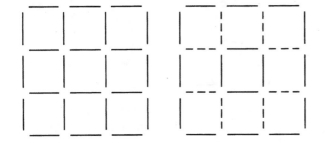

Lay toothpicks in the arrangement shown. Remove eight toothpicks so there are only two squares left.

TRICKS WITH PAPER

Tear the Rope

Materials: Paper napkin, water

Twist a paper napkin into a rope and dare everyone to tear it apart. They can't, and yet you can.

Solution: Merely wet your fingers. When you tear the paper rope, touch the center with the water on your fingers, and the napkin will tear easily.

Strong Paper

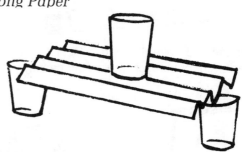

Materials: Three glasses, a sheet of paper

Ask whether anyone has seen the new strong paper that will support a glass. Show an ordinary piece of paper and lay it as a bridge between two glasses. Naturally, it won't support a glass. Then make ½-inch pleats in the paper and lay it on the two glasses again. Now it will support another glass.

Step-Through Postcard

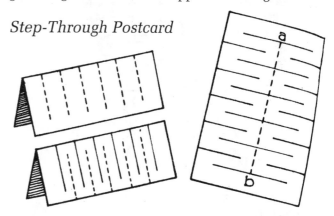

Materials: Postcard, scissors

Would you believe that you can crawl through an ordinary postcard? The answer is "yes," if you know how. Fold the card lengthwise and make cuts on the folded side, as shown by the dotted lines in the illustration. Then turn the card around and make cuts in the other direction, almost to the folded edge. Open the card and cut along line a–b. Carefully open out the card, and you will have a ring large enough to step through.

Newspaper Ladder

Follow the instructions and pictures to make a newspaper ladder.

1. Roll together several thicknesses of newspaper. Overlap about 5 inches.

2. Secure the ends with rubber bands. Flatten the tube. Tear or cut out a section from the center.

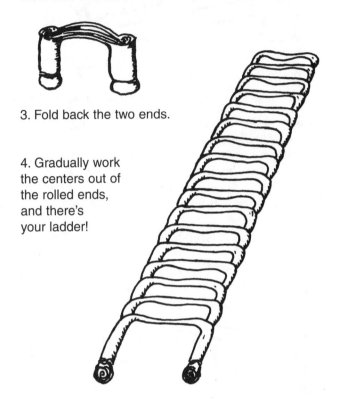

3. Fold back the two ends.

4. Gradually work the centers out of the rolled ends, and there's your ladder!

Newspaper Tree

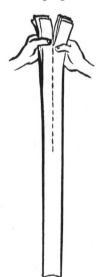

1. Make a roll of newspaper, as for the Newspaper Ladder. Flatten half the tube and tear it down the center about halfway, as shown.

2. Flatten the torn strips together and tear again down to about halfway. The four torn sections consist of several strips each. Press them down toward the rolled end of the paper so you can see an opening in the top.

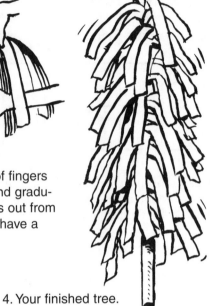

3. Put a couple of fingers in the opening and gradually pull the strips out from the top until you have a finished tree.

4. Your finished tree.

Möbius Strip

Materials: Newspaper, glue, scissors

Take a long piece of newspaper about one column wide. Give it a half-turn and glue the ends together. Cut the loop lengthwise and what do you have? Two loops? Surprise! You have one big loop.

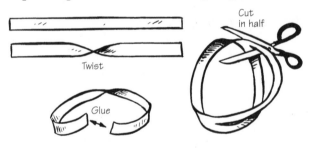

This looks like magic, but it really isn't. The Möbius strip stays together when cut in half because it has only one continuous surface. A German mathematician discovered this principle in the 1800s. You can prove for yourself that it is one continuous strip by drawing a line the length of the strip (before you cut it in half) without raising your pencil. You will come back to the starting point and will have covered both "sides" of the paper.

MAGIC TRICKS

Magic Straw

Materials: Straw, string, razor blade

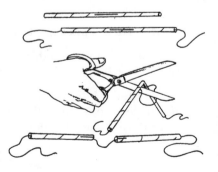

Cut a slit in the middle of a straw with a razor blade. Thread a string through it. Tell the audience you can cut the straw in half without cutting the string.

Solution: Bend the straw, pull the string out of the slit, and cut the straw. Show the audience that the string isn't cut, but the straw is!

Magic Number

Think of a number. Double it, add 10, and divide by 2. Then subtract the first number. Regardless of the number you start with, the answer will always be 5.

Magic Seed

Materials: Clear glass with seltzer water, grape seed

Drop a grape seed into a glass of water. It drops to the bottom. But at your command the seed will rise to the top and then sink to the bottom again.

Solution: What the audience doesn't know is that you are using seltzer water, not ordinary water. The gas in the seltzer clings to the seed and causes it to rise up. When the gas frees itself, the seed sinks. This will continue as long as gas is still in the water. Watch the seed carefully, and when you see it starting to rise or sink, give it your magic command.

Magic Hat

Materials: Three pieces of candy, three hats

Put three pieces of candy on a table and cover each with a hat. Lift the first hat, eat the candy, and put the hat back where it was. Do the same with the second and third hats. Now say: "You have seen me eat the candy under all three hats, but I can use magic so that all three pieces of candy are under one hat. Which hat do you choose?"

After audience members choose a hat, pick it up, put it on your head, and announce, "Now the candy is under the hat!"

The Mystifying Paper

Materials: Paper for everyone, same size and shape; pencils/pens; a boy who will be an accomplice

This is a good trick for a den meeting and requires an accomplice. Give everyone a slip of paper the same size and shape. Ask them to write a short sentence of four or five words. The words should be written plainly and not shown to anyone else. Everyone folds their papers and gives them to a person acting as "guardian." No one should try to read the papers.

Ask the guardian to hand you one of the papers. Gravely close your eyes, place the folded paper against your forehead, and remain a moment in deep thought. Then call out any sentence and ask who wrote it. The boy who is the accomplice, and did not write a sentence, claims authorship. Unfold the paper, as if to verify it, and read the sentence to yourself. Place this paper in your left hand and ask the guardian for another.

Repeat the same procedure, calling out the sentence you just read. This will be a correct answer, which one of the boys will have to admit writing. Keep this up until all players' slips have been read. The accomplice must keep your secret.

Reading Temples

Choose an accomplice and send him from the room. Tell the group that thoughts can be transmitted by feeling a person's head. Have the group select a number between 1 and 10 and call the accomplice back in. Tell him to place his hands on your temples, and after "serious concentration," name the number.

Solution: You can "transmit" the number by tightening and relaxing your jaw the required number of times, making your temples move in a way that can be felt but not seen.

Baffling Banana

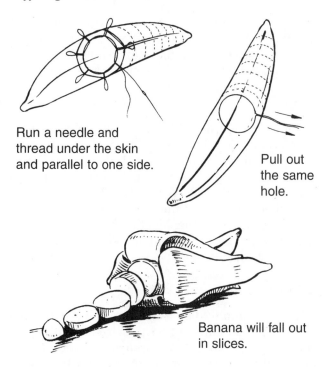

Run a needle and thread under the skin and parallel to one side.

Pull out the same hole.

Banana will fall out in slices.

Materials: A needle, thread, a banana

Run a needle and thread under the skin and parallel to one side of a banana. Repeat on each side until a circle of thread is made around the fruit. Hold the needle and end of the thread together and pull out the same hole. A cut will have been made through the fruit. Repeat this several times to cut the banana in several slices under the skin. The small needle holes will not be apparent, but when you peel the banana, it will fall out in slices.

Mysterious Money

Materials: Dollar bill, paper bag, scissors

Ask someone in the audience to give you a dollar bill. Place it in a bag and cut the bag in half. It appears that the dollar bill is cut in half, too, but then return the uncut bill to the surprised owner!

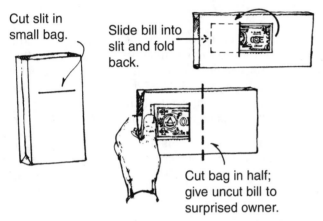

Cut slit in small bag.

Slide bill into slit and fold back.

Cut bag in half; give uncut bill to surprised owner.

Solution: Cut a slit in a small paper bag long enough for the bill to fit through. As you slide the bill into the bag, make sure that half of it goes through the slit. While you distract the audience with conversation, fold the bill over so it won't be seen or cut.

Immovable

Tell a friend you will hypnotize him so he can't raise a foot. He will be skeptical. Ask him to stand with his right side close to a wall that has no ledges or handles to hold. His right foot must be parallel to and touching the wall, while his left foot is at a natural standing distance from the right. Then "hypnotize" your friend, telling him that he can't lift the left foot slowly from the ground and keep it up. He will find that he can't!

Mind Reader

Your accomplice boasts that he can leave the room and, when he returns, name any object that the players have selected in his absence. The accomplice leaves, the players select an object, and the accomplice returns. You name one object after another, saying, "Is it [name an object]?" The answer is always, "No." You finally name the selected object and the accomplice says, "Yes, that's it!"

Trick: You name the correct object immediately after you name one that is black. This is the accomplice's signal that the next one named will be right.

Magnetized Spoon

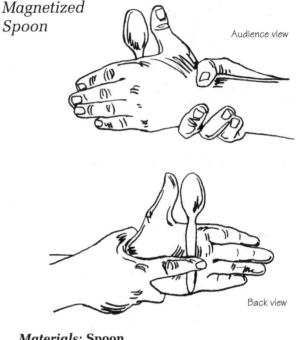

Audience view

Back view

Materials: Spoon

Rub a spoon vigorously, telling the audience that you are magnetizing it. Say some magic words. Hold the spoon as shown, showing it to the audience, who will think that it is sticking to your hand.

Balancing Egg

Materials:

Blown egg shell	Salt
Tissue paper	Hard-boiled egg
Sheet of paper	Teaspoon

This magic egg will stand upright when you hold it on the outstretched palm of your hand. It will balance in many weird ways on any flat surface.

Trick: The egg is a blown egg that contains some salt. To prepare it, pierce an egg at both ends and blow the contents out into a dish. Let the inside of the shell dry. Seal one end by pasting a tiny piece of tissue paper over it. Make a small funnel from paper and pour 2 t. salt into the shell. Seal the other end. At the end of your balancing act, place the egg out of sight.

Pick someone from the audience to try to balance the egg as you did, but give him a hard-boiled egg to use. Of course, he can't do it. Then you take the hard-boiled egg and give it a little smack as you set it on the table. The shell will break slightly and allow the egg to balance.

Money Has Power

Materials: Wooden pencil, dollar bill

Have someone hold a wooden pencil at both ends and parallel to the floor. After folding a dollar bill lengthwise, announce to the group that you will break the pencil in half with the dollar bill, and ask them to give you three chances to do so. On the first two tries, use only the dollar bill, but on the third, put your index finger in the fold of the bill and hit the pencil with your finger. The pencil will break if it is held firmly.

Magic Dust

Materials: Glass of water, ice cube, 10-inch piece of thread, salt

Place a glass of water containing an ice cube on a table. Tell your friends you can lift the ice cube using a 10-inch piece of thread. They can try, but it won't work. Lay the thread across the top of the ice cube, sprinkle some magic dust (salt) on it, and lift the thread—cube and all.

Trick: The salt makes the ice melt, but it freezes again quickly, freezing the thread to the cube.

MISCELLANEOUS TRICKS

Balancing Bat

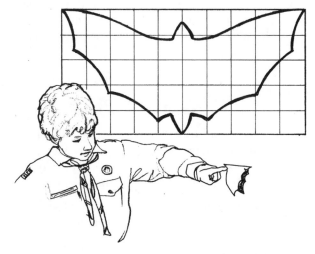

Materials: Black posterboard, scissors, tape, two pennies

Here's a balancing act to mystify your friends. The bat will balance on the tip of your finger, the edge of a table, or the rim of a glass. Enlarge the pattern and trace onto black posterboard. Cut out the bat and tape a penny to the underside of each wing tip. With a little practice, you can make it appear to fly by balancing it on your finger and raising and lowering your hand.

Windmill

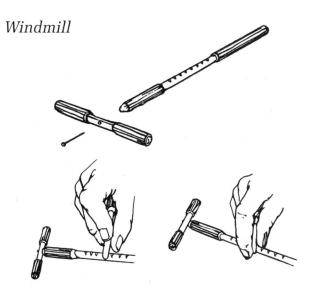

Materials: Notched stick or dowel, propeller, pin or nail, pencil

This windmill will amaze your friends. You can make the propeller revolve, stop, and reverse directions without being observed, and people will think you're doing it through your willpower. To make the windmill, fasten a light propeller to the end of a notched stick or dowel with a pin or nail. Rub a pencil along the notches of the stick to set up a vibration that will cause the propeller to revolve rapidly. You can control the direction by applying light pressure with the thumb or forefinger on one side of the notched stick or the other.

It Can't Be Done

Tell your friends that you can jump backward farther than they can jump forward, if they do exactly as you do. Prove it by grasping your toes and hopping backward a few inches. When your friends assume the same position, they'll find they can't budge when they try to jump forward.

Magic Colored Pencil

Materials: Pencil, paper

Pick up an ordinary pencil. Tell your audience that this ordinary pencil will write any color they can think of. Ask someone to name a color. Then write the color down (R-E-D, B-L-U-E, etc.) and show them.

Out of Reach

Challenge your friend to place his right hand where his left hand can't reach. When he looks perplexed, place your right hand on your left elbow.

Leaping Salt

Materials: Salt, comb

Put a small amount of salt on a table. Run a comb through your hair. Then hold the comb 1 inch above the salt. It will leap up and stick to the comb.

Red or Green?

Materials: Red paper, white paper, scissors, a light

Cut out a pig or other animal from bright red paper about 4 inches in size. Mount it on a piece of white paper. Hang the picture on the wall. Next to it, hang a large piece of white paper. With the light to your back and shining on the pig and the blank paper, look the animal steadily in the eye and count to 20. Then look directly at the large sheet of white paper. There, you'll see a green animal!

Floating Ball

Materials: Tennis ball, soda straw

Hold a soda straw in your mouth and tip your head back. Hold a table tennis ball over the end of the straw and blow softly. Release the ball. It will stay suspended above the straw as long as you blow.

Pinhole Illusion

Materials: Two business cards, pin

Punch three small holes in a business card with the point of a pin. These holes should be close together, and they must not cover an area larger than the pupil of an eye. In another business card, punch a single hole. Hold the card with the three holes as close to your eye as possible, and hold the other card about 2 to 3 inches in front of the first. When you look at a light, it will appear as if the far card has three holes in it, also.

Handkerchief Trick

Materials: Two white handkerchiefs, one colored handkerchief

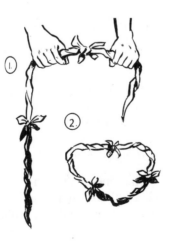

Tie two white handkerchiefs together, and then tie a colored handkerchief to one of the white ones. Ask someone to put the colored handkerchief between the two white ones without untying any of the knots.

Solution: Simply tie a third knot, making a circle of the three.

Candle Blow

Materials: Candle, matches, card

Tell your friends that you can make a candle flame move toward you.

Solution: Hold a card between yourself and the candle and blow against the card. The flame will be drawn toward you.

Disappearing Knot

Materials: 18-inch piece of string

Pull open.

Tie an 18-inch piece of string so there is a loose, open, overhand knot in the center. Now tie the ends together with several knots so the string makes a loop. Let someone examine the string and explain that you are going to remove the overhand knot without untying the other knots. Place the string behind your back for an instant, and then bring it forward and show the audience that the overhand knot has disappeared from the loop.

Solution: While the string is behind your back, open the overhand knot out wide, and move it up to join with all the other knots, where it won't be noticeable.

Super-Breath

Materials: Three small pieces of paper

Place three small bits of paper on the back of your hand. Let anyone select one of the pieces. Claim that you can control your breath so as to blow away only the chosen one. It sounds impossible.

Solution: Place two fingers on the other two bits of paper and then blow the chosen one away.

Obedient Straw

Materials: Straw, table

Tell the audience that you can make an ordinary straw obey your command. Put the straw on a table with your forefinger 6 inches in front of it. As you move your finger away from the straw, it follows.

Trick: As you move your finger, blow softly on the straw.

Disappearing Pencil

Materials: Pencil

1. Hold the hands together, fingers extended, with a short pencil crosswise under the thumbs.

2. Rotate the hands a quarter-turn (right fingers up, left fingers down), bending the right fingers over the left half of the pencil and the left hand.

3. Bring the right thumb under the left thumb and palm, and continue the rotation, allowing the hands to turn over so both palms are down.

4. The pencil has disappeared!

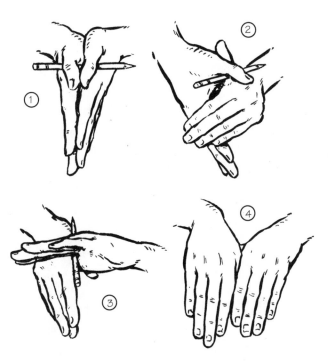

To make the pencil reappear, reverse the motion by putting the right thumb over the left thumb and pencil and rotating the right thumb toward the left wrist, along the outside of the left thumb. Bring the hands together as in the beginning, with the pencil again under the thumbs.

Disappearing Water

Materials: Napkin, glass of water, table

Put a glass of water on a table and cover it with a napkin. Tell a friend that you can drink the water without touching the napkin. Walk around the table, say some magic words, and then ask your friend to lift the napkin to see if the water is still there. When he lifts the napkin, quickly take the glass and drink the water. You didn't touch the napkin, did you?

Electric Den Chief

Materials: Small key-ring flashlight, frosted light bulb

A den chief can master this trick with a little practice. When he's ready to perform, he tells the boys he can light up a bulb in his hand with the electricity from his body.

Trick: Hold a frosted light bulb by the base, at the same time holding a small key-ring flashlight behind the frosted light bulb with the third and fourth fingers of the hand. The frosted bulb will hide the flashlight from the boys. Exert a twist with the fourth finger to turn on the flashlight and make it appear that the frosted bulb has lit.

Flip That Cup

Materials: Three glasses, table

Stand three glasses on a table in a row, with the middle one upside down. Ask someone to turn all the glasses bottom up, using three moves and picking up two glasses at a time, turning them over with each move.

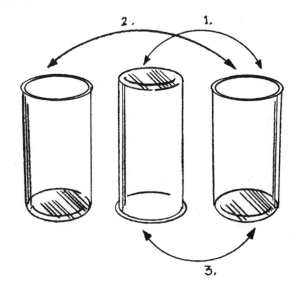

Solution: First move: turn over the second and third glasses; second move: turn over the first and third; third move: turn over second and third again.

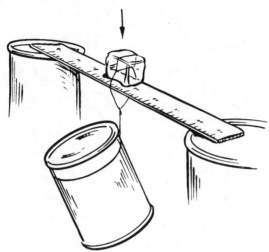

Materials: Ice cube, ruler, two tall cans, wire, unopened soup can

You may not be able to saw a person in half, but you can do a similar trick with an ice cube. Balance a ruler between two tall cans. Put an ice cube on the ruler. Twist an end of a long piece of wire around an unopened soup can or other heavy object. Run the wire over the ice and fasten it to the can so it is suspended. Soon the wire will pass through the ice cube. Has it been split in half or is it still in one piece?

SPECIAL PACK ACTIVITIES

In this chapter you'll find a broad assortment of time-tested special events that dens and packs have used successfully. Some are indoor activities, others are outdoor activities; some are suitable for the summer, some for winter, and others can be used any time of the year.

Many of the activities offer possibilities for Cub Scout advancement. It is important that you take advantage of these opportunities so that boys will not only have fun but also have a chance to learn and advance in rank.

Most of the activities require a minimum of materials and equipment. Even though they are simple and within the capabilities of Cub Scout–age boys, all require some advanced preparation on your part to be completely successful.

Planning Special Events

When planning a special activity, consider the task at hand and follow these guidelines as you evaluate your needs and resources:

Objective: Why are we having the activity? Does it help to achieve the purposes of Cub Scouting?

Leadership: Adequate adult leadership is a "must." For major pack activities, the pack committee usually appoints a chair and recruits members of an event committee to carry out the various responsibilities.

Facility: What type of facility is needed? Can the event be held in the regular pack meeting place? Is it an outdoor activity? Are reservations necessary? Will there be a charge for the facility?

Physical Arrangements: What type of seating arrangement is needed? How much space is available? If it is outdoors, what is available, and what do we need to provide?

Schedule: A written schedule or program will help the event run smoothly. When will the activity be held? What time does it begin? Who does what and when? What time does it end? And of course, let all pack families know the schedule.

Alternatives: Plan for backup leadership to fill in for emergencies. If it is an outdoor activity, have a backup plan in case of adverse weather conditions.

Public Relations: Be sure that all pack families know about the activity. Use word of mouth in your den meetings, and put an article in your pack/den newsletter. Could the event be publicized in local newspapers and other media?

Rules: For competitive events, establish clear and simple rules that everyone can understand. Be sure everyone knows the rules in advance. This will save many disagreements and help prevent hard feelings.

Judging and Awards: Any special pack activity that takes the place of a regular pack meeting should include advancement awards so that boys are recognized promptly. If it is a competitive activity, be sure that each boy receives something for participating. You should ask: "How and when should these awards be given and what type of awards will be used? Who will do the judging?" Answer these questions ahead of time.

Health and Safety: The plan should include adequate supervision and ensure the proper use of equipment. A harmless object can become dangerous when used in the wrong way. Take the necessary measures to ensure the health and safety of the boys and others taking part. Read the BSA publication *Guide to Safe Scouting* and keep it on hand for all events.

Materials and Equipment: What materials and equipment are needed? Who will provide them? Can you get donations? Check the Parent and Family Talent Surveys for resources among family members.

Finances: Estimate the cost of the activity, if any. Will the pack budget cover the expenses? If not, how will costs be covered?

Registration and Check-In Procedure: Most competitive events require some type of check-in procedure. How will it be done, and who is responsible?

Transportation: Will transportation be needed? Will each family provide its own transportation? If not, what arrangements need to be made? Are tour permits or site licenses needed?

Countdown: Does everyone involved know what is expected? Remember the secret word of Cub Scouting: KISMIF—*Keep It Simple, Make It Fun.*

BACK-DATED PLANNING CALENDAR

To ensure that nothing important is overlooked, you should develop a backdated planning calendar for each special event, such as the one shown here. List all of the steps that need to be completed before the activity, with a target date for the completion of each phase of the planning.

Six months before	Select event chair and cochair.
Five months before	Recruit event committee.
Four months before	Make a detailed, written plan with specific assignments.
Three months before	Order materials and awards. Make arrangements for the facility.
Two months before	Begin publicizing in the pack. Contact media for publicity.
One month before	Make announcement at a pack meeting, and contact other pack families. Contact media for publicity again.
Two weeks before	Make a last-minute check on materials, equipment, and the facility.
Event	Arrive early and set up if necessary. Hold the event. Have fun!
One week after	Evaluate the success of the event. Thank everyone who helped.

CALL ON THE SECOND TEAM

When planning and conducting special pack activities, don't forget to use your second team, that is, Cub Scout parents and other adults. This is a good way to get pack families to participate, to strengthen the pack, and to build spirit.

At the pack's annual planning conference, select a chair and cochair for each special activity, and identify other adults who would like to help. This way, the leadership is identified early so planning can begin early. The chair and cochair work together, so if the chair is unexpectedly out of town, the plans can continue uninterrupted.

Anniversary Week Activities

Every February, beginning on Sunday of the week that includes February 8, the Boy Scouts of America celebrates its anniversary. BSA was incorporated February 8, 1910. February is also the birth month of Scouting's founder Lord Robert Baden-Powell. During anniversary week, Scouting units are encouraged to conduct rededication ceremonies and to demonstrate Scouting's purposeful activities.

Religious Services: Many packs attend church or synagogue in uniform on Scout Sunday or Scout Sabbath. In some churches and synagogues, Cub Scouts take part in the services.

Civic Activities: Often, local government, school districts, and fraternal organizations will allow Cub Scout packs to present a flag ceremony at the openings of their meetings. This is especially appropriate during anniversary week.

Wear the Uniform: Encourage your Cub Scouts to wear their uniforms to school one day during Scouting Anniversary Week. This might be on their regular den meeting day or any other day during the week.

Cub Scouting Demonstrations: One of the best ways to mark Scouting Anniversary Week is with a live demonstration. This could be held after school or all day Saturday wherever there is plenty of pedestrian traffic (e.g., a shopping center, vacant lot, centrally located park, library, or even a large store display window). Show Cub Scouting in action—boys racing pinewood derby cars, playing games, staging skits or puppet shows. Webelos Scouts could have displays and give demonstrations of activity badge projects. Be sure to have a big sign and handouts identifying your chartered organization and unit. Include the name and phone number of a leader who can be contacted for information about joining.

Stage a skit for a Cub Scouting demonstration during Scouting Anniversary Week. Cub Scout clowns could perform various feats of skill (Wolf Achievement 1).

Good Turns: Do a Good Turn for the pack's chartered organization—or for your community. Think of a worthwhile project that involves parents and other family members as well as Cub Scouts.

Displays: Window displays will attract attention to your pack. Make arrangements early with a public library, your chartered organization, or a store to use a display area. A window display might be tied to a particular Cub Scouting theme, or it could cover the pack's activities for a whole year. Decorate with banners, flags, streamers, etc. to make the display colorful and attractive. Be sure to have a sign identifying the pack and its chartered organization, with the name and phone number of a leader who can be contacted for more information. Put your display up on time and remove it on time. Be sure to send a letter of thanks.

World Friendship Fund: Plan and get approval from your council and pack committee for a pack money-earning project to raise funds to donate to the World Friendship Fund. This BSA-administered fund provides material help to Scouts and Scouters around the world. Ask your local district or council for more information.

The Blue and Gold Banquet

Most Cub Scouts celebrate Scouting Anniversary Week with a birthday party called the blue and gold banquet. In nearly all packs, the annual blue and gold banquet, which is often the pack meeting for February, is the highlight of the year. It brings families together for an evening of fun and inspiration.

The purpose of the blue and gold banquet is to celebrate, recognize, and inspire. Recognize Cub Scouts, pack leaders, and other adults involved in Scouting at this event by presenting advancement awards, honors, certificates—or with just a hearty round of applause for service to the pack.

PLANNING THE PROGRAM

Early planning is necessary if the program is to be successful. The pack committee should recruit a banquet chair, who in turn selects others to carry out the responsibilities of the program. The committee reserves the location, makes arrangements for the banquet, sends out special invitations, decides on the theme, and takes care of the housekeeping. The committee should try to include as many people as possible in the planning. The committee should also keep in touch with the pack committee by attending the monthly pack committee meetings. Good communication is essential for a successful blue and gold banquet.

Suggested Timetable

Four months before: Select blue and gold chair and committee. Decide on the date, time, place, theme, and type of meal for the event. Reserve the location.

Three months before: Plan the program. The banquet committee reports progress and details to the pack committee.

Two months before: Determine the guest list, and mail invitations. (Include an RSVP card in the invitations so you can accurately plan for the amount of food and space required.) Boys begin work on decorations and presentations. The banquet committee reports progress to pack committee.

One month before: Boys continue work on decorations and presentations; recheck facilities; print the program. The banquet committee reports to the pack committee.

Two weeks before: Turn in award applications, complete decorations, verify RSVP counts and food preparation.

Banquet day: Set up the room, ENJOY THE BANQUET, clean up—and then relax after a job well done!

During the days after: Blue and gold committee writes a report that includes suggestions to help make the next year's blue and gold banquet even better.

THE BANQUET

The banquet may be served in a variety of ways. Your pack might choose to have dinner catered or in a restaurant. Many packs have a blue and gold dessert or ice cream social. Most often, the blue and gold banquet is a family potluck. Surprising as it may seem, the type of dinner isn't very important; it is the Cub Scouting that happens in making the event a time of family and fellowship that really counts.

If your pack decides to have a meal, ask yourself what type of meal best serves your pack. If your plan includes a potluck, be sure to have a variety of foods. One way to do this is to assign types of food by last name, for instance, A–E: salads and vegetable dishes; F–K: appetizers and breads; L–P: main dishes; Q–T: plates, beverages, and condiments; and R–Z: desserts. Another way is to divide food responsibilities by den, such that Den 1 brings salads, Den 2 brings main dishes, etc. Sometimes, the pack will provide the paper products and utensils or a large sheet cake for dessert.

It's important to make sure there is enough food for everyone. A good guideline for your potluck dish is to bring enough to serve your family plus two.

Finally, since this is a banquet for the boys, try to serve foods that will please them—the kind of things *they* enjoy and would choose themselves.

Blue and Gold Mints

Ingredients:
  6 T. margarine or butter
  2 t. peppermint extract
  3 lb. powdered sugar
  7 T. water (color half with blue and the other half with yellow food coloring)
  Dash of salt
  Granulated sugar

1. Cream the margarine or butter. Add flavoring and salt.
2. Divide into two batches. Add colored water to each batch.
3. Add 1 lb. powdered sugar to each batch. Blend with a mixer, and then knead another half-pound of sugar into each batch.
4. Shape into small balls and roll in granulated sugar.
5. Press into molds or roll out to desired thickness and cut or shape mints. Let the mints dry on a cookie sheet in the refrigerator. Store in a covered tin or airtight box to prevent hardening.

FINANCING

How will the pack pay for the banquet? Most packs include it in their annual budget and cover any costs through their regular money-earning projects. Your pack may charge for dinner, especially if it is catered (be absolutely certain *every* family feels it can afford to attend), or the chartered organization might be able to provide it as a gift to the pack. If there are any costs for the family, collect the money in advance.

THE FACILITY

Secure a suitable facility *at least* six weeks in advance—the earlier, the better. The number of people attending and the serving arrangement will determine the space you need. A good way to estimate the number attending is to multiply the number of boys by three. This will help you decide how large the facility should be. The location could be a school cafeteria, church meeting room, or large room at a civic center, town hall, restaurant, or cafeteria.

Consider these things: rental fee, if any; seating capacity and number of tables available; kitchen availability, if needed; adequate parking space; convenient restrooms; and accessibility for people with disabilities. You will need to find out whether special equipment is available, such as a public-address system, speaker's stand, etc., and whether you need to secure permission to use any special equipment.

OTHER CONSIDERATIONS AND IDEAS

- Be sure that boys are involved in the banquet preparations. For instance, dens can provide their own table decorations. Boys can make a centerpiece, place mats, place cards, napkin rings, and nut cups.

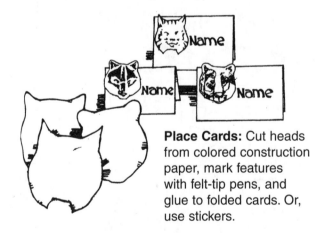

Place Cards: Cut heads from colored construction paper, mark features with felt-tip pens, and glue to folded cards. Or, use stickers.

- Enlist the help of extra parents specifically for the event. For instance, a parent who enjoys computers could make the programs. Use the Parent and Family Talent Survey to find adults with "hidden" talents.

- Invite the boys and their families, of course. You may also to wish to include some of the following special guests:
    - Head of your chartered organization
    - Chartered organization representative
    - Mayor or other local political figures
    - Police or fire department members
    - School principal
    - Scoutmaster of local Boy Scout troop
    - District executive
    - District committee members
    - Cub Scout roundtable staff
    - Unit commissioner

Banner Invitations: Use blue or gold construction paper, and write with a blue or yellow marker. Glue or tape a dowel to make a double banner.

- Include a flag ceremony in your blue and gold banquet. One of the purposes of Cub Scouting is to help boys develop habits and attitudes of good citizenship. You can find many flag ceremony ideas in the BSA publication *Cub Scout Ceremonies for Dens and Packs.*

Napkin Ring

Cut a diamond from yellow construction paper and print "Help Others" across the center. Add the guest's name, if you want. Glue the diamond to a ring of cardboard covered with blue construction paper.

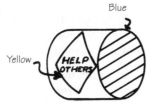

Webelos Place Mat

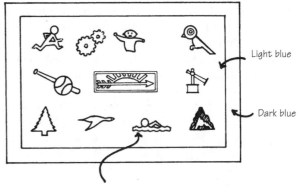

Cut activity badges from gray construction paper and glue on.

Glue an 11-by-17-inch piece of dark blue construction paper on top of a 12-by-18-inch piece of light blue construction paper. Glue on construction paper activity badges. Cut the Arrow of Light from yellow construction paper.

Neckerchief Invitation

Cut a triangle from yellow construction paper. Outline with blue marking pen and write the date, time, and place of the banquet. Fold as shown.

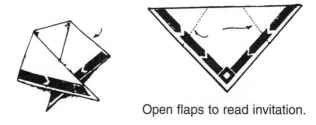

Open flaps to read invitation.

Den Cake Centerpiece

Use hat boxes and ice cream containers to build the tiers of the cake. Cover the tiers with white or yellow construction paper and add the Cub Scouting ranks with blue felt-tip markers. Place a real birthday cake on top, big enough to feed the den's families. Make the Cub Scout climbers from pipe cleaners with plastic foam balls for their heads. Make the hats and neckerchiefs from bits of blue and yellow construction paper. Don't forget to make an Arrow of Light to put on the top of the cake!

THE PROGRAM

One thing that can help guide you in your program planning is having a theme for your blue and gold banquet. A theme gives the boys an emphasis around which they can build their invitations and decorations. For instance, a "Back to the Future" theme could include place cards shaped like spaceships; an "Under the Big Top" theme invites the possibility of animal cookies decorating the dessert. Check *Cub Scout Program Helps*, where you will find the monthly theme suggested by the BSA. You will also find many program ideas to help make your blue and gold banquet special.

The banquet program must appeal to boys as well as adults. The evening can be conducted as a regular pack meeting (with songs, skits, stunts, and awards), or it can be something different and a little more special. Your pack may choose to bring in outside entertainment, such as a magician or storyteller, or have a video or slide presentation of the activities the pack participated in over the previous year. Choose a master of ceremonies who will keep the evening moving and enjoyable for all.

Include the following agenda items in the program. Move them around to suit the needs of your pack, and be sure to include applauses and stunts to fill in the gaps. Try to keep the program time to no more than 1½ hours, not including mealtime.

Preopening or Gathering Period: Have displays and exhibits, as well as games or other activities to keep younger children and the Cub Scouts busy until the meal is served.

Opening Ceremony: This doesn't need to be lengthy or elaborate, but it does need to include the boys.

Invocation: This is one way to incorporate duty to God into the program. The Cub Scouts, a pack leader, a religious leader, or someone from your chartered organization can give an opening prayer or thought. Be sure the invocation is nonsectarian.

Dinner: Allow sufficient time for everyone to enjoy the meal. If it is served as a buffet or potluck, try multiple service lines with food in the middle of the tables. Tiger Cubs usually eat the least so you may want to let them eat first after honored guests. Let the others eat by ranks—Wolf, Bear, Webelos—or randomly from a drawing or a set rotation. Some packs put numbers on the tables and draw out one or two tables every time the serving line gets small.

Welcome and Introductions: The master of ceremonies for the night, often the Cubmaster, should recognize pack leaders and special guests.

Greeting for the Head of the Chartered Organization: Give the chartered organization head and/or representative a moment to tell who he/she is and why he/she helps the pack. This is an ideal time to present the pack charter renewal certificate, if available.

Songs: Keep songs light, simple, lively, and not overly long. Provide song sheets so everyone can participate. Familiar tunes work best.

Skits, Stunts, and Entertainment: Entertainment from within the pack can't go wrong. The dens will have had plenty of time to rehearse. If you use entertainment from outside the pack, make sure it is suited to the crowd and is family entertainment appropriate for all ages.

Advancement Award Ceremony: Make this a memorable moment. This is often the most important part of the evening for many of the boys and parents.

Webelos Graduation Ceremony: If possible, involve Boy Scouts and Scouters from the troops the Webelos Scouts are joining. If your boys are bridging and/or receiving the Arrow of Light, consider inviting an Order of the Arrow ceremony team to participate (contact your district executive for details).

Recognition of Adult Leaders: Present certificates and awards to all the people who have helped make the pack "go." Include pack leaders, parents, and special guests. Make sure the awards are positive and appropriate. This is the time to make everyone feel good about his/her service to the pack and inspire others to volunteer.

Friends of Scouting Presentation: Many packs use the blue and gold banquet as an opportunity to kick off the annual Friends of Scouting (FOS) fund-raiser. This council fund-raiser helps provide money for your council's annual operating budget. Check with your local district or council to schedule a Friends of Scouting presentation.

Closing Ceremony: Be a little more serious with the closing ceremony, but don't put a damper on the evening. Try using an inspirational or patriotic closing.

Announcements, Thank You, and Good-bye: This is the time to mention upcoming events and to thank all the families and friends for attending. Most people will be ready to leave so keep comments short and to the point. Wish everyone a good night and a safe journey home.

Cleanup: Cleanup is a job for everyone. A Scout always leaves a place as clean as or cleaner than the way he found it!

BLUE AND GOLD GRACE AND INVOCATIONS

Health and Strength

(Sing grace)
For health and strength
And daily bread
We praise thy name, O Lord.

Singing Grace
Tune: "Michael Row the Boat Ashore"

God is great and God is good,
Al-le-lu-ia.
Let us thank him for our food,
Al-le-lu-ia.
By his hand, we all are fed,
Al-le-lu-ia.
Thank you, Lord, for our daily bread,
Al-le-lu-ia.

Simple Grace
Tune: "Frère Jacques"

Our Creator, Our Creator,
Once again, once again,
We shall ask your blessing,
We shall ask your blessing,
Amen. Amen.

Philmont Grace

(Spoken)
For food, for raiment,
For life, for opportunity
For friendship and fellowship,
We thank thee, O Lord.

Cub Scout Prayer

(Spoken)
O Lord, that I will do my best,
I come to you in prayer.
Help me to help others every day,
And teach me to be fair.
To honor my mother and father,
And to obey the Cub Scout Law, too.
This I ask that I may be
A loyal Cub Scout true. Amen.

BLUE AND GOLD CEREMONIES

The Light of Scouting's History

Personnel: Four readers (or prerecord narration on tape)

Equipment: Flashlight, four candles on a table

Setting: The room is completely darkened except for the flashlight held by the first reader, who passes it to the next reader, etc.

FIRST READER: In 1907, when Lord Robert Baden-Powell conducted an experimental camp for boys on Brownsea Island in England, the Scouting movement began as a tiny spark of light. *(Lights the first candle.)*

SECOND READER: On February 8, 1910, the Boy Scouts of America was born when William D. Boyce filed incorporation papers in Washington, D.C. *(Lights the second candle with the first.)*

THIRD READER: On June 15, 1916, the Boy Scouts of America was granted a federal charter by Congress. This was also the year when Baden-Powell introduced Wolf Cubbing in Europe. Fourteen years later, Cub Scouting began officially in the United States. *(Lights the third candle with the second.)*

FOURTH READER (lighting the fourth candle with the third): Just as the light in this room has grown as it was passed from one candle to the next, so the Scouting movement grew throughout the world. Today, it has millions of members in hundreds of countries. Let us take this light and spread it outward to others through our goodwill.

Will all Cub Scouts and former Cub Scouts please rise and repeat with me the Cub Scout Promise? *(Lead the Promise.)* Will everyone now please rise and repeat the Pledge of Allegiance?

The Story of the Blue and Gold

Personnel: Eight Cub Scouts

Equipment: Blue flannel board, cards for flannel board (TRUTH, STEADFAST LOYALTY, SPIRITU- ALITY, WARM SUNLIGHT, GOOD CHEER, HAPPI- NESS), yellow sun for flannel board

CUB SCOUT 1: Back in the good ol' days, the waving of school colors gave people a feeling of school pride and loyalty. Today, the blue and gold of Cub Scouting helps to build this spirit among Cub Scouts.

CUB SCOUT 2 (pointing to blue flannel board): The blue reminds us of the sky above. It stands for truth, spirituality, and steadfast loyalty.

CUB SCOUT 3 (placing the "Truth" card in the upper left corner of the board): Truth means we must always be honest.

CUB SCOUT 4 (placing the "Spirituality" card in the upper right corner): Spirituality means being concerned with and sensitive to religious values.

CUB SCOUT 5 (placing the "Steadfast Loyalty" card across the bottom): Steadfast loyalty means being faithful and loyal to God, country, and your fellow human beings.

CUB SCOUT 6 (placing the sun in the center of the board): The gold stands for the warm sunlight. (Places the "Warm Sunlight" card across the top of the sun.)

CUB SCOUT 7: Gold also stands for good cheer and happiness. We always feel better when the sun is shining, and so will those to whom we give goodwill. (Places the "Good Cheer" and "Happiness" cards on each side of the sun.)

CUB SCOUT 8: May the meaning of the blue and gold colors make us remember our Cub Scout ideals: the Cub Scout Promise and the Law of the Pack.

Blue and Gold Opening Ceremony

Print in large bold letters, one letter per sheet, B-L-U-E A-N-D G-O-L-D. Print the following script on the back of each card per page for Cub Scouts to read.

B is for BOYS—Tiger Cubs, Bobcats, Wolves, Bears, and Webelos Scouts.

L is for LEADER—The Cubmaster who guides us.

U is for UNDERSTANDING—We learn to help others.

E is for EXCELLENCE—We try to Do Our Best.

A is for ANNIVERSARY—Cub Scouting's [number] year.

N is for NEIGHBORHOOD—Where Cub Scout dens meet each week.

D is for DEN CHIEFS—Boy Scouts who help us in many ways.

G is for GOALS—For which Cub Scouting stands.

O is for OPPORTUNITY—For boys to learn and do fun and exciting new things.

L is for LIBERTY—In our country's great past and in the years to come.

D is for DEN LEADERS—Who love us and help us.

Closing Thought

NARRATOR: Lord Baden-Powell, the founder of Scouting, wrote: "While you are living your life on earth, try to do something good which may remain after you.

"One writer says: 'I often think that when the sun goes down the world is hidden by a big blanket from the light of heaven, but the stars are little holes pierced in that blanket by those who have done good deeds in this world. The stars are not all the same size; some are big, some are little, and some men have done great deeds and others have done small deeds, but they have made their hole in the blanket by doing good before they went to heaven.'

"Try to make your hole in the blanket by good work while you are on earth. It is something to be good, but it is far better to do good."

Think of Baden-Powell's words when you promise to help other people.

Ideas for Banquet Advancement Ceremonies

- Make a large papier-mâché birthday cake. (See "Crafts.") Use whipped soapsuds to ice the cake. Before soapsuds harden, insert candles (one for each year). Candles can be lit before the awards presentation and blown out after the ceremony.

- Insert boys' award into birthday balloons (orange for Tiger Cubs, yellow for Wolves, blue for Bears, and red for Webelos Scouts) before blowing them up. Write each boy's name on the outside of his balloon with a marker. All boys pop them at once.

- Package individual awards in small boxes wrapped in blue paper and tied with gold ribbons. Ask boys to wait until all awards have been presented before opening their package. Then, while boys open their packages, the rest of the pack sings "Happy Birthday."

- For more ceremony ideas, see *Cub Scout Ceremonies for Dens and Packs.*

BLUE AND GOLD SKITS

The Unknown Scout

Personnel: Cub Scout dressed as William D. Boyce, Cub Scout dressed as old-style Boy Scout, narrator

NARRATOR: It's a foggy night in London. The year is 1909. Mr. William D. Boyce, an American publisher and philanthropist, is lost. (*As the curtain opens, Boyce is onstage. He wanders around stage as if looking for a house number. He comes to a street light and peers at a slip of paper in his hand.*)

BOYCE: I don't think I can find my way in this fog. (*A Scout comes onstage.*)

SCOUT: May I help you, sir?

BOYCE: I'm looking for this address. Can you tell me where to find it? (*Shows him the slip of paper.*)

SCOUT: Yes, I can. I'll take you there (*They walk to the other side of the stage.*)

SCOUT (pointing): There you are, sir.

BOYCE: Thank you very much! And here you go, for helping me. (*Pretends to offer him money.*)

SCOUT: Thank you, sir. But I can't accept money. I'm a Scout, and this is my Good Turn. (*The Scout waves, walks across stage, and exits. Boyce exits on other side.*)

NARRATOR: Mr. Boyce was so impressed with this Scout that he found out more about the Scouting movement in England. He brought back to America a suitcase full of ideas and information. He incorporated the Boy Scouts of America on February 8, 1910. The Boy Scouts of America grew by leaps and bounds. Congress granted a federal charter in 1916—an honor given to only a few organizations. Today, Scouting is a world brotherhood, bound together by common ideals. Please stand and repeat with me the Cub Scout Promise.

Happy Birthday to Us!

Equipment: "Birthday cake" made out of a cardboard box big enough for a small boy to hide inside, a note of paper on the top

Personnel: Six Cub Scouts, one hidden in the cake

Setting: Five Cub Scouts come onstage and gather around the huge cake.

CUB SCOUT 1: Well, here we are, but where's Matt?

CUB SCOUT 2: It's just like him to invite us to a surprise party and then not be here!

CUB SCOUT 3: Does anybody know who's birthday it is anyway?

CUB SCOUT 4: It's not mine. (*Other boys shake their heads.*)

CUB SCOUT 5: Who cares? Here's a big cake, so at least we'll all get lots of it!

CUB SCOUT 1: No kidding! It's big enough to feed an army!

CUB SCOUT 2: Not with you around! I've seen you eat snacks at our den meetings!

CUB SCOUT 1: I can't help it—I'm a growing boy. The Law of the Pack says we should grow.

CUB SCOUT 3: Yeah, but I think we're supposed to grow *up*, not *out*!

CUB SCOUT 4: Hey look! Here's a note. (*Picks up the note.*)

CUB SCOUT 5: Read it—maybe it will explain what this is all about.

CUB SCOUT 4 (reading note): We're a group of Cub Scouts true, it's anniversary week, so let's all sing…

HIDDEN CUB SCOUT (jumping out of the cake): HAPPY BIRTHDAY TO US! (*Everybody joins in singing "Happy birthday to us, Happy birthday to us, Happy birthday to Scouting, Happy birthday to us!"*)

Autumn Harvest Festival

Plan a full day of fall family fun down on the farm with an autumn harvest festival. Although everyone will have a great time, it will be especially enjoyable for Cub Scouts and families who are accustomed to city living.

In preparing for this fall frolic, follow the guidelines for planning special pack activities (see page 6–1). If you know someone who owns an operating farm or ranch, you have a head start on this activity. If not, contact the county agricultural extension office for help in locating a farm that you might be able to visit. If your area doesn't have access to a working farm, you can carry out your autumn harvest activities at a public park.

The resources available to you will determine your activities. Several suggestions are included here. The pack committee chosen to oversee the event will be able to come up with lots more. Involve as many parents and other adults as possible in planning and leading the events. If the group is large, you may need to run several activities at the same time. If your pack needs to travel for the event, be sure to file the appropriate tour permit. You will also find that carpooling can help cut down on costs.

Suggested Activities

- Take a tour of the farm and learn about the daily activities of the people who live there.
- Carve pumpkins or draw faces on them or apples.
- Bob for apples. (If you have safety concerns, try tying the fruit on strings and suspending them from above rather than having a traditional apple bob in a washtub.)

- Run a turkey feather relay.
- Have a pie-eating contest.
- Have a corn-shucking contest.
- Call some hogs.
- Run a three-legged race.
- Play tug-of-war.
- Take a hayride.
- Have a wiener and corn roast or a barbecue.
- Make homemade ice cream with old-fashioned hand-cranked freezers.

Don't forget to write thank-you notes to the farm's owners, and send along some pictures of your event if you took some.

PUMPKIN-CARVING OR -DRAWING CONTEST

Provide a pumpkin for each child. If carving, children should use utensils made for carving pumpkins. Carving utensils may have a special handle for smaller hands to grip, but even so, adequate supervision is required.

Here are some carving tips:

1. Cut a hole in the top of the pumpkin angled inward so you can use the cutout as a lid.
2. Make the hole large enough to scoop out all the pulp and seeds.
3. Draw a face on the pumpkin with a pencil for cutting.
4. As you cut out features, smaller pieces such as teeth or ears can be held on with toothpicks.

If carving is inappropriate for your pack, boys can draw faces on pumpkins or apples with markers. If appropriate, award prizes for the scariest, funniest, most unusual, looks most like the Cubmaster, etc.

TURKEY FEATHER RELAY

Divide the group into teams. The first player on each team holds a long turkey feather. On a signal, each throws his feather javelin style toward a finish line. As soon as it lands, he runs to it, picks it up, and throws it again. When the feather crosses the finish line, he picks it up, runs back, and hands it to his next teammate, who repeats the action.

CORN-SHUCKING CONTEST

Have an ear of corn for everyone eating. Boys peel the husks and silk off each ear, seeing who can shuck the most, and the cleanest, corn. Since this food will be eaten, make sure boys' hands are clean. Also, handle all trash appropriately.

HOG-CALLING CONTEST

Boys and adults try to "call in the hogs" with their best "Sou-e-e-e-e-e-e-e-e—here pig, pig, pig." Select a winner on the basis of applause from the audience.

Bicycle Safety Day

This event will help make all the families in the pack more aware of bicycle safety. Adults will need enough time to set up each area before the boys arrive. If possible, ask a Boy Scout troop to help set up and run activities. You will need a large flat area, and chalk, flour, or powdered lime to set up the events.

- Every boy should bring his own bicycle. (But it is a good idea to have one or two spare bicycles for boys who may not have one.)
- *All boys must wear a helmet whenever they are riding a bicycle.*
- Plan for the event to take most of a morning or afternoon.
- The event committee should follow all guidelines for planning and running a special pack activity (see page 6–1).

- If your group is large, you may want the dens to have staggered starting times. This will allow each boy to attend the safety inspection station before beginning the course.

BICYCLE INSPECTION

If possible, include the local police department in your bicycle inspection, with a representative demonstrating the parts of a bike and how they work. Each boy should have a safety check before starting the safety course. Boys must show that they know proper hand signals and basic safety requirements before they get their "license" to ride in the bicycle safety event.

BICYCLE SAFETY COURSE

A sample bicycle safety course is shown, and the possible events described below.

Start: Mount the bike and coast, while turning your head to the left and right—but not the bike.

Intersection: Use arm signals. Obey traffic lights and signs. Make stop signs from cardboard cut into an octagon and painted for realism. Make signal lights from holiday lights or lamps with colored cellophane coverings.

Steering Course: This tests your ability to hold a straight course. Ride at a comfortable speed.

Circle Riding Area: Ride the Figure 8 1½ times.

Steering Control/Zigzag Course: Tests your ability to shift balance while changing direction.

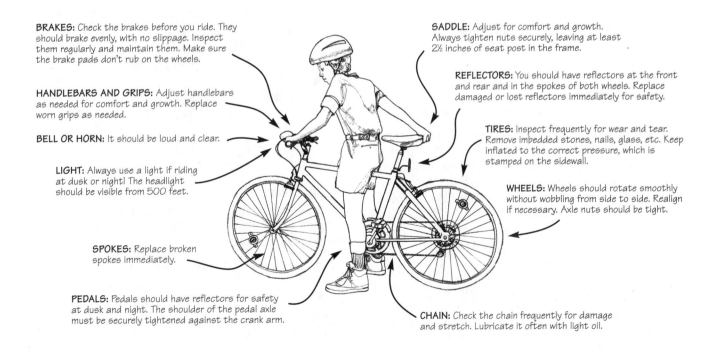

BRAKES: Check the brakes before you ride. They should brake evenly, with no slippage. Inspect them regularly and maintain them. Make sure the brake pads don't rub on the wheels.

HANDLEBARS AND GRIPS: Adjust handlebars as needed for comfort and growth. Replace worn grips as needed.

BELL OR HORN: It should be loud and clear.

LIGHT: Always use a light if riding at dusk or night! The headlight should be visible from 500 feet.

SPOKES: Replace broken spokes immediately.

PEDALS: Pedals should have reflectors for safety at dusk and night. The shoulder of the pedal axle must be securely tightened against the crank arm.

SADDLE: Adjust for comfort and growth. Always tighten nuts securely, leaving at least 2½ inches of seat post in the frame.

REFLECTORS: You should have reflectors at the front and rear and in the spokes of both wheels. Replace damaged or lost reflectors immediately for safety.

TIRES: Inspect frequently for wear and tear. Remove imbedded stones, nails, glass, etc. Keep inflated to the correct pressure, which is stamped on the sidewall.

WHEELS: Wheels should rotate smoothly without wobbling from side to side. Realign if necessary. Axle nuts should be tight.

CHAIN: Check the chain frequently for damage and stretch. Lubricate it often with light oil.

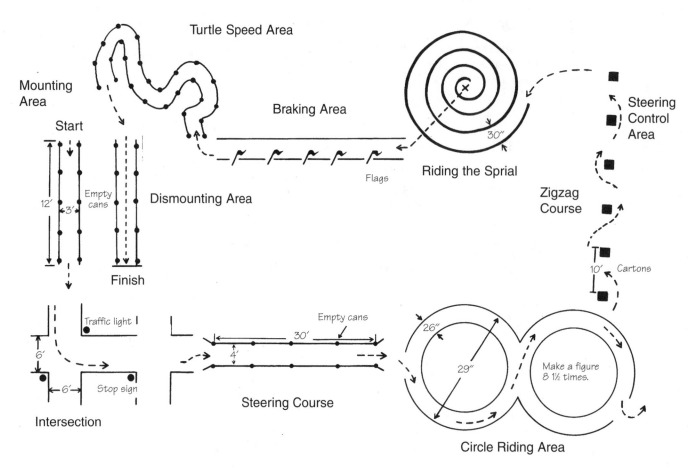

Turtle Speed Area

Mounting Area

Start

Braking Area

Steering Control Area

12' 3' Empty cans

Dismounting Area

Flags

Riding the Sprial

30"

Zigzag Course

Finish

Traffic light

6'

6' Stop sign

Intersection

Empty cans

30'

4'

Steering Course

10' Cartons

26"

29"

Make a figure 8 1½ times.

Circle Riding Area

Riding the Spiral: Ride at any speed, trying not to touch the lines. Place your foot down at the "X."

Braking Area: Keep pedaling at a comfortable speed until a whistle blows. Then stop without skidding. The leader should blow the whistle when the rider is even with any flag. The rider should stop before the next flag.

Turtle Speed Area: Ride as slowly as possible, keeping your balance on the bike.

Conservation Day

The highlight of a conservation day could be a conservation project or Good Turn. Such a project will provide Cub Scouts with an opportunity to help other people and our country, as well as show good citizenship by protecting our planet and giving something back to the community.

CONSERVATION GOOD TURN

Boys should understand *why* and *how* a conservation project is important. If, for example, the Good Turn is cleaning up and planting flowers in a park, the boys should understand that they are doing more than merely making the park attractive. They are also conserving the soil by removing potential pollutants and practicing good soil conservation by planting desirable plants that will reduce erosion.

A conservation Good Turn, such as cleaning up litter at a park or planting trees and shrubs, will show Cub Scout good citizenship in action, as well as help the community and our planet.

Consider several factors when choosing a Good Turn.

• What needs doing? Seek help from local authorities such as city and county park departments, school officials, or perhaps the head of your chartered organization. Also check with local offices of the state conservation or fish and wildlife services, soil conservation district, U.S. Forest Service, or other agencies that have conservation among their purposes. These agencies may be able to suggest projects and also will have ideas for carrying them out.

- Will the project be meaningful to the boys? Will they see the project as more than just busywork?
- Consider the number and ages of boys available to do the project. Can you complete the project within, say, a couple of hours? Can most of the work be done by boys? If adults do most of the work, the boys will learn little. Remember that projects need to be suitable for boys ages 6 to 10.

Good Turn Ideas

- Clean up a neighborhood park, empty lot, school yard, or cemetery. (Note: When cleaning up litter and garbage, always wear protective gloves.) Plant shrubs, flowers, or grass seed to reduce erosion.
- Plant tree seedlings for shade, landscaping, or ground cover.
- Make litter bags for the cars of pack families and neighbors.

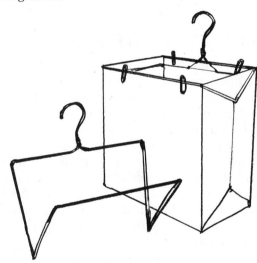

Litter Bag: Use pliers to bend a coat hanger as shown. Fold the top of a paper or plastic bag over the wire frame and fasten with paper clips or staples. If you use a paper bag, you may want to protect it from wet trash by putting a plastic bag inside of it. Decorate as desired.

- Clean out trash from a section of a stream or lakefront.
- Collect newspaper, glass, aluminum, tin, or plastic for recycling, depending on the needs and resources of your community. Recycling not only beautifies the community by removing trash, it conserves energy because it takes less energy to recycle items than to make them from raw materials. It also saves valuable space in landfills.
- With advice from a conservation agency, build brush piles to provide cover for birds and small mammals in a wild area.
- With advice from a conservation agency, plant shrubs that produce food and cover for birds and mammals.
- With advice from a conservation agency, plant wildflowers or ground cover to stop erosion on sloping ground.

OUTDOOR CODE RESPONSIVE READING CEREMONY

Equipment: U.S. flag, copy of the Outdoor Code for each participant

The Cubmaster speaks briefly about the importance to our nation of taking good care of our natural resources and then uses the Outdoor Code as a responsive reading, with boys reading the responses.

CUBMASTER: As an American, I will do my best to be clean in my outdoor manners—

BOYS: I will treat the outdoors as a heritage. I will take care of it for myself and others. I will keep my trash and garbage out of lakes, streams, fields, woods, and roadways.

CUBMASTER: Be careful with fire—

BOYS: I will prevent wildfire. I will build my fires only where they are appropriate. When I have finished using fire, I will make sure it is cold-out. I will leave a clean fire ring or remove all evidence of my fire.

CUBMASTER: Be considerate in the outdoors—

BOYS: I will treat public and private property with respect. I will use low-impact methods of hiking and camping.

CUBMASTER: Be conservation-minded—

BOYS: I will learn how to practice good conservation of soil, waters, forests, minerals, grasslands, wildlife, and energy. I will urge others to do the same.

CUBMASTER: Let us close by singing "God Bless America."

Disabilities Awareness Day

Most Cub Scouts are in good health and are physically strong and mentally alert. But according to the Bureau of the Census (1997), one in eight children between the ages of 6 and 14 has some kind of disability. A disabilities awareness day will help boys understand that some people have special needs different from their own. Through activities, the boys will be able to see some of the challenges people with special needs might face, and they may ask questions. Be prepared to answer and explore their questions.

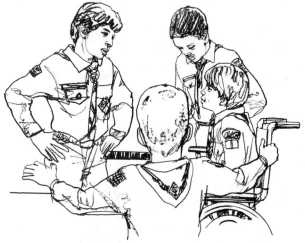

A disabilities awareness day will help boys understand that some people have special needs different from their own.

Review the guidelines for planning special pack 6–1). You should also preview information in the *Cub Scout Leader Book* as well as the "Cub Scouts With Special Needs" chapter of this book.

BLINDFOLDED OBSTACLE COURSE

Set up a course along a string guideline with stations every 20 feet. Run the string guideline between posts, with the string 30 inches off the ground for the boys to hold on to as they go. (Make posts from PVC pipe set in No. 10 cans filled with plaster. Drill holes through the PVC pipe at 30 inches from the bottom of the can to run the string through the pipe.) Remind the boys that they need to move slowly for safety reasons. Have adults at each station to direct the activities. Boys are blindfolded and move along the string from station to station.

- **Station 1:** Boys must find a chair, sit on it, stand up, and then continue.
- **Station 2:** Boys must pick up wads of paper on the ground and put them in a trash can. Tell boys how many wads of paper there are so that they can try to find all of them.

- **Station 3:** Boys peel an orange and eat it. Then they must place the peels in a trash can.
- **Station 4:** Boys pour a glass of water from a small pitcher and drink it.

WHEELCHAIR MANEUVERING

Borrow or rent a manually operated wheelchair. Set up a course that includes a left and right turn, a bump to negotiate over, and a transfer point for boys to move from the wheelchair to a bench and back without using their legs. Tie boys' legs together for added realism.

LIFE WITHOUT SOUND

Use heavy-duty headphones to cover the ears of each participant. Show each boy a written message that he must convey to another individual some distance away who also has his ears covered.

I CAN'T USE THIS HAND

Each boy writes his name first right-handed and then left-handed. Have him put his dominant hand behind his back and make a peanut butter and jelly sandwich with only one hand.

CUBMASTER'S MINUTE CLOSING

CUBMASTER: How many of you had fun today? Well, for many people, activities like these aren't so much fun. They are a necessity every day of their lives. You have had the opportunity to experience some of the challenges that other people face day to day. So now you have an idea of what might be helpful to someone in that situation. But always remember that people who have special needs aren't necessarily incapable. In most ways, they may be just like you. They might not want or require any help. So always ask whether someone wants help—don't *assume* he or she needs it.

Water Carnival

When the weather gets hot, Cub Scouts and their families will want to head for the water—so why not have a water carnival? Swimming and other activities in and on the water are fun and excellent for improving physical fitness.

For all activities in or near water, always follow the principles of Safe Swim Defense (found in the *Cub Scout Leader Book*), which include having qualified supervision and lifeguards on duty, separating boys into swimming ability groups, and maintaining the buddy system. If swimming in a home pool, follow the additional safeguards in the *Cub Scout Leader Book*.

Along with the procedures for special events at the beginning of this chapter (page 6–1), the water carnival committee should follow these added guidelines:

- Before the event, all committee members should attend Safe Swim Defense training provided by the BSA. Check with your local council for the availability of this training.

- On the day of the event, everybody should register as they arrive. Before leaving the registration area, each child should be paired with a buddy. Hold buddy checks regularly throughout the event.

- Consider having a family picnic once everyone is out of the water and hungry!

Any public swimming area—pool or lakefront—can be suitable for your water carnival, as long as a section of it can be marked off for your pack and it follows the requirements of Safe Swim Defense. (If the site is unguarded and unsupervised, water carnival committee members should arrive early to set up the required elements, including a marked swimming area cleared of obstacles and the appointment of lifeguards and a lookout.) Other possible sites are pools at schools or colleges and universities, a local YMCA, or even a local motel.

For all events, health and safety come first. Be sure to review and have on hand the BSA publication *Guide to Safe Scouting* before beginning this and any Cub Scout activity.

SAMPLE PROGRAM

Gathering Time: Registration and pairing of buddies.

Preopening: Have a free swim time for pack families. This will also allow all ability groups to have fun at their own level. (You might prefer to have free swim after events.)

Opening: Call everyone out of the water and have the song leader lead a lively "watery" song such as "Be Kind to Your Web-Footed Friends" (sung to the tune of "Stars and Stripes Forever"):

Be kind to your web-footed friends,
For a duck may be somebody's mother.
Be kind to your friends in the swamp,
Where the weather is very dark and damp.
You may think that this is the end,
Well, it is!—

Water Carnival: Choose water games from the "Games" chapter of this book. Water games and relays should include everyone. If there are non-swimmers in the group, some activities may not be suitable. Webelos Scout dens may demonstrate water rescues or how to use a mask, fins, and snorkel. End the carnival with a game of Watermelon Scramble, with enough watermelon for everybody to enjoy a slice!

Watermelon Scramble

Put a watermelon in a large plastic bag. Tape it shut so that if the melon breaks, it won't mess up the water. Toss the melon into waist- to chest-deep water. On a signal, teams jump in and try to bring the melon to a designated point.

Cub Scout Field Day

The pack field day is an afternoon of fun for Cub Scouts and their families. Allow all boys and family members to participate in this day of fun. Events can be competitive, or participants can be measured against their own abilities.

A pack field day might include energy-burning and fun dashes, relays, and sprints.

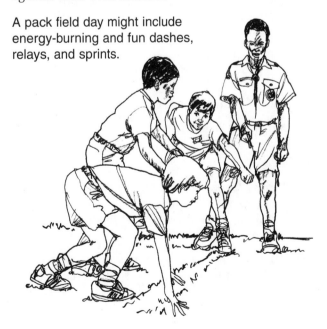

For a special recognition, make an olive leaf crown like the kind winning athletes received at the Olympics in ancient Greece. Make crowns from green construction paper, wire, and masking tape. The masking tape holds the leaves and covers the wire, which is the frame of the crown.

In preparing for the field day, the event committee should follow the guidelines for planning special events (page 6–1). Consider such things as location, promotion, sign making, instructions for events, equipment, stop watches, marking game areas, scoreboards, decorations, and prizes. Make a final check about two weeks before the event to make sure that plans are progressing smoothly. When the big day comes, the committee should arrive early to decorate and set up the games. Prepare large signs to tell families where each event is taking place and where to store their picnic suppers.

Along with a chair and the event committee members, a field day may also require a physical arrangements committee (for signs, permits, equipment setup); an awards committee; a refreshment committee; and starters, judges, and scorekeepers.

SAMPLE PROGRAM

Committee members must arrive early to set up the events, registration table, decorations, etc.

1:00–1:30	Registration and gathering time
1:30–2:00	Opening ceremonies: Each den marches in parade-style, carrying its den flag.
2:00–4:00	Events
4:00–4:30	Recognition ceremonies and closing
4:30–5:30	Picnic supper
After supper	Cleanup

EVENTS

Foot-Put: Players remove one shoe. Then lying on their backs, place the shoe loosely over their toes. With a kicking motion over their head, players see how far they can propel the loose shoe behind them.

Starting Whistle: This is a timed event. Starting at the word "Go," the boy eats two saltine crackers and tries to whistle a simple tune such as "Yankee Doodle." Measure time from the word "go" to the end of the tune. If necessary, supply a song sheet so judges can follow the tune.

30-Yard Dash: This is a timed event. Prepare a straight course with starting and stopping lines 30 yards apart.

100-Yard Relay: This is a timed den event. Lay out a course for 100 yards. Four-boy teams run the relay. The first boy begins at the starting line; the second boy begins at 25 yards, the third at 50 yards, and the forth at 75 yards. The first boy begins to run from the starting line holding a small object or baton, which he hands off to the next boy as they meet. The next boy runs the next segment of the race, and so on.

Standing and Running Long Jump: To score these events, measure from the starting line to the part of the body closest to the starting line. For the standing long jump, the boy begins with both feet on the starting line and then jumps forward as far as possible. For the running long jump, mark a running line 10 feet before the starting line. Boys run from the running line and then leap forward at the starting line in one continuous motion. This event must have a landing area on a soft surface or long jump pit made especially for this purpose, as the jumper will naturally fall forward.

Softball Throw: Each boy throws a softball as far as he can from a designated starting line.

Discus or Shot Put: Use lightweight equipment or make your own. Make a discus from two sturdy paper plates or use a commercial plastic flying disk. The shot put could be a rock, beanbag, or sandbag. Each boy throws as far as he can from a designated starting line. Someone who understands the correct throwing style of each sport could teach the boys.

Javelin Throw: Make a javelin from a broom handle or 1-inch dowel rod. Measure the distance thrown from a designated throwing line to the part of the javelin closest to the starting line. You must have a large open area for this event and take extra care for safety.

Water Bottle Relay: This is a timed team event. You will need a plastic water bottle and two buckets, one filled with water and one empty but marked with a fill line. Punch a number of small holes at random in the sides of the water bottle. In teams of equal numbers, boys fill the bottle from the full bucket, hand it off fire-brigade style, and dump it into the marked bucket. Measure the time required to fill the container to the line.

Make a winners' stand like the one they use in the Olympic Games. Use wooden boxes and make simple medals to hang around the boys' necks.

RAINY-DAY FIELD DAY

Here's a pack event that you can schedule ahead of time or use to provide a fun-filled substitute program on a day when the pack has an outdoor activity that has been rained out. You can store most of the needed items in a rainy-day box and keep for use as needed. Your rainy-day box could include feathers, uncooked beans, paper plates, table tennis balls, tennis balls, balloons, assorted buckets and jars, paper bags, straws, and string. Boys can run these events as individuals or teams, as straight races or as relays. If this activity is to be used as a backup plan, all chairs running an outdoor event should be aware of the program possibilities.

Events

Mini Shot Put: Each boy tries to throw 10 navy beans into a quart jar from a chalk line on the floor.

Balloon Volleyball: Divide boys into teams. Use string on the floor or tied between two chairs for a net. You could mark boundaries with masking tape.

Balloon Hammer Throw: Tie an inflated balloon to the end of a string. Each boy throws the "hammer" by the end of the string.

Straw and Ball Blow: Boys are given a straw and take positions around a table (a card table works well). Each boy kneels so his face is level with the tabletop. He places the straw in his mouth and his hands behind his back. A table tennis ball is placed in the middle of the table. By blowing through the straw, each boy tries to keep the ball from rolling off his area of the table. This is a good gathering activity, and play can begin as soon as two boys arrive. Additional boys join the others as they arrive.

Standing Broad Grin: Judges measure the width of grins. The widest grin wins.

Paper Plate Discus Throw: Boys throw a paper plate from a chalk line. The plate must be held flat in the hand, against the palm, with the fingers wrapped over from the top and not sailed with thumb and fingers.

Giant Shot Put: Boys toss an inflated paper bag, or a bag filled with crumpled newspaper with a string tied around the end to seal it, for distance. Boys make the throw from the shoulder as if it were a shot put.

Heel-to-Toe Foot Race: Boys walk 10 feet moving heel-to-toe as fast as possible.

Running Whistle: The boy who holds a whistled note the longest wins.

Feather Blow Relay: Blow a feather 25 feet and return, tagging the next player. A straw can be used to direct the airflow.

50-Yard Cup Hop: Each boy hops on one foot carrying a paper cup of water. The boy who gets over the finish line first with the most water still in his cup wins.

Feather Race: With one hand, boys carry five feathers on a paper plate for a certain distance. They must pick up any that drop before continuing.

Eggroll Relay: Relay teams use a stick to roll plastic eggs down a course and back.

Turtleneck Pass: The first player on each team places a tennis ball or small inflated balloon under his chin. Players pass the ball or balloon from chin-to-chin using no hands until all players have received the object.

Cub-anapolis 400

The exciting Cub-anapolis 400 allows boys and their families to be more personally involved in a car race than the ever-popular pinewood derby—because the boys are the cars, and family members are the pit crew!

The fun begins when boys and their families make the cars together. Choose an appropriately sized cardboard box for the boy to hold around him as shown. Look for one that is 24 to 36 inches long, 12 to 18 inches wide, and 12 inches deep (if a box is too deep, a boy might have trouble holding onto it). Cut holes for the head and arms—about a 9- to 10-inch hole for the head and 4-inch holes for the arms. Make a windshield if you want, folding cardboard into a triangular shape and gluing it to the box. Make four cardboard wheels with about a 4- to 5-inch radius and glue them to the box, also. Then paint and decorate as desired. Let your imaginations go wild!

Each driver must wear either glasses or goggles and a pair of lace-up shoes (such as sneakers) with socks (you'll see why in a minute...).

Lay out a racecourse as large as the meeting area can provide. An outdoor racecourse is the best, in any large, open, grassy area where the track can have turns and straightaways. The race will involve four laps around the track. You might find it easiest (and the least crowded) to run the race in heats of three cars at a time.

Just as in any long car race, cars will need pit stops. The boys' families set up their pit areas at any point along the track, but they must be far enough away from the track so they don't interfere with the other racers.

- During the first lap, the car will need to have its windshields washed. A family member washes the boy's glasses or goggles, perhaps squirting them with a spray bottle to add to the fun.

- During the second lap, the car will need fuel. The boy pulls into his pit area while his family holds out a small cup of juice or water that he must drink through a straw. (Make sure that each boy drinks the same amount of "fuel.")

- During the third lap, the car will need to have its tires changed. Each boy pulls into the pit area, and the pit crew removes his shoes and socks. They put the socks back on inside out, and then put on and tie his shoes—and he is off for the final lap.

- Cars don't stop during the last lap. Now it's a race for the finish and the checkered flag!

Award prizes as with any derby. Consider special prizes—for largest or smallest car, fanciest socks, best-looking car, or most organized pit crew.

Summer Celebration

Summer is a great time for celebration and includes many holiday opportunities for fun: Flag Day, Independence Day, and Labor Day, for instance. A summer celebration is a great way for the pack to participate in activities that will help them achieve the National Summertime Pack Award and keep them on the road to the National Quality Unit Award. Choose a theme for your celebration that will help guide your decorations and games. "Fun Across America," presented here, is an example.

The program committee needs to find a suitable (preferably outdoors) location, arrange seating, and prepare all materials. One member of the committee should coordinate an area for games and assign each den to help set up the events. The committee should follow the guidelines for planning special pack activities found at the beginning of this chapter (see page 6–1) and include lots of adult participation.

One adult should be assigned to each event. That person can choose to run the event or enlist the aid of other adults. Or the program committee can assign dens to run each event along with an adult sponsor.

SAMPLE PROGRAM

9:00   Set up events.

9:30   Opening ceremony. Choose a patriotic opening or have all dens participate in a flag salute and sing "America."

9:35   The Cubmaster or master of ceremonies welcomes all the families and asks for a moment of silence while the pack remembers those who made our country free.

9:40   The cheermaster leads off with the Sea to Shining Sea Cheer: Divide the group in half. When the cheermaster raises his/her right hand, the group on the right yells "Atlantic!" When he/she raises the left hand, the group on the left yells "Pacific!" When he/she raises both hands, everybody yells "Gulf of Mexico!"

9:45   The summer celebration chair gives directions for maneuvering the celebration games course. This will be determined by the size of the pack. For large packs, each den may be directed to a specific station at a specific time. For smaller packs, dens may choose to move in a clockwise direction. The chair also tells the pack what time the games will end and the awards ceremony will take place.

9:50   Let the celebration begin!

11:30   Recognition ceremony, advancement awards

11:45   Closing ceremony

AWARDS

You can score the following events or just play them for fun. Match awards to games, when possible; for example, award a plastic orange for the Florida Orange Peel or a carton of milk for the Wisconsin Dairy Draw. Each participant could receive a small flag or flag pin as a participation remembrance.

CARNIVAL GAMES

All timed events require a stopwatch or watch with a second hand; relays can be timed on an individual basis. If the players won't or can't eat food items for events, substitute nonedible items. For example, metal nuts could replace raisins, and coins or washers could replace cookies.

Florida Orange Peel

Materials: One orange for each participant

Time players on how long it takes them to peel an orange using their fingers only. If a player removes the peel in one piece, he gets bonus points. After the contest, the reward is eating the orange.

Philadelphia Liberty Bell Relay

Materials: Bell

Place a bell 30 feet from the starting line, where dens line up. On a signal, the first in line runs to the bell, rings it, and runs back to tag the next runner. The relay continues until all players participate.

Cajun Crab Walk

Each player crab walks for 30 feet. You can run this as a relay, or time each team member individually and figure the team average by dividing the entire time by the number of members.

Georgia Peanut Relay

Materials: One unshelled peanut per person, bowl, one wooden spoon per team, jar

Place all peanuts in a bowl and place an empty jar 30 feet away from the bowl. In relay style, each player, with one hand behind his back, scoops up one peanut from the bowl onto a wooden spoon. He then runs to the jar, drops the peanut into it, returns to the team, and hands the spoon to the next player.

Chicago Windy City Blow

Materials: Table tennis ball, soda straw for each boy

Players, on their hands and knees, place a table tennis ball on a starting line on the ground and propel it to the finish line by blowing on it through the straw.

Wisconsin Dairy Draw

Materials: For each participant, a rubber glove filled with water and suspended or held over a bucket or measuring cup

Poke a small hole in two fingers of the rubber glove. Each participant "milks" into a bucket for 1 minute. Score the contest by how much milk a player gets into the bucket. For extra fun, suspend the glove from cardboard cutouts of a cow.

Denver Mile High Cookie Stack

Materials: Lots of cookies

Participants count how many cookies they can stack in 30 seconds. If their stack falls over, they are disqualified.

Idaho Potato Toss

Materials: Water balloon for each pair of players

Partners toss a balloon filled with water back and forth, taking a step back after each toss. If the balloon hits the ground and breaks, the pair is disqualified.

Texas Rope the Steer

Materials: **Sawhorse, ropes**

Each player has five tries to lasso a sawhorse or a cutout of a steer.

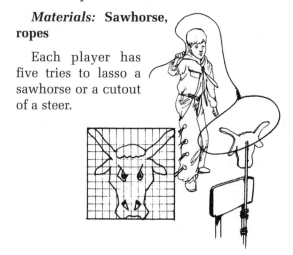

California Raisin Toss

Materials: **Paper plates decorated with California scenes from magazines or travel brochures, raisins**

Count how many raisins each participant can toss onto a plate in 1 minute from a specified location.

Seattle Space Needle Ring Toss

Materials: **Quart milk carton, rocks or marbles, paper plate, pipe cleaners**

Make a "space needle" as shown. See how many rings players can toss over the needle in a given number of turns.

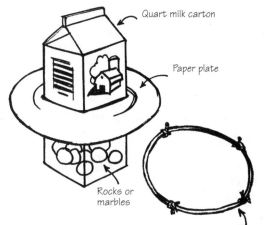

Quart milk carton

Paper plate

Rocks or marbles

Ring made from pipe cleaners with twisted ends

Welcome to the Midway

The Cub Scout midway is a series of simple games that can be played for small prizes—or just for fun. Use the midway activities described below for a Cub Scout fair, circus, festival, or any other special event. With a few balloons and some crepe paper you can make each activity into a midway spectacular.

• Bounce a ball into a wastebasket.

• Toss beanbags at a target on the floor or through holes in a tossing board.

• Turn a chair upside down. Make rings from plastic lids with the centers cut out and toss them over the legs.

• Mark a target on the floor. Pitch painted jar lids at the target.

• Mark a shuffleboard on the floor. Use a broom to push plaster-filled jar lids onto the board.

• Snap tiddlywinks disks into shallow cups or muffin tins.

• Bounce table tennis balls on a table into small bowls.

• Bounce tennis balls into a target of No. 10 cans tied together.

• Roll balls to knock down a child's bowling pins, quart milk containers, or water bottles set in a row or triangle.

• Throw an inflated paper bag for distance.

• Toss cards into a hat.

• Guess the number of beans in a jar.

• Take three tries to toss a hat onto a hat rack.

• Drive a 1-inch nail into a 2-by-4 board in five swings.

• Glue numbered paper cups onto a cardboard box. Toss checkers and give prizes according to the points scored.

OTHER MIDWAY ACTIVITIES

Hat-Making Booth: Have a good supply of paper hats and old felt hats along with plenty of buttons, ribbons, feathers, and other items to decorate hats. Have needles, thread, and glue on hand for the decorating.

Portrait Gallery: Draw life-sized folklore or comic figures on a piece of 6-by-10-foot wall board, such as shown. Cut out circles for the customers' heads. Use an instant camera to take pictures.

Paint or sketch figures on wood backdrop using the grid method to enlarge them.

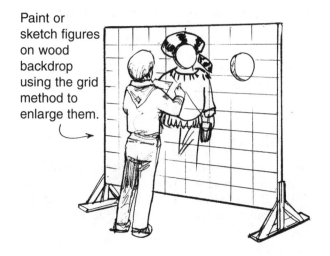

Splash 'em: Toss wet sponges at an agreeable volunteer.

Lookie Loos: Cut a small hole in one end of several shoe boxes. Make a slot about ½ inch wide on the top near the other end of the box. Paint or decorate the boxes. Put an "attraction" in each box near the slot and arrange along a table so the end holes are at eye level. String Christmas lights into the slots to illuminate the attractions. Add a sign to identify each attraction. Examples:

- A Diamond in the Rough (a lump of coal)
- A Tear Jerker (an onion)
- A Real American Hero (a hero sandwich)
- Ancient Ruins (a broken dish)
- The Amazing Aquanaut (a rope overhand knot floating in a glass of water)
- The World's Smallest Dog (a cocktail frank)
- The Best Cub Scout on Earth (a mirror)
- Rare Invisible Fish (bowl of clear water)

Marble Golf: For golf holes, bury baby food jars in the soil to the brim. Mark the holes with flags made from tiny paper triangles glued to craft sticks and numbered. Add water hazards and sand traps if you wish. Make "golf shots" in the approved knuckles-down way as for regular marbles. The winner is the player who takes the fewest shots to go around the course. This game can be played outdoors or indoors, filling a large box with 4 or 5 inches of potting soil.

Family Cake Bake

Everyone seems to love this special pack activity—because after all, at the end of it everybody gets to eat cake! Run the activity any time of year, but in February, you can use the cakes for blue and gold banquet desserts. Or you can auction the cakes and use the proceeds for pack needs or a donation to the World Friendship Fund. (If you are using this or any event as a unit money-earning project, be sure to get council approval. Complete and submit the Unit Money-Earning Application for approval well before the event.)

Just as in any other special pack activity, follow the guidelines found in the beginning of this chapter to ensure an enjoyable and well-organized activity (page 6–1).

The event chair makes sure that families are furnished with the rules, recruits judges, and procures prizes.

RULES

- Cakes should be delivered to a specified location by a specified time and date.
- Cakes must be decorated according to specified guidelines (such as the monthly theme).
- Cakes must be baked and decorated by a Cub Scout or Webelos Scout and as many family members as possible.
- All the parts of the cake must be edible, including the decorations.
- Cake mixes and canned icing may be used.

- All cakes should have a title or name, either as part of the decoration or on a card attached to the cake. Cakes should be numbered for judging purposes.
- Cakes should be placed on a disposable plate or tray.

JUDGING

Cakes will be judged and prizes awarded at the pack meeting. Here are some suggested categories for judging.

- Judge's Choice (Best of Show)
- Most Original Creation
- Best Representation of the Monthly Theme
- Most Suitably Named
- Biggest
- Smallest
- Flattest
- Yummiest Looking

Pack Picnic

On a beautiful day in the spring, summer, or fall, what better family activity than a picnic? And if you hold it in late afternoon, you could add a campfire to the program, too. The pack picnic should be an informal family affair. This doesn't mean, however, that planning is unnecessary. The location, meal arrangements, games, equipment, transportation, and other details must be thought through ahead of time.

Consider using the monthly theme for your picnic. A pirate theme brings to mind a treasure hunt rather than a scavenger hunt. A birdwatching theme might include counting how many different birds boys can find in the picnic area. Check *Cub Scout Program Helps* and attend monthly roundtables for more ideas to add spark to your pack program and special events.

Picnic activities should include lots of fun and activity for the entire family. You'll never go wrong with soccer and softball.

SAMPLE PROGRAM

Each family could be asked to bring hot dogs and buns for their family and a salad or chips to share. The pack could provide the paper plates, utensils, drinks, dessert, and charcoal/lighter. You might also assign dens to bring certain items.

4:00–4:30	Families arrive at the picnic site. Have a gathering time activity.
4:30–6:00	Organized games and play. One adult from each den reports for fire building and food preparation.
6:00–6:30	The meal
6:30–7:00	Cleanup and campfire preparation
7:00–8:00	Campfire program (refer to the "Outdoors" chapter)
8:00–8:30	Final cleanup

PICNIC ACTIVITIES

These activities have been successfully used at Cub Scout picnics. Choose activities that require lots of interaction and fun for the whole family. For instance, you can never go wrong with softball or soccer at a picnic.

Relays

For relays, the first person in each team performs a designated task, after which the next in line competes. The relay continues until all players participate. Teams could be den against den, family against family, or adults against boys. Relays are a great way to incorporate themes; for instance, a "Race for Space" theme could include throwing a paper plate flying saucer at a target. See the section on "Relays and Races" in the "Games" chapter of this book.

Miniature Golf Course

You can play this miniature golf game almost anywhere. Competition can be individual, by family, or by den. Set up a course using No. 10 cans or any straight-sided receptacle with a large opening for "holes." Place cans on their sides and shoot balls into them. Use natural hazards in your area or make your own from cardboard cutouts. Don't make the course too long. At a picnic there is lots to do, and you want to keep the boys' attention.

- Shoot balls (a rubber ball or tennis ball) underhand toward the "hole."
- Take succeeding shots from where the ball stops. In den or team play, number each player and rotate each shot by player throughout the course.
- Keep score by awarding one point for each toss. The goal is to have the lowest score.

Earth Ball

Earth balls are giant blown-up balls, typically 4 to 6 feet high, that are available at recreational supply stores. These balls create a natural activity for team play, as it usually takes more than one person to move the ball. Try earth ball relays or earth ball toss. Here's an example of an earth ball game.

No Stopping Here: You'll need one earth ball, two hula hoops, and a large playing area free of hazards. Each of two teams gets a hula hoop to use as a goal and decides where they want to place their goal. (Goal placement is an important point of strategy because a small rise can make a big difference.) To begin the game, center the ball between the goals. At a signal, players try to move the ball into the opposing team's goal.

Parachute Toss

Equipment: Parachute, soccer ball or volleyball

Like earth ball games, parachute games require a lot of cooperation. Try a parachute toss. Boys surround and stretch out the parachute and see how high or how far they can toss a ball with the parachute. See the "Games" chapter of this book for other parachute games.

Capture the Flag

Equipment: Flag for each team

Each of two teams places their flag at a designated spot. The object of the game is to take the opposing team's flag and return it to your home base first without being tagged. If tagged while holding the flag, a player can drop it to be picked up by a player from either team, and play continues. Another variation is that the tagged flag holder must return the flag to its "home."

Western Rodeo Roundup and Pioneer Day

For a fun-filled Western rodeo roundup or pioneer day, the event committee will select a suitable indoor or outdoor location and follow the guidelines for the successful planning and carrying out of special pack activities found in the beginning of this chapter (page 6–1). *Please remember to exclude Western gunfights and negative images of American Indians!*

WESTERN RODEO ROUNDUP

A Western festival is a fun way to give Cub Scouts a taste of the Old West. For extra fun, suggest that everyone come in Western attire. An easy way to dress up your uniform is to wear a cowboy hat and replace your neckerchief with a bandanna.

Wagons Ho! can be the call for your Western rodeo roundup or pioneer day.

If you are having a meal, have chuck wagon chow, such as beans, cornbread, and barbecue served from a table decorated to look like a chuck wagon.

Sample Program

6:00–6:15	Gathering time activities (preopening)
6:15–6:25	Opening ceremony
6:25–7:10	Chuck wagon meal
7:10–8:00	Contests and games
8:00–8:30	Recognition and closing
8:30	Final cleanup

Activities

Opening Ceremony: The Cubmaster or cheermaster can lead off with a loud "Howdy!"—followed by a tall story. For example: "Howdy partners! My name's Bill—the roughest, toughest cowpoke in the county. I had to travel 5,000 miles over the roughest country—full of sky-high mountains, ocean-sized rivers, mile-long rattlesnakes, and bone-dry deserts filled with hungry varmints. But it didn't take me no time at all 'cause my horse Paint was bigger 'n those mountains and could jump over the Grand Canyon in one leap. Yep, I got here on Paint. He got me here just in time although now he's all lathered up and sweaty. Ya know, I'd bring him out here and let ya'll pet him, but ya know yer not supposed ta touch 'Wet Paint.' Ya know, I thought I left them hungry varmints behind, but looks like there's a bunch of 'em right here—lookin' like hungry Cub Scouts. So let's say grace and set to eatin'."

"Johnny Appleseed"

(Sing grace)

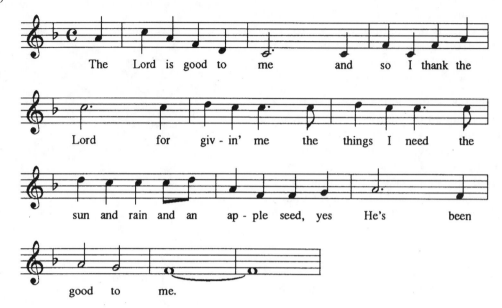

The Lord is good to me and so I thank the
Lord for giv-in' me the things I need the
sun and rain and an ap-ple seed, yes He's been
good to me.

Bronco Riding: Using a heavy fiber drum or barrel for the body of your bronc, bolt on wooden legs, rockers, head, and stirrups as shown. If possible, surround the riding area with loose hay.

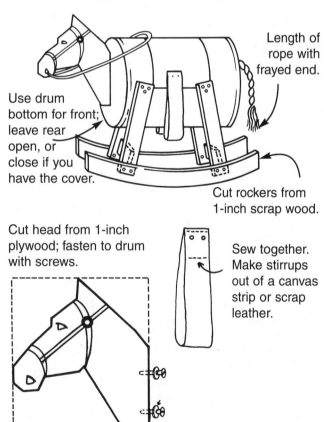

Length of rope with frayed end.

Use drum bottom for front; leave rear open, or close if you have the cover.

Cut rockers from 1-inch scrap wood.

Cut head from 1-inch plywood; fasten to drum with screws.

Sew together. Make stirrups out of a canvas strip or scrap leather.

Buffalo Wheel: Fasten an old bicycle wheel to a post that will allow the wheel to spin. Remove half of the spokes and mark scores on the remaining ones with small sheets of paper. Make a "buffalo" by filling the toes of two socks with nuts or small pieces of wood and then tying the socks together. To score, throw the buffalo into the spinning wheel and count the score of the numbered spokes it wraps around. For safety reasons, be sure to have an adult oversee the spinning wheel used in this activity.

Ten-Gallon Hat: See how many playing cards each player can toss into a 10-gallon hat from a given distance in 30 seconds.

Pony Express Relay: Divide the group into equal relay teams. Divide each team in half and station members in lines 30 to 40 feet apart. The first player on each team is given a stick horse and a pony express bag. On a signal, he rides to his teammate in the opposite line, carrying the bag over his shoulder. He transfers the horse and bag to the new rider, who gallops back. Play continues until all players have participated. For safety purposes, stick horses may be constructed using lengths of foam pipe insulation.

Chuck Wagon Contest: Each team has a chuck wagon. This can be an unadorned coaster wagon or a wagon decorated with a cloth cover on a wire frame (see illustration). Two den members are designated as horses (horses could wear paper bag masks). Behind the wagon are a number of pots, pans, and tin cans. On a signal, all team members except the horses load the cans into the wagon. When they are finished, they yell, "Wagons ho!" and the horses dash off pulling the wagon around a designated course. If an implement falls off, the horses must stop and the other den members put it back in the wagon. If you have only one chuck wagon, this can be a timed event.

Chuck Wagon: Build a wooden frame that will fit inside the box of a coaster wagon. For the wagon cover's frame, cut four 6-foot lengths of heavy wire. Drill matching holes in the wooden frame and fit the wire loops into them. Brace the wires lengthwise with wire or heavy cord. Use an old sheet for the cover. Decorate as desired.

Rodeo Clown Face Painting: Set up a face-painting area using water-soluble makeup for rodeo clown face painting.

Spino-Lariat: Paste a 13-foot strip of colorful crepe paper to a cardboard leader. Punch a hole through a sponge rubber ball with an ice pick to attach a string. Hold the string, and try some spino-lariat moves!

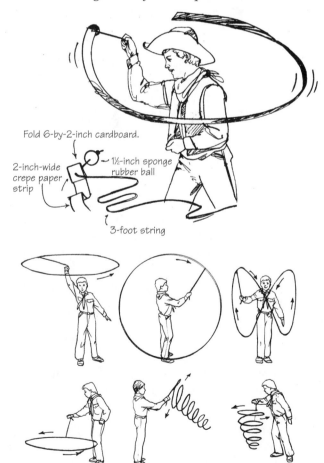

Fold 6-by-2-inch cardboard.

2-inch-wide crepe paper strip

1½-inch sponge rubber ball

3-foot string

PIONEER DAY

Remember our ancestors seeking a better place to live? Families moved westward with hopes of finding their destiny. Many were their trials and tribulations, but great was their celebration when they reached their destination. The Santa Fe Trail or Oregon Trail can be themes for a fun event filled with history and celebration. Pioneer costumes and props will add to the enjoyment of this special pack activity.

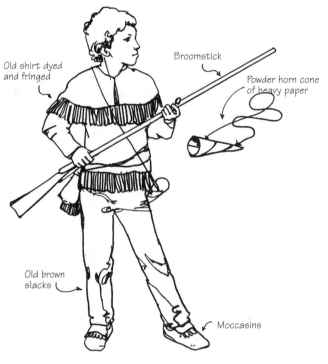

Old shirt dyed and fringed

Broomstick

Powder horn cone of heavy paper

Old brown slacks

Moccasins

Pioneer day can be part of your regular pack meeting or run as a stand-alone activity. Either way, be sure to include awards and recognition.

Follow the sample program above for the Western rodeo roundup and adapt it as needed.

Obstacle Course

Set up an obstacle course with any or all of these ideas. Start the dens at different stations to keep things moving.

- **Broken Wheel:** Roll a bicycle wheel around an obstacle.
- **Ox in the Mud:** Use this as a cooperative team-building event. Have the pack work in dens or by family to move a heavy object several feet. If used as a competitive activity, time how long it takes to move the object.
- **Dust Storm:** Set up a waist-high track of string around a series of trees or poles. Boys follow the string while blindfolded.

- **Beaver Trap:** Use a child's wading pool. Place four cutouts of beavers in the "beaver pond." Let the boys toss beanbags to "trap" the beavers. Count the number of beavers each boy traps.
- **The Narrow Pass:** Use duct tape to fasten three or four cardboard boxes together. Each boy crawls through the pass.
- **Repair Harness:** Each player joins two ropes together with a square knot.
- **Derby Wagon Races:** Set up the pinewood derby track or just a plywood board on a slant. Each boy races a self-made Conestoga derby wagon.

Conestoga Derby Wagon

You can turn a regular pinewood derby kit into a covered wagon.

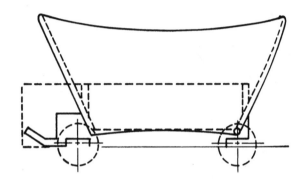

Materials: **Pinewood derby kit, 6½-by-10-inch piece of white fabric, two 10-inch pieces of coat hanger or other wire**

See the illustration for the outline of the wooden block. When finished, make holes in the wood and glue in the wire. Cover the wire frame with fabric, turning back the edges and gluing the fabric securely to the wire frame. Attach wheels, and it's westward ho!

Derbies and Regattas

All derbies and regattas have several things in common: They all require planning and preparation; they all involve competition and prizes; and they all provide fun for boys and their families. *Always remember that in Cub Scouting, it is more important to "Do Your Best" than to come in first.* Emphasizing winning too much can demoralize a young Cub Scout who does his best but doesn't win.

The program committee for every derby will need to

- Follow the guidelines for planning special pack activities found at the beginning of this chapter (page 6–1) so that nothing important will be overlooked.

- Provide each pack family with a set of simple, uncomplicated rules, including a time schedule.
- Plan and carry out appropriate opening, award, and closing ceremonies.
- Handle all aspects of awards. *Every* boy should receive an award for his participation in the derby.
- Plan for crowd control.
- Devise a fair method of judging.
- Plan and provide appropriate decorations with lots of boy participation.
- Secure a public-address system, if needed.

You can find more information on pinewood derbies, raingutter regattas, and space derbies in the BSA publication *Cub Scout Grand Prix Pinewood Derby Guidebook.*

You can use this double elimination bracket with any derby.

PINEWOOD DERBY

Ask any adult male who was a Cub Scout what he remembers most about being a Cub Scout, and he will probably reply, "Racing those little wooden cars!" The pinewood derby is one of the most popular and memorable special events in Cub Scouting. Like all successful events, it requires planning and preparation, but its value in promoting fun and positive family interaction has been proved over the years.

Pinewood derby cars are small models of specified dimensions, created, carved, and assembled by the boys under the guidance of an adult family member. The cars are gravity powered and run down a regulation track.

You can buy pinewood derby kits, with building instructions, individually or in packs from a local Scouting distributor. Often, the derby committee purchases derby kits in quantity and distributes them to pack families. The Scouting distributor also will have many derby "extras," such as spare wheels, ribbons, trophies, decals, and more.

Personnel and Procedures

Registration Team, Before the Race Begins:

- Mark unique numbers on the bottom of each car.
- Enter the number and names of each entry on a preliminary heat sheet.

Registration Team, Once the Race Begins:

- Enter the names and numbers of heat winners on semifinal sheets.
- Determine the final standing of each winning car and report the results to the awards committee.

Inspection Team, Before the Race Begins:

- Weigh the cars with an accurate scale.
- Check the overall dimensions. One easy method is to construct a small box measuring 2½ by 7 by 1½ inches. If the car fits in the box, it passes inspection.
- Act as judges for prerace craftsmanship awards, such as Most Colorful, Best Looking, Best Paint Job, Most Scouting Spirit, etc. Report results to the awards committee.

Inspection Team, Once the Race Begins:

- Help at the starter's table.

Track Operations Team:

- Set up and maintain derby track or tracks. Larger packs may find that multiple tracks make the event move more quickly and smoothly.
- Have a starter's table where cars are placed until their turn to race.
- Have a starter at the beginning of each track.
- Have two or three judges at the end of each track (two for determining first and second places, three for determining first, second, and third places).
- Have two or more gatekeepers to line up the boys.
- Report winners to the registration team.

Interim Event Crew:

- Have planned activities for boys and siblings during the preopening, while registration and inspection are taking place.
- Make paper racing flags to mark off the race area.
- Have planned activities for boys and siblings between heats and during the final awards ceremony.

Awards Committee:

- Make sure enough awards are on hand for the size of the pack.
- Inform the master of ceremonies of the name of and award for each recipient. Large packs might consider having each den come forward and present all awards to the den leader. Smaller packs might consider calling each boy in alphabetical order and presenting any and all awards won. As every boy will receive an award for his participation in the derby, no one will feel left out.

Sample Program

1:00   Preinspection allows boys and their families time to correct any problems before derby time. (If feasible, cars can be inspected the night before the derby.)

2:00   Final inspection and registration

2:30   Opening ceremony. Let the races begin! Some packs may want to award ribbons and heat winner prizes during the running of the derby.

4:00   Recognition ceremony; be sure to recognize adult committee members.

4:15   Closing ceremony

Sample Rules

- The car can't be wider than 2½ inches and longer than 7 inches.
- The car can't weigh more than 5 ounces.
- The axles, wheels, and body of the car should be made from materials provided in the kit.
- Wheel bearings, washers, and bushings are prohibited.
- Only powdered graphite or silicone may be used for lubrication of the axles.
- The car must stand alone, not riding on any kind of spring or other device.
- The car must be freewheeling, with no starting devices.
- No loose materials of any kind are allowed in the car.

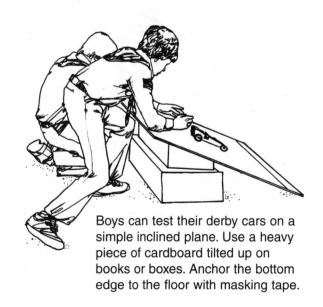

Boys can test their derby cars on a simple inclined plane. Use a heavy piece of cardboard tilted up on books or boxes. Anchor the bottom edge to the floor with masking tape.

Running the Derby

- Each boy takes his car to the registration table to have his name and number entered onto the heat sheets.

- After registration, each boy takes his car to the inspection table to have it pass final inspection and be placed, by den, on the starter's table.

- As each heat is announced, drivers retrieve their own car from the starter's table and place it at the starting gate. The starter releases the gate.

- Judges at the finish line will determine the results of the race. The car whose nose is first over the fin-

ish line wins. In case of a tie, or if judges are unsure, the race will be run again.

- After the race, cars are returned to the starter's table, in the event of additional heats.

- If a car leaves the track, runs out of its lane, interferes with another car, jumps the track, or loses an axle or any other part, it is judged as finishing last. If a car interferes with another car and negatively affects that car's result, the race should be run again. In the case of lost parts, if the car can be repaired quickly, it can be run in additional heats.

- Judges' decisions are final.

Pinewood Derby Track

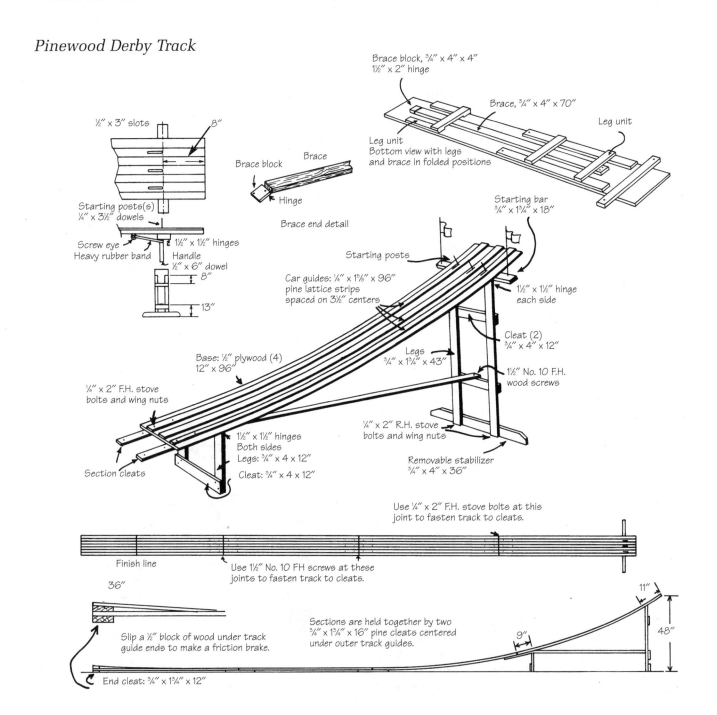

The Track

Many packs build their own tracks for use year after year. In many cases, packs work together, sharing tracks as needed. In any case, be sure to inspect each track after use and make needed repairs before storage. Equally important is inspecting each track well enough before race day to correct any problems that may have occurred during storage.

The track illustrated will allow three cars to race at one time. It can be built with ordinary workshop tools. The use of loose pin hinges makes it easy to take apart for storage.

Lane strips should be ¼ inch high. The bottom of the grand prix derby car is designed to be just ⅛ inch above the lane strip. If the lane strip is too high, the racer will drag.

Block sand all track surfaces, particularly where sections are joined. For extra strength, use white glue on all joints before fastening with screws. Also, a good grade of hard enamel paint is recommended for finishing the track.

Tips for Racer Construction

Boys should build their own racers with guidance and minimal assistance from an adult. Many packs have a separate division for cars built by adults to help share the fun and allow boys to work alongside adults.

- Paint the body parts before assembling the car to avoid getting paint on the axles.
- To remove burrs on the nail axles before adding wheels, use sandpaper or emery paper.
- If there is a mold seam on the wheels, sand very lightly. The wheels are hollow and break easily if too heavily sanded. Another danger of too much sanding is that the car will "high center" on the track.
- Use white glue or model cement to hold the pin axle in the body. Measure the distance between axles before securing.
- Fishing sinkers or other weights may be incorporated into the body to add weight, but the total weight cannot exceed 5 ounces.

SPACE DERBY

The space derby is similar to the pinewood derby only it uses miniature rockets. These propeller-driven rockets are powered by three rubber bands and travel along a monofilament fishing line. Boys carve and assemble the rockets themselves under the guidance of an adult family member.

Space derby kits with building instructions can be bought individually or in packs from a local Scouting distributor. Often, the derby committee purchases derby kits in quantity and distributes them to pack families. The local Scouting distributor also will have many derby "extras," such as space derby carriers, accessory kits, extra rubber bands, ribbons, trophies, decals, and more.

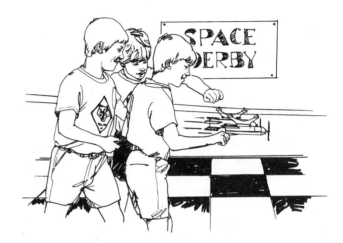

Personnel and Procedures

Registration Team, Before the Race Begins:
- Mark unique numbers on the bottom of each rocket.
- Enter the number and name of each entry on a preliminary heat sheet.

Registration Team, Once the Race Begins:
- Enter the names and numbers of heat winners on semifinal sheets.
- Determine the final standing of each winning rocket and report the results to the awards committee.

Inspection Team, Before the Race Begins:
- Check entries for use of official materials.
- Act as judges for prerace craftsmanship awards, such as Most Colorful, Best Looking, etc. Report results to the awards committee.

Inspection Team, During the Race:
- Have extra boxes of rubber bands on hand. It takes three rubber bands to fly each ship properly.
- Have small hand drills for winding rubber bands. This will help speed up the event. Check the ratio of the drill by making one revolution of the crank handle and counting the number of times the chuck turns. Most drills average a one-to-four ratio; thus, 40 turns equal 160 winds on a rubberband motor (150 to 170 winds are sufficient).

- Help boys by stretching the rubber bands 12 to 15 inches beyond the tail. One person holds the rocket while the other winds the rubber band. This is especially helpful when using a hand drill as the winder.

Launch Operations Team

- Set up and maintain launcher. Larger packs may find multiple launchers make the event move along more quickly.
- Have a starter's table where rockets are placed until it is time to race.
- Have a starter at the beginning of each track.
- Have two judges at the end of each track.
- Have two or more gatekeepers to line up the boys.
- Report winners to the registration team.

Interim Event Crew:

- Have planned activities for boys and siblings for preopening, while registration and inspection are taking place, and between heats. Boys could make paper airplanes and have target or distance throws.

Awards Committee:

- Make sure enough awards are on hand for the size of the pack.
- Inform the master of ceremonies of the name and award for each recipient. Large packs might consider having each den come forward and present all awards to the den leader. Smaller packs might consider calling each boy in alphabetical order and presenting any and all awards won. As every boy will receive an award for his participation in the derby, no one will feel left out.

Sample Program

7:00	Inspection and registration of rockets
7:30	Opening ceremony
7:40	Let the races begin! Some packs may want to award ribbons and heat winner prizes during the running of the derby.
8:30	Recognition ceremony, advancement awards, derby committee recognition
8:45	Closing ceremony

Sample Rules

- Only basic materials supplied in the kit may be used for rocket construction.
- The rocket body may be no longer than 7 inches, not including propeller and fins.
- There are no restrictions on the weight or design of the rocket.

Running the Derby

- Each boy takes his rocket to the registration table to have his name and number entered onto the heat sheets.
- Contestants report to the gatekeepers, who line them up in the order in which they will compete. At this point each boy starts to wind up the rubber band motor of his rocketship.
- As his name is called, the boy hooks his rocket in the guideline assigned to him. He must center it between the vertical dowels and lock the propeller behind the horizontal dowel on the starting gate.
- The gatekeeper starts the countdown and fires at zero by lifting the rear of the starting gate frame, which releases the rockets.
- Each race is run in heats with up to four contestants at a time. Each boy gets to try at least twice. For example, in a den of six boys, try heats of three boys each.
- The rocket whose nose is over the finish line first or travels the farthest if none passes the finish line wins.
- The winner takes his rocket to the registration table for recording.
- Judges' decisions are final.

Rocket Construction and Operation

The official kit includes all necessary materials and instructions for building your rocket. Decorate the rocket with bright colors, and apply decals.

Tips for Rocket Builders:

- Reduce air friction or drag by making all surfaces as smooth as possible. A blunt, rounded nose causes less drag than a sharp nose. A good design has all leading edges rounded and trailing edges tapered to reduce drag.
- Rubber bands should be lubricated. They are the "motor," and this will help them stay strong and flexible. Soak them overnight in castor oil. Or mix two parts green soap with one part glycerin and one part water; rub the mixture on the rubber band about an hour before race time.
- Use a sharp knife for cutting the grooves for the hanger fitting and fins. A dull knife will crush and splinter the balsa wood or foam.
- When you start a curve, remember that the end with the small hole is the rocket nose.
- A potato peeler is good for carving the shape.

The Rocket Launcher

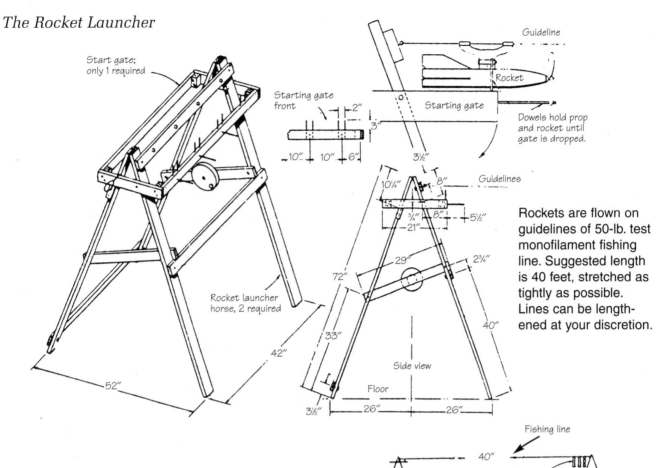

Start gate; only 1 required

Starting gate front

2"

3"

10" 10" 6"

Guideline

Starting gate

Rocket

Dowels hold prop and rocket until gate is dropped.

3½"

10¼" 8"

Guidelines

¾" 8"

21"

5½"

Rockets are flown on guidelines of 50-lb. test monofilament fishing line. Suggested length is 40 feet, stretched as tightly as possible. Lines can be lengthened at your discretion.

Rocket launcher horse, 2 required

29"

2¾"

72"

40"

33"

Side view

Floor

42"

52"

3½"

26"

26"

- To help increase rocket speed, reduce the wall thickness to a minimum of ⅛ inch. Don't weaken the area around the hanger (carrier) or carve away the nose button circle.

- Don't apply too much paint to the outside unless you sand between each coat.

- Be careful not to get glue on the plastic carrier, especially in the holes through which the monofilament line runs. Glue can interfere with smooth operation.

- Make the propeller shaft as short as possible by bending it close to the prop. Cut off excess wire with wire cutters.

- Test rocket balance by hanging it from a string through the hole of the hanger fitting. If the rocket is nose-heavy, carve or sand a little bit off that end. If it is tail-heavy, remove excess from the tail area.

Dens may wish to secure a 50-foot length of 50-pound monofilament fishing line for test runs before the derby. Secure the line at just less than 100 feet, as tight as possible.

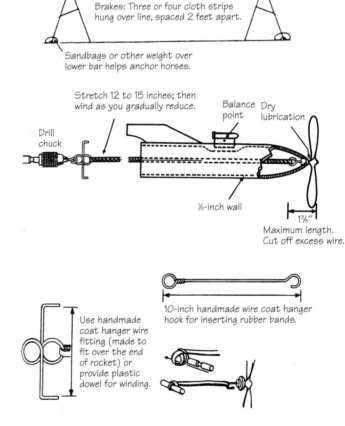

Fishing line

40"

Brakes: Three or four cloth strips hung over line, spaced 2 feet apart.

Sandbags or other weight over lower bar helps anchor horses.

Stretch 12 to 15 inches; then wind as you gradually reduce.

Balance point

Dry lubrication

Drill chuck

⅛-inch wall

1⅜"

Maximum length. Cut off excess wire.

10-inch handmade wire coat hanger hook for inserting rubber bands.

Use handmade coat hanger wire fitting (made to fit over the end of rocket) or provide plastic dowel for winding.

RAINGUTTER REGATTA

Ahoy mates! This could be the sailing regatta of the century! Although the seas are only 10-foot lengths of raingutter filled with water, and ships are a mere 6 inches long, the race is an exciting event. Each boy builds his own boat with the help and guidance of an adult. He also provides the "wind" for his sail with his own lung power.

The regatta boat kit with building instructions can be purchased individually or in packs from a local Scouting distributor. Often, the derby committee purchases derby kits in quantity and distributes them to pack families along with rules, tips on construction, and any other helpful hints. The local Scouting distributor also has many derby "extras," such as decals, ribbons, trophies, and more. The kit includes a preshaped hull, metal keel, mast, and sail. Or the pack can choose to run the regatta with rubber band–powered boats. Just be sure that the depth of the boats chosen doesn't exceed the depth of the raceway.

The personnel needed is similar to any derby event (see "Personnel and Procedures" above for the pinewood derby or space derby). The inspection team needs to measure the keel to make sure it will not drag on the bottom.

Sample Program

6:00   Preinspection allows boys and their families time to correct any problems before derby time. If feasible, inspect boats the night before the race.

6:30   Final inspection and registration

6:40   Opening ceremony. Let the races begin! Some packs may want to award ribbons and heat winner prizes during the running of the derby.

7:40   Recognition ceremony, including recognition of adult committee members

7:45   Closing ceremony

Sample Rules

- The hull cannot be longer than 7 inches or shorter than 6½ inches.
- The mast should measure 6½ inches from deck to top.
- The keel and rudder supplied in the kit must be used with no alterations.
- The sail should be no larger than the material supplied in the kit.
- There are no restrictions on color or design.

Running the Regatta

- Boys take their boats to the registration table to be checked and numbered and have their names entered on the heat sheet.
- They then take the boats to the inspection table to make sure they meet specifications.
- The race is run in heats. Boats are powered by each boy blowing into the sail of his own boat.
- Boats start with the stern touching the end of the gutter. The starter stands at the opposite end, and on a signal the boys begin to blow. With a double raceway, two boys compete at the same time. The first boat to reach the end of the raingutter wins. Once the race has started, the boys may not touch the boats with their hands. Should a boat snag, a judge will right the boat and then the boy may continue.
- Watch the boys carefully, as hyperventilation can occur.
- On courses other than a raingutter, boats must be held by the pilots at the starting line and released on a signal. Once again, the use of hands is not allowed, and boats cannot be pushed. If any boat runs afoul, the heat is considered a no-contest and is run again.

The Course

This practice raingutter regatta course can be set up in almost any backyard.

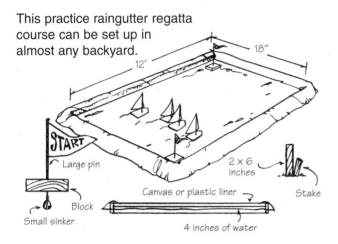

One popular course is simply a standard 10-foot-long raingutter set in groves on wooden supports (see illustration). Another method is to place the 10-foot lengths of raingutter at either side of a long table. Once the raingutters are in place, put a small amount of water into each gutter to make sure it is level. Even on the most level ground, some adjustment may be necessary. Two 10-foot lengths of raingutter will hold approximately 8 gallons of water, so once full, they are difficult to move without causing a minor flood. After making any adjustments, fill the gutter to about ½ inch from the top.

Regattas may also be held in small inflatable pools, swimming pools, or lakes, as long as Safe Swim Defense is followed and appropriate health and safety regulations are met.

Construction Tips

- Sandpaper the hull to the desired shape, adhering to the specifications required. First use a medium-grade sandpaper, then finish with a fine-grain sandpaper.

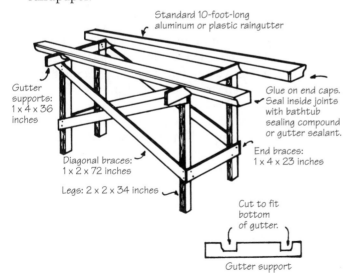

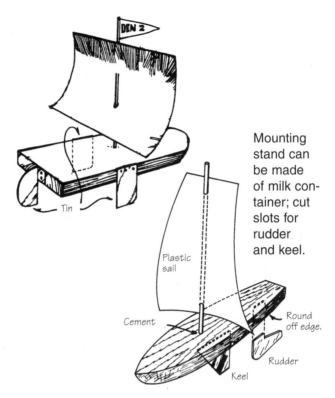

Mounting stand can be made of milk container; cut slots for rudder and keel.

Cement keel and rudder in slots where indicated on hull bottom.

- Give the boat two coats of sanding sealer.
- Paint the boat with two coats of colored lacquer or acrylic paint. Don't use water-based or tempera paints.

CUBMOBILE DERBY

The Cubmobile derby is a thrilling pack activity that is fun for the entire family. Planning for the derby should begin several months in advance so Cub Scouts and adults from each den can build a racer. That's right! Each den builds its own Cubmobile, with plenty of adults to help supervise construction. There is no engine; the Cubmobile runs by gravity.

Personnel and Procedures

Program Committee: Besides the general responsibilities of the program committee noted above (page 6–1), the program committee for a Cubmobile derby should make arrangements for a rescue squad of first aiders to be on hand for emergencies. Remember: Boys are the drivers. The committee chair is responsible for getting any required city permits for use of public streets or right-of-ways and for securing approval from the appropriate city, county, or park authority to close off the street to traffic.

Inspection and Registration Team:

- Make a cutout of cardboard or wood to check the overall dimensions of the Cubmobile.
- Check for correct attachments of safety requirements, paying special attention to the brake system and seat belts.
- Make sure that a bicycle helmet is available for each driver.
- Number each car.
- Act as judges for craftsmanship awards. Report winners to the program committee.
- Register each boy and give him a number within his den.
- Enter each car and driver for each run on a tally sheet, to keep track of who runs each heat.
- Get times from timekeepers at the finish line and record them.
- Determine the final standing of each den car and report the results to the program committee for presentation of awards.

Track Operations Team:

- Assign at least two gatekeepers to line up cars.
- Have at least two starters to operate the starting ramp (one for each lane).
- Have official timers with stopwatches at the finish line (one for each lane).
- Mark lanes with chalk, and rope off racing area as necessary.
- Provide hay bales or sand pits at the end of the track to make sure Cubmobiles stop.
- Report official times to the registration team.

Sample Program

(This is designed for a Saturday.)

9:00	Registration and gathering time
9:30	Opening ceremonies
9:45	Events
11:15	Recognition ceremonies and closing
11:45	Cleanup

Running the Derby

- The derby is run in heats. Each den has one Cubmobile, and each boy in the den races the car one time. The den with the lowest average racing time wins.
- Each den reports with its Cubmobile to the inspection station, where the car is inspected and numbered.
- Cub Scouts bring the Cubmobile to the registration table where boys' names are listed on the heat schedule.
- As the master of ceremonies calls his name, each boy reports to the starting gate. He is helped into the car. An adult checks to see that his seat belt is fastened and helmet is secure.
- All drivers should wear protective gear, including a helmet and knee and elbow pads.
- When cars are released from the starting gate, drivers should try to stay in their own lane.
- No pumping or pushing with the feet is allowed.
- After driving, each boy should join the spectators' section to cheer his den on.

The Track

The track should be a smooth-surfaced street with a gradual slope that is neither too long nor too steep. The suggested track length is 150 feet, plus additional stopping space. The lanes should be marked with chalk. Crossing over from one lane to another will happen, especially with inexperienced drivers, but boys should be instructed to stay within their own lanes. Judges should observe the race for any fouls. If a driver is fouled, he should be given another run.

The Starting Ramp

Usually, a ramp is set up to start the cars. Cubmobiles start from a standstill, rolling down the ramp and the slope to the finish line because of gravity. The starting ramp may be as simple or elaborate as the derby committee wishes. Sheets of heavy plywood are effective and can usually be rented. These can be elevated from the backside with cement blocks. Another type of starting ramp is shown here. Consider safety factors when determining the angle of the starting ramp. The ramp should allow room for the number of cars starting at one time.

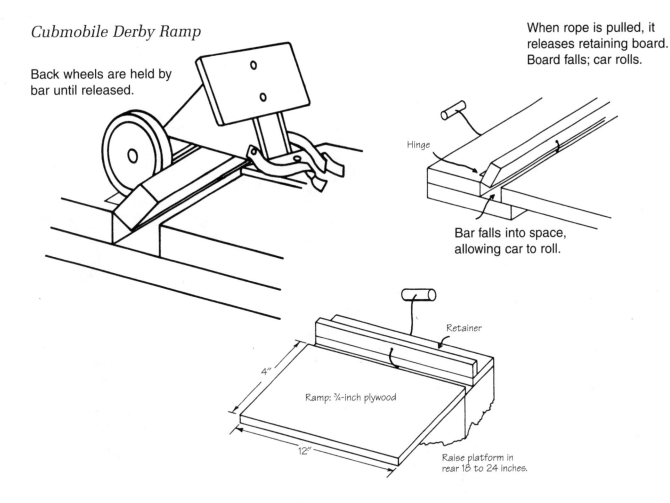

Cubmobile Derby Ramp

Back wheels are held by bar until released.

When rope is pulled, it releases retaining board. Board falls; car rolls.

Hinge

Bar falls into space, allowing car to roll.

Retainer

4"

Ramp: ¾-inch plywood

12"

Raise platform in rear 18 to 24 inches.

Cubmobile Specs and Parts

- See the illustration for building materials and hardware.
- Wheels may not exceed 12 inches in diameter.
- All wheels must be equipped with rubber tires.
- The car frame is made from 2-by-4-inch construction lumber.
- The overall length of the car is a minimum of 5 feet; the wheelbase is a maximum of 4 feet. The outside circumference of the wheel may vary from 30 to 36 inches.
- Use roundhead ½-inch bolts to hold the frame. Screws are a second choice. Nails are NOT suitable, because they may work loose.
- All cars must have a seat with a braced backrest so the boy can comfortably steer with his feet.
- Cars must be equipped with an adequate safety belt securely fastened to the frame of the car.

- Steering is done with the feet, placed on the front axle, and by the hands holding a rope fastened to the front axle.
- If threaded axles are used, the nuts must be secured with cotter pins or wire.
- Cars must be equipped with a hand brake. Its rubbing surface must be faced with a rubber material such as a strip of an old tire. This will stop the car when dragged on the ground.
- During the race the two 2-by-4-inch blocks fastened ½ inch from the centerboard will limit the turning radius. See illustration.

Publicity

A Cubmobile derby will have considerable appeal to the general public. Invite photographers from local newspapers to take pictures. Make sure the boys are properly uniformed in either full uniform or matching T-shirts. Use this event as a recruiting opportunity, *but a boy must be registered with the pack to race a Cubmobile.*

Cubmobile Specs and Parts

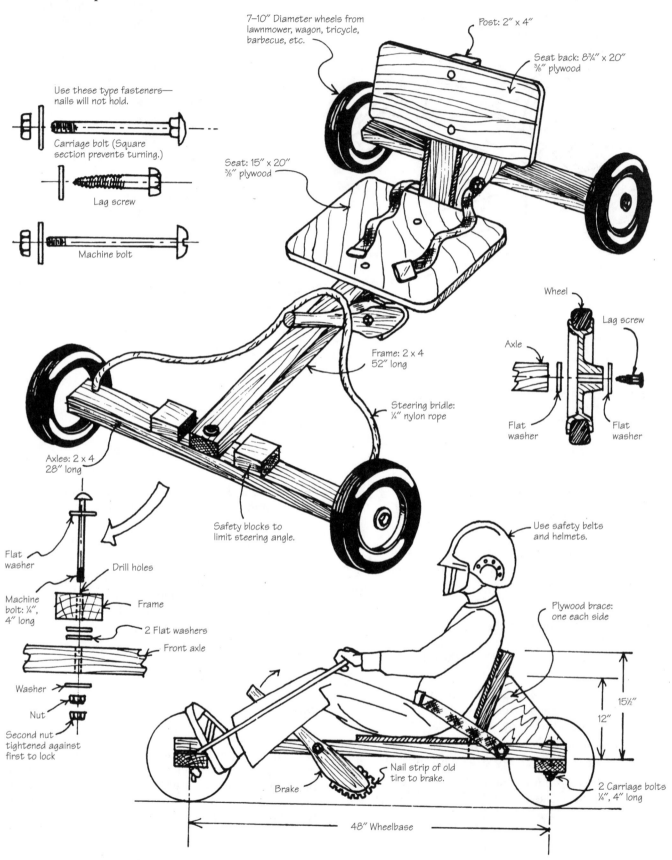

7–10" Diameter wheels from lawnmower, wagon, tricycle, barbecue, etc.

Post: 2" x 4"

Seat back: 8¾" x 20" ⅜" plywood

Use these type fasteners— nails will not hold.

Carriage bolt (Square section prevents turning.)

Lag screw

Machine bolt

Seat: 15" x 20" ⅜" plywood

Frame: 2 x 4 52" long

Wheel

Lag screw

Axle

Flat washer

Flat washer

Steering bridle: ¼" nylon rope

Axles: 2 x 4 28" long

Safety blocks to limit steering angle.

Flat washer

Drill holes

Machine bolt: ¼", 4" long

Frame

2 Flat washers

Front axle

Washer

Nut

Second nut tightened against first to lock

Use safety belts and helmets.

Plywood brace: one each side

15½"

12"

Brake

Nail strip of old tire to brake.

2 Carriage bolts ¼", 4" long

48" Wheelbase

ALL-DERBY RACE DAY

If it has wings, wheels, or rudders, it can happen on all-derby race day. This event may include as many of the derby activities as there are adults to staff the events. It requires lots of hands-on participation, so you may consider combining with other packs or holding it as a district- or council-level event. As with all derbies, the purpose is not to win or lose but to have fun.

Preplanning is a must for this special event. Follow the guidelines from the beginning of this chapter so that nothing will be overlooked (page 6–1). Boys and their families are invited to bring any Cub Scouting–recommended derby car, rocket, or boat and race against each other for fun. This is also a great opportunity for dad to dust off his own derby car from when he was a Cub Scout—or to make a new one.

Personnel

- **The race-day chair** will oversee and coordinate the race-day events, secure the site, and provide necessary information to the families.
- **The deputy chairs** for each event are responsible for securing tracks or equipment needed for their area.
- **The adult assistants** for each event are recruited by the deputy chairs.
- **The registration committee** will register each participant and help with crowd control. A registration sheet is filled in for each activity a boy wishes to enter. The sheets are given to the area deputy, who will call the names of participants for each race.

Events

Include pinewood derbies, Cubmobile races, space derbies, and raingutter regattas as your resources and personnel permit. For recognition, you can use mini-stickers or gummed stars in gold (first), silver (second), and blue (third) and place them on the bottom of the cars, sides of rockets, or tops of boats to indicate place. But the primary idea of race day is to *have fun*.

To run an event, call names in the order they appear on the registration sheets. If someone is at another event, move his name to the bottom of the list until all racers have participated.

Sample Program

1:00   Registration. Complete a sheet for each event a boy wishes to enter. Any weighing or measuring is done at this time. After registering, the car, boat, etc., is turned over to that committee and stored until that race is called.

1:30   Opening ceremony

2:00   Let the races begin! Packs may choose to award ribbons and heat winner prizes during the running of each derby.

4:00   Recognition ceremony, including recognition of adult committee members

4:15   Closing ceremony and cleanup

FISHING DERBY

There are two kinds of Cub Scout pack fishing derbies, and both are fun for boys and adults. One is a joint Cub Scout and adult partner fishing trip to a nearby lake or river where adults and boys can fish off the banks. Prizes are awarded for such things as the biggest fish, first fish, and the most caught. Unless the fish are to be eaten, fishing should be done under the catch-and-release plan. The other type of fishing derby is a family outing with games and contests related to fishing.

The fishing derby committee should follow the guidelines for planning special events (see page 6–1). Planning for either type of fishing derby includes securing a site, arranging transportation, and coordinating activities. The committee must be aware of and obtain any required licenses or permits. The committee duties also include providing prizes and making sure there is enough fishing gear for every child to participate. If a meal is included, arrangements must be made to assure enough nutritional food for everyone. The committee might try some special promotional ideas, such as sending fish-shaped invitations or inviting local anglers to help.

For the family outing derby, make signs for each contest area. Use ropes, posts, or colored streamers to mark game areas. Fishing areas should also be marked off and watched, as many families will have small children attending. Consider the need for a public-address system and always remember safety.

Sample Program

The activities and schedule below pertain to a family fishing derby with games and contests.

10:00–11:00	Committee arrives ahead of time to set up activities.
11:00–12:30	Free time for fishing. As the boys arrive, set up adult and boy with fishing gear and get them started. It is a good idea to have experienced anglers available to help those who are new to the sport.
12:30–1:30	Lunch and cleanup. Roast corn and fried fish might be prepared by the fishing derby committee; or have a picnic of hot dogs, baked beans, and watermelon; or have a family potluck.
1:30–2:30	Special contests
2:30–3:00	Awards ceremony
3:00–3:15	Final camp cleanup

Contests

Guessing Game: How many fish eggs are in the jar? Fill a jar with miniature red jellybeans (count as you fill the jar). Have slips of paper and a drop box so players can write down their names, write their guess on the paper, and drop it in the box. Whoever guesses closest to the actual number of "fish eggs" gets the jar and the jellybeans as a prize.

Just Fishin': Fill several 2-L. bottles with water and reclose. (The more water, the greater the challenge.) Use a ½-inch dowel and attach a 30-inch string that has a 3-inch ring tied to the end for a pole. Place the filled bottles or "fish" on their sides. Catch a fish by standing the bottle upright.

Are They Biting? Cut out cardboard fish. Mark the underside of the fish with a point value. Apply a piece of magnet to the tail of each one. Use poles with magnet strips on the end to catch a fish. (Opposite polarity magnets will attract each other.) Add up point totals after a set time.

Cross the Pond: Have a den relay where each boy wades barefoot through six pans of water. Or cut out two large circles of paper for each team. These are the team's "rocks," which they must step on to cross the pond and return. Mark off or designate a 10- to 15-foot strip of ground as the "pond." Place the paper rocks in the pond a few inches apart. The first boy steps from the "bank" onto the first rock, then the second. Since this leaves no rocks to step on, he must turn around and pick up the rock from behind him and place it in front of him to make the next step without falling into the pond. If a participant falls into the water, he must start back from the bank he just left.

KITE DERBY

A pack kite derby can be one of the best spring or summer activities. It may include various kite demonstrations and contests and may also include a picnic lunch or supper. Some kite derbies are held just for fun, with no special contests or prizes. Others include contests with prizes for each participant.

Follow the guidelines for planning special activities found in the beginning of this chapter (page 6–1). The kite derby committee must consider the location (an open field), the layout of the field, and the meal if any. If contests are to be included, decide on entry requirements, which events will be held, and the rules and prizes for each. You will need an announcer, a starter, and one or two judges.

The kite derby plan should be developed far enough in advance so the boys and families will know the types of events and rules before they begin making kites. The "Crafts" chapter of this book contains information on making several types of kites. The den meetings leading up to the derby would be a good time to discuss kite-flying safety rules with the boys (see below).

Sample Program

10:00	Registration, exhibits, display and judging of kites
11:00	Opening ceremony
11:15	Kite contests
12:30	Picnic time!
1:00	Recognition
1:15	Closing ceremony

Entry Requirements

The kite derby committee will want to set some rules beforehand to help prevent any misunderstanding or disappointment. Here are a few suggestions:

- All kites must be made by boys and adult partners.
- Boys may enter only one kite.
- Each kite must be numbered.
- Each boy may have his adult partner help him get his kite into the air and help him catch it when it comes down.
- Only wood, fabric, or plastic may be used to make kites. No fighting kites are allowed; glass, razor blades, and metals are not permitted.
- No wire kite lines are permitted.
- Kites caught in power lines are considered lost and may not be retrieved.
- Kites may be adjusted and modified any time during the derby.

You may want to measure the kite cords before the competition and mark them at 100 yards to aid judges in determining how high they are flying. Or the kite derby committee could provide premeasured standard cords.

Judging

Kites should be divided into three groups for competition:

- Bowed or tailless kites
- Flat kites or those with tails
- Box kites or combination kites

You may wish to establish a point system for judging in order to make it easier to determine the winners of some of the awards. Preflight judging can be done for design, workmanship, and creativity. Prizes could be awarded for

- Smallest
- Largest
- Most comical
- Most unusual
- Best craftsmanship
- Most original
- Most beautiful
- Most Cub Scout–ish

During flight, kites could be judged for

- First in the air
- Highest after 5 minutes
- Highest after 15 minutes
- Most stable flier
- Most graceful in the air
- Fastest climbing

You could also judge boys for

- Best sportsmanship
- Most persistent flier

Kite-Flying Safety Rules

- Always fly a kite far away from electric or power lines, transmission towers, TV and radio antennas, and ponds.
- Don't fly kites on rainy days; never fly a kite in a thunderstorm.
- Use wood, fabric, or plastic to make the kite. Never use metal.
- Always use dry string. Never use wire for a kite line.
- When flying a kite, avoid public streets, highways, and airline or railroad right-of-ways.
- If your kite gets snagged in a power line, treetop, roof, or high pole, never try to remove it.

Kite Contests

100-Yard Dash: The contest starts on a signal, with launching in any manner. Kites must be flown to the end of a 100-yard cord and then wound back to the hand of the flier. An assistant may remain under the kite as it is wound in to catch it before it falls to the ground. The race ends when the flier has rewound his cord. At the finish, the flier must be on the starting line with his kite and cord wound back into his hand.

Altitude Race: Fliers start on a signal and run out from the flying line, working the kite up to its highest possible altitude. At the end of five minutes, judges determine which kite is flying the highest.

Messenger Race: All players send their kites up to a specific length of line—about 50 yards. A paper messenger is attached to the flying lines and allowed to blow up the kite. (See the "Crafts" chapter for making kite messengers.) The boy whose messenger first reaches his kite wins the race.

7

CUB SCOUTS WITH SPECIAL NEEDS

Every boy has needs. Three important ones are to feel accepted by a group, to feel a sense of competence as he approaches a task, and to feel a sense of self-satisfaction at its completion. For some boys, these needs are easily met. For others, it takes a little more thought and planning on the part of leaders to help the boys. That's what this chapter is about.

The parents of a boy with special needs will be the best resource for information about their son's abilities, limits, and goals. Other resources include the boy's teachers and the *Cub Scout Leader Book*.

Feeling Accepted in the Den

Many people wonder how a boy who is different from other members of the den will be accepted. You will find that with proper preparation of the den, these boys are accepted into the fellowship of the den easily.

Before a boy with special needs joins the den, the den leader should plan some time to prepare the boys to meet their new member. During the two meetings before the new boy's joining the den, devote part of the regular meeting time to activities that will prepare everyone. The assistant den leader and den chief will need to take part in planning these activities and will need to understand the needs of the new Cub Scout.

FIRST DEN ORIENTATION

Materials: **Chalkboard, chalk, appropriate simulation items (blindfolds, newspapers, rope, etc.) to simulate the new boy's disabilities**

Announce that you are having a "rap session." Tell the boys that a new member is joining the den. If they don't already know, tell the den his name and tell them that he is a little different from them. Don't mention the boy's disability yet. Ask the boys to name all the things they can all do (run, jump, see, ride bikes, hear, etc.).

If the den does know the new boy, have them share any experiences they have had with him. Ask the boys whether they have already helped him in some way. List these on the board. Also list the ways the new boy is just like the boys in the den.

- Point out that no one can do everything. Each of us needs help at certain times. Identify things the individual members of the den and the leaders need help with.

- Describe the disability in simple terms, explaining that the new boy may do some things differently from other boys. Use the Cub Scout motto "Do Your Best" to explain that everyone does his best in everything he undertakes and that each den member's "best" is different.

Simulation Game: After a discussion of the boy's condition, ask the den members whether they have an idea of what it would be like not to be able to do something they enjoy or take for granted. Suggest a game to find out. For example, if the new Cub Scout is blind, blindfold each boy in turn and ask him to bring you a specified object. If the new Cub Scout is deaf, have boys communicate without talking. If the new boy has trouble focusing on a task or performing tasks at a normal pace, play a version of "Simon Says." In this version, all commands are to be followed. Begin slowly, allowing time for each boy to complete the command. Then speed up the game until the commands are coming at so rapidly that no one can keep up.

SECOND DEN ORIENTATION

With the den, plan the next meeting when the new Cub Scout will attend for the first time. Learn a welcome song such as "We're Glad to See You Here" from the *Cub Scout Songbook*. Have everyone make suggestions for activities for the day. Follow the meeting structure outlined in the *Cub Scout Leader Book*. You may want to plan for special refreshments during this welcome meeting so that it seems more like a party.

With some boys with special needs, a "buddy system" can be very effective. If it is appropriate for the new Cub Scout, explain the system to the den. Each week, a different den member will be responsible for helping the new Cub Scout during the meeting. Emphasize that the important factor is to "Do Your Best" and that the boy who is helping must be *patient*—not only because of the special needs of the Cub Scout but because the new boy is new to Cub Scouting. Practice the planned activities, with each boy taking a turn at helping and being helped. Often, boys learn more about helping others when they themselves are helped.

FIRST DEN MEETING WITH THE NEW CUB SCOUT

The process described here is a good one for planning all den meetings. Consult *Cub Scout Program Helps* and the *Webelos Leader Guide* for weekly den meeting ideas that follow the monthly theme or activity badge.

The purpose of this first den meeting is to introduce the new Cub Scout to the members of the den. Use a ceremony from *Cub Scout Ceremonies for Dens and Packs* to welcome the new boy.

Icebreaker

Choose an icebreaker or two to help everyone get to know one another. You can use a simple one from *Group Meeting Sparklers* or use one suggested here.

Have You Ever?: Visit with the parents of the new Cub Scout to find out what his interests are. Find out about things he has done that he especially enjoyed. Armed with that information and similar knowledge about the den members, devise a list of questions. Direct the boys to raise their hands when the answer is "I have." The questions should demonstrate that not all members of the den have done everything and that the new Cub Scout has something in common with other members of the den. Consider questions such as the following:

• Have you ever been to the circus?
• Have you ever found a snail?
• Have you ever eaten a snail?
• Have you ever caught a fish?
• Have you ever traveled out of the state?
• Have you ever spent the night in a tent?
• Have you ever cooked your own breakfast?
• Have you ever cooked breakfast for someone else?
• Have you ever been to a ball game?
• Have you ever talked to the mail carrier?

Who Am I?: Ask den members to line up in two rows facing each other about 6 feet apart. Ask the new boy to stand at the head of the two lines and throw a ball to the boy whose name the leader calls at random. The boy whose name is called should be encouraged to act silly, wave his hand, or in another way attract the attention of the new Cub Scout. This should reveal personalities and help the new Cub Scout learn the names of the den members.

Game

Choose a game from the ones at the end of this chapter (they are arranged by specific disability), choose one from the "Games" chapter of this book

(keeping in mind everyone's abilities), or adapt a game so that everyone can play. Information on how to adapt games is provided in the "Feeling of Competence" section below.

Activity Period

The activity period should include only things that all the boys can easily do. Choose from one of the many projects in the "Crafts" chapter, keeping in mind everyone's abilities, or use the one suggested below. (Most Cub Scouts can do this with a little help.)

Scout Calendar

Materials:

    11-by-17-inch piece of heavy paper or cardstock
    9-by-13-inch piece of paper with calendar for the month printed on it
    Tempera paint
    Sponges cut into small pieces
    Stickers to designate den meeting days and pack meeting
    Clothespins
    Glue

Wet the sponges with water and squeeze the water completely out of them. Using the clothespins to hold the sponges, dip the sponges into the tempera and press onto the 11-by-17 paper, leaving a print. This should be repeated in a haphazard manner, using different colors of tempera if desired. When dry, glue the calendar in place, leaving a border of the sponge print around it. Attach stickers to the days for den meetings and pack meetings. Write the time and place down on those days.

Closing

For the closing of the meeting, the den leader should give a brief talk on what is expected of each den member—that he *do his best*. Then tell boys what they will be doing at the next meeting. If the new Cub Scout's abilities are such that familiarity with the activities before den meetings is helpful, be sure that his parent is aware of this. A den take-home note or newsletter for all the boys could be a subtle way of communicating with the parent. Close with a Living Circle (see *Cub Scout Ceremonies for Dens and Packs*).

DEN DISCIPLINE

A boy knows that he is cared for when he knows that others care about his behavior. A boy's parent will be the best resource for understanding what a boy is able to do and how strict the code of conduct should be. If it is necessary to relax the rules for one Cub Scout, it will be necessary to relax them for all den members. The "Accentuate the Positive" chapter of this book has several helpful ideas for monitoring boy behavior in the den. Clear communication about what is expected and appreciated is a key to a boy's developing self-discipline.

For instance, instead of the usual "Good job!" try saying something like this: "I felt _____ when you _____ and it made me want to _____." When encouraging (or discouraging) particular behavior, it is helpful to fill in these blanks as specifically as possible. It isn't necessary to have them in this order. Other examples: "I was so happy when you shared your special ball with Matt that it made me want to shout"; "I just wanted to tell you how proud I was when you helped Matt with his project"; "When you asked Matt to sit next to you so he would feel welcome, it made me so pleased that I want to shake your hand."

"IT'S NOT FAIR!"

It isn't uncommon for boys or adults to notice when one boy is getting special treatment. Then, you might hear the phrase, "It's not fair!" First, be sure that all boys are being treated equally—that no one is being corrected for something that others are not. If all the boys are being treated equally, then it may be time for you to choose one or more of the following activities to do with the individual who is complaining or with the den as a whole.

- Discuss the concepts of *fair* versus *equal*. "Fair" means that the needs of everyone in the den are being met. Because those needs are not the same, treatment is not the same. Ask whether adults in their family get more on their plates at dinner than they do. Why is that? Would it be fair to expect everyone to eat as much as the adults do? When someone is sick in the family and has to have supper in bed instead of with the family, would it be fair to make everyone have supper in bed? Ask the boys to come up with another example. End the

conversation with, "Is it fair that some boys don't have all the abilities that others do?"

- Replay the simulation game that you played in the preparation meeting for the new Cub Scout. Now that everyone is familiar with the limits of the boy with special needs, this game may have more significance.

- Redo the rap session from the first den orientation meeting. This time, focus on what each of the boys can do, including the boy with special needs, and then focus on who is the best at different activities. The den leader may have to suggest several things at which each boy is the best.

Feeling Accepted in the Pack

For the first pack meeting with a boy with special needs, the Cubmaster should consider these suggestions:

1. Have the den introduce their new member to the pack and do a cheer.

2. Use the normal induction ceremony, including the induction of the boy's parents, but emphasize the Law of the Pack and the Cub Scout motto, particularly "to help other people."

3. Be sensitive: Try not to embarrass the new Cub Scout or his family in any way.

Feeling of Competence

Every boy should feel "I can do that!" when each project is presented to him. Often, a boy with special needs hasn't had that feeling before. Because the Cub Scout program is flexible and based on the idea of a boy doing his best, it is important to consider every boy's abilities and modify activities or advancement requirements when necessary. Each boy should feel challenged but not feel that anything is beyond his capabilities. Meeting the challenge will build a sense of competence.

It is important for all concerned to consider how complete the activity is rather than how incomplete it is. No boy's level of achievement should be used as a measuring stick for any other boy. Celebration needs to occur when improvement has been made or when it has been determined that a boy has done his best.

ADAPTING ACHIEVEMENTS

The *Cub Scout Leader Book* has directions for the Cubmaster and pack committee on how to substitute requirements for an achievement. When modifying an achievement, consider these things:

- It is imperative that boys feel that they are working and *earning* achievements. An achievement should not be modified so much that boys feel it is being *given* to them.

- Consider reducing the number of repetitions of a particular activity.

- Substitute an activity that will be a stretch for the boy but still within his capabilities.

- If the boy can't physically do the activity itself, can he teach or lead someone else through the activity?

- If applicable, consider substituting dictation for writing.

- Allow for extra time for completion.

ADAPTING CRAFTS

In addition to altering achievements, you may have to adapt some crafts.

- Some part of the project may need to be precut for ease of construction. For some boys it is best to put "their" materials in a bag so that they know whose is whose. If that is the case, use bags for every boy in the den. This can be a subtle way to ensure that some boys get a bag with more of the preconstruction done for them.

- Keeping instructions simple and few in number will help those boys who have trouble focusing or retaining information. Crafts that take a long time to complete should be divided up into several short tasks for such boys.

- It may be necessary to allow additional time for some boys to finish a project (perhaps at home or after the meeting) while the rest of the den moves on to something else.

- Some crafts may require an adult to help the Cub Scout with special needs in addition to the help he will receive from his "buddy of the week."

ADAPTING GAMES

Games can be a problem for boys with special needs, but you can adapt them with great success. Sometimes, helping a boy merely means clarifying directions. Perhaps the rules need to be simplified so that all boys can easily understand them. Often, a "practice game" helps clarify the rules and cement the order of play for boys who have trouble with retaining auditory directions. Some boys will need to see written directions. Competing against a clock or for a "personal best" rather than competing against other boys can be a good way to enable everyone to be a winner.

There are many ways to adapt games. For example, if a game involves throwing a paper airplane but making the airplane is too complicated, substitute throwing a piece of paper wadded up into a ball. If a game involves running a short distance and one boy can't run, perhaps he can use his arms to move from one point to another, much like a soldier in the field. Perhaps *all* the boys could do this. Consider ways, for instance, that a boy in a wheelchair can mimic the actions of a boy on a bike or running. Choosing games carefully and adapting them can make this part of Cub Scouting fun for all.

ADAPTING SKITS

Skits should include everyone. When planning them, be sure that everyone in the den has a significant part. Remind boys that announcers and narrators are important. So are the people who do special effects, sounds, and lighting. Make sure that everyone rotates through these positions so that everyone has his time behind and on stage.

When writing skits, don't overlook the contributions that can be made by boys who have trouble maintaining focus. Because they pay attention to everything at once, they often associate two things that are wildly different from each other—which can be the basis for skit humor.

ADAPTING THE DEN MEETING

Structuring the den meeting with the Cub Scout with special needs in mind may help him be more successful in the den. Boys who have trouble paying attention thrive when activities change frequently—particularly when an "active" game or activity follows a "quiet" one. If a boy still needs additional activity, ask him to run little errands—go and get the glue, etc. A den leader should always have an extra activity ready for those days when the planned activities have been exhausted.

Feeling of Self-Satisfaction

Every boy wants to be proud of his achievement. Advancement and achievement may be especially important to the boy with special needs—he wants to feel he did it just like everyone else. Often, these boys are not able to master an activity at the same level of others in the den, but they are able to improve. The best way for them and the den leader to see improvement is to measure it.

When introducing a new activity, ask all the boys to do their best to accomplish it without any instruction. Make a chart. Measure the activity in some way. Maybe there is a written comment, a picture is taken, or a number of repetitions is noted. Then give the instruction and set goals for each boy based on their ability. Do the activity again. Measure again. Celebrate improvement with a cheer, a pat on the back, or something tangible. Reevaluate the goals: Were they set too high for some? Too low for others? Repeat the activity. Measure. Celebrate any improvement. When the boys have reached their goal, *or* when it has been determined that a boy has done his best, declare the activity completed and celebrate immediately. Advancement recognition for all boys should occur as soon as possible.

Special Activities

Careful planning, choosing appropriate activities, and adapting them when necessary should create an atmosphere in the den in which all members are successful. The following activities are grouped by specific disabilities, but consider using one from a different category if you know your boys and think it will work. It is hoped that these suggestions will help you learn how to create and adapt other games and crafts to introduce to the den. These tested activities have been enjoyed by all boys—not just those with disabilities.

FOR BOYS WHO HAVE VISION IMPAIRMENTS

Choose activities that don't require sight. Since every boy likes a mystery, why not try one of these?

Kim's Game

Materials: **Bag, variety of objects familiar to the boys**

Place all the objects into the bag out of sight of the boys. Allow each of them to place their hand in the bag without looking and feel each of the objects. They should then write down or whisper to the game leader all the things they can remember.

Don't Eat Pete

Materials: **Sheet of construction paper divided into nine equal spaces, nine wrapped candies that will fit in the game spaces**

Each boy takes a turn leaving the room while the rest decide which candy will be "Pete." When the Cub Scout returns, he chooses a candy, by touching it, to eat—hoping it isn't "Pete." If it is, the rest of the den will shout, "Don't eat Pete!" If it isn't "Pete," he is allowed to eat the candy.

What Is That Sound?

This is a good game to play outdoors or as a night hike. All members of the den should close their eyes and be silent for 2 minutes. At the end of that time, they should write down or whisper to a leader all that they heard and could identify.

Ball Wrestle

Materials: **Basketball, blindfold**

Two boys kneel facing each other with a basketball between them. (The boy whose vision is not impaired should wear a blindfold.) They place one hand on the ball and the other behind their backs. The object of the game is to wrestle the ball away from the opponent and stand with the ball held overhead in one hand. If no one wins in 2 minutes, declare the game a draw.

FOR BOYS WHO ARE EMOTIONALLY DISTURBED

Choose one of the noncompetitive games found in the "Games" chapter of this book, or have boys compete for a personal best rather than against one another. Choose crafts that are process-oriented rather than achievement-oriented.

Flying Bat

Materials: Box, black paper for paper airplanes

Cut a hole in a box and decorate the exterior as a cave. Each boy makes a paper airplane out of the black paper and then throws his "bat" into the bat cave. Allow each contestant as many turns as time allows.

Roll the Marble

Materials: Shoe box, five marbles per boy

Take the lid off a shoe box and turn it upside down. Cut two or three "doors" in one of the long sides. Boys shoot their marbles through the doors. Allow as many turns as time permits.

Variation: Increase the distance, reduce the number of doors, or use marbles of different sizes.

FOR BOYS WHO ARE AUTISTIC

- Choose games and activities that have simple directions and can be completed in a short amount of time.
- Clearly and simply state the directions several times.
- Many autistic children are very artistic and can complete detailed artwork.
- Present all the steps to a project as an overview, and then allow the den to work on the project one step at a time. It is important to the autistic boy to know what is coming next.

Fly the Airplane

Materials: Wire coat hanger, paper for paper airplanes

Each boy makes a paper airplane. Create a target for the airplanes by stretching the hanger into a circle and hanging it at the boys' chest level. The object is to throw the airplane through the hoop. To vary the game, change the height or swing the target from side to side.

Making a Paper Airplane

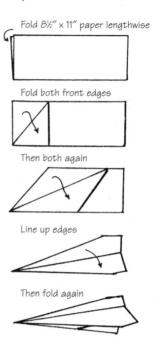

Fold 8½" x 11" paper lengthwise

Fold both front edges

Then both again

Line up edges

Then fold again

Ring Toss

Materials: Washers or plastic rings, pan for the target

Toss the washer or plastic ring into the target. Score one point for each successful attempt.

FOR BOYS WHO HAVE LIMITED MOVEMENT

Choose activities that keep participants in a small area.

Tin Can Bowling

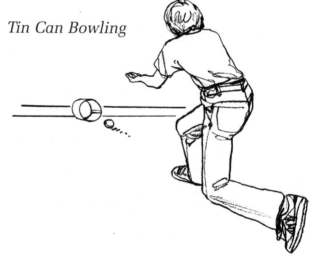

Materials: 48-oz. empty can with lid cut off, one per team; rubber ball, one per team

Place the empty can against a wall on its side with the open side toward the players. Two teams stand 12 to 15 feet away from the can. Each team member bowls or rolls the ball toward the can. The object is to get the ball to stay inside the can rather than bouncing back out. Score one point for each successful attempt.

Pass It

Materials: **One lemon per team, small paper cup per player**

Balance the lemon on the small paper cup. Without dropping the lemon, transfer it to the next boy's paper cup. If dropped, pick up the lemon at that place in line. The first team to transfer the lemon to the back of the line wins.

FOR BOYS WHO HAVE DOWN SYNDROME

Choose games that don't require much coordination or energy.

Clothespins in a Bottle

Materials: **Narrow-mouthed jar, five clothespins per team**

Place a narrow-mouthed jar on the floor. Boys hold a clothespin at chin level and drop it into the bottle. It looks like it won't fit, but it will! The team with the most clothespins making it into the bottle wins. The leader keeps the cumulative score. As this is not a race, each boy can have the time he needs.

Leaf Prints

Materials: **Variety of leaves, thin paper, crayons or soft pencils**

Place thin paper on top of a leaf that has been placed vein side up. Using a crayon or soft pencil, color over the leaf so that the veins of the leaf are visible. Repeat using other leaves and colors.

FOR BOYS WHO HAVE BREATHING DIFFICULTIES

Choose indoor activities involving little or no physical activity.

Bean Jacks

Materials: **20 dried beans per boy**

Arrange the beans in a single layer on a table or the floor. Each boy picks up one bean with his left hand, transfers it to his right hand, and with his right hand, places the bean on the back of his left hand. Repeat until one bean falls off.

Toothpicks and Peanuts

Materials: **Toothpicks, plastic foam peanut packing material**

Using toothpicks to join the peanuts, allow the boys to make anything they want. This makes a mess, but boys love it. To make this craft a game, challenge boys to create an animal, an invention, or whatever fits the monthly theme. Judge the entries and give prizes. Every boy should get a prize. To vary the activity, use glue and craft sticks.

FOR BOYS WHO HAVE ATTENTION DEFICIT DISORDER

Most of the time boys with attention deficit disorder merely need more time to process the directions to a game or art project. Demonstrating the game or art project can be very helpful because of the additional processing time that demonstration allows. Divide the directions up into steps and let each step "register" before moving on. Limit the number of directions given at one time.

Egg Carton Paper Clip Drop

Materials: **Egg carton per team, paper clip per boy**

Open the egg carton and write a number at the bottom of each cup so that it is visible. Give each boy a paper clip and line the teams up at the opposite side of the room. Each boy runs to the egg carton, holds the paper clip at nose level, and drops it into one of the egg carton cups. If the paper clip bounces out, he should pick it up and try again until the paper clip stays in a cup. The leader records his score. The boy then runs back to his team and tags the next player.

Splatter Painting

Materials: **Tempera or acrylic paint, old toothbrush per boy, plastic gloves, paper or object to be painted**

This is a great way to decorate many things: a painted box or bookshelf, paper to be folded for note cards or invitations, etc. The boy dips the bristles of the toothbrush in the paint and rubs his thumb across the bristles (wearing the gloves) so that the paint splatters onto the object. Use single colors or lots of colors for different effects.

FOR BOYS WHO HAVE ATTENTION DEFICIT DISORDER WITH HYPERACTIVITY

In addition to having the problems that boys with attention deficit disorder have, these boys are unusually active. The key to helping them is switching activities often.

Cup Stacking

Materials: **Lots of small paper cups per boy**

Challenge the boys to build a tower of paper cups with only one cup as the base. The tallest standing tower wins. The trick is to place cups alternately on their top and then their bottom.

Fill the Basket

Materials: **Large basket or other container, as many balls as possible**

This is a den–against–den leader game. Boys unite and try to fill the basket by throwing the balls into it. The leader tries to keep the container empty by tossing the balls as far away as possible. The winner is determined by where the majority of the balls are located after a given time period.

FOR BOYS WHO ARE GIFTED AND TALENTED

These boys will need enrichment activities to keep them interested because they finish projects quickly.

Marble Mazes

Materials: **Assorted cardboard tubes (from toilet paper or paper towels, etc.), tape, chair, several books, marbles**

Give the boys several cardboard tubes to make a marble maze with. They will need to tape them together or cut some of the longer ones for corner pieces. When their maze is completed, they can use the chair and several books for support so that the beginning of the maze can be elevated. Then let the good times roll!

FOR BOYS WHO HAVE HEARING IMPAIRMENTS

Boys with hearing impairments can play most games. Depending on the severity of the impairment, however, the leader may have to help them keep track of the game.

Hat Pantomime

Materials: **Slips of paper with directions written on them, hat**

Write directions on slips of paper such as "Wash the dog," "Buckle your seat belt," "Take out the garbage," or "Do your homework." Place them in a hat. Boys take turns drawing one out of the hat and pantomiming the action for the rest of the group. The player who guesses first what the boy is doing is next.

Doughnuts on a String

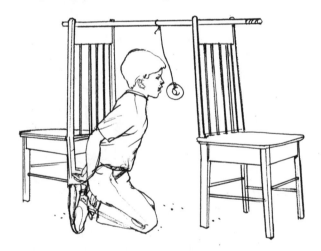

Materials: **Doughnut, string, broom, two chairs**

Tie a doughnut onto a string. Suspend it from a broom handle and attach the broom handle across the backs of two chairs. With their hands behind their backs, boys must get down on their knees and try to eat the doughnut.

FOR BOYS WHO HAVE MEMORY PROBLEMS

Be sure to write down directions to all activities so that boys with memory problems can refer back to them.

Alphabet Scavenger Hunt

Materials: **Paper with alphabet listed vertically, pencils**

Each boy has a pencil and specially prepared paper. Assign them a designated area of the room or outdoor area. Ask them to write down the names of things they see next to the appropriate first letter of the object. Example: A—apple.

Leather Neckerchief Slide

Materials:

Scraps of leather	**Leather stamps**
Hammer	**Glue**
Plastic ring	**Markers or leather stain**

Provide several leather stamps for boys. Let them choose a piece of leather and stamp their desired design on it. They can color it with markers or stain it with leather stain. When finished, they can attach a ring to the back with glue.

FOR BOYS WHO HAVE LIMITED VITALITY

Boys with limited vitality do best with short activities and need frequent breaks.

Marble Croquet

Materials: **Paper clip for each boy, marble for each boy (preferably different colors), plastic centers from pizza delivery boxes**

Each boy bends his paper clip to form a miniature croquet club. Use the plastic centers from pizza delivery boxes to make wickets for the course. Each boy can use his club to move the marble through the course.

Earth, Water, Air, and Fire

Materials: **Beanbag**

Boys sit in a circle with one boy in the center holding a beanbag. He throws the bag at someone and shouts "earth," "water," "air," or "fire." If it is "earth," the chosen boy must reply with the name of an animal before the boy in the center can count to 10. If it is "water," he must think of a fish; if "air," a bird; and if "fire," he must whistle for the fire engine. Once a creature has been named, it may not be named again. If a boy can't reply with a new item in time, he changes places with the thrower.

RESOURCES

Included here is a list of BSA resources referred to in this book as well as BSA resources that leaders will find helpful in their Cub Scouting positions.

Leaders should always remember that a wealth of information is available to supplement that provided in this *Cub Scout Leader How-To Book.* Use your local library! Also, don't forget the resources and ideas available from your local council, such as roundtable and pow wow. And, of course, the ever-expanding World Wide Web is an exciting source of games, crafts, stories, and tricks for boys.*

BSA Resources

Bear Cub Scout Book, No. 33107

Boys' Life magazine

Campfire Program Planner, No. 33696A

Cub Scout Academics and Sports Program Guide, No. 34299

Cub Scout Ceremonies for Dens and Packs, No. 33212B

Cub Scout Grand Prix Pinewood Derby Guidebook, No. 33721

Cub Scout Leader Book, No. 33221A

Cub Scout Magic, No. 33210

Cub Scout Program Helps, No. 34304 (yearly)

Cub Scout Roundtable Planning Guide, No. 34239 (yearly)

Cub Scout Songbook, No. 33222

Cub Scouting's BSA Family Activity Book, No. 33012A

Den Chief Handbook, No. 33211A

Group Meeting Sparklers, No. 33122

Guide to Safe Scouting, No. 34416B

Local Tour Permit Application, No. 34426B

Pack Program Planning Chart, No. 26-004

The Pack's First Three Months, No. 13-010

Family Talent Survey, No. 34362

Scouting magazine

Tiger Cub Handbook, No. 34713

Unit Money-Earning Application, No. 34427A

Webelos Leader Guide, No. 33853A

Webelos Scout Book, No. 33108

Wolf Cub Scout Book, No. 33106

ADVANCEMENT

Webelos Activity Badge pocket certificate, No. 33423

Arrow of Light Award pocket certificate, No. 34219A

Arrow Point pocket certificate, No. 34233

Bear Cub Scout Badge pocket certificate, No. 34221

Bobcat Cub Scout Badge pocket certificate, No. 34218

Cub Scout Den Advancement Chart, No. 34192A

Cub Scout Insignia poster set, No. 4648

Cub Scout Insignia stickers, small, No. 34457

Cub Scout Insignia stickers, large, No. 34650

Immediate Recognition Kit, No. 01804

Pack graduation certificate, No. 33751

Webelos Scout Advancement Chart, No. 34187A

Wolf Cub Scout Badge pocket certificate, No. 34220

---

*Please note that some activities found on Scouting Web sites may not be appropriate for boys of Cub Scout age. Furthermore, information on BSA policy is accurate only on the official Web site of the Boy Scouts of America National Council at www.scouting.org.

INDEX

Index